The Southern Ming

THE

Southern Ming

1644–1662

LYNN A. STRUVE

YALE UNIVERSITY PRESS
NEW HAVEN AND LONDON

Published with assistance from the Office of Learning Resources,
Indiana University.

Designed by James J. Johnson
and set in Bembo Roman type by
Asco Trade Typesetting Limited.
Printed in the United States of America by
BookCrafters, Inc., Chelsea, Michigan.

Library of Congress Cataloging in Publication Data

Struve, Lynn A., 1944–
    The Southern Ming, 1644–62.

    Bibliography: p.
    Includes index.
        1. China—History—1644–1795.   I. Title.
DS754.2.S77   1984   951'.03   83–23341
ISBN 0–300–03057–6

10   9   8   7   6   5   4   3   2   1

For those Ming martyrs who
"knew it was no use, but went on anyway."

The Analects, XIV: 38

Contents

List of Maps

Genealogical Chart of the Major Southern Ming Claimants

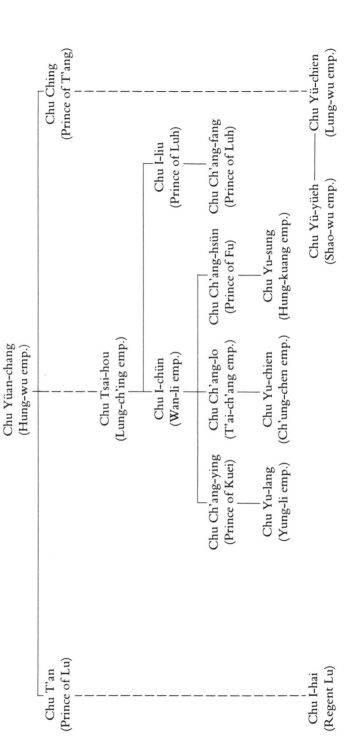

Chu T'an (Prince of Lu)

Chu Yüan-chang (Hung-wu emp.)

Chu Ching (Prince of T'ang)

Chu Tsai-hou (Lung-ch'ing emp.)

Chu I-chün (Wan-li emp.)

Chu I-liu (Prince of Luh)

Chu Ch'ang-ying (Prince of Kuei)

Chu Ch'ang-lo (T'ai-ch'ang emp.)

Chu Ch'ang-hsün (Prince of Fu)

Chu Ch'ang-fang (Prince of Luh)

Chu Yu-lang (Yung-li emp.)

Chu Yu-chien (Ch'ung-chen emp.)

Chu Yu-sung (Hung-kuang emp.)

Chu Yü-yüeh (Shao-wu emp.)

Chu Yü-chien (Lung-wu emp.)

Chu I-hai (Regent Lu)

Preface

A S far as anyone knows, the Southern Ming was not called the "Southern Ming" by a Chinese writer until the middle of the nineteenth century,[1] that is, until the Ch'ing dynasty, which had displaced the mortally wounded Ming in the seventeenth century, itself had become plagued by the dual evil of "internal chaos and external calamity" and was lurching into its own final decades. This late appearance of the term Southern Ming is understandable because, paralleling the long-accepted designations of other dynasties in Chinese history, especially the Southern Sung, it implied respect and legitimacy for a series of political regimes that the Ch'ing officially had striven to dismiss as benighted and insignificant. Most Ch'ing authors referred to the period 1644–62 as the "[twig]-end" or the "last [season]" of the Ming, as the time of the "southern territories," or with classical allusions to fallen states of ancient times. But with the downfall of the Ch'ing in the first decade of the twentieth century and the consequent venting of anti-Manchu sentiment in the republican period, those who had resisted the Ch'ing in times past were extolled, and the term Southern Ming came into general use. In this book, however, it is used simply as a terminological convenience, not as a means of ascribing any particular status to the period in question—except, perhaps, one of respectability as an object of historical study.

The Southern Ming scarcely has been touched in Western scholarship. During the past decade, studies of various aspects of China's seventeenth century have increased in number and quality, but a great gap has been left at midcentury. This neglect—or avoidance—of the Ch'ing conquest and the Southern Ming probably has been due to the scattered, fragmentary, and otherwise highly problematical condition of the all-too-voluminous source materials. I began

puzzling over them as a graduate student in 1970, submitted a doctoral dissertation on some of them in 1974,[2] and have continued to find them exasperating
for almost another decade now. But over the years I have developed a modicum
of bibliographic control and have learned a good deal about which works and
other materials truly constitute the primary record of the Southern Ming. I have
striven to base this book on only the most credible sources, written by men who
actually observed the events they describe, or who conducted conscientious
inquiries soon after such events occurred. I have excluded from use not only most
Ch'ing secondary and tertiary renderings, but also writings that, although they
were produced by contemporaries of my preferred authors, seem too derivative
or inaccurate to warrant much attention. Consequently, readers who have some
knowledge of Southern Ming history may be surprised to find that certain
familiar titles appear seldom or not at all in my notes and bibliography. Although
I cannot claim to have examined every last shred of good primary material on the
Southern Ming—some surely having escaped my notice, and a few important
texts having remained outside my reach[3]—in general, the omission of a well-
known work may be regarded as an indication of my negative judgment on it.
As for the large amount of twentieth-century writing on the Southern Ming,
much of it is heavily journalistic and propagandistic in aim, so I have cited only
the portion that I have found to be of value for scholarship.

    The history of Chinese writing on the Southern Ming is fascinating in itself.
From the late 1640s to the present day, Chinese historians have seen that period as
pregnant with meaning in ways that have metamorphosed frequently, reflecting
various changes—some subtle, some radical—in the conditions of intellectual
endeavor in China during the past 340 years. If I were to discuss intermittently in
the text of this work just how my treatment of Southern Ming events conforms
to, departs from, or seeks a middle path among the multifarious interpretations
of three centuries, the pattern of my narration—already complex—would
become thoroughly obscured. And if I were to discuss in the notes of this work
the hundreds of questions that arise in judging the veracity of source materials on
the Southern Ming, I soon would overstep the limits of one volume. In view of
this, and in response to the interest expressed by colleagues, I intend separately to
write a historiography of the Southern Ming, which will be both a study in the
"sociology" of historical knowledge in China and a guide to sources.
Meanwhile, students of this period may find helpful my bibliographic article on
Southern Ming studies which will appear in the *Cambridge History of China*,
volume 7; and they surely will join me in welcoming the publication of an
expanded and revised edition of the monumental bibliography *Wan-Ming shih-
chi k'ao*, by the late Hsieh Kuo-chen.[4]

    The seventeenth century was one of the most crucial in all of Chinese

history. Many waves of change that had been building for decades seem to have
crested at midcentury and broken into a swirling surf of events that mesmerize
but also seem to defy systematic research and explanation. Most Western scholarship on this century has concentrated on the relatively stable earlier and later
decades, eschewing the task of figuring out what happened in between. Those
bold enough to tackle the middle decades have adopted various laudable approaches: Close examinations of events and changing conditions on the local
level have shown how certain factors intersected in certain places; moreover,
these local studies have brought forth the personal element in ways that satisfy
our desire to know "how it was." Such studies have been aided, but not wholly
shaped, by the work of others who interpret the period primarily from the
perspective of economic change and resulting social-class antagonisms. More
traditionally, there has been much emphasis on the moral and administrative
acumen—or, rather, the lack of it—in governmental officials of the time. And,
of course, there have been numerous portrayals of famous Ming loyalists and
other colorful figures in every stripe and hue—portrayals which may seem
melodramatically stereotypical but often are quite true to the times. As one
colleague aptly has pointed out to me, "Southern Ming events were surrounded
as they happened by dense clouds of role-playing and fabulation; [and] even when
one sticks to the best and closest primary sources, the people and events seem
almost incredible...."[5]

I find validity in all these approaches but feel that a great deal more work
must be done, by many scholars working in various but related ways, before a
well-founded, synthetic treatment of the mid-seventeenth century will come
within reach. Moreover, in my view work on midcentury affairs has been
inhibited mainly by a dearth of clear and balanced explications of the major
political and military developments of those decades. Because other American
colleagues have been working on the conquest period by focusing on the
"Ch'ing side,"[6] and because of my relative familiarity with sources on the
"Ming side," I have felt that the best contribution I might offer under present
circumstances would be an account such as this one, which treats fully yet
sparingly the general history of the Southern Ming. Those who are interested in
such large questions as why the Ming declined, how the Manchus succeeded,
how Ming Neo-Confucian culture affected loyalist behavior, or what structural
relation there may have been between socioeconomic disjunctures and the
political upheavals of the century will find that some light is shed on these and
other matters in this study. I have tried to cast that light intelligently, but
answering such questions has not been my goal. Rather, I have sought to present
a precise yet panoramic view, through geopolitical lenses, of a kaleidoscopic age.

Over several years, financial support for this research has been provided by the American Council of Learned Societies with funds from the National Endowment for the Humanities, the Pacific Cultural Foundation of T'ai-pei, the Mellon Foundation through the University of Pennsylvania, and, at Indiana University, by the President's Council on International Programs and the Office for Research and Graduate Development. Of course, the views presented in this book are entirely my own and do not necessarily represent those of any of these generous institutions.

I have benefited immensely from the hospitality and assistance of the scholars and staff members of the Institute of History and Philology and the Institute of Modern History of the Academia Sinica in T'ai-wan. I am especially indebted to the late Professor Ch'ü Wan-li, whose gracious sponsorship enabled me to make extensive use of the Fu Szu-nien Memorial Library and other facilities there, as well as materials in the National Central Library in downtown T'ai-pei. At National T'ai-wan University, Professor Juan Chih-sheng introduced me to the rich periodical collection in the Graduate Library, and Professor Yang Yün-p'ing kindly has sent me copies of several of his publications. Also, in the early stages of my research, the late Mr. Huang Yü-chai, a well-known private scholar of T'ai-wan history, generously provided me with offprints of his ground-breaking articles. In mainland China, the Institute of History of the Chinese Academy of Social Sciences enabled me to make the acquaintance of several prominent scholars of seventeenth century Chinese history during my tour as a member of the Ming-Ch'ing History Delegation in 1979; and the Institute also has provided me with copies of publications that otherwise would have been difficult for me to obtain. The staff of the National Library of China in Pei-ching, too, has been cooperative in sending me microfilms of rare texts. And at Hongkong University, Professors Chin Fa-ken and Tu Wei-yün have been helpful in many ways, as have the staff members of the Feng P'ing-shan Library there.

In the United States, the efforts of Professor Frederick Mote have made it possible for me to participate in the Ming History Project and to utilize the superb Gest Oriental Library, as well as the services of the Department of East Asian Studies, at Princeton University. At the University of Pennsylvania, my thanks go to Professors Nathan Sivin, Susan Naquin, and Victor Mair, and to the East Asian librarian, Nancy Cheng, all of whom assisted me during my year of residence and research at Penn in 1980–81. The list of other persons to whom I am grateful certainly is headed by Professors Frederic Wakeman, Jr., of the University of California at Berkeley, and John E. Wills of the University of Southern California, without whose unflagging encouragement and support, in numberless large and small ways, I might never have persisted in this work. Also, special recognition should go to Mr. J. M. Hollingsworth of Cartographic

PREFACE   xvii

Services in the Department of Geography, Indiana University, whose patience
and skill were essential in producing the numerous maps for this volume, and to
my colleague Professor Richard Chi, whose calligraphy graces the front.

Others who have offered help and advice include Professor Emeritus
Charles O. Hucker of the University of Michigan, William Atwell, Lecturer in
the School of Oriental and African Studies of London University, Professor
Beatrice Bartlett of Yale University, and Professor Ronald Toby of the University of Illinois at Urbana-Champaign. The seemingly inexhaustible hospitality
of Betty and Richard Liu extended and enriched my last trip to Hongkong. And
at home, I scarcely could carry on my research without the continual assistance
of Indiana University's librarian for the East Asian Collection, Shizue Matsuda.

The Southern Ming

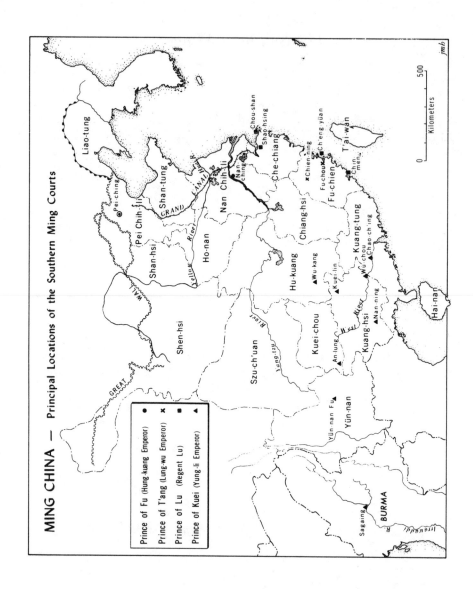

MING CHINA — Principal Locations of the Southern Ming Courts

Prince of Fu (Hung-kuang Emperor) ●
Prince of T'ang (Lung-wu Emperor) ✕
Prince of Lu (Regent Lu) ■
Prince of Kuei (Yung-li Emperor) ▲

Liao-tung

Shan-tung

(Pei Chih-li)
⊙ Pei-ching

GRAND CANAL

Shan-hsi

Ho-nan

Nan Chih-li
Nan-ching

Chou-shan
Shao-hsing ■
Che-chiang

Chien-ning ✕
Fu-chou ■ Ch'eng-yüan
Fu-chien
Ch'üan-men ■

T'ai-wan

Shen-hsi

GREAT WALL

Yellow River

Huai River

Chiang-hsi

Hu-kuang
▲ Wu-kang
▲ Kuei-lin

Kuang-tung
Wu-chou ◀
▲ Chao-ch'ing

Kuei-chou

An-lung ▲

West River

Kuang-hsi
▲ Nan-ning

Hai-nan

Szu-ch'uan

Yung-tzu River

Yün-nan Fu ▲
Yün-nan

BURMA

Sagaing ▲

Irrawaddy R.

0   500
Kilometers

jmb

Introduction

WHEN did the Ming dynasty really end? That question is as much philosophical as historical, and is more or less answerable depending on one's purposes.[1] For textbooks and chronological charts of the major Chinese dynasties, the year 1644 has sufficed. The events of that year certainly were momentous: the suicide of the Ming Ch'ung-chen emperor, as the rebel forces of Li Tzu-ch'eng overran the northern capital, Pei-ching, and penetrated the imperial palace grounds;[2] the alliance between the Ming regional commander at Shan-hai Pass, Wu San-kuei, and the Manchu regent, Dorgon, which enabled the Manchus to rout the rebels from Pei-ching and subsequently to occupy the whole North China Plain.[3] But, formally speaking, 1644 marks neither the end of Ming nor the beginning of Ch'ing. The Manchu leader Khungtaiji proclaimed himself emperor of a new dynasty, the Ch'ing, in 1636; and the last Ming prince to claim sovereignty over China, as Yung-li emperor, was not eliminated until 1662.

If the beginnings and endings of polities are pursued for heuristic purposes, then many interesting possibilities appear. Numerous studies of the Manchus prior to 1644 naturally have emphasized their evolution from common tribe to unique state and the crucial accomplishments of their Great Ancestor, Nurhaci (1559–1626).[4] As for when the Ming really was finished—in other words, when the forces of decline and defeat became irreversible—that is a more dismal and yet more lively question. Was it the 1620s, when usurpation of power by the notorious eunuch Wei Chung-hsien made it "appear probable that at no time in Chinese imperial history were court politics and ethics more debased"?[5] Or was it in the 1630s, when, despite the accession of a conscientious emperor, the weakened and demoralized Ming government was able neither to prevent the

I

Manchus from pressing on, and occasionally breaking through, the Great Wall in the northeast nor to confine the "roving bandit" armies to Shen-hsi Province in the northwest?[6] Others find the roots of these disasters in the preceding Wan-li reign (1573–1620), blaming the emperor's unprecedentedly long and stubborn refusal to handle state affairs for a "constitutional" crisis that reverberated through the remainder of the Ming.[7] However, when one looks to problems in fiscal management, which invariably beset major dynasties by midterm, the earlier Chia-ching reign (1522–66) seems to emerge as the time when disjunctions between a rapidly changing economy and relatively fixed state financial practices became chronic in ways that thwarted Ming efforts to deal with other large-scale problems, especially military ones.[8] And so on, back through time, toward the ultimate encounter with those who always can find the genes for death in the embryo.

This study simply places the end of the Ming dynasty per se at the point after which there were no more genuine Ming dynasts, while showing how that point came to occur fully eighteen years after the fall of Pei-ching. Although no attempt is made herein to precisely measure or analyze the various factors that combined to weaken the Ming and prevent its reinvigoration, before or after 1644, two themes are given special emphasis, because they emerge unmistakably and continually in the record of the Southern Ming's struggle to survive, and because they highlight two important difficulties of the Ming dynasty as a whole: (1) the inability to balance and integrate civil and military affairs (and concomitant denigration of the military), and (2) dilemmas in providing assistance for the emperor.

Both problems were perennial in Chinese history, especially since the Late T'ang and Sung (i.e., the turn of the second millennium, A.D.), and both were especially marked in the Ming. They remained largely distinct, converging in just a few clear instances, during the greater part of the Ming period; but in the Southern Ming, when military capability and effective leadership at the top literally became matters of life and death, they intersected continually and directly in ways that were disastrous for the loyalists' cause. Intimately related to both was the carefully nurtured and jealously guarded preponderance of the civil bureaucracy, which became more self-righteously (and, in the end, suicidally) exclusive during the Ming than during any other period in Chinese history.

It is ironic that a state founded and consolidated in the spirit of "Vast Martiality" rapidly turned its regard away from military matters. The Great Ancestor of the Ming, T'ai-tsu (1328–98), had expelled the Mongols and defeated his domestic rivals with a combination of political shrewdness and skill in both land and naval warfare that was approximated in the imperial line only by his fourth son, Ch'eng-tsu, who battled to wrest the throne from his nephew at the turn of the fifteenth century. But Ch'eng-tsu chose the reign title "Eternal Happiness"; and T'ai-tsu, despite his awesome reign title and the attention he devoted to creating a military aristocracy, had not wished to perpetuate or propagate martiality among the general populace. Rather, his desire to relieve the average citizen of the burdens of military service and support underlay one very consequential part of the Ancestor's Order: the segregation of military men from others in the society by making them a hereditary caste—this at a time when Chinese sociopolitical values already had largely spurned heredity in favor of merit for assigning prestige, position, perquisites, and other rewards.[9]

The hereditary nature of the Ming military system was twofold: First, common soldiers and officers alike were drawn from eternally designated "military households" (*chün-hu*). They supposedly maintained themselves in readiness while cultivating state farmlands in military colonies (*chün-t'un*) and were administered and trained through a network of strategically located garrisons (*wei* and *so*). Second, there were military nobles (*hsün-ch'en*), who held in perpetuity titles as dukes, marquises, and earls, conferred on them by emperors for outstanding service. These men usually filled such high-ranking positions as Military Commissioner-in-Chief or Commander of the Capital Guard and could pass on their noble titles (and, in some cases, their positions) to heirs without diminution in rank.[10] In the fifteenth and early sixteenth centuries, both the system of military colonies and garrisons and the status of military nobles declined drastically, as civil officials, especially those in the Ministry of War, increasingly dominated military affairs.

Partially as a result of fiscal mismanagement, but also out of simple disregard and disdain on the part of the civil bureaucracy, the living standards of military households and the service conditions of soldiers on duty were allowed to deteriorate almost shockingly, adding material hardship to the social stigma of hereditary military status. Desertion, absconding, and empty rosters became common. Garrison strengths sank far below their designated levels, and those soldiers who remained often were employed in nonmilitary tasks, as transport or construction workers and even as officers' domestic servants.[11] Efforts to make up for shortfalls in the system of hereditary military colonies by instituting nationwide militia systems (*min-ping* and *min-chuang*) either failed for lack of volunteers or, under the control of local civil officials, gradually metamorphosed into means for raising extra revenues rather than extra troops.[12] Indeed, because the payment of silver in lieu of militia service became such a staple of Ming civil administrative revenues, in 1637 when reactivation of the militia system was proposed at court, the idea was rejected because the government could not afford the loss of income that would result. Consequently, the innumerable local defense corps that formed in response to banditry and conquest in the 1640s aimed strictly at local self-preservation; they rarely were coordinated from any higher level or directed toward regional defense goals.[13]

As numbers of hereditary soldiers and militiamen proved insufficient, the government was forced to rely more and more on paid recruits (mu-ping); and the steady increase of this expenditure, exacerbated by general escalation in the costs of warfare in the sixteenth and seventeenth centuries, proved too great for Ming fiscal and logistical practice to bear.[14] Moreover, unpaid recruits were more dangerous than uncompensated soldiers from military colonies. The latter usually had homes to which they could return, whereas recruits were gotten from the flotsam of society—rootless, often desperate men who, once armed and trained in the techniques of violence and then deprived of material support, were prone to mutiny and to directly seize their due from the citizens they were hired to protect. As mutinies, rampages, and other social disruptions grew more common, it became easier to raise fighting men on short notice for perhaps temporary pay; but such men correspondingly proved more difficult to train or control. Commanders in the field, forced to use irregular expedients to maintain their units, came to have semiprivate armies of surly, restive men whom they were wiser to mollify than to discipline. The armies of the so-called peasant rebels of the late Ming were constituted in large proportion of such dregs of a society that accorded no human dignity to the common soldier.[15]

Thus, it is no surprise that the Ming looked to what was regarded as a marginally human element for its best fighters. The "wolf troops" from a certain tribe of aborigines in remote Kuei-chou Province were as famous for their ferocious fighting as they were notorious for their rapacity toward the civilian population.[16] "The bandits [went through] like a coarse comb, the [regular] troops like a fine one, but the aboriginal soldiers were like a shaver!"[17] Used only for limited campaigns and sent back to their tribal territory as quickly as possible, the wolf troops epitomized the separation of civil and military in Ming times.

A different sort of notoriety became attached to the military nobles, who frequently were characterized as spoiled, incompetent "fancy pants" by civil officials. The largest number, and the most prestigious, of the military noble lines had been established in the beginning of the dynasty, during the reigns of T'ai-tsu and Ch'eng-tsu; but since the latter part of the fifteenth century scarcely any new investitures had been made,[18] and the institution became even more anachronistic. Moreover, although military nobles always retained the high rank that pointedly had been accorded to them in the founding reigns, their powers and prestige dropped steadily over the years. Most telling in this respect are the evolutionary histories of the Five Chief Military Commissions and the Capital Guard. Both groups originally were the exclusive preserves of the highest-ranking military nobles, but both gradually became more subject to control by the Ministry of War; and in both cases the functions of the military nobles were encroached upon by eunuchs, as well as by civil officials.[19] In assignment to important tasks they also lost ground to nonnoble military men who had passed the military *chü-jen* and *chin-shih* examinations, conducted regularly (as a lesser counterpart to the civil service examinations) by the Ministry of War beginning in the late fifteenth century.[20]

The deterioration of the Ming military establishment often is attributed to "long periods of great peace." But was this really the case? Certainly the Ming was not subject to the prolonged and heavy pressures that the Sung dynasty felt. But she had considerable trouble with both internal rebellions and her southern neighbors, the Burmese and Annamese; and the Mongols in the north, always a potential threat, menaced Pei-ching intermittently. In one "ridiculous incident," the emperor, who had been led out on a foolhardy campaign by his head eunuch, was captured by the chieftain of the Western Mongols and held at ransom for over a year, precipitating a great crisis in the Ming court.[21] Frederick Mote has examined "the Chinese failure to learn the right lesson" from this debacle,[22] and the same judgment could be applied to other Ming military endeavors.[23]

Defense installations on "China's third frontier,"[24] the maritime southeast, also declined with startling rapidity in the early fifteenth century, completely reversing the surge of naval power that had attended the Ming founding.[25] When attacks by so-called dwarf [Japanese] pirates became especially virulent in the middle of the sixteenth century, coastal defenses were in a deplorable state. Special forces had to be raised and new commands established. The court's most able general in this struggle, Ch'i Chi-kuang, ultimately was successful against the marauders, but "he had virtually to create a new army" in order to do so.[26] Because the lessons of Ch'i's experience were not carefully read, in the seventeenth century the government resorted to employing the brigands themselves in order to keep some semblance of peace along the seaboard.

Frequently Confucianism either gets the blame or gets the credit for "old China's" derogation of the military. On the negative side, long-robed Confucian scholar-officials are criticized for lording over and wasting the talents of more pragmatic, rough-and-ready men, and for making the country vulnerable to invasion by barbarians. On the positive side, they are praised for maintaining civil control over the military and for holding the arts of harmony over the techniques of violence. John K. Fairbank, writing about "Varieties of the Chinese Military Experience," stressed that Chinese officials regarded fighting as the last of an array of approaches that they preferred to keep at their disposal for dealing with multifaceted problems. "The resort to *wu* (warfare) was an admission of bankruptcy in the pursuit of *wen* (civility)." They took "the larger view that seeks to maintain the established order without the use of violence." But even if hostilities became unavoidable, still, "war was too complex a matter to be left to fighting men."[27]

The latter characterization is overly generous if applied to the Ming. True craftsmen keep a spread of tools at hand, each one respected and maintained in fine working order. As craftsmen of peace and harmony, Ming officialdom fell short of this. Military might was not just controlled by civil government; it was stultified. Military men were not just subordinated by civil officials; they were degraded. Far from being esteemed as junior partners in a common cause, generals and soldiers were regarded with fear, suspicion, and distaste.[28] As one critic put it shortly after the fall of the Ming:

> Since T'ang and Sung, civil and military have split and gone down two separate paths. Thus, in positions from the Chief Military Commission at the center to the units stationed inside and outside our borders, both civil and military officials have continued to be used. But only in the Ming were they kept absolutely segregated. Although civil officials serving as viceroys or provincial governors were involved in military matters, they took all responsibility for supervisory control and maintained a distance between themselves and the soldiers. Those who had contact with the troops had no part in planning for supply; and those who planned for supply had no contact with the troops. The supervisors never got to lead troops; and the troop leaders never got to supervise. This, of course, was precisely the use of a dog-toothed, intersecting system to ensure that no one ever got the power to rebel.[29]

As the above passage suggests, by no means were all Ming civil officials necessarily moronic in military affairs, nor did prevalent Ming attitudes and policies toward the military go entirely unquestioned by contemporary statesmen. Nevertheless, stellar careers were not made from martial achievements, and the man who could lead either a campaign or a court conference with equal facility was a very rare anomaly. Although lip service was paid to the principle of integrating *wen* and *wu* in men of elite status, in actuality officials clung to their civil identities. In Ming China there were no Dwight Eisenhowers or Alexander Haigs, or lieutenant colonels who later became governors or mayors, proud to tell constituents of their record in military service. Such role changes were unthinkable for the Ming scholar-official.

Confucianism was responsible to some extent for this civil bias. But ideologies are not held for long or mouthed incessantly unless they serve the interests of those in power. Although individual ministers suffered unprecedented maltreatment, especially under the despotic first emperor of the dynasty,[30] by mid-Ming times the civil bureaucracy was in its heyday, and scholar-officials strove to make themselves more elite than any other elite. Military nobles, imperial clansmen, powerful eunuchs—all were bombarded with ammunition from the Confucian arsenal and regarded as morally unqualified to lead society because they were not schooled in the literature of the civil service examinations. In times of relative peace such exclusivity may have been functional. But in the Southern Ming, when the dynasty was in a life-and-death struggle and needed to concentrate the best capacities of all its elites, the alienation that had been engendered between civil officialdom and other elements, especially the military, proved too great to be overcome.

The history of the Southern Ming can be seen, through one lens, as the painfully gradual, conflict-ridden displacement of civil by military structures and methods, until, in the end, the court's sole support was from military organizations that were not even directly of Ming origin. The next phase in the elliptical cycling of *wen* and *wu* would have been the emergence of civil management from within the military organizations of Cheng Ch'eng-kung in the far southeast and of Sun K'o-wang in the far southwest, and there were some signs of this. But the Ch'ing did not give those incipiences much chance to develop.

The civil bureaucracy, though ascendant and exclusive in Ming times, was hardly monolithic and, moreover, was fatefully dependent on a strong emperorship in two ways: First, for its very existence. Throne and bureaucracy really were codependent institutions, and, though they often irritated one another, it was a "vital tension," necessary to the health of the traditional Chinese state. Significantly, the Ming marked the height of both monarchical autocracy and bureaucratic monopoly in Chinese history. The groveling of ministers before the Ming throne had a masochistic air; they had, "in the kowtow, self-aggrandizement through self-abasement."[31] Second, the bureaucracy needed a strong, decisive emperorship to actually wield the ultimate authority vested in it by "Heaven" and thereby control bureaucratic factionalism. Chinese government is and always has been heavily factional, because China always has provided the institutional conditions in which such fluid power arrangements thrive. That is an observation of political science, not a pejorative statement.[32] Factions are the oil of bureaucratic machinery everywhere. The question for historians should be: Under what circumstances does everyday factional competition become virulent, fratricidal, and eventually suicidal for the organization concerned? In Ming times, the primary cause of bureaucratic high blood pressure and deadly factional strife was the problem of assistance to the emperor.

I have said that the emperor*ship* was important to the bureaucracy, because that institution, in most dynasties, normally included the emperor *and* his legitimate delegates, one or two prime ministers or chief councillors. But the Ming dynasty departed from this pattern in 1380 when ever-suspicious T'ai-tsu executed his prime minister on charges of sedition, abolished the prime ministership entirely, and stipulated the death penalty for any official who ever proposed instituting it again.[33] This meant that, above the level of the Six Ministries (of Personnel, Revenue, Rites, War, Justice, and Public Works), only the emperor remained to handle the enormous number of complicated matters that routinely were referred to the top of the state pyramid. T'ai-tsu managed to do it almost alone, but his successors either could not or would not assume such a burden. Subsequently, the gap between emperor and administration was filled, so to speak, by two "illegitimate" or "unconstitutional" elements: eunuchs and grand secretaries. The Ming was troubled by eunuch power more than any other dynasty, and it has been suggested that their exaggerated role was a natural concomitant of autocracy.[34] But more accurately, their role should be seen as deriving from the *failure* of Ming emperors to rule as true autocrats (as distinct from ruling arbitrarily) within an autocratically constructed system. And the same can be said for the evolution of the Grand Secretariat.

Even in T'ai-tsu's day, a certain amount of high-class clerical help for the throne had been borrowed from the Han-lin Academy, the realm's paramount official institute of learning, where the cream of each triennial crop of civil service doctoral examinees usually began their careers. Gradually these Han-lin secretaries were relied on more heavily for decision making. In the second quarter of the fifteenth century they came to constitute a true Secretariat and received supernumerary rank assignments that placed them above all others in the administrative hierarchy, and in the third quarter of that century it became customary to designate one man as Chief Grand Secretary. Moreover, the grand secretaries' function evolved from that of simply writing up the emperor's orders to that of previewing memorials before they reached the emperor and penning for him suggested decisions or courses of action. Earlier emperors used such advice as no more or less than that; but later emperors tended to accept the wisdom of their grand secretaries—as processed by the chiefs—and simply approved with little change the "draft rescripts" that were sent to them.[35] Thus, grand secretaries acquired indirect executive and legislative powers, and the capturing of positions in the Grand Secretariat, via the Han-lin Academy, became one of the prime goals of national politics.[36]

But this did not resolve the problem of assistance for the emperor, because, however functionally necessary the Grand Secretariat may have been, it remained institutionally ambiguous, suspended uncomfortably between emperor and bureaucracy and wholly trusted by neither side.[37]

> The manager's assistants, so to speak, never became assistant managers. The grand secretaries had no formal executive powers, and they were constantly subject to the whims of the emperor. Moreover, despite their nominal concurrent appointments in the ministries, they remained essen-

tially members of the inner court and could not expect united support and cooperation from the outer court. Some grand secretaries nevertheless became strong and influential, usually in alliance with imperially favored eunuchs. But it would seem almost inevitable that they should have been frustrated and undone by resentment among officials in the outer court. The problem was how to become a prime minister under a system that did not permit a prime ministership.[38]

If the chief grand secretary had been part of the Ancestor's Order, rather than an unplanned institutional accretion, then the capture of that position by one or another bureaucratic faction might have had stabilizing effects on court politics, since one faction then would have to be accepted, even if grudgingly, by the others as preponderant. But because the powers of that office remained ambiguous, its occupiers always could be challenged for overstepping their duties, especially if they tried to take a firm hand in government and exercise leadership as a prime minister might have done. Consequently, factional strife was exacerbated, since any important faction that failed to dominate the Grand Secretariat could attack that body on constitutional grounds (which usually were formulated in ethical terms). The position of chief grand secretary was a hotseat for even the most cautious, mild-mannered incumbents, who always could be made scapegoats for the failings of the emperors.[39] And those who tried to make a real impact on government through that office were excoriated for attempting to usurp imperial prerogatives, or for leading the emperor astray.[40] Indeed, it was the strong-willed administrative reformism of Chief Grand Secretary Chang Chü-cheng (1525–82) which gave rise to the strident "anti-administration" movement, led by the Tung-lin politico-literary society, toward the end of the Ming.[41] And since both eunuchs and grand secretaries had moved in to occupy the vacant territory between emperor and bureaucracy, it is no wonder that the Tung-lin leaders went on to martyrdom under the tyranny of Wei Chung-hsien in the 1620s, and that the successor to Tung-lin, the Fu She, identified the strongest chief grand secretary of the 1630s, Wen T'i-jen, with the anathematized "eunuch faction."[42]

It was bad enough that the lack of a prime ministership in the Ming aggravated the age-old problems of monarchical incompetence and bureaucratic factionalism. Worse, it also aggravated an age-old, fundamental divergence among Chinese scholar-officials, that is, between those who often are called "idealists," on the one hand, and "realists," on the other. Although individual men seldom were purely of either type,[43] in policy debates on virtually any matter of state, apposite arguments tended to emerge. The former had a clear edge in rhetoric, the latter in practice. And the give-and-take was more than just a matter of opinion, since, consonant with traditional Chinese sociopolitical discourse in general, it was seen as directly reflecting the basic views of human nature and, hence, the moral grounding of those involved.

For present purposes, suffice it to point out that one common distinction between Chinese idealists and realists lies in their differential tolerances of, and approaches toward dealing with, human weakness. The former generally hold that all men are perfectible—or at least can be improved considerably—through reform of the spirit or will. So their approach to changing men's behavior tends to be ethically instructional and exhortatory—often, though not necessarily, self-righteous in tone. The latter, however, are more inclined to accept, work around, or work upon men's shortcomings. And their approach to getting things done tends to be more canny and manipulative—often, though not necessarily, cynical in tone. Applied to the problem of assistance for the emperor, this divergence resulted in a conflict between two points of view: On one hand, those who were willing to accept as virtually unavoidable some incompetence and irresponsibility in the imperial line also were willing to meet that eventuality by augmenting the power of some figure such as a chief grand secretary. Such ready accommodation to the imperfect was opposed by those who insisted that the "root of the state," no matter how deficient he might be, could be taught, guided, and thus enabled to keep the reins of government in his own hands. In other words, one sort of minister was inclined to think, "If the emperor can't handle things, let's give him someone who can"; whereas the other sort tended to say, "The emperor *must* handle things, and we are responsible to see that he can and does" (within the bounds of custom and precedent, of course).

With this in mind, it may be easier to see why the issues of the Wan-li reign resulted in upheavals so great that the Ming bureaucracy never fully regained its footing. Chang Chü-cheng was seen by the Confucian revivalists (particularly those who began the Tung-lin movement) not only as presumptuously acting in the emperor's stead, in ways that the emperor, if enlightened, would not approve, but also as self-servingly insulating the monarch from contact with those who could enlighten him. And later they defiantly opposed this benighted sovereign for delaying the formal designation of—and, hence, the beginning of regular (Confucian) instruction for—the heir to his throne. Having been deprived of influence over the present emperor (who refused to see his ministers at all for the greater part of his forty-seven-year reign), they now were losing their chance with the next one as well. They were full of anxiety that if the succession matter were not resolved expeditiously, then the country would go to the non-Confucian dogs, that is, to self-aggrandizing eunuchs or chief grand secretaries. They were right. It went to the dogs first, and then to the barbarians. But both losses might have been avoided or deferred if the protests of the "righteous" Confucian revivalists had not been so shrill, thus alienating or immobilizing moderates and inviting severe counterattacks. In the Southern Ming, also, we will see that the problem of assistance to the emperor was never solved and generated rhetoric and rancor to the very end.

General judgments on the late Ming never fail to mention widespread corruption in officialdom as a cause of the dynasty's downfall. But "corruption" is a vague term that begs for both specific definition and sociological analysis. (What behaviors were customary or made necessary by institutional or economic conditions?) In any case, it seems to be much more the result than the cause of other things. Officials take bribes, engage in larceny, cheat or "squeeze" their constituents, and so forth, in unwarranted ways when they recognize no relation between those actions and the future of the government of which they are a part. Whether that future is assumed to be one of perpetuation or of demise, the lack of personal identification with the enterprise is similar. And this sort of corruption-breeding alienation, though not wholly attributable to virulent factional conflict, surely must increase when an organization loses *ésprit* as severely as did the Ming bureaucracy in the first forty years of the seventeenth century. Moreover, for reasons discussed above, it scarcely could have been combatted by discipline imposed from the top.

Two other problems, both also peculiar to the Ming dynasty, emerge notably in the record of the Southern Ming: (1) the ubiquity of, but general lack of leadership qualities among, the Ming imperial princes; and (2) pandemic social unrest and disruption, which were accentuated after Pei-ching fell and the authority and powers of local governments thus were called into question in 1644. These serve secondarily as themes, relative to the problems explained above, not because they are of lesser importance in understanding the sociopolitical conditions of midcentury. Rather, it is because, in this work on the Southern Ming, I have chosen to place primary emphasis on problems internal to that series of regimes; whereas the Ming imperial princes and widespread social unrest proved to be at least as problematical for the Ch'ing as for the Ming.

Unlike other dynasties, the Ming ennobled, and provided with stipends in perpetuity, all male descendants of the Great Ancestor—as well as their aunts, sisters, and daughters. Only the heir-designate was retained in the capital. The other male offspring of the emperor, when they reached adulthood, were assigned to large estates (with numerous tenants and retainers) scattered throughout the realm. Eldest sons succeeded to these princes' titles and estates, while younger sons and other descendants also were given titles and maintained on imperial clan lands, concentrated in certain prefectures but present in every province. Initially, the purpose of this system was to augment dynastic security by placing blood relatives of the emperor in every corner of the country. But after a series of high-ranking princes led revolts against the throne, this system came to be valued more as a means of keeping princes and important clansmen separated, circumscribed, and distant from the capital. Gradually they became subject to a great many restrictions—for instance, princes were not allowed to leave their estates without permission from the emperor, and neither they nor their estate officials were to have any hand in political or military affairs. Moreover, all imperial clansmen were forbidden to take up occupations, enter the civil service, or function as anything other than salaried dignitaries.[44]

In the beginning of the dynasty, when the system of imperial princes was established, it was not anticipated that the number of princes and other stipended clansmen would expand, nor that their support would become a drain on state revenues to the extent that this happened in the sixteenth and seventeenth centuries. In 1553 it was estimated that the cost of supporting imperial clansmen from revenues retained in the provinces each year came to over twice the total revenues forwarded to Pei-ching. At this time, their total number was over 23,000; but by the late Wan-li reign they numbered over 80,000, and the government simply no longer was able to provide for them as before. Although the estates of the major princes continued to grow, stipends for others were reduced and delayed, as were marriages and successive investitures; and many lower-ranking clansmen became impoverished. In 1590 a portion of the clansmen were permitted to give up their status as such and pursue common occupations as farmers, artisans, merchants, and the like; and in 1606 clansmen of all ranks below that of prince were permitted to compete in the civil service examinations, on the stipulation that successful ones always would be assigned to minor posts in the provinces, never to the capital.[45] Although scholar-officials generally recognized the need to do something about the situation of clansmen, they did not welcome them wholeheartedly into the civil service, regarding them as lazy, ignorant, and ethically unreliable.

During the Southern Ming the numerous imperial princes and clansmen were both blessing and bane. On one hand, wherever Ming loyalists gathered, there also was likely to be some prince or another who would serve as a rallying figure or, more rarely, assume actual leadership of resistance groups. But since these princes never had been in contact with one another previously, nor had they any experience in national politics, their perspectives and followings tended to be parochial, and their leadership produced many disparate, often competing centers of loyalist activity. As for those clansmen whose status had brought ennui or destitution to them under the Ming, when the Ch'ing offered them honorable treatment if they submitted and material support at their due level for the rest of their lives,[46] many changed allegiances easily to the Ch'ing side. Of course, the Ch'ing too had a good deal of trouble with these ubiquitous princes and clansmen, both as opponents and as untrustworthy collaborators. And the cost of maintaining such completely parasitic symbols was difficult for the Ch'ing as well to bear, especially in view of the urgent need for revenues to carry out the conquest. But fear of adverse political ramifications if they reneged on their promise to the Ming imperial clansmen kept the Ch'ing committed to their policy of hospitality.[47]

The condition of the Ming imperial princes was but one case of the erosion of status in the late Ming. In virtually every social sector one can find evidence of severe strain on traditionally accepted relations between superiors and inferiors—for instance, landlords and tenants, masters and servants, employees and workers, literati and nonliterati. The first half of the seventeenth century stands out in Chinese history for the frequency and virulence of such things as: revolts of indentured servants against household heads, from whom goods, freedom, and self-humiliation were demanded; rent-withholding against land-lords, which was incited by a variety of unfair practices; strikes by mining, industrial, and transport personnel, stemming from both governmental mis-management and regional or periodic economic disjunctions; counterattacks by religious sects and illegal, underground organizations against the suppressive authorities; the aforementioned army mutinies and mass rural uprisings, usually because of starvation wrought by both bureaucratic and natural calamities; and banditry of every kind—local or regional, from the hills or lakes, marshes or seas—which fed on all the other kinds of disruption. Of course, when a dynasty is in decline, things go wrong more badly and more irreparably than in healthier times. But the late Ming is distinctive for the blatancy and pervasiveness of the spirit of revolt in its society. Modern scholarship has tended to see this as a period of emergent class struggle and has focused mainly on landlord-tenant and master-bondservant conflicts.[48] But wider inquiry has shown that breakdowns in status relationships were occurring even within social classes, for instance, between older and younger, or senior and junior members of the same family or organization.[49]

It seems undeniable that this social destabilization was caused at least as much by the multiple forces of early modern economic change as by the failings of Ming government, and that the climate of fear, apprehension, and distrust in late Ming society hindered the formation and success of grassroots resistance movements in the Southern Ming.[50] But this condition, and the general militari-zation of the society that it entailed, were exceedingly troublesome for both the Ming and the Ch'ing.[51] Suffice it to point out here that by the mid-1640s these social "contradictions" had developed to the point that the arts of peace had to await the application of the arts of war. No ameliorative social policies could have been instituted by either the Ming or the Ch'ing until one side or the other took and held communities by force, not only from the other, but also from all the forces of armed conflict that abounded. The cutting edge of the conquest literally was military, and it was in the military sector that the Ming had engendered its most serious case of status repudiation.

CHAPTER ONE

First Stand:
The Hung-kuang Regime

I N early April 1644, as the rebel armies of Li Tzu-ch'eng were advancing inexorably across northern Shan-hsi Province toward the northern capital, Pei-ching, officials in the southern, auxiliary capital, Nan-ching, grew more anxious about confused, irregular, and forbidding reports of developments in the North. On April 12, the Ch'ung-chen emperor in Pei-ching authorized the transfer of any loyal forces that could aid the northern capital, and he specifically ordered Shan-tung Regional Commander Liu Tse-ch'ing to come to his defense.[1] But Liu disregarded this order and instead moved southward, and other commanders in the Yang-tzu region never received orders to head north. In any case, they were not prepared to do so. Although the southwestern parts of the Southern Metropolitan Area (Nan Chih-li), had repulsed threats from the "roving bandits" several years earlier,[2] that area now had no large, standing army apart from the regular garrison commands designated for the defense of the Yang-tzu River and Nan-ching. Moreover, officials there had reason to believe that the heir-designate, or the emperor himself, might soon come to Nan-ching, in which case it would be important to have all lower-Yang-tzu forces in readiness there.[3] Ming forces upriver, in the central lakes region, were substantial in numbers but also were occupied with restoring control in Hu-kuang Province, which recently had been vacated by the rebel army of Chang Hsien-chung; and, anyway, they were too distant. Armies that might have responded, those in Nan Chih-li north of the Huai River, were in disarray under pressure from units of the Great Shun regime (of Li Tzu-ch'eng). Plagued by mutinies, desertions, and cowardice, they were more concerned to seek refuge south of the Huai than to save the emperor in Pei-ching.[4]

Not long after midnight on April 25, as rebel forces swarmed the capital and began penetrating the Forbidden City, the Ch'ung-chen emperor committed suicide by hanging himself in a red pavilion on Coal Hill just north of the Inner Palace.[5] But not until May 5 did even the news that Pei-ching had fallen reach the Ming governor at Huai-an, where "half the people who heard this did not believe it."[6] The next day when the southern capital was informed, the senior official there, Nan-ching Minister of War and Grand Adjutant Shih K'o-fa, met with his fellow high-ranking officials and issued a call to arms (*chiao*), intending to assemble an army to "succor the sovereign" (*ch'in wang*). But then they thought, into what situation would such a force be heading? Conditions in the South were unsteady and those in the North still were unclear. For instance, where now was the sovereign whom they wished to succor? Shih K'o-fa crossed the Yang-tzu and began making preparations at the P'u-k'ou garrison; but beyond that little was done, and those who had begun organizing volunteers from the "grasses and marshes" further south were told to desist.[7]

> Each time the important elders of the South gathered at the Discussion Hall, they could only look at each other with knit brows and nothing to say. Some would just look up at the room screens and exclaim in anguish and frustration, "What can be done when we don't know what's happening?" Finally, they would kick the floor with the toes of their boots, sigh heavily, and one by one depart.[8]

On May 15 the first reliable word of the Ch'ung-chen emperor's death reached Huai-an, and within three days the top officials in Nan-ching realized that they would have to form a new court.[9]

This news greatly shocked the southern leadership, and as they moved to cope with such destabilized conditions, their need to reinforce unity, cooperation, and a common identity was expressed in both symbolic and pragmatic ways. Ironically, what ensued was the self-destruction of a composite political elite. In accommodating dissatisfied elements, the officials who established the first Southern Ming regime in Nan-ching were especially eager to placate the military. This was natural, since the exigent situation put a premium on military capability. But the military proceeded to push its gains to lengths, and in ways, that the most prestigious leaders of the bureaucracy and of the southern scholar-official stratum were unwilling to accept. To garner support in their bid for increased power, the militarists promoted alliances among themselves and other resentful elements that had been shunted aside by the bureaucracy in general, and by the "righteous" element in particular. Eager to ally themselves with the militarists were imperial clansmen, eunuchs, and officials whose careers had been obstructed by the now preponderant Tung-lin and Fu She factions, especially those who had been blacklisted as members of the "eunuch clique" and dismissed from government after the downfall of Wei Chung-hsien eighteen years before.

These alliances, and the crudeness with which they were brought into play, soon elicited a reaction from the "righteous" leaders, which ended the spirit of compromise and marked the advent of a determined struggle over power and principles. The gradual defeat of the "pure" faction, and the failure of even respected moderates to survive this political strife, left the Nan-ching court almost devoid of statesmen—and of popular support. Those who "won" this conflict did so at the expense of destroying their prize, the ability to exercise the power and influence that they felt had been wrongly denied them in the past. Stung by the severity of "righteous" rebuffs, the leader of the ascendant elements soon was put on the defensive; and, in order to bolster his position, he adopted many nearsighted policies, the deleterious effects of which he later was unable to contain. His regime became paranoid, isolated, and, along with the monarch to whom it was wed, unable to govern. The history of this court traditionally has stressed heavily the character of a few major figures—heroes and villains, martyrs and traitors; and the present account, too, will assign some praise and some blame. But these personalities should be viewed within a configuration of political forces that seemed to have a dynamic of its own.

Competition began immediately over the choice of a new ruler. It began in earnest because, of the several princes then in the South,[10] the one who was most readily available and most directly related to the imperial line, the Prince of Fu (Chu Yu-sung), had reason to hold a grudge against the Tung-lin. Moreover, he had fallen into the hands of the most powerful militarists. It was precisely this prince's deceased father, the offspring of the Wan-li emperor and his most beloved, Imperial Concubine Cheng, whom the Tung-lin partisans had barred from being named Heir in favor of the emperor's firstborn son, several decades before.[11] The partisan controversies spawned by this case had kept the bureaucracy in turmoil ever since. Even though those controversies had not affected or interested the current Prince of Fu or his father on their opulent estate in Ho-nan, different elements in the bureaucracy respectively hoped and feared that the trenchantly contested issues of three past reigns,* which to a certain extent had been decided in favor of the Tung-lin in 1629, could be reevaluated under a Fu monarchy.[12]

In view of this, some temporized, pointing out that they still did not know what had become of the Ch'ung-chen emperor's heir-designate or his two younger sons,[13] all of whom had been in Pei-ching just prior to its fall. What would happen if some prince were enthroned and the heir later appeared to claim his right to rule? Others invoked the principle of "selecting worthiness

---

*Wan-li (1573–1619), T'ai-ch'ang (1620), and T'ien-ch'i (1621–27).

over seniority [in descent]" and advanced the candidacy of the Prince of Luh
(Chu Ch'ang-fang), who also had fled his estate in the North and entered Nan
Chih-li. Even though this latter prince was known chiefly as a literary dilettante,
with a passion for antiques and "fingernails six or seven inches long, which he
protected with bamboo tubes," [14] still, he could be touted as more worthy than
the Prince of Fu, who had a reputation for lasciviousness, ignorance, and
irresponsibility. But few people, even high officials, knew much at all about these
princes, and most were indifferent about the choice. At the same time, there was
great anxiety that *some* prince be elevated soon to stabilize the South and much
self-interested concern among political figures that they each be seen as having
supported all along *that* prince, whoever it was to be. Consequently, in the few
days after news of the emperor's death reached Nan-ching, much furtive consultation, cautious jockeying for position, and covering of tracks took place among
the leading civil and military officials of Nan Chih-li.

But a consensus in favor of the Prince of Fu formed rapidly when it became
known that he was being protected in the Huai region, and supported for the
throne, by the military commanders in northern Nan Chih-li upon whom
defense of the Southeast now would depend. Two figures who joined this
military coalition somewhat belatedly but then became its leaders were the
aforementioned regional commander, Liu Tse-ch'ing, and the Ming viceroy at
Feng-yang, Ma Shih-ying. Both men had reason to resent the dominant element
in the civil bureaucracy and to hope for enhanced status if the "pure stream"
could be blocked. [15] In Nan-ching, certain military nobles and other political
opportunists picked up on this tune, and when the "hundred officials" convened
to ceremonially report their choice of the Prince of Fu to the Ming dynastic
ancestors, an ugly altercation erupted. Certain prominent civil officials were
charged with having obstructed the selection, and the senior military noble in
Nan-ching, Commissioner-in-Chief for River Control Earl Liu K'ung-chao,
actually drew his sword on the outspoken head of the Han-lin Academy, Chiang
Yüeh-kuang. [16] Similar tense confrontations between civil and military officials
marred all the subsequent stages in setting up the new regime.

Having been transported down the Grand Canal by a large task force
assembled by the commanders north of the Yang-tzu, the Prince of Fu, somewhat disheveled, arrived by boat at the main moorage northeast of Nan-ching on
June 3. And the following day, when he formally was greeted there by the
ranking civil officials and military nobles of the southern capital, he was very self-
effacing and declined to consider enthronement, bewailing both the hardships he
had endured and his unworthiness to rule. [17] Nevertheless, on June 5 he was
escorted in full procession, via the Great Ancestor's tomb, into Nan-ching's
palace compound. Common people lined the way, looking on respectfully in a

happy mood, putting out fragrant flowers and colorful lanterns, as good omens circulated among them.[18]

But when the prince again received the welcome and advice of various officials in his temporary quarters, the *ya-men* of the grand commandant, the proceedings were disrupted by the loud complaint of Marquis T'ang Kuo-tso that the Ministry of Revenues was holding back military provisions. T'ang soon was shut up by Acting Minister of Rites Lü Ta-ch'i;[19] but the military nobles were vociferous again when discussion was held over whether the prince should be urged to take the throne directly as Emperor, or whether he first should assume the tentative title of Regent (*chien-kuo*)[20] until circumstances had become clearer. Most officials favored a temporary regency, perhaps with enthronement following in about a month. But Earl Liu K'ung-chao was among those who pressed for immediate enthronement, and his cohort continued to cast suspicion of obstructionism, and of "having other ideas" about the selection, on civil officials who argued for a more moderate pace.[21] Moreover, at this same time deliberations began on the selection of grand secretaries and top ministers for the new court. Wishing to accommodate the malcontented military, civil officials broke precedent and allowed some military nobles to participate in the nominating court conference (*hui-t'ui*) whereby recommendations for such important positions customarily were decided upon.[22] Liu K'ung-chao then surprised the assembled officials by nominating himself to be a grand secretary; and when he was told that there was no precedent for military nobles serving in the Grand Secretariat, he proposed as a substitute for himself Ma Shih-ying.[23]

On June 6 the Prince of Fu, who previously had said that he "just wanted to take refuge in Eastern Che-chiang" and probably was sincere in disclaiming any desire for the throne, responded to the customary "three urgings" of the Nan-ching officials by agreeing to become Regent.[24] This was followed just two weeks later by his enthronement as Emperor, with the reign title Hung-kuang.[25] The proclamations that were issued on these two occasions constitute virtual catalogues of remedies for the ills of late Ming sociopolitics and of palliatives for all classes of people.[26] They remind us that political leaders of the day were acutely aware of many problems and not totally absorbed in petty, self-centered clique squabbles and machinations. But unless ways could be found to reverse disintegrative tendencies among factions in the bureaucracy and other components of the political elite, little could be done about those ills.

Consequently, when decisions were made in appointing charter ministers for the new government, care was exercised to maintain a "righteous" majority while also appeasing other elements. On the "righteous" side, grand secretaryships went to Shih K'o-fa and Chiang Yüeh-kuang; Chang Shen-yen was made Minister of Personnel; and the influential post of Censor-in-Chief was offered to the doyen of the "purists," Liu Tsung-chou; while several other important ministries were put into the hands of Tung-lin and Fu She sympathizers. For moderates, there were two grand secretaries, Kao Hung-t'u, an upright and reasonably capable man, formerly the Nan-ching Minister of Revenues, who had managed to maintain an independent stance in partisan politics, and Wang To, a man of literary repute whose record in governance was indifferent. And a number of lesser positions went to men who held no clear factional allegiance. As a concession to the military, and as a reward for "merit in setting the plan" (i.e., for supporting the Prince of Fu), Ma Shih-ying also was made a grand secretary and given high rank through concurrent ministerial appointments and the bestowal of honorifics; initially, however, he was instructed to continue functioning as Viceroy at Feng-yang.[27] By this arrangement, Ma formally was placed on the same level as the leading figure in Nan-ching, Shih K'o-fa (who remained, concurrently, Minister of War), while at the same time he was kept away from the court.

But a reversal of the positions of these men, Shih and Ma, quickly followed, and this had important consequences for the Hung-kuang regime. Simultaneously two movements occurred. Ma Shih-ying, without waiting for authorization, moved his large army (on twelve hundred boats) from Feng-yang to Nan-ching and was there in person to enter the Grand Secretariat when the new emperor was enthroned. Also, the various commanders in Nan Chih-li north of the Yang-tzu, led by Liu Tse-ch'ing, clamored for Shih K'o-fa to come into the field and serve as a coordinator among them.[28] The prospect of this turnabout alarmed many in Nan-ching, and some extreme public statements were made, comparing Shih to maligned worthies and Ma to traitorous villains of the past.[29] But Shih, perhaps unenthusiastic about working closely with either Ma or this emperor, perhaps feeling that he was the best man for the coordinator's role, and, in any case, wishing to accommodate the commanders, publicly expressed his desire to atone for his failure to save the former emperor and to be allowed to lay his life on the front lines.[30]

To understand the negative reaction of the southern sociopolitical leadership to this change, we must look more closely at the backgrounds of Shih and Ma, both of whom probably looked on themselves in much the same way, that is, as prominent civil officials who, appropriate to the current emergency, had considerable experience in military affairs. But the differences between them, though exaggerated by others, were crucial at that time and reflect prevailing attitudes about the proper relation between *wen* and *wu*. Shih approximated the ideal of the all-around statesman. A native of traditional China's heartland, Honan, he was poor but well schooled as a boy, and he became the favorite protégé of a Tung-lin leader who was martyred in opposing Wei Chung-hsien. Shih's

early record in local, civil governmental affairs had been exemplary. And in the
1630s, when he was assigned to help defend southwestern Nan Chih-li against
rebel attack, he performed so well that he soon was placed in charge of defense in
the whole middle-lower Yang-tzu region. He was admired for immersing
himself in the action, braving dangers and sharing hardships right along with his
troops. But he led the military men under him patronizingly, by offering a
sterling example of active, effective civility, and by showing his men that he as
their superior really cared about them and their common cause. He was averse to
applying coercion, except against an implacable enemy, and above all he saw
himself as a harmonizer. Indeed, he devoted himself more consistently and
sincerely to reconciling conflicts than any other figure in the Southern Ming.[31]

Ma Shih-ying, on the other hand, was a native of remote Kuei-chou
Province in the relatively undeveloped far Southwest (and later he appropriated
a contingent of wolf troops from there to be his personal guard). He could boast
of no special literary talent or association with outstanding scholar-officials, and
he chafed at being considered rather crude. His first tour of duty in local
government had ended in charges of corruption, removal from office, and
banishment to the frontiers, after which he bided his time in Nan-ching, com-
miserating with other political losers. Through the machinations of a figure who
was anathema in "righteous" circles, he had been recalled to office and made
Viceroy at Feng-yang in 1642.[32] Although he was criticized for the rapacious
liberties he allowed to the soldiers under his command,[33] he was a competent
strategist and got along well with generals by seeming to be one of them, as well
as one with them, in the business of fighting.

> Since Shih-ying long had consorted with the Four Commanders [north of
> the Yang-tzu, when they came to visit the court], he even more [assidu-
> ously] exhausted every means to fawn on them and do their bidding ... [to
> the point of] ordering his son to serve them wine, and to kneel and rise as
> though he were their son or nephew. [Chiang] Yüeh-kuang heard of this
> and asked Shih-ying if it was true. Shih-ying knew what he meant, and after
> a long, nervous pause, said: "Sure. So what? In all that I do, I'm never afraid
> to condescend. The pride of men like that mustn't be injured...." Chiang
> replied: "... Each official station has its proper form and, moreover, exists
> to pursue only the Great Way, You should much abide in the Correct to
> lead them, and amass absolute Sincerity to move them. Thereby you
> will awaken their resolve. No one is devoid of Goodness...." Shih-ying
> laughed heartily at this, thinking it abstruse and far off the mark in
> human affairs.[34]

Among military men, also, there were different attitudes about the proper
relation of *wen* and *wu*. By no means was obstreperousness on the part of
commanders in the field always attributable to rejection of, or dissatisfaction

with, the traditional subordination of military to civil. Rather, they wanted to have their just due in that relationship, and they wanted the civil officials to live up to their side of it. Recalcitrance often appeared when soldiers and officers perceived civilians and civil officials as not only failing to do their part, but also as hampering the military's fulfillment of its traditional role. This attitude seems to have characterized most of the Hung-kuang commanders. But others in the military really wanted to reslice the pie of power. The ambitions of the hereditary military nobles were manifest and not difficult to understand. Those of Regional Commander Liu Tse-ch'ing, however, were more complex.

Early in life Liu had exhibited two contradictory propensities: to style himself as a literatus, and to kill people coldbloodedly. Because of the latter, he had been barred from taking the civil service examinations and instead had passed the military tests, eventually achieving success as a general. But his physical features were quite fair, and in many ways he sought acceptance among litterateurs, becoming pathological when they refused to grant him the respect he coveted.[35] When he addressed the emperor in court audience, Liu declared,

> The world of the [Ming] ancestors has been completely ruined by white-faced schoolboys. This whole bunch should be tied up in a high tower until after I have beaten the rebels. Then they could be taken and put to work dusting and cleaning, perhaps to earn some favor that way. Today I request terminating the civil service examinations to facilitate matters.[36]

He went on to urge, also, that an outstanding general be employed in an advisory capacity on par with the chief grand secretary. Naturally, he was inimical to Grand Secretary Chiang Yüeh-kuang (who at one point objected to the emperor's addressing the commanders as "Sir"); and it was to Chiang that he expressed his determination to kill all Tung-lin adherents, whom he blamed for ruining his father's career.[37] On the other hand, he naturally got along very well with Ma Shih-ying.

> Ever since [Liu] Tse-ch'ing murdered the censorial official [Han Ju-yü], people had treated him coolly. Now, when he came to court, people even more looked askance at him. Tse-ch'ing felt this and kept trying subtly to excuse his action. But Shih-ying laughingly scolded him, saying, "That murder really was nasty of you!" and went on teasing him vulgarly, startling those who overheard.[38]

Although Ma Shih-ying had the unsavory reputation of catering to military men, actually it was Shih K'o-fa who initiated plans to give the leading generals unprecedentedly free rein in managing their armies. Naturally, as Minister of War and Grand Adjutant, Shih had been prompt to submit plans to reorganize and strengthen the lower-Yang-tzu defense system and the Nan-ching imperial

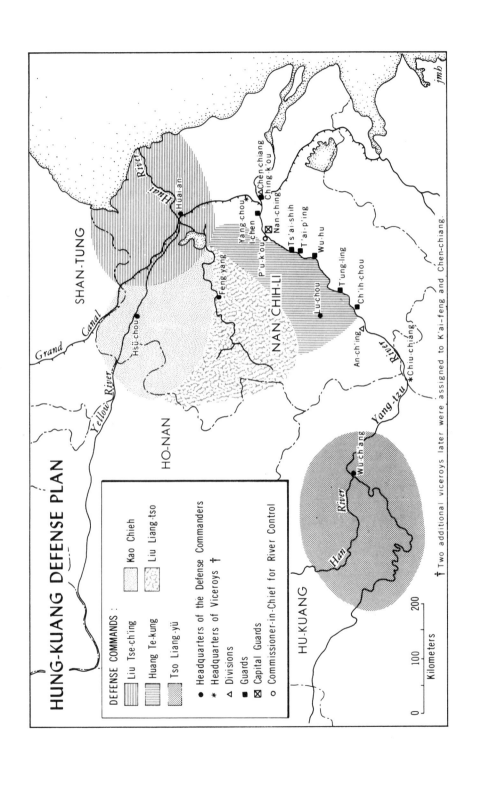

HUNG-KUANG DEFENSE PLAN

DEFENSE COMMANDS :

Liu Tse-ch'ing
Huang Te-kung
Tso Liang-yü
Kao Chieh
Liu Liang-tso

● Headquarters of the Defense Commanders
✻ Headquarters of Viceroys †
△ Divisions
■ Guards
⊠ Capital Guards
○ Commissioner-in-Chief for River Control

† Two additional viceroys later were assigned to K'ai-feng and Chen-chiang.

SHAN-TUNG

HO-NAN

NAN CHIH-LI

HU-KUANG

Grand Canal

Yellow River

Huai River

Hsü-chou

Feng-yang

Huai-an

Yang-chou
Liu-chen
P'u-k'ou
Pai-chou
Ch'ih-chou
T'ung-ling
Wu-hu
Ta'i-p'ing
Ts'ai-shih
Nan-ching
Ching-k'ou
Chen-chiang

An-ch'ing

*Chiu-chiang

Yang-tzu River

Wu-ch'ang

Han River

Kilometers

0   100   200

jmb

guard, which was changed to conform to the Pei-ching pattern.[39] But beyond that, in consultation with the other grand secretaries, and reflecting general anxiety about the dangerously chaotic state of affairs among the armies in Nan Chih-li north of the Yang-tzu, Shih proposed that certain powerful and recently ennobled generals, with their semiprivate armies, constitute four defense commands (*chen*), which would radiate northward and westward from Nan-ching (see map 2).

(1) Kao Chieh was to station himself at Hsü-chou, to hold jurisdiction over the area between the Yellow* and Huai rivers in northwestern Nan Chih-li, and to be responsible for offense and defense in northern Ho-nan; (2) Liu Liang-tso was to station himself at Feng-yang, to hold jurisdiction over west-central Nan Chih-li south of the Huai River, and to be responsible for offense and defense in central and southern Ho-nan; (3) Huang Te-kung was to station himself at Lu-chou, to hold jurisdiction over central Nan Chih-li north of the Yang-tzu, and to be responsible for backing up Liu and Kao to his north (as well as guarding against possible untoward developments upstream on the Yang-tzu); and (4) Liu Tse-ch'ing was to station himself at Huai-an, to hold jurisdiction over that prefecture, and to be responsible for offense and defense in northeastern Nan Chih-li and southern Shan-tung. (Later an important fifth *chen* was designated, i.e., Tso Liang-yü and his sprawling, disparate army in central Hu-kuang Province.) The soldiers of each command were to supply their own food by cultivating abandoned or marginal lands; weapons, equipment, and other materiel were to be purchased with the proceeds of various taxes in each command's jurisdictional area. Moreover, each command, authorized to maintain 30,000 men (for Tso, 50,000), was to receive from the central government allocations of money and provisions at a level of twenty taels per soldier per year. Any territory recovered by a command was to become part of its jurisdiction; anyone who restored a locality was to be appointed the official there.[40]

This plan virtually gave away civil oversight in half the territory subject to Nan-ching's control. But it was hoped that, thereby, some semblance of order could be brought to the scene north of the lower Yang-tzu, where armies were contending with one another—and against stubbornly resistant townspeople—for major urban centers, the most readily available sources of walled protection, domicile, and requisitions. As it was put by a specially deputed troubleshooter, Wan Yüan-chi:

> Yang-chou, Lin-huai, Liu-ho—everywhere soldiers and civilians are in conflict. On the soldiers' side, there is little discipline; on the citizens' side, of

---

*During this period, the Yellow River flowed to the south of Shan-tung and joined with the Huai River at a point west of Huai-an.

late they have been even more contrary. So it has become a standoff across
city walls. The people take the soldiers to be bandits and will die before
letting them in, while the soldiers see the people as refractory and attack
them in cycles with no respite. If suddenly the [real] bandits should arrive,
the people surely will be taken by surprise and run away [rather than
defending their locales]. This truly is the greatest worry of the present
day.[41]

Especially troublesome were armies that recently had been displaced from other
regions under chaotic circumstances, or that were constituted in large proportion
by surrendered erstwhile roving-bandit forces. But even those that had been in
place for some time grew restive as other armies crowded in on them, worsening
breakdowns in normal supply patterns. Simply declaring the institution of four
defense commands did not immediately resolve these difficulties. When Huang
Te-kung, who had been at loggerheads with Kao Chieh, was being read an
authoritative peacemaking order from the Hung-kuang court, he got up, flailing
his arms, and, forcing the emissary to rise also, shouted: "Go away. Fast! Get out!
I don't recognize this proclamation!"[42] Viceroys and governors still were
assigned to duties both inside and outside the defense commanders' jursidictions.
But relations between these civil officials and the various *chen* were tense, as the
former strove to maintain their own revenues and protect the populace, and it
was all they could do to avoid open hostilities.[43] This was especially true in the
case of Shih K'o-fa, who established his headquarters at Yang-chou in order to
coordinate the four defense commands.

Shih's first and greatest difficulty as commander-in-chief north of the Yang-
tzu was dealing with Kao Chieh, a former rebel general under Li Tzu-ch'eng
who (because he had stolen Li's wife) defected from the rebels in 1635.[44]
Although Kao's men—the same stout fighting stock from Shen-hsi who made
Li's armies so formidable—had performed as well as any on the government
side, they remained very much Kao's personal force and never shook the onus of
being "bandits" who raided at will. In spite of this, Shih K'o-fa saw the best
potential in Kao for reasserting Ming power in the North, and it was imperative
that Kao be disentangled from the conflicts he had caused near the Yang-tzu and
moved to the front lines on the Yellow River. But Kao insisted on occupying the
wonderfully rich and beautiful city of Yang-chou as a place to "safely lodge his
family" before he could concentrate on the northward campaign. This first was
contested by other commanders, who also were "drooling over" that famous
entrepôt on the Grand Canal; then it was contested by the people of Yang-chou
themselves, who barred the gates and responded in kind to assaults by Kao's
soldiers on townspeople. Violence escalated and tempers flared, until a *chin-shih*
degree-holder, who tried to mediate the dispute but showed signs of favoring

Kao, was cut to pieces in the very presence of city officials by an angry mob.[45]

Partly in order to neutralize and pacify Yang-chou, Shih chose that city to be his own headquarters. But when he arrived there, he vowed not to enter until the trouble with Kao Chieh had been resolved. "Orders? What orders?" asked Kao disdainfully, brushing aside a document issued by Shih. "Didn't you see me earlier when I rode my horse in the Hall of Great Majesty [in the Nan-ching imperial city]?"[46] Relinquishing his personal guard as a gesture of trust, Shih entered Kao's camp and stayed there—some say under virtual house arrest—for over a month, trying to influence Kao by personal example, "like water working on a rock." Although many have extolled Shih's virtue in this effort and fulsomely portrayed the great transformation that Shih's presence wrought in Kao's attitude, others closer to the scene saw Kao as having the upper hand, alternately ingratiating himself and applying pressure on Shih.[47] At considerable length, Shih was able to get the various commanders, including Kao, to assume their designated stations in the defense commands, but only by making concessions in ways that caused him to lose respect and leverage with the people of Yang-chou, as well as with the commanders.[48] Shih never achieved the effectiveness that his position implied. Always constrained by the four defense commanders, rather than vice versa, he often failed to place his own men where they were needed. Thus, it is not surprising that, when the chips were down, some of Shih's own frustrated lieutenants submitted readily to the Ch'ing and became leading figures in the subsequent conquest of southern Nan Chih-li and northern Chiang-hsi.[49]

Shih K'o-fa's relation with Kao Chieh, and its effects, illustrate a problem which was to grow steadily more serious in the course of the Southern Ming. That is, civil officials clung tenaciously to moral suasion and righteous exhortation as the only valid means of handling the military. They rejected or ignored as unfit company those who did not respond to such appeals, rather than working—by deception and force, if necessary—on the material and organizational problems that fostered rebellious attitudes. Shih K'o-fa was much less deluded in this way than many of his peers and successors; nevertheless, he pursued harmony at a regrettably high price and eschewed coercion when persuasion failed. In spite of Kao's encouraging response to Shih's influence, the hatred he had earned among other generals resulted in his being assassinated at a crucial point in the southern defense; and Shih K'o-fa's hopes, which he had placed on the character of this one man, collapsed along with Kao's army.[50] This style of leadership among scholar-officials became even less effective as conditions in the South became more thoroughly militarized, and especially as larger and larger portions of the Southern Ming fighting force came to be made up of former rebels who had "come to their proper allegiance" rather than submit to the Ch'ing.

Regardless of the extent to which Shih K'o-fa created his own problems with the four defense commanders, scholar-officials south of the Yang-tzu were inclined to blame their truculence on Ma Shih-ying, who was charged with encouraging them, by both covert direction and overt example, to throw their weight around, expect undeserved rewards, and interfere in court politics. This criticism sharpened dramatically in mid-July when the prestigiously "pure" scholar and philosopher Liu Tsung-chou (who had demurred when offered the post of censor-in-chief and first had sought assurances of the emperor's support) submitted a series of scathing memorials. In these he lambasted certain hereditary military nobles, eunuchs, political opportunists, and—with special vigor—Ma Shih-ying and the four defense commanders, calling them "small men" who were dragging down the level of the court. Liu charged that they had speciously claimed "merit in setting the plan" so that, in the commanders' case, they could acquire noble titles, and in Ma's case, he could presumptuously insert himself into the Grand Secretariat. Moreover, Liu urged that Ma be sent forthwith back to Feng-yang, "and then if any generals do not follow orders, they immediately should be dealt with according to the great laws of the court." [51] This was directly reinforced by a crusading censorial official who, in an extremely emotional court audience (which he referred to as a "suicide mission"), charged Ma with "ten capital crimes" and led the dumbstruck emperor temporarily to consider accepting Ma's resignation. [52]

But Ma really did not intend to resign. Instead, faced with this sort of opposition, he hardened and closed ranks more tightly with all those who had reason to resist the idealistic element in the bureaucracy. In so doing, Ma achieved his short-term goal of expunging rivals and consolidating his power. But he also unleashed forces and encouraged tendencies that went beyond his power to control, soon weakened the Hung-kuang regime, and hastened its demise. [53] Let us examine developments in Ma's "constituencies" one by one:

1. The *hereditary military nobles* and the *defense commanders* became thoroughly politicized. The former pressed outrageously for institutional changes, such as selecting grand secretaries and ministry heads through the Chief Military Commissions, rather than through court conferences conducted by the Minister of Personnel, and making consultation mandatory with the hereditary military nobles in all matters of civil personnel appointments, ministry procedures, and governmental planning by the emperor. [54] Though none of these was approved, the military nobles still managed to affect civil governance in

more negative and disorderly ways. They violently attacked, both verbally and at knife-point, Minister of Personnel Chang Shen-yen, criticizing him for appointing only civil officials to posts, thereby neglecting military men, and for forming a clique by nominating certain figures whom they did not favor.[55] In spite of protests from officials who pointed out that Chang had complete authority to make whatever civil appointments and nominations he saw fit, whereas the nobles had none, and in spite of urgings from both the emperor and Shih K'o-fa to resolve this conflict between *wen* and *wu*, Earl Liu K'ung-chao in particular was unyielding. Through an ally in the bureaucracy (who coveted Chang's position), he charged that Chang had been one of a group that had opposed the military nobles by trying to obstruct the emperor's enthronement, and he soon succeeded in hounding Chang out of office—the first casualty on the "righteous" side.[56]

In the course of this, Liu K'ung-chao did succeed (with Ma Shih-ying's approval) in getting the emperor formally to open the "channels of remonstrance" (*yen-lu*), that is, grant censorial impeachment powers, to hereditary military nobles. This authorization soon was rescinded;[57] however, military leaders, the defense commanders in particular, began to indict court officials and memorialize to the throne on political matters without inhibition.

> Huang Te-kung kept a keen eye on the courtiers, always thinking about who was up to what. If anyone so much as nipped at him, a memorial would go up immediately demanding that the party be sent before his army and executed.[58]

But it was Liu Tse-ch'ing who led the counterattack against Liu Tsung-chou, saying that he should be put to death for endangering the throne by urging the emperor to personally lead a campaign northward, and for fomenting unrest among the commanders by threatening to remove their newly bestowed titles.[59] The spectacle of a super-righteous censor-in-chief being impeached by a homocidal militarist set scholar-officialdom agape. The emperor admonished all parties, saying,

> This contention between *wen* and *wu* grows more severe day by day.... If this fire-and-water [relation] is not resolved, and spears and shields are turned and raised [internally], then affairs of the world will deteriorate insufferably. Moreover, what kind of ruler do you think I am [to countenance this]?![60]

But Liu Tsung-chou's predictably sharp retort, that Tse-ch'ing in one stroke had wiped away all the organizational principles, laws, and regulations of the dynasty, and calling for him to be tried by a court assembly, charged the atmosphere even more.[61]

The politicization of the military did not work uniformly to Ma Shih-ying's favor, however. In particular, the most powerful commander upriver, Tso Liang-yü, though illiterate (like most generals who came up through the ranks), had been deeply impressed early in his career by the character of a Tung-lin activist under whom he had served. Consequently, he was predisposed to dislike Ma Shih-ying, who reciprocated by delaying Tso's designation as the fifth defense commander and otherwise withheld cooperation, while avoiding any open breach with a figure whom he feared justifiably. Tso, now old, ill, and losing his judgment, was easily swayed by those around him and listened credulously to talk of how the court was being corrupted by Ma.[62] Indeed, it was Tso's eventual decision to intervene actively in court affairs that spelled Ma's downfall.

2. Leaping into the fray enthusiastically were certain *imperial clansmen*, who made charges against figures inimical to Ma in order to gain his favor and thereby receive appointments to bureaucratic positions, which otherwise they probably could not have obtained. These men were criticized for intruding on central governmental affairs, as well as for circumventing the proper channels in submitting their memorials. But the emperor was partial to the clansmen, who, after all, were "his own family," and screened them from further criticism. Largely as a result of attacks on him by the imperial clansman Chu T'ung-lei, Grand Secretary Chiang Yüeh-kuang left office (after a bitter row with Ma Shih-ying) on October 9, 1644—the second casualty on the "righteous" side.[63]

3. Most explosive, however, was Ma Shih-ying's tactic of reemploying *blacklisted bureaucrats*. The first and most controversial case of this, which opened the door to many others, was Ma's recommendation of the one figure, branded as part of the "eunuch clique," who was most abominated by the Fu She—Juan Ta-ch'eng. Ma and Juan had been associates for many years, ever since they had found themselves together, bitter and out of office, in Nan-ching in the mid-1630s. Subsequently Juan Ta-ch'eng, though still not able to reenter government himself because of his condemnation in the "cases of perniciousness" (*ni-an*) early in the Ch'ung-chen reign, did manage to effect Ma Shih-ying's return to office and his appointment as Viceroy at Feng-yang. For this, Ma owed him a debt of gratitude; and because one of Juan's personae was that of military strategist and patron of "knights-errant," Ma was able to recommend him as talented in martial matters.[64]

Indeed, Juan's propensity to surround himself somewhat theatrically with footloose swordsmen had provided the impetus in 1638 for the Fu She in Nan-ching to issue a "Manifesto to Thwart Chaos in the Auxiliary Capital,"[65] which heaped social ostracization on top of political purgation and steeled Juan's resolve to some day reap vengeance on his persecutors. The depth of hatred felt toward Juan by the Fu She activists is not easy to explain. His dealings with those in power during the ascendance of the eunuch dictator, Wei Chung-hsien, were neither unique nor blatant and did not justify the opprobrium that later was hurled at him by the purists. Basically, the latter seem to have felt that Juan's overweening desire for public office, combined with his calculating, egotistical, and vengeful character, made him a man of sinister potential. Events of the Hung-kuang interlude bore out such fears; but to the extent that Juan was excessively goaded and humiliated by the partisans, their suspicions also may have been self-confirming.

> [Juan] was like a fierce tiger trapped in a well, surrounded on all sides by men who attacked it with all their might. On the day when he jumped out, those who escaped his bite were few![66]

Ma Shih-ying's initial recommendation of Juan on July 9, to be a vice minister of War, elicited a furor that took even Ma aback and thoroughly bewildered the politically naive emperor, who could not understand why so much fuss was being made over one man. Ma temporarily was blocked by the insistence of opponents that recommendations for such high offices be made through court conferences, a route that Ma was unwilling to take. And censorial officials, in particular, beat the drums against betraying the will of the former emperor by overturning the "cases of perniciousness" and allowing men such as Juan to be reemployed.[67] But Ma bided his time and tried again in late September, whereupon Juan was appointed by a "direct edict" from the emperor.[68] This circumvention of customary review by high-ranking ministers had aroused great controversy and led to calamity in the T'ien-ch'i and Ch'ung-chen reigns;[69] and now the emperor's refusal (under Ma Shih-ying's presumed guidance) to renounce either the use of "direct edicts" for appointments or the restitution of previously blacklisted men, led to the resignations of not only Liu Tsung-chou—another major casualty on the "righteous" side—but also the astute moderate, Kao Hung-t'u, whose departure from the Grand Secretariat in early November left Ma Shih-ying with virtually an open field on that level.[70]

Ma did not immediately make a clean sweep of the rest of the court. But gradually, as figures associated with the "righteous" element left office—in disgust or under fire from Ma's faction—they were replaced by "pernicious" figures, others who had been at odds with the Fu She, and a few factional turncoats who prostituted themselves to Ma for their own advantage.[71] Not until the early spring of 1646 did the court become completely dominated by the so-called Ma-Juan clique.

If this had been a complete political changing of the guard, then the court might have become more effective as its leadership was made more homogeneous. But this was far from the case. First, the competition between factions thoroughly partisanized everything the regime tried to do, from the most symbolic to the most pragmatic. For instance, numerous honorific gestures were made to assuage and propitiate the spirits of historical personages who had been wronged under the Ming dynasty (especially ones associated with the southern capital).[72] This soon became a public contest to see which faction would get honors granted or restored to its own forebears and denied or removed from the forebears of the opposition.[73]

More serious was the question of policy toward Ming officials in the North, who almost automatically had fallen under suspicion of having aided, or at least of having failed to resist, the rebel takeover. Popular feeling against collaborators was strong,[74] and maintaining a "hard line" against them was one means of keeping alive the sense of outrage that would have to undergird any restoration of Ming control in the North. On the other hand, the Hung-kuang regime needed the support of capable officials wherever they might be, and Shih K'o-fa soberly reminded everyone that it was not just those caught, by chance, in the North who were culpable for the Ch'ung-chen emperor's demise.[75] Moreover, as it became known that many in the North had turned to serving the Manchus, it seemed wiser to announce severe punishments for a few undisputed traitors while leaving paths open for the majority to return to the fold.[76] Balancing these considerations and making judgments in individual cases (usually in the absence of clear evidence or information) would have been difficult even under stable circumstances. But in the midst of clique warfare, the matter became grossly distorted. Many who had behaved unpardonably in the North went unmolested in the South, and some even were reemployed in government, while others were persecuted mercilessly in order to implicate their innocent relatives and associates.[77] This erratic, arbitrary manner kindled more outrage against the Hung-kuang regime than against the rebels, and it was ineffectual in undermining collaboration with the Ch'ing.

Moreover, the ascendance of the Ma-Juan faction was pushed to a vengeful extreme that neither Ma nor the military leaders fully condoned. In fact, the term "Ma-Juan" is misleading, because after Ma secured Juan's appointment, the two actually did not associate closely. Rather, Ma found himself in the position of having to brake Juan's purgative schemes and even Juan's ambitions to rival Ma's own power; thus, a state of enmity developed between them.[78] Others besides Juan, such as Grand Secretary Ts'ai I-ch'en, Minister of Personnel Chang Chieh, and Censor-in-Chief Yang Wei-yüan, pursued real or supposed enemies to foolishly counterproductive lengths, and sought to bolster their positions by admitting to office large numbers of men whose chief qualification was the means to pay the "fees."[79] Yang, in particular, pressed on obsessively, even as all civil and military order crumbled around the Hung-kuang regime, to have republished the *San-ch'ao yao-tien* ("Essential Matters of Three Reigns"), an anti-Tung-lin "white paper" first issued in 1626 at the behest of Wei Chung-hsien.[80]

> As for [Ma] Shih-ying, he basically did not intend to harm the dynastic altars, but they became a mound [of ruins]. He had no taste for heavy bribery, but the gates of graft were opened wide. He had no desire to cut down the pure element, but it was completely driven out.... How could anyone say that he was not a world-class criminal?[81]

4. The situation among the *eunuchs* was typical for the Ming: The chief eunuchs were sought after as allies by leaders of factions in the bureaucracy. Outer Court politics thus became entwined with politics inside the eunuch establishment; and the eunuchs' role in affairs expanded or contracted in inverse relation to the strength of various emperors and chief grand secretaries.[82]

The (eunuch) Grand Commandant and Director of Ceremonial for the auxiliary capital, Han Tsan-chou, long had been on good terms with Juan Ta-ch'eng. Moreover, it is said that Juan also made a special effort to host eunuchs who came fleeing to Nan-ching from conditions in the North in 1644, in order to use them and Han to inform the southern monarch about Juan's virtues and educate him in partisan affairs.[83] But Han, who had long experience in the Directorate of Ceremonial, found more favor in "righteous" circles for knowing and trying to maintain the proper way of doing things, which included "knowing his place." And a split soon developed between Han and the emperor's own eunuchs, who had been with him during his days as the Prince of Fu in Ho-nan, and who not only were ignorant of court principles and protocol, but also tended to encourage the emperor's indulgence in wine, women, and song. Han eventually resigned because of this.[84]

More sinister was the reestablishment, in spite of numerous protests from officials, of the infamous Eastern Depot, a eunuch agency in the Inner Court which had operated like a secret service, capable of incarcerating, interrogating, and torturing officials apart from regular judicial procedures.[85] Of course, the reactivation of this feared and hated institution was a prelude to the various political persecutions that grew in intensity through the Hung-kuang period. Although Ma Shih-ying probably welcomed the eunuchs' diversion of the emperor's attention away from court business, it cannot validly be claimed that he approved their expansion into inquisitorial activities.

5. The *emperor*, Chu Yu-sung, was the wrong man in the wrong place at the wrong time. For good reason he had been reluctant to assume the throne. Reared in luxury and theretofore having been strictly barred from national politics, he never had developed the strength of character, decisiveness, or knowledge of public affairs that the times now required. Nevertheless, having been propelled to

the pinnacle of state by the ambitions of other men, he did try hard in the first months of his reign to fulfill the duties of Emperor, freely acknowledging his need for guidance and for the assistance of able grand secretaries. Contrary to common assumption, however, Ma Shih-ying was not his favorite from the beginning. The emperor only came to rely on Ma out of childlike fear and desperation as political feuds drove away Chiang Yüeh-kuang and the man the emperor most preferred, Kao Hung-t'u.[86] At one point when Ma was under double indictment (by Liu Tsung-chou and by the censorial official Huang Shu) and had offered to resign, he secretly memorialized the emperor.

> "That Your Highness gained the throne was due to the efforts of this official and the four defense commanders. All the others were intent on supporting the Prince of Luh. If I am dismissed today, the Prince of Luh will be exalted tomorrow." The emperor believed his words and cried like rain for a long while. After that, he left all court affairs completely to Ma and just wandered around madly in the palace gardens, as though he had lost his heart and mind.[87]

Ma knew well how to play on the emperor's feelings of helplessness, insecurity, and ineffectuality. While "righteous" figures heightened these by urging the emperor to boldly seize the handles of power, exercise his sagely wisdom in discerning right and wrong, inspire the people by personally leading a campaign northward, and otherwise be a paragon of imperial activism, Ma began with a "Secret Memorial Stating a Great Plan for the National Founding":

> It is essential that the Sage's [i.e., the emperor's] heart be at peace before general affairs can be undertaken. The root base [i.e., the emperor] must be firm before wrath against the enemy can be aroused.

Thus, Ma urged that the first order of business should be to ease the emperor's mind by (1) rescuing the empress dowager (his stepmother) from Ho-nan; (2) conferring posthumous honorifics on the emperor's father, who had been killed by the rebels; (3) bringing the latter's remains to Nan-ching for proper dispensation; (4) selecting fine women to become imperial consorts and ladies-in-waiting; and (5) asserting control over the movements and associations of the other imperial princes.[88]

Ma had the right idea for the short-term goal of gaining this ruler's confidence. But he did not really need to push himself on the emperor nor take pains to convince him of the nefariousness of the Tung-lin and Fu She. With this true grandson of the Wan-li emperor, he had only to wait—and not very long. The emperor knew little about Ming governmental institutions, court procedures, or the factional situation in the bureaucracy. This ignorance was a continual source of embarrassment and frustration to him, since he always felt that he was either disappointing or being duped by his ministers. Basically irresolute, he was agonized by the sudden demand that he decide all manner of weighty and momentous questions—only to be told politely that his decisions would not do because they conflicted with some precedent or another. And the dogfights at court audiences, which everyone expected him to resolve, left him redfaced and speechless. He was magnanimous or indifferent about who had supported or opposed his father as heir-designate long ago, or himself as monarch recently; but, unhappy as he became when these issues repeatedly were raised, he did not have the force of will to stop the polemic. These irritations, and the high-minded admonitions of the "righteous" officials, only drove him more quickly back to the inner chambers.[89]

By midautumn, the Hung-kuang emperor was staying secluded, "unaware of the bad government being perpetrated by those under him."[90] Public ceremonies began to be canceled or delegated to ministers; and, although stories of his sexual perversity must be regarded skeptically,[91] it seems true that through the winter and the following spring the emperor became almost totally absorbed in the business of selecting women for the palace, planning his marriage cere-mony, and holding private galas with his eunuchs and theatrical players.[92] The thoughtless procedures by which lovely young virgins were hunted out in Nan-ching and Hang-chou caused considerable bitterness among the populace;[93] the wildly lavish expenditures on the inner apartments and the imperial wedding bankrupted the treasury;[94] and at one point the emperor's indulgence in sensual pleasures became so excessive that he collapsed and almost died.[95] Later, as the Ch'ing armies were within days of reaching Nan-ching, the emperor was half oblivious to, half unwilling to know what was happening. Of course, it was to Ma Shih-ying's advantage that so much was left in his own hands. But the emperor's abdication of responsibility was such that popular support for Ma's regime was undermined and, in the end, completely lost. For the "righteous" element, conscious of the institutional history of the chief grand secretary, it was an enactment of the ultimate worst-case scenario.

The sectional developments discussed above produced, by the spring of 1645, a dominant political coalition that was isolated, paranoid, and obsessed with combatting enemies on the home front. This, and the frenetic state of the popular psyche, is best illustrated by an almost incredible succession of "three suspicious cases," each of which might have been handled with dispatch, judi-cially or diplomatically, but which instead festered and brought about the final internal disintegration of the Hung-kuang regime. The dilatory handling of these cases is attributable to, first, the use of each by competing factions to damage or embarrass one another, and second, the public's championing of anyone (the more colorful or romantic the better) who could make trouble for this unpopular regime. Few had much interest in clear evidence, and the historical accounts reflect this.

The first case was that of a monk with the clerical name Ta-pei, who was arrested in Nan-ching on January 12 allegedly for impersonating the Ch'ung-chen emperor. Official reports of the subsequent secret interrogations said that Ta-pei dementedly posed first as one imperial prince, then another, "as though talking in his sleep," and that all his claims patently were false. It was thought by others, however, that he possessed knowledge about the Prince of Fu that men in power did not wish to have brought to light. In any case, whether Ta-pei genuinely was insane or was a charlatan feigning derangement, the Minister of Punishments and others in charge of the case sought to bring it quickly and quietly to a close. But Juan Ta-ch'eng, wishing to make use of the case, drew up a blacklist of 143 persons, headed by "Eighteen Lohan," who purportedly had favored the Prince of Luh and had instigated Ta-pei to upset the court. In this instance, however, Juan was restrained by Ma Shih-ying, and the matter ended with the public execution of the "Mad Monk" on March 27.[96]

On that same day the nightmare of the southern court began to come true: It was reported to the throne that a young man who claimed to be the Ch'ung-chen emperor's eldest son and heir had been found in Che-chiang. Repeatedly, since the founding of the Hung-kuang regime, attempts had been made to squelch belief in the survival of the heir—by publishing as fact rumors of his death, and by assigning to him posthumous honorifics[97]—but hope persisted among the people that he would be found alive. Consequently, when the young man in question was brought to Nan-ching, he initially was treated with cautious respect. Subsequently, he was questioned several times, first in open session by officials and later under confinement by the notorious Embroidered Uniform Guard. The young man seems to have recognized some persons whom the heir should have known but not others, and to have correctly answered some questions about the heir's experiences but not others; each session, though declared conclusive by some officials, was found unsatisfactory by others. Physical evidence, verifiable by eunuchs who were familiar with the heir's anatomical peculiarities, apparently never was solicited. Those who had most power over the proceedings soon declared that the young man had confessed to being Wang Chih-ming, the grand-nephew of an imperial in-law. But others said that this identification was fabricated, and that the young man had consistently maintained his claim to be the true heir-designate in spite of many humiliations.

In any case, the emperor, who earlier had said that he welcomed discovery of the heir, under pressure from his advisers accepted the decision that the person in question was an impostor. And he expressed this conviction repeatedly in responses to memorials from commanders in the field who had become alarmed by rumors that the heir-designate was being slandered and mistreated by villains at court. Such rumors were intensified when three men, who supposedly had put "Wang Chih-ming" up to this masquerade, were placed under increasingly severe interrogation in an effort to uncover a wider plot by persons hostile to the court.[98]

Complicating the historical question of the fate of the genuine heir, and the feelings and opinions of men at the time, has been the fact that three months earlier another person who claimed to be the Ch'ung-chen heir-designate had appeared in the North, giving rise to a case in the Ch'ing court every bit as delicate, enigmatic, and fraught with political consequences as the one in Nan-ching. The Manchus eventually executed the northern claimant;[99] but greater internal insecurity prevented the exercise of this option in the South, where, despite the lack of firm evidence, it became widely and often fanatically believed that the "False Heir" was real. Fearing insurrection, either by certain commanders or by the people of Nan-ching, the court did not dare kill the young man whom it had "proven" to be an impostor; and many on the "righteous" side who also doubted his genuineness were glad to let him remain alive as a thorn in the side of the "pernicious" clique.

Even as the interrogation of the False Heir was taking place, a certain Madam T'ung, who claimed to be the former concubine of the Hung-kuang emperor, was being escorted from Ho-nan into Nan-ching. There, however, unexpectedly she was conducted straight into the palace prison, since the emperor angrily and summarily had declared her story to be bogus and refused to hear any more of the matter, even against the advice of Ma Shih-ying. Though some accounts tell of how movingly she wrote and spoke of her past relationship with the prince, others say that she soon turned to claiming that her mate had not been the Prince of Fu, but rather the Prince of Chou, whom she mistakenly thought had been enthroned in Nan-ching. In any case, the "False Imperial Concubine" was grievously maltreated, slandered as having had illicit relations with men who sought to harm the court, and allowed to die in prison of illness or starvation. The unexplained callousness of the emperor toward this woman added to his unpopularity and even fomented suspicions that *he* was the impostor![100]

All of the conditions described above, and others, grew worse in the year 1644–45 partly because circumstances hindered the Hung-kuang regime from formulating clear strategic objectives for dealing with the North. Granted, the regime needed time to organize and build its strength before launching a campaign to reconquer the Central Plain. If that time had been spent with an unambiguous goal or a single source of threat before everyone's eyes, then unity might have been forged and preserved, and fewer senseless, wasteful things might have occurred. But that year was spent more in passive waiting than in active preparation—waiting for the situation in the North to sort itself out, after which the South could direct its capacities more specifically. The psychological effects of this suspended state on the military, the bureaucracy, the throne, and the populace all were deleterious. And the effects on government finances were disastrous.

The Hung-kuang regime's first month witnessed an impressively rapid transformation of the auxiliary capital, with its skeleton administration consisting largely of sinecures, into the nerve center of the country, as it had been in the first century of the dynasty.[101] The new regime had to recreate almost the entire Pei-ching governmental structure, including the capital guard system, redirect the flow of tax revenues and transport services, rearrange administrative circuits, and rebuild or renovate the halls, temples, and living quarters which had fallen into disuse within the old imperial palace compound.[102] All this was done with admirable dispatch, considering the confusion of the time. And the nearby tomb of the Great Ancestor became an important source of renewed pride in Ming accomplishments and basic institutions.

But against what entity did this restored government take its stand? What were the northern rebels doing or planning? Had any action been taken by the Liao-tung army under Wu San-kuei? If so, what may have been the response of the Manchus? And what about the rebel leader Chang Hsien-chung in Szu-ch'uan? Would he stay there or try to reinvade the Yang-tzu region? Those who called for an immediate campaign to chastise the rebels and restore the dynastic cauldrons in the North were mostly civil officials of "righteous" pedigree who had no experience in military affairs.[103] But the zeal to take revenge forthwith on the rebels was not exclusively a "righteous" property, nor were caution and gradualism—often pejoratively referred to as "satisfaction with one part [of the realm]" (p'ien-an)—especially characteristic of the "pernicious" element. Shih K'o-fa, who in May of 1644 had wanted to "succor the sovereign" as soon as a force could be organized, in June had come to the more moderate view that the four defense commanders should establish themselves securely in their jurisdictions in order to prepare for a general advance at the appropriate time—a view that was widely shared among officials.[104] The commanders certainly were willing to adopt a long-range perspective on preparation. Liu Tse-ch'ing, for instance, asserted that one or two years would be required to bring the southern forces to a state of readiness.[105]

Wishfully simple-minded solutions also were proposed by both civil and military officials, with a significant difference: The former tended to exhibit "show-the-flag-ism," assuming that restoration could be effected simply by arousing the spirit of loyalty among people in the North; whereas the latter were inclined toward "sweeten-the-deal-ism," assuming that important collabo- rationist generals could be brought back to Ming allegiance if they could be offered sufficiently handsome material and titular inducements.[106] Both ap- proaches ignored difficult but necessary organizational matters, which would require that civil and military personnel work closely together.

Generally, however, during the first several months of the Hung-kuang regime, enmity overwhelmingly was directed toward the northern rebels under Li Tzu-ch'eng. After all, they were responsible for the death of the Ch'ung-chen emperor, desecration of the imperial palace in Pei-ching, and the current predica- ment of the southern court. And representatives of the Great Shun regime, pressing on locales in the Huai region, initially were much more visible than the Manchus.[107] This remained true well after Nan-ching learned, first, that Li had been defeated by Wu San-kuei and driven back into Shen-hsi and, later, that Pei- ching and much of Pei Chih-li had been occupied by the Manchus. Although the Manchus' propaganda, beginning early in June (which Nan-ching received a month later), made clear their intention to dominate China proper,[108] their potential actually to do that never was taken seriously enough by Ma Shih-ying and other leaders in the South. Centuries-old stereotypical ideas about the northern "slaves" or "barbarians" came into play: that deep in their often benighted hearts they "knew the principle" of self-subordination to the Han Chinese and, thus, might well be sincere in their vaunted determination to punish the rebels for heinous acts against the Great Ming; if not, that they always could be appeased or bought off; and if that didn't work, they and their horses would never like the watery South, so they soon would lose interest in aggressive ventures and leave. In any case, it seemed wisest for the South, which needed time anyway, to attack neither the rebels nor the Manchu-Ch'ing for the present, but rather to wait for them to fight each other and then deal with much weakened adversaries, taking the proverbial "fisherman's profit."[109]

The next question was, would the rebels and the Manchus do this? Or would one or the other move against the South first? Or might they form an alliance against the South? Or might the Ch'ing attack Li Tzu-ch'eng in such a way as to drive his armies before them into the Yang-tzu region? Because of these uncertainties—and the political geography of China—the Hung-kuang regime found itself in the dilemma of having to defend five approaches to Chiang-nan:*

---

* "Chiang-nan" was, and still is, a common term for the whole lower Yang-tzu region. During the Ch'ing Shun-chih and early K'ang-hsi reigns it also was the specific name of a province, i.e., what formerly had been Ming Nan Chih-li. Subsequently this was divided into the modern-day provinces of Chiang-su and An-hui.

The Manchus might come (1) through southern Shan-tung on either side of the Grand Canal to challenge Hsü-chou, Su-ch'ien, or Huai-an, or (2) through the leg of far southern Pei Chih-li and the part of Ho-nan north of the Yellow River to challenge Lo-yang, K'ai-feng, and Kuei-te. Li Tzu-ch'eng's armies might (3) come across central Ho-nan into the Huai lakes region or (4) move more immediately southward into northern Hu-kuang via the Han River to challenge Wu-ch'ang. And Chang Hsien-chung might (5) retrace his steps back down the Yang-tzu River through Ching-chou into the central lakes region.[110] Setting priorities among these with inadequate intelligence information and planning to some degree for all eventualities with limited resources were very difficult problems for the South. In the end, Nan-ching was faced with enemy offensives on the Shan-tung, Ho-nan, and Hu-kuang fronts simultaneously. Although an unwise choice of priorities at that time contributed to the disastrous outcome, under these and other burdensome circumstances the regime's defenses probably would have failed anyway.

After the Manchus' first proclamation to the South was made public, some officials in Nan-ching began to think that they should be contacted. So an ambassadorial mission was planned, the stated purposes of which were to: (1) ensure proper burial of the Ch'ung-chen emperor and other members of the imperial family; (2) bestow a noble title and congratulatory gifts on Wu San-kuei; (3) present gifts of thanks (that is, indemnities) to the Manchus for their service in driving the rebels away from the northern capital; and (4) induce the Manchus to withdraw by offering them all the territory outside Shan-hai Pass and a yearly payoff of 100,000 taels.[111]

But, partly because the South had difficulty finding men who were willing to go on such a mission, there was considerable foot-dragging until the late summer and early autumn. By that time, Ch'ing troops had supplanted rebel troops in southern Shan-tung and had become an even greater threat to towns and cities in the region just north of the Huai River. Moreover, the South had learned that Wu San-kuei definitely was serving the Ch'ing. Fear grew that if Ch'ing bellicosity were not checked with force, and that if envoys were not sent soon to ascertain the Manchus' position, the latter would continue to strengthen their bargaining stance and would be even more difficult to deal with later.[112]

Consequently, several urgings to depart were delivered to the three men— an odd combination—who had been chosen to carry out the mission: Tso Mou-ti, formerly a minor censorial official and a member of the Fu She, was appointed as chief civil emissary. He had volunteered to go so that along the way he could perform his filial duties to his mother, who recently had died in T'ien-chin, and he wore mourning garb throughout the mission. Moreover, he had an extremely supercilious attitude toward the Manchus, whom he stubbornly regarded as a subject people, not comparable to the Liao dynasty in its relations with the Sung in the eleventh century, and he seemed more bent on accomplishing his own martyrdom than on accomplishing the mission.[113] Moreover, he objected to the assignment of the second civil emissary, the former bureau secretary Ma Shao-yü, who Tso felt had favored the Manchu side in negotiations that had been conducted secretly under the Ch'ung-chen emperor.[114] Nor did Tso get along well with the military envoy, former regional commander Ch'en Hung-fan, who had been recommended by Liu Tse-ch'ing and Kao Chieh, and who was being sought just then by the Ch'ing court as a likely person to act as go-between in persuading the South's leading generals to defect.[115]

On August 22 the mission commenced haltingly and proceeded up the Grand Canal route very slowly because of provisioning and transport problems (service personnel having long since deserted the now-empty waterway), and because of encounters with bandits in the no-man's-land between Ming-controlled Huai-an and Ch'ing-controlled Chi-ning, which the southern emissaries did not reach until October 5. In Ch'ing territory they were received very inhospitably, offered no accommodations, and subjected to many restrictions, which increased as they neared Pei-ching. Treated as tribute bearers from a subordinate state rather than as representatives from an equal, at length they were held virtually captive in the Court of State Ceremonial and were spurned in their attempts to contact Wu San-kuei. Twice they were visited by Manchu Grand Secretary Ganglin, who berated them and the southern government for dilatoriness, confiscated the gifts they had brought, and refused to allow any sacrifices to, much less reburial of, the Ch'ung-chen emperor. Moreover, Ganglin summarily dismissed negotiations now as pointless, since, he said, the Ch'ing already had launched a campaign against the South. The ambassadorial party finally was allowed to leave Pei-ching on November 25, but soon it was overtaken by a Ch'ing contingent, which seized Tso Mou-ti and Ma Shao-yü. Ch'en Hung-fan, who by this time certainly was collaborating with the Ch'ing, was allowed to return to the South, perhaps to act as a secret agent there. He reentered Ming territory in late December and reported to the Hung-kuang court in mid-January 1645.[116]

Thus, a full half year was spent awaiting the outcome of a completely futile diplomatic mission, months during which the Ch'ing greatly increased their strength in southern Shan-tung and their pressure on key locations in northernmost Nan Chih-li.[117] When Shih K'o-fa, who had been laboring mightily to keep such crucial cities as Su-ch'ien out of Ch'ing hands, learned of the failure of the Tso mission, he sent a passionate memorial to the emperor imploring him to arouse the court from its stupor: "Civil officials are serene, and military men play around" while the Manchus proceed southward, he warned. We are totally unprepared to defend the Huai River, he added, much less to threaten the rebels in Shen-hsi. We deservedly are the laughingstock of the enemy, and we will suffer for our inaction unless we immediately concentrate all our capacities on resisting the Ch'ing. "Yes, people's hearts still *can* be stirred! And Heaven's favor still *can* be brought back!"[118] But Ma Shih-ying still "took a stack of eggs to be a pile of faggots," saying that the Manchus were constrained at one side by the rebels and that, anyway, the force of peoples like them from the far northeast (e.g., the Jurched Chin) historically had been inconstant and easily blocked.[119]

One result of this waiting and indecision vis-à-vis the North was to allow the attention of the military to be drawn more easily toward internecine conflict and court politics. Examples of this among the defense commanders north of the Yang-tzu and in Hu-kuang have been cited above. The same phenomenon also appeared in the less militarized Su-Sung delta south of the Yang-tzu and in northern Che-chiang Province, which together comprised the nation's economically most advanced region. There conflicts arose not only between soldiers and citizens and among regular army units that had been brought in from different areas but also between regular troops and volunteer auxiliaries, a problem which was to become worse in subsequent Southern Ming regimes. These conflicts readily became politicized because southeastern Nan Chih-li and central Che-chiang were the hotbeds of Tung-lin and Fu She activism. Consequently, the Ma-Juan element in the Hung-kuang regime always suspected that their political enemies were behind, or were ready to manipulate, any military movements in that region and were plotting thereby to threaten or take over the court.

A good example of the deleterious effects of factional politics on military preparedness is the case, in Tung-yang, Che-chiang, of a volunteer army organized by Hsü Tu, a Chin-hua prefectural student noted for his interest in military affairs, who had been executed early in 1644 after his movement ran afoul of the local magistrate.[120] After the fall of Pei-ching, Hsü's followers had continued to militate for action by volunteer forces such as themselves, encouraged, no doubt, by similar demands that were being made by prominent "righteous" leaders on balky officials in Che-chiang.[121] Consequently, in September of 1644, the man who previously had handled the Hsü Tu uprising, Tso Kuang-hsien, a Fu She leader and now the provincial governor of Che-chiang, was impeached, allegedly for having tried to cover up matters in the case, removed from office, and eventually ordered to submit to arrest.[122]

Of more serious consequence for the immediate defense of the southern capital were the multiple problems that arose in Chen-chiang, where the Grand Canal meets the southern bank of the Yang-tzu, and in Ching-k'ou, the nearby garrison which guarded the canal locks. This was the key point for crossing the great river in the lower Yang-tzu region and also a prime location for either protecting or attacking Nan-ching. Ming soldiers there first had to staunch the attempts of generals north of the Yang-tzu, especially Kao Chieh, to cross from Kua-chou and thus gain a foothold in the rich territory south of the river. Next, hostilities erupted there between a unit detached from the command of Shih K'o-fa, which was unpopular with the citizenry, and other more socially conscientious units which had been transferred there from Che-chiang. And next, local boatmen became involved in friction that developed between naval units brought to Ching-k'ou from Che-chiang and Fu-chien.[123] These latter disruptions, especially, consternated the Ma-Juan element in the Hung-kuang regime, which feared that the military forces from Che-chiang—or even those from Fu-chien—might be part of a "righteous" plot to overthrow them.[124] Consequently, the governor who had jurisdiction over Chen-chiang, Ch'i Piao-chia, a disciple of Liu Tsung-chou, was pressured into resigning, and responsibilities at Chen-chiang subsequently were given to members of Ma Shih-ying's cohort who were better known for artistic than for martial brilliance.[125] Thus, it is no surprise that when the Ch'ing carried out their momentous crossing of the Yang-tzu in the summer 1645, Chen-chiang defenses collapsed like a house of cards.

Like the military, the common citizenry, too, having no external enemy in sight, turned to venting their wrath on enemies at home. Genuine patriotic indignation probably accounts in large part for attacks—verbal and physical—on the persons, families, and properties of men who were suspected of having served the rebels. But in many instances the charge of collaboration appears to have been a pretext for settling old scores, airing social resentments, robbing vulnerable refugees, and just plain looting. Prohibitions were issued against disruptive armed gangs that formed on the pretense of "succoring the sovereign," but incidents continued to flare throughout southern Nan Chih-li.[126]

In Nan-ching, the sense of having nothing urgent or immediate to do contributed to a run on titles, status designations, and minimally functional official positions—all with their entailed privileges—as social climbers took advantage of the insecure regime's desire to attract support and please everyone. Fittingly, those who cried first about this stampede were the very ones who had led the way in challenging the elite status quo: the hereditary military nobles and the imperial clansmen. Too many people, they cried, were spuriously claiming *their* status and perquisites, diluting the dignity of rank, wreaking havoc on the uniform, insignia, and sumptuary codes, and using their elevated footing to seek official position for cunning and vengeful purposes! Complaints that "imperial relatives fill the streets" led to prohibitions on clansmen seeking office or even entering Nan-ching. And military men below the rank of full general were forbidden, futilely, to ride in palanquins rather than on horseback.[127] It was a time when the government needed to "break form" (*p'o-ko*), that is, set aside its usual standards and qualifications to employ expeditiously men of ability in dealing with turbulent conditions. But this idea instead was used to give away a superfluity of unimportant positions to flocks of mediocre men. Some attempts were made to brake this tendency and to find the right men for genuine service in the more exposed and threatened territories, but to little avail.[128] People were anxious and self-protective. Moreover, Chiang-nan had become filled with men who had been displaced from their homes or posts in the North, and who were desperately willing to pay whatever they could to acquire or maintain official status, which afforded opportunities for peculation and entitled them at least to a small salary, deferential social treatment, and a modicum of physical protection. Thus, as a popular ditty put it:

> Drafters are found everywhere; Han-lin scholars fill the streets.
> Supervisors are numerous as sheep; bureau secretaries are low as dogs.
> For hereditary privilege, the dust of a thousand years is stirred.
> Men enter the National Academy by just raising their heads.
> And all the cash of Chiang-nan is swept up,
> To stuff the mouths of the Ma family.[129]

Bribe-taking for appointments became so flagrant and widespread that it verged on being a standard, public practice. This was especially so because the government, following the precedent of many beleaguered Chinese governments in the past, resorted to the sale of minor degrees and titles, and to requiring graded payments from officials and degree-holders, as means of augmenting inadequate state income.[130] The Ministry of Revenues in the southern capital had never operated on a grand scale. In late Ming years it had handled annually only about 1,400,000 taels in silver and payments in kind, and in 1643–44 it had seen serious shortfalls.[131] Now, despite reorganizations that aimed to substitute Nan-ching for Pei-ching as the fiscal center of the empire, the Hung-kuang court never was able to meet its expenses. And this condition grew worse as the regime waited, its armed forces "sitting and eating," through the winter and spring of 1644–45.

True, the lower Yang-tzu region was the wealthiest in the country, but not independently so. Because of the commercialization of its economy, which appears to have been especially rapid in the latter part of the Ming period, Chiang-nan lands increasingly had been used to grow industrial and specialty crops rather than the basic food grain, rice. The region had become heavily dependent on other regions, especially Hu-kuang, for the bulk of its rice supply, and on the free flow of interregional trade, especially between North and South, for its livelihood.[132] Now two of the main transport arteries that maintained the health of the Chiang-nan economy were cut off. The Yang-tzu River and the

Grand Canal both had become defense zones, where all commercial boats were subject to being halted or requisitioned for military purposes, a condition that effectively stymied the important trade in salt, as well as other commodities. Hu-kuang had been devastated by rebels and now could not feed Tso Liang-yü's huge army, much less deliver grain to Chiang-nan. And the greatest single reason for the nodal position of Chiang-nan, the sale of goods from the South to the capital and other cities in the North, had been nullified.[133] Moreover, although the economic prosperity and unusually high rates of taxation in Chiang-nan had made it the fiscal mainstay of the national government, tax collection there long had been peculiarly difficult, for both geographical and political reasons, and the region was notorious for arrearages.[134] Now, with conditions so uncertain, local officials and taxpayers alike were inclined to sit on their monies. Literally, though in an ironic sense, they were waiting for a rainy day, since, on top of other troubles, 1644 was a year of prolonged drought in Chiang-nan, with no precipi-tation from June until December. This not only affected crops but also made waterways so shallow that trade was interrupted even more.[135]

These economic and fiscal problems naturally grew worse as the months passed. Estimates of income and expenditure for the Hung-kuang regime proved to be woefully high for the former and low for the latter. Originally Shih K'o-fa expected that the court could sustain an annual military budget of over 6 million taels if it economized in other areas. But the view of the supervising secretary for Public Works, Li Ch'ing, was pessimistic: maximum total revenues, less than 6 million; minimum expenditures on the military alone, over 7 million. As it turned out, the shortfall was even worse than Li predicted.[136] Army ranks first swelled with men who had lost other means of livelihood; they then starved or turned mutinous for lack of pay and provisions. Meanwhile, ministers at court were unable to restrain the profligate spending of the emperor.[137]

Revenues were sought in a variety of ways, all of which weakened the governmental fiber more than they strengthened the treasury. Added to the sale of offices, degrees, and titles were fees for exemption from civil service qualifying examinations and from certain criminal punishments. And numerous miscella-neous taxes were instituted or increased—for instance, on domestic and foreign, commerce, liquors, fishing, pearls, salt, and shoreline reeds.[138] In spite of protests from officials, eunuchs were sent to "expedite" the forwarding of various taxes to Nan-ching, especially the "gold-floral silver" that went directly into the emperor's privy purse.[139] At the founding of the Hung-kuang regime, all of the extra levies that had been imposed from Wan-li through Ch'ung-chen to deal with the rebels and the Manchus were canceled, and large remittances were granted to parts of the country that had suffered from the rebellions, in an attempt to garner public favor. But this policy gradually was mitigated and then reversed for the territories still under Hung-kuang authority.[140] Moreover, the defense commanders were allowed to milk their jurisdictions in any ways they wished—ways that grossly interfered with people's livelihoods in those areas.[141] And there were many who took advantage of this fiscal juggling and confusion for their own illicit gain—quietly under the table of the *ya-men* or noisily at the doors of frightened and bewildered citizens.

The result of all this was that popular support for the Hung-kuang regime withered rapidly, and people became prone to believe the stories of villainy and debauchery that they heard about Ma, Juan, and the emperor. Worse, the court not only relinquished all fiscal and administrative control over the defense commands, it also had to renege on its commitment to supply them at certain levels, causing mass discontent among soldiers and officers. These factors, plus the fear that Li Tzu-ch'eng would descend on Wu-ch'ang from southern Shen-hsi, eventually instigated Tso Liang-yü's army to rebel. Having convinced Tso that he should launch an "eastward campaign" to "cleanse the surroundings of the emperor," in late April 1645, his men went on a rampage down the Yang-tzu, burning and pillaging from Chiu-chiang onward until they were stopped in the vicinity of Ti-kang.[142] This revolt led Ma Shih-ying to transfer forces westward just as the Ch'ing armies were approaching the Huai River, thus further reducing any possibility of checking their advance.[143]

CHAPTER TWO

First Defeat: The Ch'ing Conquest of the Yang-tzu Region

THE strategic question for the Ch'ing leadership at this stage was a mirror reflection of that for the southern leadership: What could and would the rebels do? Was the southern court hostile, and what action might *it* take? Both sides faced a common enemy. Although early in 1644 the Manchu regent, Dorgon, had attempted to contact Li Tzu-ch'eng to discuss forming an alliance against the Ming,[1] now the Manchus' advantage clearly lay in augmenting their image as saviors of the Chinese people and avengers of the Ch'ung-chen emperor against the bandit horde. But Nan-ching at least had to evince a determination to repossess the North, whereas the Ch'ing appear to have been unsure at first about conquering the South.

Since early in the seventeenth century, the Manchus clearly had harbored a desire to invade China proper, that is, penetrate inside Shan-hai Pass;[2] and as Li Tzu-ch'eng's movement had burgeoned in Shen-hsi and Shan-hsi in 1643–44, they certainly had been aware of the opportunities that Li's success might bring to them. Indeed, eighteen days after the fall of Pei-ching, but a week before receiving a proposal of cooperation from Wu San-kuei, the Ch'ing had designated Dorgon as plenipotentiary to lead a campaign to secure "the Central Plain" (i.e., China north of the Yellow River); and other proposals at this time spoke of the territory "north of the [Yellow] River," the "Central Plain," or more vaguely of the "interior."[3] Wu San-kuei's appeal for help and his subsequent willingness, under pressure, to bear allegiance to the Ch'ing court were great windfalls. Wu's overriding desire to vanquish the rebels, who not only had killed, in effect, his ruler-father, but who also actually had tortured and murdered his true father, enabled the Ch'ing to drive Li Tzu-ch'eng and his main force out of Pei-ching and out of Pei Chih-li within days after Li's resounding defeat near Shan-hai Pass on May 27.[4]

46

On June 6 (just as the Prince of Fu was becoming the Ming regent in Nan-ching) Regent Dorgon ceremoniously entered strife-torn Pei-ching in the very palanquin that the surprised but exhausted capital officials had prepared to receive the Ming heir-designate. Acting for his seven-year-old nephew, the Ch'ing Shun-chih emperor who recently had been enthroned in Shen-yang, Dorgon set about "ruling the whole world." [5] And about this time he issued a public edict to the officials, soldiers, and citizens of the southern court, saying:

> In the past my country has wished to live in harmony with your Great Ming and enjoy eternal peace. But our several missives went unanswered, causing us to make four incursions in the hope that you would regret [your attitude] and realize [our position]. Who would have thought that you would remain rigid and not respond? Now [the northern court] has been ex-tinguished by roving bandits, so those matters belong to the past and need not be discussed. Moreover, the world [t'ien-hsia] is not one person's; rather, it is to be occupied by the virtuous. And the soldiers and civilians are not one person's, but are to be ruled by the virtuous. We have come here in your behalf to liquidate the enemies of your ruler-father. We will break our axes in sinking their ship; and we swear that as long as one bandit goes unvanquished, we will not turn back our chariots! In all the locales we pass through, those who can shave their heads [in the Manchu style] and submit, opening city [gates] and offering valuables [as tokens of submission], will be given titles and salaries and for generations will hold elite status. But if some resist and do not respect us, then when our great troops arrive, they will not separate jade from rock but will unrestrainedly carry out massacres. For men of resolve, now is the time for great accomplishments! If we lose credence [in all the above], then how can we expect to lead the world?[6]

But "the world" had ideas of its own and was not about to be subdued by this or other proclamations alone. An order of June 7 that all Chinese men, on pain of punishment, shave their pates and braid their remaining hair in the distinctive Manchu queue was rescinded twenty days later, perhaps in response to the popular revolts that this and other Manchu practices provoked.[7] Moreover, one must keep in mind that, although Manchu sociopolitical organi-zation was fundamentally paramilitary and their soldiers probably were the best fighting men on the East Asian continent at this time, nevertheless, the Manchus were very small in number compared to the Han Chinese whom they hoped to rule. Moreover, economic conditions had been hard in Manchuria, and the Ch'ing armies (in which Manchu companies numbered less than one-third, the others being composed of allied Mongols and Liao-tung Chinese subjects) were not in peak fighting condition.[8] Ch'ing soldiers in Pei Chih-li at this point, including the army of Wu San-kuei, probably numbered about 280,000.[9] In the South, just those armies that were supposed to be directly subsidized by the Hung-kuang court were conservatively estimated to number 350,000 (those in western Ho-nan, Szu-ch'uan, Kuang-tung, and other outlying areas being innumerable).[10] And the army of Li Tzu-ch'eng, although its numerical size has defied even general estimation, surely was formidable, especially in its Shen-hsi stronghold.[11] These and other inhibiting circumstances led Dorgon to resist acting immediately on the continual urgings of collaborating Chinese civil and military officials, who seem to have been more bellicose than the Manchus themselves about conquering all of China.

Thus, in a formal proclamation, which was delivered by courier to the South in mid-July, Dorgon was more circumspect and tentative. He opened by fulsomely praising Ming T'ai-tsu and the Ch'ung-chen emperor, roundly excoriating the rebels, and reciting Ch'ing merit in providing proper burials for deceased members of the imperial family. Then he went on to say:

> We are deeply grieved that no princes of your Ming dynasty have survived [in the North], leaving conditions precarious. For this reason, we have moved the Great Ch'ing to *domicile in this northern territory*. We are drilling our soldiers and feeding our horses, determined to annihilate the villains [i.e., the rebels] and purify the myriad locales. We have no desire to grow rich off the world; in truth, we plan just to rescue China. North and south of the [Yellow] River, everyone [of every status] laments the former dynasty in his heart and hopes to wash away the shame [of its loss]. We will not stint in giving all [such men] noble titles and elevating them with special honors. As for those who have not forgotten the Ming [imperial] house and have supported and enthroned a worthy prince, putting forth their fullest effort with unified hearts to protect the lower Yang-tzu, *that is as things should be. We will not stop you.* But you should contact us for peaceful, amicable discussions and not rebuff our dynasty. Feel in your hearts our benevolence in continuing what was cut off, and look with kindness on a *friendly neighbor.* Those who have the strength to trust, rather than to be inimical, and sincerely proffer their allegiance to the North, each should belabor his strong forces to assist our westward campaign [against the rebels]. If, perchance, others can eliminate remaining bandits in their own areas and be of service in that way, we would welcome it with open hearts and be glad to share success with them.... When a country is without a definite ruler, people cannot be of one mind. If some falsely enthrone a stupid and weak man, that, in effect, will give rein to evil plotting by the rampant and defiant. And if some overtly go along with my dynasty but covertly do [snake-in-the-] grass treachery, then they will be as insects who rob the people and as bandits hated by their countrymen. Just wait until we take and secure Shen-hsi. Then we will turn our forces southward to chastise them, and that kind of monster will be made extinct!...[12]

This proclamation reflects the Manchus' decisions, also of mid-July, to make Pei-ching their capital and bring the Ch'ing emperor there to reign, and also to defeat the rebels in Shen-hsi first (and perhaps in Szu-ch'uan, as well) before gradually working to stabilize the situation in the Southeast.[13] It also reflects uncertainty about the strength of the South and a desire to blunt, for the time being, any hostility from that quarter.[14] While making clear that the Ch'ing claim to rule the North should be respected, they threaten to invade the South only if the leadership there proves to be dishonorable (i.e., uncooperative) or unworthy (i.e., inept).

Clouding perceptions between North and South at this time was the utterly chaotic condition of Shan-tung Province, which lay in between the northern and southern Metropolitan Areas. In many locales, remnants of the Great Shun rebel regime clung to power; however, as they gradually were defeated or driven out by indigenous forces, struggles ensued over which armed element would reassert control.[15] Attacks and counterattacks by "bandits," gentry-led forces, and scattered Ming regulars kept the province in turmoil (and this was another factor that slowed the progress of the Hung-kuang ambassadorial mission). The Ch'ing had to assert themselves there as rapidly as possible, not only to protect their southeastern flank from rebel attack as they turned mainly southwestward, but also to ascertain the Ming influence there and staunch any offensive through Shan-tung by the southern court. Thus, in late July the Ch'ing began to move concertedly into northern Shan-tung, and by the end of October they had established a weak front along the southern border of that province, as well as on the northern side of the Yellow River in far northern Ho-nan.[16]

The generals and officials who hammered out this defensive, probing, secondary front almost all were Chinese, the Ch'ing having reserved their Manchu units or transferred them to the more crucial western front (north and east of Shen-hsi). The task of these men was frustrating, inglorious, and precarious, with rebels still active to their rear, substantial Ming forces not far away or threatening to encircle them by sea, and duplicitous, fence-sitting militarists all along the thirty-fifth parallel.[17] Erstwhile Ming generals were eager to earn merit in Ch'ing eyes by persuading their peers in the South to defect. They made many optimistic claims in this vein, and feelers were sent out.[18] But both the men who initiated these feelers and those who responded positively were distrusted by the Manchus, who needed go-betweens but at this early stage preferred to minimize contact between newly surrendered Chinese generals and their former colleagues on the Ming side. This circumstance partially accounts for the virtual quarantine of the Hung-kuang ambassadorial mission while it was in Ch'ing territory.[19]

Dorgon did have a taste for personal diplomacy on the highest level, however. On August 28, 1644, he sent a letter to Shih K'o-fa which can be considered a model of the sort of missive employed regularly by the Ch'ing to win over officials from the Ming side. That is, it contained: praise of the addressee's accomplishments and reputation; the names of his friends, relatives, or colleagues who already were serving the Ch'ing; profession of Ch'ing respect for the "former Ming"; allusions (however inaccurately drawn) to analogous circumstances in Chinese history and the Classics; and citation of the favorable treatment already accorded to the Ming nobility and others of the addressee's own status who had submitted to the Ch'ing. In this particular letter, Dorgon needled Shih about the South's failure to take action against the rebels:

> Now we are waiting for the crisp height of autumn to send our generals on a westward campaign, and we have transmitted a call to Chiang-nan to join forces with us in going up the [Yellow] River. . . . We hardly expected that all the fine men in the southern region would shiftlessly be satisfied with a day-to-night [existence] and not deeply consider the current situation, fecklessly hoping to gain empty reputations and lumpenly forgetting the actual harm [in such attitudes]. I am very disturbed by this. My country was able to sooth and stabilize Yen-tu [i.e., Pei-ching] by getting it from the Ch'uang bandits [i.e., Li Tzu-ch'eng], not by taking it from the Ming. The bandits destroyed the Ming dynasty's temples and its ruler, their insults reaching to the ancestors. My country, with no fear of how taxing it would be, mobilized its humble fighters and set about washing away this shame for [you]. How [much] the filial and humane [should] appreciate and repay this benevolence! But now you take advantage of the bandits' still awaiting punishment while we temporarily rest our troops, and you hope to occupy Chiang-nan like heroes, sitting and enjoying the fisherman's profit. This goes against human feeling and reason. How can it be called fair?

And Dorgon went on to urge that the South depose its emperor and return him to princely status, in which he would be fully respected and comfortably maintained by the Ch'ing.

> Now if you raise up [another Ming] reign title and declare respect for [a new emperor], causing Heaven to have two suns and showing strong enmity [toward us], we will select some of our armaments going westward and turn our war flags for an eastward campaign. Moreover, we might also release the rebels from heavy punishment and order them to be our forward guides.[20]

From this we can see that by late August the Ch'ing no longer would concede the propriety of setting up a Ming court in Nan-ching; but they still hoped to bully the South into acknowledging Ch'ing hegemony without launching a full-scale attack.

In his reply of October 15, Shih K'o-fa expressed surprise at the content and tone of Dorgon's letter, explaining that he had not thought it appropriate to communicate personally before the completion of the ambassadorial mission, which then was under way. He politely told Dorgon that the latter was mistaken in both his perception of and judgments on the attitudes of southern officials, and he pointed to not only the legitimacy but also the popularity of the Hung-kuang emperor at the time of his enthronement.

> Suddenly word was received that *our great general, Wu San-kuei,* had borrowed troops from your honorable country and had broken and expunged the perfidious [Li Tzu-]ch'eng, that *he had* declared mourning and carried out full ceremonies for the [Ch'ung-chen] emperor and empress and swept clean the doors to the palace, soothing and drawing together the common people. Moreover, *he rescinded* the order for [all men] to shave their hair, showing that he had not forgotten his own dynasty.

As for repaying the Manchus' benevolence, the ambassadorial mission would deliver suitable gifts and, further, would arrange with them for joint action against the rebels. (In direct contrast to the view of the chief emissary, Tso Mou-ti) Shih suggested as a model the harmonious relationship between the Sung dynasty and the Khitan Liao, who had been content to occupy their northeastern corner and receive yearly deliveries of gold and silk, and who had been of assistance to the Chinese without coveting their whole territory.

> But if you take advantage of our misfortune, casting away amity and exalting enmity, looking on this land as [your due for] limitless virtue, this would be to start in righteousness but end in profit-seeking and would be snickered at by the rebels. How could your honorable country do such a thing?[21]

Thus, Shih sought to downplay the Manchus' achievements in the North, to impress on Dorgon the importance of the ambassadorial mission, and also to challenge the Ch'ing to make good on their rhetorical claims to be acting on behalf of the Great Ming.

The first intelligence reports that the Manchus received about the South had induced caution and defensiveness.[22] But on October 25, Dorgon began to receive word of developments in the contact between Ch'ing officials and Ch'en Hung-fan, the chief military emissary from the Hung-kuang court, who was not in accord with the chief civil emissary, Tso Mou-ti, about the extent to which they should adjust their ambassadorial objectives in view of the Ch'ing strength they were encountering.[23] During the following month the Ch'ing attitude changed, and by November 20 Dorgon's younger brother, Dodo, had been ordered to prepare for an imminent campaign on Chiang-nan.[24] That campaign proceeded in three stages (see map 3):

1. First the Ch'ing needed to *consummate their ongoing campaign against the Great Shun* in Shen-hsi.[25] By early November they had accomplished their first westward objective of securing all of Shan-hsi Province,[26] and on November 17

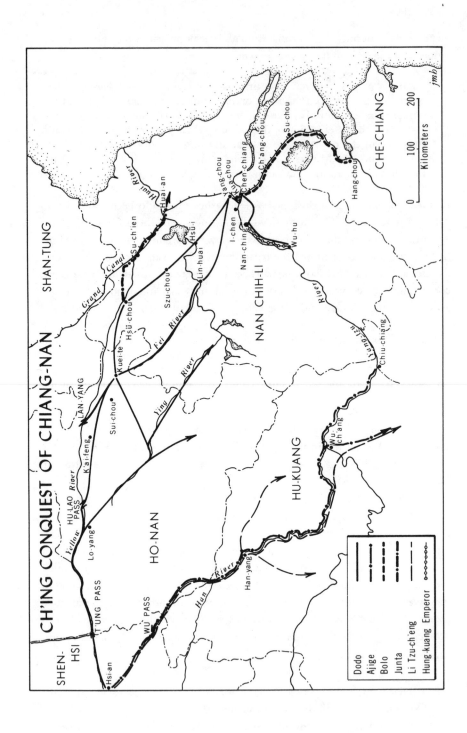

CH'ING CONQUEST OF CHIANG-NAN

SHEN-HSI

SHAN-TUNG

CHE-CHIANG

NAN CHIH-LI

HO-NAN

HU-KUANG

TUNG PASS

WU PASS

HULAO PASS

T'UNG PASS

Hsi-an

Lo-yang

Yellow River

Sui-chou

K'ai-feng

LAN-YANG

Kuei-te

Hsü-chou

Szu-chou

Lin-huai

Hsü-i

Su-ch'ien

Huai-an

Grand Canal

Huai River

Fei River

Ying River

Han River

Han-yang

Wu-ch'ang

River

Chiu-chiang

Nan-ching

I-chen

Wu-hu

Yang-chou

Chen-chiang

Kua-chou

Ch'ang-chou

Su-chou

Hang-chou

Kilometers

0   100   200

jmb

Dodo
Ajige
Bolo
Junta
Li Tzu-ch'eng
Hung-kuang Emperor

Dorgon's elder brother, Ajige, was appointed Generalissimo to lead the campaign to destroy Li Tzu-ch'eng's stronghold in southern Shen-hsi by attacking through Yen-an to the north. Dodo was to depart from Pei-ching on November 25 and simultaneously pursue his campaign on the South,[27] probably through Ho-nan. But reports soon indicated that Shun rebels, coming out through strategic T'ung Pass at the juncture of Shen-hsi, Shan-hsi, and Ho-nan, had become perilously active in northwestern Ho-nan and might threaten the success of both campaigns. So Dodo was then instructed to first quell rebels in northwestern Ho-nan and join with other Ch'ing forces there in attacking T'ung Pass, thus forming pincers with Ajige on the rebel capital, Hsi-an. If they were able to defeat the rebels there, then both generalissimos were to wait for further orders before proceeding, either southwestward or southeastward.[28]

This phase of the Ch'ing plan was carried out in January and February of 1645. A crack force of only five or six thousand men under Dodo crossed the Yellow River at Meng-ching just north of Lo-yang, defeated Shun rebels to the west, and received the surrender of semi-independent stockade defenders and Ming generals to the south and east. Then Dodo proceeded with his whole army to assault T'ung Pass, which was penetrated, after a week of heavy fighting, on February 8. As Ajige pressed down on Hsi-an from the north, Li Tzu-ch'eng abandoned southern Shen-hsi and fled with his still large but disintegrating army southeastward through Wu Pass toward Yün-yang and Hsiang-yang in extreme northwestern Hu-kuang.[29]

Meanwhile, in spite of continuing unrest in Shan-tung, the Ch'ing intensified their pressure on the northern border region of Nan Chih-li and northeastern Ho-nan.[30] This activity was perceived as very threatening by Shih K'o-fa and other commanders near the Ming front lines, and considerable effort was expended in redeploying Ming units to meet the challenge.[31] But for the Ch'ing it appears to have been a diversionary tactic and a "softening up" of Ming defenses in preparation for the later use of a real offensive force. The Ch'ing commander-in-chief for the area north of K'ai-feng, Kuei-te, and Hsü-chou was not authorized to cross the Yellow River. That step was reserved for a fresh army, which was dispatched from Pei-ching on February 9 and arrived near the end of that month.[32]

2. The stage was set for the Ch'ing *conquest of the region between the Yellow and Yang-tzu rivers*. This comprised two theaters of action far removed from one another. To the west, Ajige pursued Li Tzu-ch'eng down the Han River valley into north-central Hu-kuang, where most of Li's units became separated in their desperate dash for survival. It was this deluge from the north, the approach of which was realized in Wu-ch'ang by late March,[33] which prompted the army of Tso Liang-yü to launch its aforementioned "eastward campaign" down the

Yang-tzu toward Nan-ching. Li Tzu-ch'eng himself crossed the Yang-tzu at a point midway between Wu-ch'ang and Yüeh-chou and entered the hilly border-land between Hu-kuang and Chiang-hsi near T'ung-shan. There, riding almost alone with only a small reconnaissance unit, he is said to have been killed by peasants, probably in early June 1645.[34] However, this was not known for some time by Ajige, who had been occupying devastated Wu-ch'ang and Chiu-chiang and chasing various parts of Li's 200,000-man army around central Hu-kuang. Ajige did send some Ch'ing forces to help in securing Ho-nan and Chiang-nan,[35] but that was incidental to the main action in those areas.

Shortly after March 11, Dodo, after "mopping up" around Hsi-an and outside T'ung Pass, received orders to proceed with the original plan to invade Chiang-nan.[36] This drive was made much easier by the dramatic assassination of Kao Chieh at Sui-chou in early February by the Ming general Hsü Ting-kuo, who for some time had been making overtures to the Ch'ing side, and even longer had harbored hatred toward Kao for the evils and atrocities he had committed.[37] Hsü's feelings toward Kao were shared by other commanders north of the Yang-tzu, so little could be done to reconstitute Kao's army as it rampaged all the way from Sui-chou back to Yang-chou, and beyond there to Kua-chou, where cannon fire from Chen-chiang prevented some units, com-pletely out of control, from crossing to the south side of the Yang-tzu.[38]

Hsü Ting-kuo's subsequent surrender and service to the Ch'ing, and the chaotic collapse of the strongest army on the Ming side, were new windfalls but not decisive developments for the Manchus, who would have gone forward with their plans anyway. Consistent with their usual pattern of launching three-pronged campaigns, the Ch'ing sent forces into eastern Ho-nan simultaneously along three routes, through the Hu-lao and Lung passes east of Lo-yang and at the Lan-yang crossing east of K'ai-feng, beginning on April 1, 1645. Their main forces met at Kuei-te in the latter part of the month, while contingents were sent to take over stockades and towns across the broad drainage of eastern Ho-nan.[39] On April 30, Dodo again led his armies out along three routes, aiming to cross the Huai River at Lin-huai, Hsü-i, and Huai-an; and they proceeded "like breaking through bamboo," as Ming forces surrendered, collapsed, or fled before them.[40]

Shih K'o-fa had been in the midst of moving forces northward to meet the Ch'ing challenge at Hsü-chou when he was ordered by the Hung-kuang court to come westward. This was because, although Tso Liang-yü himself had died at Chiu-chiang, his army continued to pillage down the Yang-tzu toward Nan-ching, and Ma Shih-ying, fearing this threat more than he feared the Manchus, suddenly had pulled several commanders out of the northern defense lines to halt the Tso advance. Although Shih, among others, vigorously protested—"I don't know how Ma Shih-ying can be so stupid as this!"—he could not disobey an imperial edict.[41] As Shih predicted, the disorganized Tso army was dealt with easily by the riverine commands, while the Ch'ing crossed at Lin-huai and Hsü-i unopposed.[42]

Shih rode without stopping through mud and rain from P'u-k'ou back to Yang-chou, reaching there only four days before the first Ch'ing units arrived on May 12.[43] Most of Shih's command had become separated in the recent frantic movements north and west. Of those lieutenants who did rejoin him in Yang-chou, several tried to force him to flee the city with them. Shih resisted this but did not try to stop them from leaving. Many residents of Yang-chou also had left. Those who remained were hardbitten and experienced in defending the city; but they also were disgusted with the Ming military, especially Kao Chieh's army which recently had raked through again, and with Shih's having allowed Kao's martial wife and her base unit to billet inside Yang-chou.[44] So a stiff citizens' defense was mounted against the Ch'ing, but there were few Ming regular troops and little internal cohesion.

As the Ch'ing armies gradually surrounded Yang-chou, Dodo repeatedly sent letters urging Shih K'o-fa to surrender—all to no avail. On May 19 they began to bombard one city wall with cannon; the following day it was breached, and Manchu troops poured in. Stories of what then happened to Shih are more legend than fact, but it appears most probable that he was captured after attempting suicide, brought before Dodo, and then executed when he still refused to submit.[45] His body never was found in the carnage.

Because Yang-chou was the first city in Chiang-nan to stubbornly resist the Ch'ing, and perhaps because the Manchus wished to set a clear example for the rest, a general massacre of the city was ordered and continued for more than ten days. One Yang-chou denizen was fortunate to survive and be able to record his horrifying experience:

> A general conflagration was taking place at that time all around the city. More than a dozen places close by were on fire, while farther off the number of burning buildings was too great to count. The crimson light was reflected like lightning or a sunset; the cracking sound went on thundering in my ears without cessation. Again, we heard faintly the flogging and whipping of people, while the wind sobbed with a bitterness entirely beyond my power to describe.

> The women wore long chains around their necks, like clumsy strings of beads, and they stumbled at every step so that they were covered with mud. Here and there on the ground lay small babies who were either trodden under the hooves of horses or the feet of men. The ground was stained with blood and covered with mutilated and dismembered bodies, and the sound of crying was heard everywhere in the open fields. Every gutter and pond

was filled with corpses lying upon one another, and the blood turned the water to a deep greenish-red.

Where the sword hilts clattered and fell, waves of bitter cries arose and hundreds begged for their lives. Whenever soldiers appeared, all the southerners, no matter how great their number, squatted down and dropped their heads. None dared to flee, but each stretched out his neck, expecting the stroke of the sword.

Suddenly I saw a very handsome man of less than thirty wearing a Manchu-style hat, a red coat, a pair of black shoes, and carrying a two-edged sword hanging by his side, accompanied by a follower, also very gallant and brave in appearance, wearing a yellow jacket.... The man in the red coat looked into my eyes and said, ... "Tomorrow His Highness the Prince [Dodo] will order the swords to be sheathed and all of you will be spared."[46]

During this time the Ch'ing eastern-route army, under the Manchu noble-man Junta, had been proceeding more slowly from Hsü-chou toward Huai-an, encountering considerable resistance along the way from units under Liu Tse-ch'ing's command. But as Junta approached Huai-an, Liu and the canal governor there boarded ships and retreated out to sea, while other officials surrendered the city. This Ch'ing army continued to secure territory east of the Grand Canal while Dodo's main force proceeded to the Kua-chou area. There they deployed on May 30, preparing to cross the Yang-tzu.[47]

3. The next objective was to *capture Nan-ching and southern Nan Chih-li*. The naval units at Ching-k'ou and army units at Chen-chiang held back the Ch'ing crossing temporarily; but they were nervous, since most had been transferred there relatively recently from Che-chiang and Fu-chien, and, as explained above, there had been politically caused discontinuities in the chief command. Consequently, the Ch'ing were able, by a distracting ruse, to plant a very small force on the southern bank during the foggy night of June 1; the following morning, discovery of Manchu troops close by threw the Ming soldiers into a panic.[48]

> On the other side of this River stood the Army of China, which was so numerous, as if they had but cast off their very shoos, they had erected such a Rampart against the Tartars, as all the Horse would hardly have sur-mounted it. But it is the resolution and valour in War carries the Trophies, not the number of men: for hardly had the Tartars set foot in their Boats, but the Chineses ran all away, as Sheep use to do when they see the Wolf, leaving the whole shore unfenced to their landing.[49]

As the Ming forces scattered before them, wreaking destruction as they went, the Ch'ing armies in orderly fashion occupied Chen-chiang and swung southwest-ward to Chü-jung, planning to approach Nan-ching from the east and southeast.[50]

As the Ch'ing armies amassed on the Yang-tzu, the Hung-kuang court, which only recently had been grandly celebrating the defeat of Tso Liang-yü, became paralyzed with indecision. No one was willing to take the initiative for either defense or flight, and there was an aura of simply not wanting to know what was happening.

> The emperor assembled his various ministers, but they all were silent. "People outside say that I am about to go 'on tour'," he said. [Grand Secretary] Wang To asked where he had heard such talk, and the emperor pointed to a young eunuch. Wang then unctuously told the eunuch that outside rumors did not warrant repetition, and he went on to request that the emperor set a date for the Court Lecture [on the Classics]. "After the Dragon Boat Festival [May 29]," he replied,

and went back to his inner-court pleasures.[51] In fact, many officials were surreptitiously leaving the capital, and those who remained were making plans to strike a deal with the Manchus, whether by surrendering or by paying them off.[52] Then on the night of June 3, the emperor, without telling either Ma Shih-ying or the empress dowager, charged out the southwestern gate of the city with a band of eunuchs and one thousand horsemen, hoping to find refuge elsewhere. And the next morning Ma Shih-ying, with his personal army and the empress dowager, also headed southward in pursuit of his own survival, not the emperor's.[53]

In their wake, the palace was ransacked and the residences and persons of especially unpopular officials were attacked by irate citizens, as two centers of authority competed for the allegiance of the townspeople: The "False Heir" was released from prison by a frenzied mob, "enthroned" in the palace by a group of minor degree-holders, and began holding court and issuing imperial edicts to the populace; while from his headquarters the commander-in-chief of the capital guard, Earl Chao Chih-lung, tried to keep civil order, waiting to hear the Ch'ing response to his offer—presumably to turn over the city whole and trouble-free in return for favored treatment. On June 6 Chao received the reply he had hoped for and moved to squelch the farcical court of the "heir."[54]

The next day a Ch'ing advance brigade arrived outside the city gate just south of the imperial palace compound; and on June 8 Dodo was received there by a motley assortment of Ming civil and military officials, standing abjectly in the heavy, incessant rain. For a week Dodo camped there, confidently receiving more surrenders, making certain that all was secure inside the city, and enjoying the convivial hospitality of Chao Chih-lung.[55] The latter issued not only his own proclamation to the citizens of Nan-ching castigating the Hung-kuang emperor and his officials, but also Dorgon's proclamation to all the people of Nan Chih-li, Che-chiang, Chiang-hsi, and Hu-kuang faulting that "nest of rats," the southern court, for taking no action against the bandits, prematurely setting up a new monarch, and managing civil and military affairs so badly as to provoke internal rebellion. Death or enslavement was promised for any who opposed the Ch'ing; however, forgiveness, recognition, elevation in rank, and good treatment were promised for those who submitted willingly—including the Prince of Fu. The common people were not to be fearful.[56] Moreover, Dodo ordered that all Chinese *military* men who submitted were to shave their heads and cultivate queues in the Manchu style.[57] The collaborating erstwhile Ming civil and military officials, for their part, also issued an edict to publicize their support:

> Ever since the Liao, Chin, and Yüan [dynasties], those who have entered China from the [northern] deserts, although they [have purported to] replace the wayward with the Way, all have cast aside the good, wrought cleavages, and made accusations [as pretexts] to call up armies. But for raising troops to beat bandits, stirring righteousness to come and rescue, driving out the bandits that our country abominates, avenging the hatred that would not let our former emperor rest in peace, washing away shame and expelling evil—in a thousand years of history has there ever been any like the Great Ch'ing? . . . Since ancient times there never have been troops as humane and well-behaved, as peaceful in manner and civilly self-controlled as those of the Great Ch'ing. Aiding the trustworthy and assisting the submissive, they have brought Man back into accord with Heaven. When they crossed the Great [Yang-tzu] River, the god of winds was behind them; as they entered Nan-ching, the sun came out brightly in the sky. A thousand soldiers and innumerable horses were so quiet, there was not a sound; little children gathered to watch, and the morning markets went on without interruption. The soldiers of the Three Reigns [of golden antiquity] have appeared again today![58]

On June 16, Dodo entered the city and the southern gate of the imperial palace compound on horseback, in full ceremonial array. He asked for the names of all persons on the Ming side who had sacrificed their lives during the occupation of Nan-ching and learned that they totaled twenty-eight.[59]

The Hung-kuang emperor, who had fled to the camp of Huang Te-kung southeast of Wu-hu, was captured there in mid-June after Huang was killed in a confrontation with his erstwhile compatriot, Liu Liang-tso.[60] Liu and his new Manchu comrades then brought the emperor—now just the Prince of Fu again—back to Nan-ching on June 18. Having been reviled along the way by angry crowds, he was subjected to more verbal abuse at a banquet, where he was seated below the "heir" whom he had refused to recognize (but who now temporarily was honored as genuine by Dodo to gain favor with the people of Nan-ching). Sweat soaked his clothing as the rejected Son of Heaven, head held low, stammered inaudibly in response to Dodo's jabbing questions. But for the time being, he was spared physical harm.[61]

Then Dodo sent another expeditionary force, under his cousin Bolo, southeastward along the Grand Canal to help secure the Su-Sung area and to seize Hang-chou, where a rump assemblage of Hung-kuang civil and military officials, and the empress dowager, persuaded the reluctant Prince of Luh to assume the title of Regent on July 1. No governmental measures were taken under this regency, however, apart from sending the perennial intermediary, Ch'en Hung-fan, to negotiate with the Ch'ing. When Bolo's army reached Hang-chou in force on July 6, the regent, the provincial governor, and the townspeople surrendered without resisting. Indeed, the latter were glad to be relieved of the scourge of disorderly Ming troops who, in retreat from debacles on the Yang-tzu, had been milling around the city in large numbers.[62] An ironical threesome—the Prince of Luh, the Prince of Fu, and the "heir"—was taken to Pei-ching in the autumn of 1645, and none of the three seems to have survived very long thereafter.[63]

Most remarkable about all of this was the overwhelming military superiority of the Ch'ing, not only in fighting but, equally important, in controlling their troops when they were not engaging the enemy. A concomitant of this was the ready surrender, *and subsequent active collaboration*, of almost the entire Ming military leadership north of the Yang-tzu.[64] By the time the Ch'ing reached Nan-ching, they had received the submission of twenty-three regional commanders, forty-seven colonels, eighty-six lieutenant-colonels and majors, and 238,300 soldiers.[65] These numbers did not include the core units of Tso Liang-yü and Liu Tse-ch'ing, which also surrendered with little trouble.[66] At this most crucial stage in the history of the Southern Ming, the professional military establishment clearly led the way in scuttling a ship of state that had not done right by them, in favor of a regime, the Ch'ing, that seemed to offer them better conditions and opportunities for success, even as "two-timers."

Having come this far by military means, the Ch'ing now turned to the social, economic, and political aspects of pacification in Chiang-nan, the security of which was recognized as essential to success in future stages of the conquest. Because they overoptimistically believed that the Yang-tzu delta region held great stores of rice which could relieve a prolonged grain shortage in Pei Chih-li, Ch'ing officials long had been concerned to restore service on the Grand Canal, which for two years had been virtually unused and, like the Yellow River dikes, was in dire need of maintenance.[67] They also moved quickly, for both symbolic and fiscal-administrative reasons, to depute their own officials to various prefectural and district seats to collect the local land and tax registers.

Also demanding attention was the restoration of some form of civil government in what the Ming had treated as its "southern capital" in its Southern

Metropolitan Area. Soon the Ch'ing court decided not to follow the Ming pattern in this respect, but to rename Nan-ching as "Chiang-ning" and to make it the seat of the *province* of Chiang-nan (i.e., what had been Nan Chih-li).* The Nan-ching bureaucracy, thus, was to be trimmed down and reorganized. By late August Dodo had recommended 372 Han Chinese for provincial posts in Chiang-nan, besides also incorporating 374 former Ming military nobles and officers into the Ch'ing military system.[68] Moreover, in early August the extraordinarily able and dedicated collaborator, Hung Ch'eng-ch'ou, was appointed to be Viceroy for all regions of the South under Ch'ing control and, as such, from his headquarters in Nan-ching to handle all political, organizational, and logistical affairs.[69] This appointment marked an important transition for the Ch'ing, that is, to placing more balanced emphases on the sociopolitical and military aspects of their "great undertaking."

Of more immediate concern for the populace were thirty-eight items of policy, which were promulgated in Pei-ching to take effect in the South from June 24. Similar to those announced the previous year for the North, these included a general amnesty; cancellation of all late Ming supernumerary taxes, irregular levies, odd revenue schemes, and arrears accumulated because of these; harsh punishment for official abuses and corruption; tax remissions, especially in areas that submitted obediently to the Ch'ing; judicious employment of good civil and military officials who came to allegiance sincerely, and extension of invitations to other officials, nobles, and talented social leaders of the former dynasty; revival of trade; care for the destitute and reunion of families; restoration of properties grabbed by local bosses or bullies, and resettlement of people in their former homes; reinstitution of the government school system and the civil service examinations; and other pronouncements designed to win the compliance of the people to Ch'ing rule. Toward enemies not yet subdued, the Ch'ing offered various inducements: leniency to surrendering rebels; employment with no reduction in rank, title, or level of emolument for Ming resistance leaders who might surrender willingly; and dignified treatment, including state subsidization, for Ming princes who presented themselves to the Ch'ing authorities.[70]

One of these items, however, departed sharply from previous Ch'ing policy. This was the order, issued from Pei-ching on June 28 and from Nan-ching on July 21, that all nonclerical adult male citizens demonstrate their allegiance to the Ch'ing by adopting the Manchu hairstyle and cut of dress. Generally it was recognized that a considerable length of time would be needed

---

*The names Nan-ching and Nan Chih-li are used throughout this writing, both for consistency and to maintain the Ming perspective.

for everyone's clothing to be altered or made anew with the high collar, narrow sleeves, and open-pleated lower garment of the Manchus; but shaving of the head, leaving only a small, round patch of hair at the back for a braided queue— derisively called the "coin[-sized] rat's tail"—was a different matter. This was to be enforced on pain of death within ten days of the order's receipt in each locality.[71]

As mentioned above, the Manchus previously had rescinded this order in the North, and when they took Nan-ching it was made very clear that only military personnel were to adopt Manchu styles, presumably so that enemies and allies could be distinguished in battle.[72] On the surface it appears that, having secured both Ming capitals, the Manchus now thought (perhaps prematurely) that they were in a position strong enough to again insist that "rulers and subjects be of one body." From the diary of Regent Dorgon we also learn, however, that just two days before promulgation of the hair-and-dress order in Pei-ching, he had been angered by the argument of some Chinese that, according to their "system of rites and music," shaving the head was improper. Dorgon retorted that the Manchus *too* had a system of social and ceremonial norms which should not be dismissed as inferior to that of the Chinese.

> There may be some sense in the idea that one's hair and skin are from one's parents and, thus, ought not to be harmed. But I will not stand for this droning on about the [Chinese, hence, universally normative] "system of rites and music." Thus far I have been tolerant with officials and have not pressed them to shave their heads; but now, hearing these arguments, I am going to insist on this for officials and common people alike.[73]

Whether it arose from cool calculation or from pique, or both, the sudden reinstitution and draconian enforcement of this decree to "lose your hair or lose your head," more than any other factor, inflamed the people's spirit to resist.

In the Yang-tzu region, countercurrents of resistance arose in three large areas: Nan Chih-li south of the Yang-tzu, central Chiang-hsi, and central and northeastern Hu-kuang. Although conditions in each of these areas varied greatly (as did conditions in various locales within each area), some generalizations can be made about this stage in the Ming struggle. First, in each area the normal Ming military infrastructure had collapsed, and regular commands remained only in fragments. Consequently, attempts to mobilize armed resistance were disjointed, ad hoc, and feverish, with little or no regional coordination, or even much communication among leaders in proximate locations.

Second, this basic weakness on the Ming side was made worse by conflicts and failures to cooperate among (1) the *civil element*, which here includes Ming civil officials and the military units (whether mercenaries or militia) under their

A Ch'ing-period barber prepares to tidy up the bristled pate of a customer in his "head-shaving parlor."

Male patrons of a Ch'ing-period bathhouse display their queues, one hanging down the back in the usual manner and the other wound around the pate for convenience.

Two gentlemen of Ming times, wearing the typical loose-necked robe tied with a sash at the waist. Both have full heads of hair, tied back at the crown in one case, or allowed to fall freely in the other.

Two gentlemen of Ch'ing times, both with shaven pates (and queues not visible from the front). Both wear the typical high, stiff collar, buttoned snugly across the right shoulder. One wears the cinched-up belt and tapered sleeves characteristic of Manchu riding apparel, whereas the other wears the free-falling robe and voluminous sleeves of the literatus.*

*The author extends heartfelt thanks to the respected Ming-Ch'ing historian and bibliophile Mr. Su T'ung-ping, of the Institute of History and Philology of the Academia Sinica, who provided these illustrations from the *Wu-chün ming-hsien t'u chuan tsan* and the *Ch'ing-su chi-wen*.

personal direction; local degree-holders and other notables, with the semiprivate forces they raised using their own fortunes and civic contributions; and volunteer, auxiliary units composed of commoners in their own locales; (2) the *professional military element*, which here includes regional and garrison commanders of both land and naval forces; and (3) the *outlaw element*, which here includes remnants of the large roving-rebel armies, local bandit and pirate groups, and other armed, illegal organizations such as underground gangs. Certainly for actors in the resistance tragedy, things were not as clear-cut as in the statements above. There was much blurring of identities, as parts of one element coalesced mercurially with parts of another, in a tangled profusion of activities. For instance, erstwhile outlaws—common fighters as well as some outstanding leaders—constituted a large portion of the professional military by this time, adding greatly to problems of control in that sector. And even volunteer soldiers turned to outlawry when that was necessary for survival. But as a means of grasping the panorama of Yang-tzu resistance within the context of Southern Ming history as a whole, the above categories appear serviceable.

Best known is the resistance in southern Nan Chih-li, which was most intense in the economically most advanced areas, Ch'ang-chou and Su-chou prefectures in the east and Hui-chou prefecture in the west. In the former, regional military authority had been weakened earlier by the removal of Ch'i Piao-chia as governor of the Su-chou circuit; and it was smashed when the regional defense forces, which had been concentrated at Chen-chiang, were routed by the Ch'ing as they crossed the Yang-tzu from Kua-chou. While troops from other provinces were fleeing back to their home garrisons, the new circuit governor himself had stopped only briefly in Su-chou before retreating with just his personal guard into southern Che-chiang; and the regional commander of Su-Sung navies had been so weakened that he scarcely was able to do more than find respite for his remaining forces among the pirates and waterborne vigilante groups on the eastern side of T'ai Lake.[74] In southwestern Nan Chih-li, the depredations of Tso Liang-yü's army and the subsequent arrival of the Manchus under Ajige had removed from action the viceroy at Chiu-chiang, Yüan Chi-hsien, and thrown the other Yang-tzu defense commanders between An-ch'ing and Nan-ching into a flurry of retreat—many all the way out to sea. The death of Huang Te-kung near Wu-hu removed the last chance for regional military coordination in that area.

Moreover, as the Hung-kuang regime collapsed, Nan-ching was taken over, and as Ch'ing officials were deputed to claim administrative records and occupy the various *ya-men*, almost all the magistrates and prefects in southern Nan Chih-li had abandoned their posts. They did so in view of threats both from the Ch'ing and from increasingly bold dissident and lawless social elements—bands of indentured servants who sought release from their contracts and revenge on their masters, secret religious organizations that sought redress for past suppressions, Mafia-like clubs that now found freer rein for engaging in "protection" and extortion, and private armies raised by local bullies and bigshots who tried to arrogate to themselves public funds and supplies, to cite a few of the kinds.[75] This meant the disappearance not only of regional authority, but also of local authority over the self-defense forces that had been organized in most locales. There ensued macabre games of hide-and-seek, king-of-the-mountain, and musical chairs, as various armed groups sought to eliminate local enemies and vied for control of the *ya-men*.

In many places loyalist figures stepped forward and attempted either to forestall the complete collapse of, or to restore Ming leadership in, the seats of their home or assigned districts and prefectures, especially when word of the hair-and-dress decree stirred anger among the people. These men mostly were degree-holders, former officials, incumbent local officials who had been displaced by the Ch'ing, and second-string local officials who had fallen heir to *ya-men* responsibilities when their superiors had fled. This predominantly civil resistance leadership tried manfully to piece together credible defense forces from the disparate armed elements at hand, and from branches and fragments of regional armies and navies nearby. But in almost no cases were they able to maintain control of their shaky coalitions, having had little or no previous experience in military affairs. In the end, most lost the support even of their peers, the local gentry, who wished mainly to avoid military hostilities and to restore social order. If that could have been done under leaders who stood for the Ming, then all the better (for despite everything, Ming dynastic symbols still elicited positive responses from all classes of people). But when the best chance for civil order seemed to lie, rather, in cooperating with Ch'ing representatives, who were Han Chinese themselves and might be able to keep the Manchu horsemen away if Ming resistance could be stifled, then the support of the local social elite often was withdrawn from the loyalists.[76] (For the discussion below, see map 4.)

Resistance in southern Nan Chih-li began in late July and early August in districts of Ch'ang-chou and Su-chou that were among the first to receive the hair-and-dress decree—Chiang-yin, Chia-ting, K'un-shan, Sung-chiang. But these locales had no natural defense advantages, aside from the many waterways that made cavalry and artillery movements inconvenient. District city gates and walls simply became fodder for Ch'ing cannon, and the efforts of resisters to counter sabers with bamboo poles and crossbows with flung pots of excrement can only be characterized as pathetic. Cities that fought stubbornly in this way

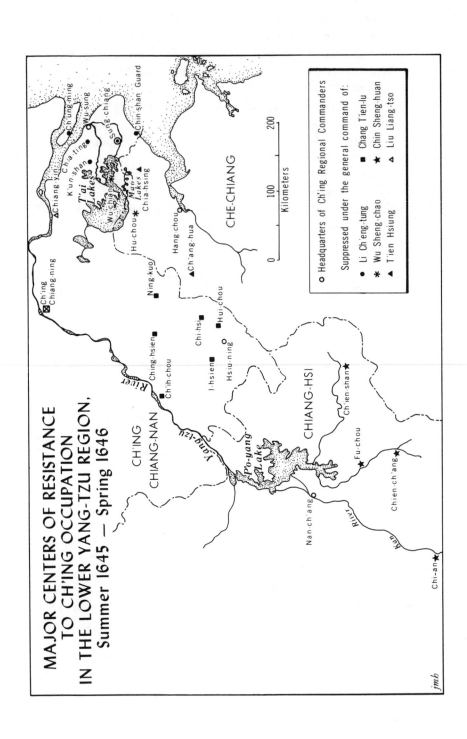

MAJOR CENTERS OF RESISTANCE
TO CH'ING OCCUPATION
IN THE LOWER YANG-TZU REGION,
Summer 1645 — Spring 1646

CH'ING

CHIANG-NAN

Yang-tzu River

CHE-CHIANG

CHIANG-HSI

River

River

Ch'ung-ming
Wu-sung
Sung-chiang
Chin-shan Guard
Chia-ting
Chiang-yin
K'un-shan
Tai Lakes
Wu-chiang
Mao Lakes
Chia-hsing
Hu-chou
Hang-chou
Ch'ang-hua
Ning-kuo
Ch'eng-ning
Ch'ing
Chiang-ning
Ch'ing-hsien
Chih-chou
I-hsien
Chi-hsi
Hsiu-ning
Hui-chou

Po-yang Lake
Nan-ch'ang
Chien-shan
Fu-chou
Chien-ch'ang
Chi-an

Kilometers
0   100   200

○ Headquarters of Ch'ing Regional Commanders

Suppressed under the general command of:

● Li Ch'eng-tung   ■ Chang T'ien-lu
✻ Wu Sheng-chao   ★ Chin Sheng-huan
▲ T'ien Hsiung   △ Liu Liang-tso

jmb

were put to the sword as mercilessly as at Yang-chou, the primary "butcher" here being a general from Shih K'o-fa's command who had surrendered to the Ch'ing at Hsü-chou, Li Ch'eng-tung.[77]

Open rebellion began somewhat later in Hui-chou, Ning-kuo, and Ch'ih-chou prefectures to the west. And it persisted longer there, also, in part because Ch'ing units needed more time to reach that area in force, in part because of the exceptional ability of the Hui-chou resistance leader, Chin Sheng, but perhaps most important, because of the natural defensibility of the intermontane corridor that stretches from Ning-kuo to Hsiu-ning. Suppression in this area was not so brutal as in the delta, however, thanks to the more humane policies of the Ch'ing regional commander-in-chief, another who formerly had been under Shih K'o-fa, Chang T'ien-lu.[78] Although incidents continued to erupt, especially to the southwest of Nan-ching, through the spring of the following year,[79] most of the open, land-based resistance in southern Nan Chih-li was broken by early December 1645.

For the Ch'ing, whose strength was based on cavalry, the activities that were most difficult to counter at this stage were those of loyalists who joined forces with pirates, fishermen, and remnants of Ming naval commands on Ch'ung-ming Island in the mouth of the Yang-tzu and on T'ai Lake in the center of the delta. While resisters in Ch'ang-chou Prefecture sought aid from Ch'ung-ming, those on T'ai Lake struck out to the east, south, and west, to bolster comrades in such cities as Su-chou, Wu-chiang, Hu-chou, Ch'ang-hsing, and I-hsing. Although Li Ch'eng-tung rounded out his suppression campaign by establishing (tenuous) Ch'ing control on Ch'ung-ming in the early winter of 1645, the core of the lacustrine movement was not soundly defeated by the Ch'ing regional commander-in-chief for Su-Sung navies, Wu Sheng-chao, until May of 1646.[80] (For the following discussion, see map 6.)

Regional military command in northern Chiang-hsi had been weakened and destabilized by the depredations of Chang Hsien-chung's roving rebel army before the fall of Pei-ching. And, similar to the case in southwestern Nan Chih-li, it had been almost completely ruined by the successive waves of Tso Liang-yü's army and the pursuing Ch'ing from Wu-ch'ang. As Viceroy Yüan Chi-hsien was being captured near Chiu-chiang, the provincial governor had fled southward from Nan-ch'ang. But a renegade Ming colonel, who became disgruntled when the townspeople and local defense corps of Wan-an fought back against the raping and pillaging of his troops, seized the governor and presented him as a token of surrender to the Ch'ing authorities.[81]

At this time "the Ch'ing authorities" at Nan-ch'ang and Chiu-chiang were little more than the staff of Chin Sheng-huan, another general from Shih K'o-fa's command who had been assigned to assist Tso Liang-yü. When Tso's army

surrendered to the Ch'ing, Chin had incorporated a portion of the rebel army of
Li Tzu-ch'eng that spilled over from Hu-kuang, and had moved quickly to take
over the P'o-yang Lake region in late June and early July, hoping to earn special
merit with the Ch'ing by promptly delivering into their control the whole
province of Chiang-hsi.[82]

These events rendered insignificant the few incidents of resistance within
Chin's sphere in the northern part of the province and, from the outset, moved
the front line, so to speak, of loyalist activity down to central Chiang-hsi—Lu-
ch'i, Chien-ch'ang, Lin-chiang, Yüan-chou. But no loyalist united front should
be imagined. On the eastern side of the Kan River, resistance activity centered on
restoring, losing, restoring, and losing again such major urban centers as Chien-
ch'ang and Fu-chou. There the most prominent leaders were minor Ming
imperial princes, reflecting the especially great concentration of imperial clansmen in that region. Little is known about their efforts, except that they were
sporadically persistent, in spite of their lack of experience or provisions.[83]
Typically parochial in outlook, these minor princes do not seem to have had the
ability or inclination to extend communications or enter into organized cooperation with loyalist forces to their east and west. For assistance, they and their
supporters drew mainly on aboriginal fighters and mountain bandits from the
infamous Chiang-hsi, Fu-chien, Kuang-tung border region[84]—hardly the stuff
with which to rebuild the military infrastructure of the province. The continuation of loyalist action in this theater can be attributed in part to trouble within
the ranks of Chin Sheng-huan (see chapter 5), in part to the proximity of refuge
in the mountains to the east, and in no small measure to the attempts—though
frustrated and uncoordinated—of commanders from Fu-chien to come to their
aid (see chapter 3).[85]

The devastation in northeastern Chiang-hsi throughout the 1640s was
especially severe, and its effects were to persist for many years, despite the
nominal establishment of Ch'ing authority there. One merchant, traveling
through this region into Che-chiang as late as 1654, was appalled to find that

> inside the walls of every city I went through—An-jen, Kuei-ch'i, Ko-yang,
> Kuang-hsin, Yü-shan—there were only several dozen households. And on
> the river I scarcely saw any boats—only that of a man from Hui-chou, who
> came along and moored with me. He said it was because the garrison
> general, a man named K'ang from Ho-nan, daily sent toughs into the
> villages to attack the rural people and return, while calling it [the work of]
> "hill bandits." They slaughtered and pillaged just about everywhere. In the
> whole prefecture of Kuang-hsin, no district had all its villages, no village
> had all its families, no family had all its members, and no man had all his
> womenfolk. To pursue my salt business, I made haste to pass right through,
> and no one ventured to hail me down. In the [formerly] rich households of

the prominent clans, everyone sat around waiting for death. When they got a pint of my grain or a pinch of my salt, they were very pleased and said [self-deprecatingly], "We want it but are not worthy." When I heard such words, I covered my ears and left in haste.[86]

To the west of the Kan River, resistance was more organized and the elements of success were more in evidence. Most local officials still were in place, and they were reinforced by prominent officials from the Ch'ung-chen and Hung-kuang courts whose homes were in Chiang-hsi. Moreover, large numbers of Ming regular troops, which had been specially recruited from Yün-nan and Kuang-tung in the previous two years, had stopped in western Chiang-hsi when they learned of the fall of Nan-ching and now were eager to fight.

The Kuang-tung troops went barefoot, but they could leap across mountain valleys as though flying. The Yün-nan troops had especially hard armor and sharp weapons, and their muskets and repeating crossbows could pierce men's chests like punching holes in notebooks.[87]

But the elements of success did not fuse, for the civil officials in charge could not control the conflicts that arose between the "host" and "guest" military units, and between the soldiers and the populace, which itself had been fraught with widespread revolts by indentured laborers. One troop-supervising censor, appealing for aid to Fu-chien, put it this way:

Generals now are fighting with generals and in turn with the civil officials. Troops are fighting with other troops and also with the people. . . . Although there are several very conscientious censorial officials in the area, they can scarcely just keep the peace; and it is no wonder that [the new viceroy] is at his wit's end. I recommend that *no more troops* be sent to this area, since that would only make matters worse. Rather, you should send *officials who can get the troops back in order.*[88]

In spite of these problems (and again, partly because of troubles on Chin Sheng-huan's side), the loyalists were able to advance from the southwest and restore Chi-an in the late autumn of 1645.[89] But then the powers of Viceroy were given to the former Hung-kuang Vice Minister of the Court of the Imperial Stud, Wan Yüan-chi, who had extensive experience in military affairs, but who does not seem to have had the right touch with his "outside" regulars.

[Previously] the Yün-nan generals Chao Yin-hsüan and Hu I-ch'ing had been pleased to be treated very respectfully as guests, so they fought bravely and had considerable success. . . . But then Wan [Yüan-chi] tried to control them by talking about the "body and system," and they became unhappy.

Wan, in turn, treated them even more superciliously and sought, instead, to rely on temporarily cooperative bandit forces that were supposed to come from the mountains to the southeast. A new Ch'ing counterforce arrived first, however. Wan's defenses collapsed, and Chi-an was lost again.[90] This occurred in May of 1646, when Ch'ing forces also were quelling the last major incidents of rebellion in the northeastern corner of the province.[91] Thereafter, popular resistance in Chiang-hsi was confined largely to Kan-chou Prefecture in the far south.

In central Hu-kuang the Ming resistance began under even more chaotic conditions than in Nan Chih-li or Chiang-hsi. But because of the herculean efforts of a few especially able officials, and because the Ch'ing position in Hu-kuang initially was the weakest and most difficult to reinforce, organized loyalist opposition held out much longer there. Regional military control first had been undermined in Hu-kuang when Chang Hsien-chung broadly occupied the center of that province in 1643.[92] Ming generals who escaped destruction during that time did so by retreating into the mountainous periphery of the south, where they survived and held their men together by hook or crook. And after Chang abandoned Hu-kuang for Szu-ch'uan, they remained warily independent, never willing to submit fully again to central direction or coordination from Wu-ch'ang.[93] Moreover, when the army of Tso Liang-yü rebelled, the viceroy for Hu-kuang, Ho T'eng-chiao, barely escaped with his life and the clothes on his back after being kidnapped and taken downriver into Chiang-hsi. When he finally made it back to Hu-kuang, he had to recreate provincial civil and military government at Ch'ang-sha virtually from nothing.[94]

Complicating matters immensely for both the Ming and Ch'ing sides were portions of Li Tzu-ch'eng's and Tso Liang-yü's armies that had become scattered over the entire central Yang-tzu region from Ching-chou to Chiu-chiang. Most of these units either had feigned surrender to the Ch'ing and then broken with them as soon as circumstances permitted, or they had made gestures falsely indicating a willingness to submit[95]—all in a frantic scramble for food (which had become extremely scarce in this region), more secure positions, and at least brief respite from the exhausting and disorienting movements of the past few months. While some of Tso Liang-yü's generals came back up the Yang-tzu and offered their services to Ho T'eng-chiao from Yüeh-chou, the two largest remaining parts of Li Tzu-ch'eng's army, now having lost their supreme leader, sought acceptance under the Ming banner from Ho in the Ch'ang-sha and Hsiang-yin area, and from the new provincial governor, Tu Yin-hsi, near Ch'ang-te.[96] Ho T'eng-chiao, who at first did not even know who the rebels were, hardly considered all this convergence to be a boon, since he, as Viceroy, thereby became responsible for stationing and supplying several hundred thousand soldiers of every stripe and hue, when only a small fraction of them actually could be supported adequately in that devastated province.

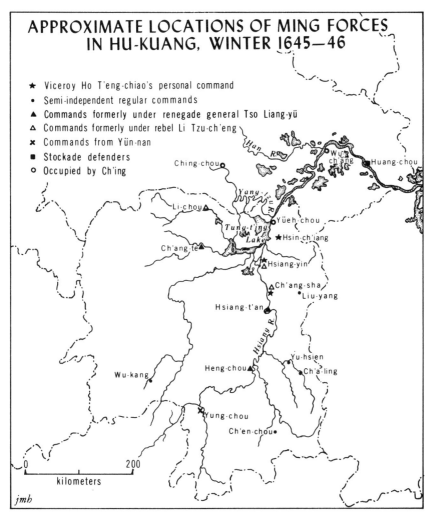

APPROXIMATE LOCATIONS OF MING FORCES
IN HU-KUANG, WINTER 1645—46

★ Viceroy Ho T'eng-chiao's personal command
• Semi-independent regular commands
▲ Commands formerly under renegade general Tso Liang-yü
△ Commands formerly under rebel Li Tzu-ch'eng
× Commands from Yün-nan
■ Stockade defenders
○ Occupied by Ch'ing

Han R.

Ching-chou○ Wu-ch'ang Huang-chou

Yang.

Li-chou▲

Tung-t'ing Lake Yüeh-chou
★Hsin-ch'iang

Ch'ang-te▲

▲Hsiang-yin

△Ch'ang-sha
★ •Liu-yang

Hsiang-t'an

Hsiang R.

Yu-hsien

Wu-kang Heng-chou▲ ★Ch'a-ling

×Yung-chou

Ch'en-chou•

0   200
kilometers

jmh

Consequently, although Ho assigned his various commanders to certain positions, he could do little but acquiesce when they pillaged and moved around at
will, trying to survive (see map 5).[97]

Ch'ing officials at Ching-chou and Wu-ch'ang, also, were justifiably anxious and frustrated, feeling surrounded by an amorphous but dangerous and
unpredictable enemy, and lacking sufficient soldiers or supplies to deal with the
situation. Plaintive appeals to Nan-ching and Pei-ching yielded results only
slowly, for the limited number of reliable Ch'ing forces were deeply involved
elsewhere. Moreover, in seizing Chiang-nan the Ch'ing had fallen heir to the

Hung-kuang court's basic problem vis-à-vis Hu-kuang, that is, the reversal of the usual economic relation between the two regions, calling for Chiang-nan to supply Hu-kuang with grain, rather than vice versa. Besides, much of the Yang-tzu delta's already depleted grain stores had been sent to relieve long-standing shortages in Pei Chih-li.[98] Like the Hung-kuang court, the Ch'ing also found themselves in the dilemma of having to cut back on tax remissions and reinstitute canceled levies, while realizing that the agricultural population sorely needed some relief from these exactions in order to restore production.[99] Because of these circumstances, not until late February of 1646 did a Manchu commander-in-chief of princely rank, Lekdehun, reach Wu-ch'ang to take charge of the suppression campaign there.[100]

Ho T'eng-chiao soon found that he could not rely on the "highwaymen" from Tso's army, that the erstwhile Shun rebels had their own pressing needs and customary leadership practices, and that the virtually autonomous commanders of Ming regulars in Hu-kuang would respond to his orders only when it suited their convenience. Consequently, at the advice of his remarkable assistant, Chang K'uang—one of the very few examples of all-around excellence in both civil and military management in the Southern Ming—Ho created de novo his own viceroy's command, largely from Yün-nan troops who subsequently remained devotedly loyal to him (Ho also being a native of the Southwest). By tireless shuffling, maneuvering, and squeezing blood from the stone of southern Hu-kuang resources, Ho and Chang were able to maintain a stout and sometimes offensive front against the Ch'ing just south of Yüeh-chou. And they even managed to send some help to northwestern Chiang-hsi for more than a year, from the early winter of 1645 until the early spring of 1647.[101] This was not done, however, without placing intense pressure on the populace.

> Suddenly a levy was added for "righteous provisions," and at the same time [they] wanted to call up a whole year's land tax from the people at over six times [the regular rate] per mu. When that was not enough, [they] invoked the precedent of having the tax captains produce [the needed amounts], and so the local headmen and minor officials all used [their own] properties to acquit themselves. And when that was not enough, then requisitions were declared. Wicked people then secretly made accusations against the well-to-do, and the fines [assessed on the latter] for provisions completely ruined them.... The people of southern Hu-kuang gradually became [so] disoriented and dislocated that more than half of them did not survive.[102]

Even after the arrival of Lekdehun's task force, the Ch'ing were not able to concentrate on challenging the loyalists' front in Hu-kuang until they cleared up some peculiar trouble to their rear. The slopes of the Ta-pieh Mountains, which separate Wu-ch'ang and Huang-chou prefectures in northeastern Hu-kuang from Ho-nan Province further north, were filled with hundreds of stockades and barricades. Especially since the first promulgation of the Manchu hair-and-dress decree in Hu-kuang, these fortifications had been manned and fiercely defended by common people and miscellaneous military officers who refused to submit to Ch'ing rule. In most cases, groups of stockades put up united defenses, and there is some evidence of communication between the leaders of this activity and Ho T'eng-chiao's men across the Yang-tzu to the southwest. But no regional command ever evolved that could have seriously put pincers on Wu-ch'ang. The stockade defenders were stubborn, heroic, and isolated, epitomizing the condition of the whole popular resistance effort at this stage. Ch'ing forces, spearheaded by the intrepid colonel, Hsü Yung, gradually defeated them, locale by locale, through 1646,[103] while Lekdehun concentrated on breaking up or driving back remnants of Li Tzu-ch'eng's army that still were threatening Ching-chou and the middle Han River area to the northwest.[104]

By the end of 1646, the Ch'ing had become convinced that Ho T'eng-chiao could not be persuaded to surrender; moreover, for the time being they considered their campaigns against rebels to the northeast and northwest of Wu-ch'ang to be completed.[105] So in late September 1646, a generalissimo and two commanders-in-chief were named to undertake a fresh campaign on the far South. This was the famous trio of ennobled collaborating generals, K'ung Yu-te, Keng Chung-ming, and Shang K'o-hsi.[106] When these men attacked in force south of Yüeh-chou in late March 1647, Ho T'eng-chiao's armies, plagued by poor communications and internal resentments (especially of Ho's own regulars against the less disciplined "savages" from the Tso and Li armies) simply collapsed and scattered. The Ch'ing then took Ch'ang-sha, while Ho and Chang K'uang were forced to retreat south of Heng-chou.[107] For the time being, the whole Yang-tzu region seemed to be firmly in the Ch'ing grasp; however, especially in Hu-kuang, chaos still was more prevalent than order. As the Ch'ing regional inspector for southern Hu-kuang reported after his first tour:

> Since 1642, every year [the area] has suffered burning and killing, and every place has been a battleground. Add to that the unusual natural calamities of this spring, [and so] the roads are full of skeletons and rotting flesh, the town walls full of tangled weeds. From Yüeh-chou to Ch'ang-sha, ... I did not see a single hut nor a single person on the road. No painting could depict my anguish and horror. Ch'ang-sha was occupied for several years by pernicious groups who long since had thoroughly scraped off the people's fat; and as they prepared to retreat, they also massacred the towndwellers. [So now] the people have completely abandoned the city and fled far away. However, in the high hills and along the lakeshores there still are some people who, in time, can be summoned to return. ... In Heng-chou, besides the killing and enslavement [of the people] by troops and bandits for several years in a row,

last year not a grain was harvested, so this spring and summer the price of rice has surged upward, and more than half the people have died of starvation.[108]

From these developments and circumstances it should be evident that the long struggle between the Ming and Ch'ing was not so much a direct clash between two states as a competition to see which side would prevail over, or be defeated by, a third state, so to speak, that of sociopolitical anarchy, which engulfed locales one by one in the middle decades of the seventeenth century. In the whole eighteen-year span of the Southern Ming, there were not more than a handful of instances in which the Ch'ing had to fight to wrest control of a community from Ming officials and military forces that had been in place there prior to the dynastic crisis. The problem for the Ming had been to maintain control, and for the Ch'ing it was to reestablish control, over a patchwork quilt of districts, prefectures, and circuits the size of a subcontinent. Generally speaking, the Ming lost in this competition more rapidly than the Ch'ing won.

CHAPTER THREE

Second Stand:
The Lu and Lung-wu Regimes

RESISTANCE to Ch'ing occupation of the Yang-tzu region was abetted (symbolically for the most part, and physically to some extent) by two Southern Ming courts, which were established separately but almost simultaneously in Eastern Che-chiang* and in Fu-chien after the failure to sustain a regency at Hang-chou. Although these two regimes were different in several respects, and had their differences, so to speak, as well, both suffered from the same kinds of problems in military operations and top-level decision-making as were characteristic of the whole Southern Ming.

In the second week of July 1645, as the Manchu prince Bolo took over Hang-chou, Ch'ing agents quickly crossed the mouth of the Ch'ien-t'ang River[†] and entered the two most prosperous prefectures in Che-chiang, Shao-hsing and Ning-po, on the southern side of Hang-chou Bay. There, as in the Yang-tzu delta area, most local Ming officials simply left their posts, and Ch'ing replacements took over the prefectural and several district ya-men, receiving the welcome of some local elders before other residents had time to organize any opposition.[1] But also, as previously was the case, issuance of the Ch'ing hair-and-dress decree in this area was the spark that ignited the fire of popular resistance. Uprisings against Ch'ing officials began in Yü-yao on July 31 and quickly spread to K'uai-chi, Yin, and Tz'u-ch'i.[2] Within days the thin Ch'ing presence in Eastern Che-chiang had been removed. Moreover, compared to the resistance in southern

---

*I.e., Che-chiang east of the Ch'ien-t'ang River and south of Hang-chou Bay. Che-chiang west of the river and north of the bay commonly was called "Western Che-chiang."

†Strictly speaking, this river is called the Ch'ien-t'ang only in its lowermost section where it separates Hang-chou and Shao-hsing prefectures. But for convenience, in this writing the whole watercourse, from Hang-chou southwestward past Ch'ü-chou, is called the Ch'ien-t'ang River.

Nan Chih-li, that in Eastern Che-chiang, a "land of bells and drums" where people took pride in their upright traditions, soon exhibited a considerably greater degree of social cohesion and effective leadership on the part of the local scholar-official elite.

In view of the spontaneous eruption of this resistance, various officials and social leaders sought out the Prince of Lu (Chu I-hai), who, having fled his estate in Shan-tung, had been assigned to reside in T'ai-chou, Che-chiang. There the prince acceded to requests that he step forth and lend the aura of the imperial house to the Ming restoration movement in that area. He soon was transported to the prefectural seat of Shao-hsing and assumed the title of Regent some time in late August or early September.[3] Well before the regent's arrival, leaders of auxiliary, volunteer, and regular land and naval forces had begun moving spiritedly to establish a protective arc around Eastern Che-chiang, from Yen-

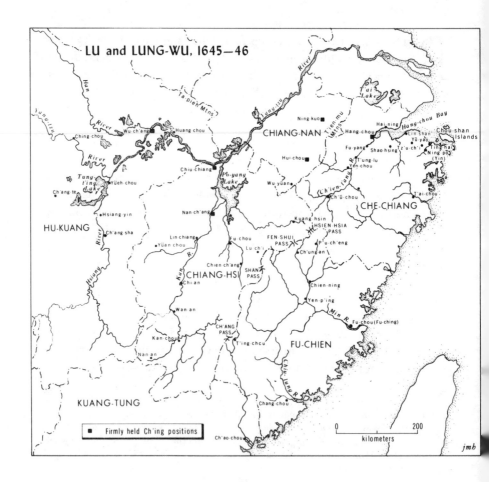

chou Prefecture on the middle Ch'ien-t'ang to the naval base at Ting-hai near Ning-po, with encampments most dense between T'ung-lu and Lin-shan. (For this chapter, see map 6). Thus fortified, and with offensive footholds across the waters at Fu-yang and Hai-ning, the loyalists hoped to link up with compatriots in Western Che-chiang and southern Nan Chih-li to make the Ch'ing position in Hang-chou untenable.[4]

During this time, another Ming prince, whose estate originally was in Ho-nan, had been traveling through Che-chiang on his way to a newly assigned residence in Kuang-hsi. The Prince of T'ang (Chu Yü-chien), when first approached by officials who wanted him to assume the regency, deferred to his generational senior, the Prince of Luh. But when the Luh regency dissolved, the Prince of T'ang, by then in the middle Ch'ien-t'ang area, accepted the formal "three urgings" of the former Hung-kuang minister of Rites, Huang Tao-chou, and at Ch'ü-chou on July 10 announced his intention to become the next regent.[5] From there he was escorted over Hsien-hsia Pass into Fu-chien by Regional Commander Cheng Hung-k'uei, who, having abandoned the Yang-tzu defense at Chen-chiang, then was hastily moving his army back into their home province.[6]

At each step along the way—P'u-ch'eng, Chien-ning, Shui-k'ou—the Prince of T'ang primed himself and the populace for an exemplary reign; and he praised the preparations of the one man who, more than any other, would make the inception of that reign possible, the real military power in Fu-chien, (Cheng Hung-k'uei's elder brother) Earl Cheng Chih-lung. When he arrived outside Fu-chou, the provincial capital, on July 26, even before formally assuming regental status, the prince named a full array of grand secretaries, ministers, and other officials, and began expounding the principles of his court. Three days later he entered Fu-chou city and proclaimed his regency with an earnestly regal flourish. And on August 18 he ascended the imperial throne, established the reign title Lung-wu, declared Fu-chou to be the temporary capital of the country, and confirmed his younger brother as successor to the title Prince of T'ang.[7]

The new emperor immediately ordered that his enthronement proclamation be publicized in Chiang-hsi, the Hui-chou area of Nan Chih-li, and southwestern Che-chiang. He issued a spate of invitations and appointments to prominent men who were vaguely thought to be potential Ming-restorationist leaders in those areas; and after he had been on the throne only a week, the Lung-wu emperor had to be restrained from launching forthwith a "personally-led campaign" out the northwestern passes to check the Ch'ing advance.[8] The emperor then settled down somewhat to the business of establishing an imperial government in Fu-chou and to making more adequate military preparations, but he remained committed to "going out the passes" as soon as possible.

As yet, neither the Lu nor the Lung-wu court knew of the other. There ensued one of the most lamented sequences of events in the history of the Southern Ming. Some time in early October 1645, the Lung-wu regime learned that it had a rival in Che-chiang. An emissary carrying a copy of the Lung-wu ascension proclamation was dispatched immediately to Shao-hsing, where his arrival discomfited and divided Lu official ranks. Regent Lu was willing, at first, to step down in favor of his "august uncle" in Fu-chien (the Prince of T'ang being one generation senior to him, both genealogically and in age), and several respected figures urged that the Shao-hsing court subordinate itself to the larger cause.[9] However, Grand Secretary and Minister of War Chang Kuo-wei passionately stated the opposing arguments: that "the whip [of command] was not long enough to reach" all the way from Fu-chou, that the resistance movement in Eastern Che-chiang (though heroic) was fragile and would collapse if the regent withdrew, and that a transfer of loyalties at that point would constitute a rupture of trust between sovereign and ministers. Regent Lu was persuaded by such pleading, other officials felt constrained to show unanimity in rejecting the Lung-wu proclamation, and emissaries were sent back with a restatement of Chang's position.[10] Consequently, although many Lu officials and generals secretly requested or accepted Lung-wu appointments and titles, no practical accommodation was sought formally by the Lu court, and a "fire-and-water" relation developed between the two regimes.

The following February 1646, the Lung-wu emperor sent a long, moving, personal letter to his "nephew prince" expressing heartfelt disappointment that the latter had declined to recognize him as Emperor, stating his own unselfish reasons for claiming a prior right to rule, imploring Regent Lu to cooperate toward the goal of restoration, and pledging nonbelligerence while citing strategic reasons why he could not avoid planning military action in Lu territory.[11] But it is not known whether this letter ever reached Shao-hsing. Later that spring, a censorial official was sent by the Lung-wu emperor with a large amount of silver to reward and encourage military units stationed on the Ch'ien-t'ang River. But this official received no protection from Lu authorities and was killed with impunity by unruly troops.[12] And in the early summer, a Lu emissary to Fu-chien was imprisoned and executed by the Lung-wu emperor, probably because he was suspected of seditious collusion with Cheng Chih-lung.[13]

Explanations of this failure to cooperate between two sincerely restorationist regimes reveal something about the geography of southeastern China, but more about some chronic weaknesses of the Ming side. First, a point of geopolitics: Several thick bands of mountains always had blocked direct travel between the populous areas of Fu-chien and Che-chiang, and rapid communication between Fu-chou and Shao-hsing never had been possible even in the best of times. Fu-chien, though noted for its maritime trade, also was notably insular vis-à-vis its neighboring provinces. In the Lu versus Lung-wu rivalry, however, Fu-chien cannot be faulted as the more parochial. The resistance effort in Eastern Che-chiang was special in spirit, and it was a local specialness. Long after the Lu regime was forced off the mainland into the maritime zone, its small leadership— all men from Eastern Che-chiang, a stronghold of "righteousness"—remained more cohesive and dedicated to a common cause than that of any other Southern Ming regime. In fending off the Manchu wolf at the door, Eastern Che-chiang could not draw on abundant material resources and did not effect any tight organizational discipline; rather, it relied heavily on just the common spirit among its people to resist the "slave-barbarians." Thus, given the geopolitical circumstances of Fu-chou and the psychosocial circumstances of Shao-hsing, it is less puzzling that officials such as Chang Kuo-wei eschewed direction from the Lung-wu camp. The divisiveness to which this eschewal gave rise may well have seemed less threatening to the Eastern Che-chiang resistance movement, in the beginning, than a sudden withdrawal of legitimacy from Regent Lu.

But Fu-chien and Che-chiang supposedly were sister provinces in one great Ming nation. Why now was only lip service rendered to this principle? Simply put, there was no center of preponderant power that could realize principle with force, whether applied or held in reserve; and without this, Chinese political tradition offered little guidance to similarly legitimate regimes that might seek to deal with one another as equals. The Lung-wu emperor knew very well that Fu-chou was not, and could never be, another Nan-ching or Pei-ching. He strove mightily to leave the Min River region and succeeded admirably in drawing under his aegis officials and generals in Chiang-hsi, Liang-Kuang,* Hu-kuang, and even Szu-ch'uan. But for reasons discussed below, he did not succeed in sending any army northward even past the twenty-ninth parallel. Without military and police capability, the aura of the Great Ming, strong as it still may have been in the hearts and minds of the people, could not be put to real effect.

Considerations of the failure of Fu-chien and Che-chiang to cooperate must also take into account the personalities of the two sovereigns involved. Both were disposed, by opposite character traits, to hold on to their positions. And an examination of their different styles of rulership also leads to observations on something they had in common, that is, the perennial Ming problem of assistance for the emperor.

Regent Lu was weak in his physical constitution and often ill (especially with asthma). But now and in years to come, he never shrank from endangering

---

*Literally, the "two Kuangs," Kuang-tung and Kuang-hsi.

himself or his family by holding court near the front lines of those who fought for the restoration of his dynastic house. Quiet, kind, and mild-mannered, he confined his actions largely to the proper execution of court formalities and allowed his ministers and generals to exercise all initiative.[14] He was not a man of exceptional vision, intelligence, or leadership ability; however, he was very warm and conscientious in his personal relations and, in a dignified way, formed close bonds with men who followed him. These traits fostered good feelings among civil officials, but they did not promote clear-cut decision-making, nor were they effective in controlling the military.

In the course of his year in Shao-hsing, Regent Lu appointed a handful of grand secretaries, but most of them remained at positions in the field, and only one or two were kept at the regent's side to handle paperwork.[15] Chang Kuo-wei certainly was the most important and influential of the Lu grand secretaries. But he never approximated the functions of a prime minister, as chief grand secretaries before him had done. Similarly, although ministers were appointed, ministries were not really formed. In short, appropriate to the collegial spirit of the Eastern Che-chiang civil leaders and the unassertive personality of their regent, the Lu regime lacked structure. When the challenge of the Lung-wu court arose, although Regent Lu could not bring himself to reject the entreaties of men who had supported him ardently, one can hardly say that a consensus was reached or that a governmental decision was made on the issue—surely none ever was systematically enforced. The regent just tacitly allowed every man to follow his own conscience on the matter. Consequently, as problems mounted and infighting increased, the loyalty question festered and was used irresponsibly to discredit some able men.[16]

The Prince of T'ang, on the other hand, was a real anomaly among the late Ming imperial clansmen—ascetic in his living habits, strong in body and mind, assertive and ambitious, well-educated in the statesman's curriculum, and concerned about public affairs. These traits had made him a very troublesome prince during the Ch'ung-chen reign, when he persistently advocated broadening the role of imperial clansmen in government and national defense, but now they seemed to make him an almost ideal ruler figure. Moreover, he had been steeled by peculiar trials in his earlier life to bear the hardships of a restorationist emperor.

Indeed, the Prince of T'ang had spent most of his life incarcerated. From the ages of three to twenty-eight he had lived with his father in a private prison on the T'ang estate, after the latter had fallen from favor with *his* father, the current Prince of T'ang. By the time Chu Yü-chien was released from this confinement and allowed to succeed to the title that his father had been unjustly denied, Ho-nan was being menaced by roving-rebel armies and Pei-ching by bellicose

Manchus. The prince's attempts to respond to these perils by building up the military defenses of his locale, and by leading an army to "succor his sovereign" in 1636, had violated dynastic restrictions on the imperial princes and resulted in his imprisonment again—this time for nine years in the penitentiary at Feng-yang for errant members of the imperial clan. During this incarceration, he suffered inhumane treatment and survived only through the self-sacrifice of his devoted wife and the intercession of some concerned provincial officials.[17] Eventually, because of amnesties granted by the Hung-kuang court, he had been released from the Feng-yang stockade as a commoner and ordered to go to the far South.[18] Now in Fu-chien, it was as though all his frustrated pride and potential had been offered the ultimate avenue of expression and fulfillment in the emperorship.

Pouring himself zealously and conscientiously into the task of being Emperor, the Prince of T'ang vowed to follow in the footsteps of the Great Ancestor by expelling the northern barbarians from the land. Blaming the decline of government on cruel and avaricious officials, he moved perhaps too summarily to execute some popular Fu-chien officials whom outsiders accused of corruption. And hoping to set an example of austerity for officialdom and the populace alike, he wore plain clothes, ate only common, unseasoned food, refused to have a palace built or opulent quarters prepared for him, and kept only a small domestic staff. Moreover, he declined to take any concubines in addition to the still childless Empress Tseng, who also was well educated and was relied on as the emperor's closest adviser in public as well as private affairs. In contrast, he gladly accepted valuable gifts of books, especially those on history and governance, and he carted along thousands of volumes even when he went out "on campaign."[19]

Having convinced himself that he was *the* prince to save the dynasty, it was unthinkable that he should climb down from his throne and defer to another, especially one who was his junior and only had become Regent, whereas he had become Emperor—and at an earlier point in time. Naturally, he was bound to address the Prince of Lu respectfully for diplomatic and strategic reasons. But there was a lack of magnanimity and a corresponding strain of meanness in his attitude toward that "nephew prince," which sharpened over time and was vented on Lu emissaries and others who were not wise enough to evince a clear allegiance to Lung-wu. Though he long had championed the interests of imperial clansmen and now publicly pledged to restore titles and stipends to all minor princes who had become orphaned or displaced, the Lung-wu emperor also was wary of and disdained any who, like him, showed leadership ability— such as those who were leading the resistance effort in northeastern Chiang-hsi.[20] And one, the hapless Prince of Ching-chiang, who (ignorant of both the

Lu and Lung-wu courts) failed in an almost farcical attempt to assume the regency in faraway Kuang-hsi Province, was brought in shackles the whole distance from Kuei-lin to Fu-chou. There his chief supporters were executed, and the prince was tried, stripped of rank, and callously allowed to die in detention as a warning to others of his status.[21]

But apart from his suspicion toward potential rivals in the imperial clan, the Lung-wu emperor was very open-hearted toward others and eager to draw capable men into his service. He awarded positions with scant regard for established procedures or standard qualifications, and he was easily moved to admiration by stirring memorials from often mediocre men who wished to gain official employment. This propensity, on the one hand, helped to make the Lung-wu regime more national in scope than that of Regent Lu, since appointments were extended to men in and from several provinces. On the other hand, it resulted in overstaffing and the assignment of many men to tasks that they really could not carry out.[22] The most pertinent example of this is the Lung-wu Grand Secretariat. In all, the emperor appointed *over thirty* men to be grand secretaries; and although some did not come and others were sent into the field, a large number of prominent and intelligent men were kept waiting around the emperor's offices with little to do. Little to do, because the emperor was both decisive in affairs and talented in literary composition, so he wrote almost all of his own edicts and proclamations and seldom consulted with the bevy of grand secretaries that he had assembled.[23]

Of course, this was a waste of talent and manpower. More lamentable, however, was that the emperor, despite his acumen, needed but did not obtain the procedurally regular and institutionally legitimate counsel of one or two astute statesmen—that is, of someone like a prime minister. As it was, the Lung-wu emperor had too many counselors and, thus, no true counselors. Being basically an enthusiastic man, his mind continually was jerked in one direction, then another, by this possibility and that; as a consequence, he issued many confusing and contradictory statements and directives.[24] Needless to say, the times themselves were frenetic, and even the most stable, well-guided mind could not have undertaken the Lung-wu emperor's mission without experiencing or causing some confusion. But whether the case was that of the Hung-kuang court, in which a power-seeking chief grand secretary acted in capacities that were not "constitutionally" authorized, or that of the Lu and Lung-wu courts, in which no decision-making figures came to the side of the ruler, the absence of a prime ministership in Ming institutions exacerbated some already very difficult situations.

The emperor was most erratic in strategic matters. This was partly because of his tendency to be stirred to action by any news, good or bad, that came from the contested provinces (Che-chiang, Chiang-hsi, and Hu-kuang), and to give orders first before fully considering feasibility. But it also arose from the complicated strategic situation of Fu-chou at this juncture, and the difficulty of obtaining quick and accurate information about what was happening outside the passes. In comparison, the situation of the Lu regime was simple—the enemy will come, or we will go, across the Ch'ien-t'ang or across the bay—and developments in Western Che-chiang and the Yang-tzu delta (the only areas that really concerned the Lu adherents) were fairly easily ascertained. But for the Lung-wu emperor to move the seat of his government from Fu-chou to a more offensively advantageous location had to be a long-range undertaking. Deciding on the first and subsequent destinations for such a move involved the consideration of several fluidly changing, if not imponderable factors: the relative strength, cohesion, and progress of the Ch'ing and the Ming resistance forces in several theaters of conflict, from Hu-kuang to Nan Chih-li; the ability of loyal armies in those areas to "meet the imperial carriage"; the potential of the Lu regime not only to keep the Ch'ing blocked at Hang-chou, but to interfere with Lung-wu movements, as well; and, not least, the adequacy in numbers, training, and supply, and the degree of commitment of Fu-chien soldiers for a long, arduous drive into unfamiliar regions.

The emperor's first intention was to return the way he had come, that is, to go back across Hsien-hsia Pass, through the northeastern shoulder of Chiang-hsi, and back down the Ch'ien-t'ang River to restore Hang-chou, from whence he then would press onward to Nan-ching. But several circumstances soon reduced the attractiveness of this strategy. The Ch'ing were found to be strong and menacing in the Ning-kuo and Hui-chou area and in the T'ien-mu Mountains to the northwest of this route.[25] Moreover, the two strongest Ming military leaders along the Ch'ien-t'ang, Chu Ta-tien and Fang Kuo-an, although both had pledged allegiance to Lung-wu as well as to Regent Lu, hated one another irreconcilably and could not be relied on to cooperate in action.[26] Third, despite the Lung-wu emperor's appeals, the Lu court persisted in withholding formal recognition from him and, thus, was unpredictable. Moreover, the regional naval commander Huang Pin-ch'ing, who had been ennobled and sent off with fanfare to penetrate Hang-chou Bay, thus to form a pincers movement with imperial troops that were supposed to go down the Ch'ien-t'ang, had stopped on the Chou-shan Islands and refused to move further.[27] Without seaborne reinforcement, a direct challenge to Hang-chou or Nan-ching was even less feasible.

But during the winter of 1645–46, successes in the Ming resistance in

Chiang-hsi and Hu-kuang (see chapter 2) led the Lung-wu emperor to consider a second preference, going "east of the lake." That is, once through Hsien-hsia or Fen-shui Pass, he would turn northwestward and, on the eastern side of P'o-yang Lake, converge with Ming forces coming from southern Chiang-hsi via the Kan River and from central Hu-kuang via the Yang-tzu. These combined armies and navies then would either defeat or co-opt Chin Sheng-huan's organization at Nan-ch'ang and Chiu-chiang and proceed to launch a riverine campaign on Nan-ching by driving further down the Yang-tzu.[28]

Desiring to maximally extend the scope of his regime, the Lung-wu emperor had been prompt to confer official titles, promotions, and honorifics on the resistance leaders in Chiang-hsi and Hu-kuang. For instance, Wan Yüan-chi's appointment as Viceroy at Chi-an had emanated from the Fu-chien court. And the emperor had done his best to reinforce the less organized popular resistance in northeastern Chiang-hsi by sending Fu-chien troops over the Fen-shui and Shan passes, the most dedicated and effective leader in this effort being the troop-supervising censor Chang Chia-yü.[29] Moreover, the emperor not only confirmed and raised the official positions of such men in Hu-kuang as Ho T'eng-chiao, Tu Yin-hsi, and the Ming commanders formally under them; he also (at Ho's request) conferred noble titles, high military rank, and even some new, imperially selected personal names on such erstwhile Shun rebel leaders as Li Chin, Kao I-kung, and Heh Yao-ch'i.[30] Largely in response to Lung-wu orders, some Hu-kuang forces went overland to aid the resistance in western Chiang-hsi; and the Lung-wu emperor hoped for a time that the still weak coordination among the three parallel provinces could be strengthened by planning a concerted campaign on the P'o-yang Lake region. But in the spring of 1646, Ch'ing actions in Chiang-hsi confined viable Ming resistance to Kan-chou Prefecture in the far south, and conditions in Hu-kuang remained much too precarious for Ho T'eng-chiao to contemplate any advances outside that province.

Gradually the Lung-wu emperor came to think more about South Kan, as the Kan-chou circuit was called. From the outset he had maintained close contact with the leadership there, sending some of his most valuable officials to coordinate affairs and to bring in aid from Kuang-tung.[31] And as the Ch'ing extended their control further southward in Chiang-hsi, he became increasingly concerned that if Kan-chou also were lost, then all the major overland approaches to (and escape routes from) Fu-chien would be closed off. But whether or when he actually would go there, and where he would go from there, never became clear. If conditions took a favorable turn in Chiang-hsi, he might lead a campaign down the Kan River to restore Ming control of that whole province. Or he might make Ch'ang-sha his "temporary capital" in Hu-kuang, from there to plot the restoration of Ho-nan and a future campaign on Pei-ching! But there were others who feared that Kan-chou would (or would appear to) be a way station for retreat into Kuang-tung.[32]

Moreover, travel through southwestern Fu-chien had become hazardous because of severe social disruptions which attended the dynastic crisis. Large bandit organizations from the chronically ungovernable triprovincial border region separating Fu-chien, Chiang-hsi, and Kuang-tung had swollen and become bold again. Some made marriages of convenience with Ming resistance leaders in Chiang-hsi, while others devastated locales in Hui-chou and Ch'ao-chou prefectures in Kuang-tung, and in adjacent T'ing-chou Prefecture in Fu-chien. This activity was related to virulent peasant revolts in other parts of T'ing-chou against the long-standing practice by "local bigshots" of using unfairly large measuring devices to collect tenants' rents in kind.[33] These were but the most large-scale and violent of the many sorts of social disobedience and outlawry that spread throughout Fu-chien in 1645–46 and became blatant even near the seats of imperial government. In view of this, the emperor feared to leave, and yet feared not to leave, the province in such an unstable condition.

As a result of these complicated considerations, the Lung-wu emperor's movements and plans to move were perpetually in a state of suspension. Having been dissuaded from returning northward in early September 1645, directly after his enthronement in Fu-chou, the emperor then definitely set October 7 as the date of his "campaign out the passes." But his departure was postponed repeatedly after that, and he was not able to get under way until January 22 of the following year. Subsequently, he established an interim "imperial campsite" upriver at Chien-ning and remained there indecisively until March, when he moved back somewhat to Yen-p'ing, closer to the southwestward travel routes. His only consistent indication during this time, regarding the immediate destination of his campaign, was that he never would fall back to Fu-chou.[34]

Aggravating the social unrest, as well as the vacillation of the emperor, were the limitations of Fu-chien for financing a large-scale war effort. Indeed, in the beginning of the Lung-wu interval, it was estimated that the cost of adequately manning the major passes and the hundred or so other possible points of entry to Fu-chien through the winter of 1645–46, and then launching dual offensives into Chiang-hsi and Eastern Che-chiang the following spring, would require 200,000 soldiers and over twice the annual revenues of Fu-chien and Liang-Kuang combined.[35] In terms of both manpower and revenues, this was out of the question. Later it was more soberly estimated that 40,000 men would be needed to hold the major passes and maintain internal security, and that their minimal upkeep would cost 862,000 taels per year. But if an offensive campaign were undertaken, then the total cost for weapons, armor, horses, tents, transport, and so forth, would climb to 1,560,000 taels.[36] From the beginning of his reign, the Lung-wu emperor had directed that all revenues be used first to meet military needs. One official stated that Fu-chien's yearly tax proceeds for military supply should be 1,200,000 taels,[37] but actual revenues do not seem to have approached this even remotely. Scattered records indicate that the Lung-wu regime drew at least 163,600 taels in revenues from Kuang-tung and Kuang-hsi and that an additional 260,000 in patriotic contributions were raised in Fu-chien. But when the 1,560,000-tael military budget was announced, the emperor lamented that it could not be met even by the full current capacities of those three provinces.[38] That amount, moreover, did not include sums that needed to be sent intermittently to forces fighting under the Lung-wu banner in other provinces.

Needless to say, every corner of the provincial economy was swept vigorously, and the platters of the people were licked clean by the constant demand for revenues. The Lung-wu emperor, who sorely wished to be a benevolent ruler, was loath to formally increase the basic tax rate and even felt obligated to declare remissions for bandit-ravaged areas. But taxes often were forcibly "borrowed in advance," and citizens were pressed so hard for "voluntary" contributions that the effective rate of taxation soared.[39] As under the Hung-kuang regime, incumbent officials were assessed in graded amounts, and—although the practice was condemned by the emperor—offices and civil service degrees in fact were sold to anyone, so that

> musicians and entertainers, menials and slaves all joined the ranks of those in caps and robes.... The wiliest among them borrowed carriages with canopies, hired servants and bearers, paid visits to the ya-men, and cracked the whip in their neighborhoods. ... But still there was a dire shortage of provisions.[40]

District granaries were tapped for emergency troop rations, and convenient sources of silver were found in the "reserves for consoling the people," as well as in various district and prefectural treasuries,[41] so that such publicly maintained cushions against disaster were removed by the very state to which the people looked to keep them in place. Moreover, the heaviest burdens fell on the "upper drainage" of Fu-chien, centered on the Min River and including Fu-chou and Chien-ning. With the growth of maritime commerce in late Ming times, this region had fallen behind the "lower drainage," centered on the Chiu-lung River and including Chang-chou, in commercialization and, hence, in public wealth. Inland transport had not advanced appreciably, and facilities for carrying people and goods over the northwestern passes simply could not bear the load of large armies.[42]

A fuller understanding of Lung-wu logistical problems, however, requires an examination and comparison of the roles and images of the two most important officials in the regime: Grand Secretary Huang Tao-chou, and Marquis Cheng Chih-lung. The conflict and contrast between these men illustrates well the civil-military disharmony of the late Ming, which also was reflected in the emperor's own disillusionment about reconciling *wen* and *wu*.

Cheng Chih-lung (known to Europeans then in East Asia as Nicholas Iquan) had begun his career as an assistant and multilingual interpreter in the perilously competitive trade that had been flourishing between China and Japan, despite restrictions imposed by the governments of both countries, in the late sixteenth and early seventeenth centuries. He had achieved notoriety first as an uncommon brigand who was exceptionally good at organizing and disciplining his men, who seemed inclined to exercise social leadership, and who showed a related tendency to cooperate intermittently with governmental authorities. In 1628 Ming officials in Fu-chien, employing the expedient of using pirates to control pirates, succeeded in obtaining his surrender. From that time he had gone on to increase his power under the aegis of the Ming military establishment, eventually rising to the post of regional commander, as did his brother, Hung-k'uei. During these years, he gradually had become the grand mogul of Chinese southeastern ports and coastal waters and, like his son later on, a legend in his own time.[43]

Initially, the Lung-wu emperor had been very pleased and grateful to receive the support of such a powerful figure. Cheng Chih-lung's noble status as an earl, which had been granted by the Hung-kuang court, soon was raised to that of marquis in recognition of his merit in establishing the new court in Fu-chou. And, less conventionally, the emperor approved Cheng's use of the informal title *hsün-fu*, "military noble and chief minister," implying status equal to that of a grand secretary. In the same vein, although Cheng was a military official, and although civil officials were appointed as ministers of Revenue, War, and Public Works, Cheng was given full authority over the affairs of those three ministries that pertained to current military operations.[44] Because almost all governmental activities in Fu-chien at that time pertained to current military operations, this made Cheng, in effect, concurrently the director of three ministries in what formally was the preserve of the civil service. Since Cheng was not only an important military commander but also the head of a prominent clan and the "boss" of an extensive politico-mercantile organization, the emperor also initially indulged the filling of many civil and military posts with Cheng relatives and hangers-on. Indeed, being still childless, the emperor even went so far as to symbolically adopt Chih-lung's impressive eldest son, Cheng Sen, bestowing on him the imperial surname, Chu, a new given name, Ch'eng-kung,* the rank of an imperial son-in-law, and many special privileges and responsibilities[45] (see chapters 4 and 7).

Naturally, not everyone was as pleased with Cheng Chih-lung as the emperor was. Civil officials disapproved the extension of powers for this poacher-turned-gamekeeper, and social leaders blamed him for the strong-arm tactics that often were used to raise funds and materiel, to the point that many withheld even regular tax payments.[46] Moreover, as time went by, the emperor, too, began to regret his dependence on Cheng, and even to doubt his loyalty. In the first place, the emperor's plans to leave Fu-chou (and later Chien-ning) "on campaign" repeatedly were delayed because, under Cheng's direction, military preparations never seemed to be complete.[47] Moreover, at an early point, the emperor designated the two most powerful secondary leaders in the Cheng organization, Cheng Hung-k'uei and the brothers' clan-cousin, Cheng Ts'ai, to be the "right and left wings" of his advance guard and, as such, to clear the way for later imperial offensives in southwestern Che-chiang and northeastern Chiang-hsi, respectively. But both men performed dilatorily and never proceeded far beyond the outer approaches to the Hsien-hsia, Fen-shui, and Shan passes.[48]

As the emperor's displeasure grew at what increasingly seemed to be the procrastination and cowardice of these three commanders, one official pointed out that the Cheng forte was in naval, not land, warfare, and that sending their men inland to face the superior Ch'ing cavalry was like "driving sheep forward to defend against wolves." It would be wiser to apply their maritime strength—which the Northerners (as the Ch'ing were called) could not match—to occupy the Chou-shan and Ch'ung-ming islands and strike at the Yang-tzu delta from the sea.[49] Correct as this observation may have been, significantly, the Chengs do not appear ever to have offered to use their maritime capacity to fight for the Lung-wu cause. Rather, Chih-lung was inclined to undercut those who did try to approach Nan Chih-li by sea.[50]

Thus, the Lung-wu emperor's great eagerness to "go out the passes" increasingly became an eagerness to free himself from the ball and chain not only of limited Fu-chien resources, but also of the Chengs' stand-pat attitude. Since he was in no position to express his anger at Chih-lung directly, it sometimes was vented in the pointedly harsh treatment of men with whom the latter had close personal relations. In particular, the emperor went to deceptive lengths to effect the execution of the last emissary to come from the Lu regime, Ch'en Ch'ien, whose friendship Cheng had prized from times past. Because of such incidents,

---

* Thus, Cheng Sen became most commonly known in history as Cheng Ch'eng-kung and by the appellation Koxinga, which is a latinization of the Amoy-dialect pronunciation of Kuo-hsing Yeh, "Master [who has the Ming] Dynastic Surname."

the Lung-wu emperor's suspicion that Cheng Chih-lung intended to defect may have been self-confirming.[51]

Traditional historiography is so biased against Cheng Chih-lung that it is difficult to assess the man objectively. Certainly he was able, cunning, ambitious, and powerful in a certain sphere. Certainly he hoped that by supporting the Lung-wu emperor he could extend the scope and depth of his sway in Fu-chien. But it seems clear, also, that he was unwilling to sap or sacrifice his hard-won, lucrative maritime power base for any campaign that might carry the court into another province. Genuine difficulties probably account in large degree for his failure promptly to field a Lung-wu war machine. But his merely lukewarm responsiveness also must be attributed to a basic conflict between his own advantage and the purposes of his sovereign. In any case, the heavy dependence of the Ming emperor at this time on the irregular powers and semiprivate organization of this one militarist is sadly telling.

Completely the opposite of Cheng Chih-lung in outlook, but no more effective, in the end, was Grand Secretary Huang Tao-chou, the most esteemed civil official in the Lung-wu regime. A native of Chang-chou Prefecture in southern Fu-chien, he long since had achieved national prominence as a leader of the Tung-lin political faction and a crusader for "righteous" causes throughout the T'ien-ch'i and Ch'ung-chen reigns. Naturally, his bureaucratic career had not been smooth, and at one time he even was imprisoned for his outspokenness. But otherwise, he had spent his intervals out of office lecturing on the Classics and philosophy in private academies of the Southeast, and he numbered many officials and social leaders among his pupils.[52] He had accepted an unimportant position in the Hung-kuang court, but he had excused himself on a pretext in the spring of 1645 and happened to be in Che-chiang when Nan-ching fell the following summer. After urging the Prince of T'ang to assume the regency in early July, Huang had remained behind in Che-chiang for a while and, thus, did not reach Fu-chou until August 26; but then he immediately assumed the role of, in his words, "the morning rooster" of the Lung-wu court.[53]

To understand Huang's conception of a restorationist government, one can look to the recommendations he submitted previously to the Prince of Luh when the short-lived regency was established at Hang-chou. Huang then argued that the fall of Nan-ching had been due entirely to a loss of determination among officials and a consequent loss of the people's trust, not to any unwillingness to fight or any slackening of vigilance among the generals or soldiers in the defense zones. Thus, he recommended that seven steps be taken within ten days "so that [the Manchus], hearing of it, will think that the sages have reappeared; the elders of Chiang-nan, seeing it, will think that [the ancient] rites and music have risen again; and then anything under Heaven will be possible": (1) gather the officials of all localities to inquire about the conditions of the common people, and personally go to all quarters of Hang-chou to see that their sufferings are alleviated; (2) go out to the schoolhouses of the area and dispense cloth, rice, and meat to the elderly; (3) gather all local education officials to inquire about selecting men by examination, and give a special test to obtain good ideas from men of exceptional ability; (4) gather all civil and military officials who have fled from Nan-ching to inquire about the fate of the Hung-kuang emperor, then report to the ancestors and issue a list of criminals who have harmed the nation; (5) summon all officials who are out of office in the nearby prefectures, while soliciting recommendations from the governors of surrounding provinces; and last (7), lead the "hundred officials" in personally conducting a review of all military forces in the area, reward special skills and courage in low-ranking soldiers, and have important officials station military units at strategic points to the north.[54] This was Huang's scale of priorities when Bolo's army was only days away from Hang-chou!

Apparently the experience in Che-chiang had heightened Huang's sense of urgency about military matters, for in Fu-chou he made no mention of idealized sagely gestures. Rather, immediately upon his arrival, he preempted even the Lung-wu emperor in requesting that he, Huang, lead a campaign to show the flag outside the northwestern passes, to stabilize the people's hearts, and to erase any impression that the court would be "fecklessly satisfied" with its isolated position in Fu-chien.[55] Forestalling the emperor's plan to do the same thing, Huang, then sixty years old, left Fu-chou going upriver on September 14 (just two and one-half weeks after his arrival) with no experience in leading troops and, indeed, with no troops and only 4,500 taels for provisions and expenses. But he had great confidence that, because of his good name among the people, sufficient men and supplies would come to him along the way, and that he probably would be able to strike directly at Nan-ching within a month's time.

> I am as though with one hand and a naked body, with neither a big army nor many supplies. Moreover, the way is long and far, so the glib-tongued may make light of me. But I only need Your Majesty to broaden the road ahead and turn obstinacy to vastness of heart, so that all intentions will flow together like water....[56]

But "the perspicacious already knew the bad trend of the times and that, once [Huang] went out, he never would return [alive]."[57]

As though in the first acts of a tragedy, Huang's expectations were borne out to some extent. Over half the silver that Huang took from Fu-chou had been contributed by sympathetic officials. And in Yen-p'ing, Chien-ning, and Ch'ung-an, he "borrowed" over 5,000 taels from the treasuries of cooperative local officials and received 1,450 taels in donations from gentry in those areas.

Moreover, he was joined by enough local volunteers and forces led by his relatives and friends from Chang-chou to constitute twelve companies, or about 4,600 men. At no point did he receive the service of any regular troops or officers or any logistical support from the Ministry of War (i.e., Cheng Chih-lung). Nevertheless, Huang calculated that to take such an army on a two-month campaign outside the passes would require half again more than the 10,890 taels he had at Ch'ung-an, which he knew had exhausted the resources of the "upper drainage." Moreover, it had rained heavily, causing his men to struggle piteously in the mud; then, when Huang allowed them to drink from the flood-swollen river, almost all were overcome with illness, and some even died.[58]

In view of these circumstances, Huang could not bear to press his scarcely trained units into even greater hardship and danger. So he remained stuck and frustrated in the upper reaches of the Min River until mid-November, when he finally proceeded into Kuang-hsin Prefecture, the junction for travel into northeastern Chiang-hsi, Hui-chou Prefecture in Nan Chih-li, or southwestern Che-chiang. From there the situation looked even worse. Reports—and silences—were ominous from the centers of resistance on which Huang had placed his hopes. And although one chronicler says that he raised over 10,000 men in Kuang-hsin purely out of righteousness, rewarding them with exhortations in his own calligraphy, which they prized more than any imperial conferment,[59] Huang himself complained of niggardliness and irresoluteness among the people there and said that the gentry raised well under 3,000 untrained, poorly supplied household servants and volunteers.

> With only 4,000 sick men [of my own], I dare not strike straight out for Nan-ching, but neither can I bear to half-heartedly sit behind the barrier [of the passes] and procrastinate like other officials and esteemed persons [i.e., the Chengs].[60]

Thus, distraught that his physical strength did not match his heart, but hoping to rely on "the strength of people in the end-alleys and villages of Chiang-hsi and the virtuous heart of loyalists in Che-chiang," Huang dispatched contingents into various adjacent areas and set out on his first attempt to capture Wu-yüan in late November. He had only 1,200 men under his own banner (even though he had told the court that it would take at least 36,000 men to succeed in this campaign).[61] After several encounters with the overwhelmingly stronger enemy, Huang's forces grew weaker and more dispirited. Finally, Huang was captured at Wu-yüan on February 9 or 10, 1646, and was executed with several of his loyal aides in Nan-ching the following April.[62]

Throughout this ordeal, Huang continually bemoaned his lack of ability in leading an army and the fact that those who might join with him to aid the loyalists in Hui-chou, like himself, were "of the upper stratum and not versed in military matters. So it is not surprising that they are like rabbits used as tiger bait." [63] Even so, he had no respect for military men and frequently berated them for incompetence, cowardice, and opportunism. Accounts of Huang's role in the Lung-wu regime seldom fail to recount the incident in which, at a banquet given by the emperor for his top ministers, Huang , citing the Ancestor's Order, bested Cheng Chih-lung in an altercation over who should be seated first, a marquis or a chief grand secretary. [64] This is the stuff from which melodramas about the Southern Ming later were made. More telling, perhaps, is Huang's own testimony that when real "big heroes" had come hoping to join his army in Kuang-hsin, and he had offered them positions as only advisory majors, captains, and lieutenants, they had thrown the documents on the ground, saying that from the court they could get appointments as full lieutenant-colonels or regional vice commanders. But Huang was troubled about exceeding his proper authority in the field and, moreover, could not bear to allow such men, with no accomplishments, to take advantage of his dire situation to obtain high positions. [65] His attitude illustrates the close association during the Southern Ming between "righteousness" and opposition to the professional military. Although the Lung-wu emperor adamantly refused to allow his court to be overrun by Hung-kuang-style conflicts between remnants of the "pure" and "eunuch" cliques, he was able neither to reconcile the civil and military sectors nor to break the association of "righteousness" with *wen* and "perniciousness" with *wu*. [66]

In the beginning of his reign, the Lung-wu emperor had been emphatic about the equal importance of, and the necessity to harmonize, civil and military functions; he had, in addition, evinced a desire personally to embody the complementarity of *wen* and *wu*. While collecting heavy tomes, composing eloquent edicts, and otherwise displaying his erudition, he held to the spartan life of an ideal general and swelled with inspiration when urged to emulate the great rulers-on-horseback in Chinese history, especially the "Shining Martial Emperor," Kuang-wu Ti, who fought to restore the interrupted Han dynasty in the first century A.D. But as time went on, he grew more frustrated with the military, decrying their rapaciousness and disobedience. [67] And in a vain attempt to offset the pending complete militarization of society, which he unhappily perceived, the emperor stubbornly pushed ahead with plans to conduct civil service examinations in Fu-chou, despite multiple hazards, difficulties, and the opposition of Cheng Chih-lung. [68] In the history of the Southern Ming, there was no more appropriate figure than the Lung-wu emperor for achieving a balance of *wen* and *wu*; but it could not be done through the posturings of the ruler alone, however sincere.

Under Regent Lu in Eastern Che-chiang, conflicts between civil leaders and militarists took somewhat different form, but they were equally serious. From the beginning, Lu forces, estimated to have numbered over 200,000,[69] had been a complicated, scarcely coordinated interspersion of, on the civil side, militiamen, volunteers, and corps of fighters retained by wealthy families; and, on the professional military side, armies that had fled southward or returned to their home bases in Che-chiang after the Ch'ing penetration of southern Nan Chih-li. Leaders in the former category included: from Yin District, Ch'ien Su-yüeh, a Fu She member and a former bureau vice director in the Ministry of Punishments; from Yü-yao, two other "righteous" activists, Sun Chia-chi, a former assistant surveillance commissioner for War, and Hsiung Ju-lin, a former supervising secretary for Revenue; and in Shao-hsing, the former prefect and then Ning-Shao Circuit Intendant, Yü Ying, who had worked closely with Liu Tsung-chou.[70] In the second category, leaders included Fang Kuo-an, formerly a regional commander for the middle Yang-tzu under the Hung-kuang regime (who now harbored Ma Shih-ying and Juan Ta-ch'eng in his territory); Wang Chih-jen, the regional naval commander at Ting-hai; and a martial licentiate named Cheng Tsun-ch'ien, who became a military official and assumed leadership of the same "knight-errant" element that previously had gravitated to Hsü Tu (see chapter 1).[71] As the Ch'ing gradually had more success against the waterborne resistance in the Yang-tzu delta region in 1645–46, the defenders in both of these categories were rudely disrupted by remnants of Ming naval commands arriving from farther north.[72] But such intrusions could have been controlled if internal problems of military organization had been worked out, rather than allowed to grow worse.

Of course, there were disagreements about strategy and tactics, not to mention the stresses caused by conflicting personalities; however, these cut across both the civil and military sectors. The only significant exception to this was the tendency of Hsiung Ju-lin and some other "rightous" zealots to dash into battle incessantly, with little advance preparation or coordination, and heedless of the losses incurred.[73] More serious were the tendency of "righteous" Tung-lin adherents to trenchantly criticize men of "pernicious" background who were given authority over logistical matters and the countertendency of leading militarists to charge these literati with obstructionism.[74] Related to this, and even more corrosive, was the "controversy over dividing supplies and dividing territories," which sharpened as the resources of Eastern Che-chiang were strained past their limit.

As mentioned above, the Lu regime was not highly structured, and, consonant with the general Ming tendency toward decentralization in finance and military supply, no central Ministry of Revenue ever was established. Operations began under the loose principle that Ming regulars were to draw from the governmental tax proceeds of the prefectures in which they were based,

whereas auxiliary and volunteer forces were to be supported by patriotic contributions from the districts in which they originated. The professional military
men, especially, found this arrangement unsatisfactory and pressed to have all
monies and materiel accrued for the war effort placed under their control, or at
least under the Ministry of War, for allocation according to strategic need.
However, leaders of "righteous soldiers"* balked at such centralization. They
distrusted the militarists, fearing that the latter would try to keep everything for
themselves, squeeze out the civil leaders, and subsume all soldiers under the
regular military command, thus destroying the unique spirit of the Eastern Che-
chiang resistance. Moreover, they worried that if their own personal connections
with the gentry in their home locales were severed in this respect, then voluntary
contributions would dry up, and the whole effort would suffer. Some even
proposed an absolute separation of civil and military commands. As things
turned out, all units, regular and volunteer, competed with one another in
drawing any sustenance they could—tax proceeds, patriotic contributions, or
forced requisitions—from the locales nearest to them geographically, and no
organized logistical plan ever evolved.[75]

Needless to say, under these conditions, little could be done to correct the
chronic lack of coordination among Lu units. Disorder led to chaos through the
winter of 1645–46, as increasingly severe shortages induced regular troops to
steal provisions meant for volunteer units. And as starvation among Lu forces
became common, many "righteous" units simply disbanded and went home,
while regular troops turned to looting and extortion to survive.[76] This was the
situation on the Southern Ming's front line when the Manchus decided to
resume their southeasterly advance in the late spring of 1646.

*In Chinese, to fight voluntarily for a cause ipso facto is "righteous." In this case, the soldiers
also were "righteous" in the additional sense of following men who were associated with the "pure
element" in late Ming politics.

CHAPTER FOUR

Second Defeat: Initial Ch'ing Conquest of the Southeast and Far South

C H'ING activity in Hang-chou had been strictly a holding operation. Through the fall of 1645, Lu forces were prevented from expanding on the "western" bank from their footholds at Fu-yang and Hai-ning, and from seriously threatening or encircling Hang-chou City from the west or east. And, by early 1646, the Lu front lines had been pushed into the waters of the Hang-chou Bay and Ch'ien-t'ang River (which had become hazardously shallow and silt-clogged because of continuing drought conditions in Che-chiang). But the Ch'ing viceroy for the region was instructed to make no major offensive movement, probably because Ming resistance to his rear in southern Nan Chih-li had not been satisfactorily quelled.[1] By late spring, however, favorable developments in the T'ai Lake region, Hui-chou Prefecture, and northeastern Chiang-hsi apparently made the time seem ripe for another general advance.[2] Consequently, on April 13 Bolo was designated as Generalissimo of the Southward Campaign, and he returned to Hang-chou with Manchu reinforcements on June 30.[3] The subsequent Ch'ing conquest of the far South and Southeast proceeded in four stages:

1. The *occupation of southeastern Che-chiang and Fu-chien* (see map 7) began with a concerted crossing of the Ch'ien-t'ang in mid-July. Originally the Manchus had planned to embark on boats from the dikes south of Hang-chou City; but the water level in the Ch'ien-t'ang had become so low that upstream, at a point strategically not very remote from Shao-hsing, bathers had found that men and horses could wade across easily. So a two-stage crossing was planned. On July 10, as Ch'ing cavalry rode across the river near T'ung-lu, Fang Kuo-an's army there completely collapsed and ran chaotically toward Shao-hsing, with

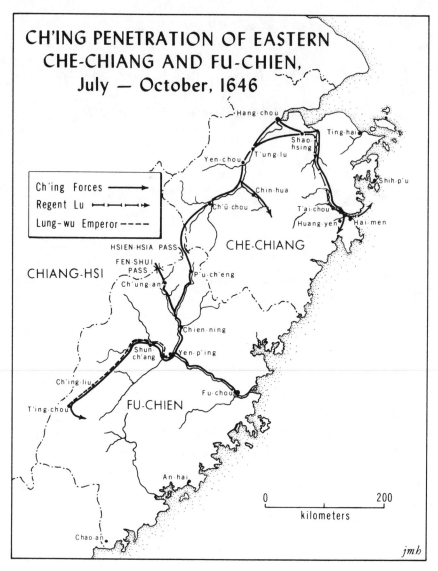

CH'ING PENETRATION OF EASTERN CHE-CHIANG AND FU-CHIEN, July — October, 1646

Ch'ing Forces ⟶
Regent Lu ↦⊢↦⊣↦➔
Lung-wu Emperor ----

Hang-chou
Ting-hai
Shao-hsing
T'ung-lu
Yen-chou
Shih-p'u
Chin-hua
Ch'ü-chou
T'ai-chou
Huang-yen
Hai-men
HSIEN-HSIA PASS
CHE-CHIANG
FEN-SHUI PASS
CHIANG-HSI
P'u-ch'eng
Ch'ung-an
Chien-ning
Shun-ch'ang
Yen-p'ing
Ch'ing-liu
Fu-chou
T'ing-chou
FU-CHIEN
An-hai
0   200
kilometers
Chao-an

jmh

the Ch'ing hot on its heels. On July 13 this Ch'ing force converged near Shao-hsing with another that had been ferried across the mouth of the Ch'ien-t'ang from Hang-chou, according to the original plan. All Ming regulars on the river were scattered, and Shao-hsing succumbed with little resistance.[4]

Regent Lu had fled Shao-hsing when he heard that Fang's men were scrambling toward the city, apparently fearing either the destruction they would perpetrate or that he would be taken captive and used by Fang to bargain with the Manchus for favorable terms of surrender. Having sent his family by boat to Ting-hai, the regent traveled swiftly overland back to T'ai-chou, hoping to hold that prefecture. But there he narrowly escaped being kidnapped by an agent of Fang Kuo-an, so he took to sea from Hai-men and soon found refuge with a Ming naval commander, who then transported him to the Chou-shan Islands.[5] Fang Kuo-an eventually was cornered and induced to surrender at Huang-yen; and subsequently he used his knowledge of Ming defenses to guide the Ch'ing in a fiercely bloody suppression of the resistance in Chin-hua Prefecture, led by Fang's old nemesis, Chu Ta-tien.[6] Aside from Fang, however, very few active Lu supporters surrendered, most of them meeting martyr's deaths or escaping to carry on the fight from the Szu-ming Hills or the coastal zone.[7] For the time being, the Ch'ing did not pursue the regent or his surviving adherents. Rather, they pressed on from Ch'ü-chou in Che-chiang and from Kuang-hsin in Chiang-hsi to penetrate Fu-chien through the Hsien-hsia and Fen-shui passes, which already had been abandoned at the order of Cheng Chih-lung.[8]

The Lung-wu emperor, then at Yen-p'ing, learned of the emergency in Eastern Che-chiang in late July and early August.[9] Although he tried to send some aid, he could do little even to prevent the gradual withdrawal of his own troops back inside the passes, and from the mountains to the littoral region, as a defeatist atmosphere pervaded his court. On September 4, in a dramatic effort to rekindle a loyal spirit among his supporters, the emperor produced at court over two hundred intercepted letters of surrender from Lung-wu officials to the Ch'ing. In an especially moving performance, he admonished those present to reform their hearts and minds, and he had all the letters burned without looking at the signatures.[10] This display, although it may have earned the emperor even greater admiration, could not stem the dissolution of his government.

For some time, the Lung-wu emperor had been planning to take his "campaign" to Kan-chou. So when the enemy was reported to have entered Hsien-hsia Pass, he decided that the time definitely had come to embark, in spite of a persistent, debilitating summer heat wave. His entourage left Yen-p'ing in orderly fashion on September 29–30; but two days later, at Shun-ch'ang, news that the Manchus already had reached Yen-p'ing threw the imperial party into a panic. Many members became scattered and lost, while others tried to follow the emperor, who galloped on horseback with a small guard to T'ing-chou. There he was overtaken by a Ch'ing contingent and summarily executed with his empress on October 6.[11]

When Manchu troops reached Fu-chou unopposed on October 26–27, the city was almost deserted. Those people with the means to do so had fled to the countryside with all their valuable possessions, including caskets which often were bought years in advance of actual need, so that a popular saying arose:

"Keep your hair, but not your life; keep your coffin, but not your house."[12] Cheng Chih-lung, who had withdrawn from Yen-p'ing on the pretext of having to deal with pirate threats to the coast, had blown up his arsenal at Fu-chou and retreated further to his home base in An-hai. He probably had been in contact with the Ch'ing side for some time but still was uncertain about the terms of his submission. Now, however, when the Ch'ing offered to give him the top regional civil post of Viceroy for Fu-chien and Kuang-tung, he disregarded the opposition of his most important subordinate commanders and the tearful dissuasions of his eldest son, and with only 500 men he proffered his allegiance to the Ch'ing at Fu-chou on November 21. Very shortly, however, his men were dispersed and Chih-lung was taken to "see his [new] emperor" in Pei-ching, where subsequently he was kept in comfortable circumstances but under de facto house arrest. While Ch'ing forces proceeded from T'ing-chou and Fu-chou to take over the "lower drainage," other surrendering Lung-wu officials and commanders were given the opportunity to redeem themselves by aiding the Ch'ing conquest of Kuang-tung.[13]

2. Meanwhile, the Ch'ing *subjugation of Kan-chou Prefecture* had been proceeding more haltingly. The Ming viceroy there, Wan Yüan-chi, though a zealous patriot, was arbitrary in handling affairs and did not get along well with the commanders of the more than 40,000 troops that eventually were amassed in South Kan. These were a disorderly hodgepodge of Ming regulars, many of whom had been recruited very recently from all of the southern provinces, aboriginal mercenaries from Kuei-chou and eastern Chiang-hsi, former river pirates, and armies of mountain bandits from the aforementioned triprovincial border region. Although disagreements and mutinies over supply shortages were frequent among these elements, still, because the people of South Kan long had been afflicted by bandits and were good at fighting, especially with firearms, they were easily organized into effective self-defense corps. So after the fall of Chi-an in early May 1646 (see chapter 2), the Ch'ing command in Chiang-hsi, itself fraught with leadership problems and low troop morale, moved within striking distance of Kan-chou City but did not immediately try to advance further. Several skirmishes between the two sides were inconclusive, and a stalemate developed.[14]

Under Wan Yüan-chi there ensued a repetition of the pattern of events at Chi-an. Wan continued to treat the Ming regular forces superciliously and to undercut their importance by unwisely relying on assistance from erstwhile outlaw elements, in this case a naval force composed largely of river pirates who were supposed to come to the aid of Kan-chou from upstream near Nan-an. Those forces took a long time to prepare, however. Meanwhile the Ming regulars lost their fighting spirit, and the Ch'ing renewed theirs. Consequently, when the riverine flotilla finally approached Kan-chou on October 1, it was completely destroyed by the Ch'ing in a nocturnal attack, and months of waiting came to naught for the Kan-chou command. The largest units of Ming regulars were alarmed at this tremendous loss of men and materiel, and at the extension of Ch'ing strength upriver. Even more, they were disgusted with Wan's attitude and poor judgment, and they soon deserted the South Kan theater. Wan, equally disgusted with them, in effect said good riddance. He then dismissed other regulars who had not deserted and vowed to die defending the prefectural city with only the five to six thousand troops who remained there.[15]

By early November 1646, Kan-chou had maintained a defensive footing for six months, and exhaustion was setting in. On the night of November 9, a defector led some Ch'ing troops over the city wall, and the following day all of Kan-chou succumbed. Viceroy Wan Yüan-chi as well as Yang T'ing-lin and Kuo Wei-ching, the Lung-wu ministers of war and personnel, all committed suicide. Over one hundred other Ming officials also lost their lives, as inhabitants of the city were slaughtered or enslaved. But all of the remaining generals surrendered.[16]

3. The Ch'ing now were in position to begin their *initial occupation of Kuang-tung* by invading along two routes: from Chao-an in extreme southern Fu-chien, and from Nan-an just outside Mei Pass, on the border between Chiang-hsi and northeastern Kuang-tung. An explanation of their subsequent actions, however, first requires an understanding of what Ming loyalists in Liang-Kuang had been doing prior to this time.

In 1645 when news of the Hung-kuang emperor's demise had reached the far South, many officials there had favored enthronement of the Ming prince who by birth was next in succession after the Prince of Fu, Chu Yu-ai, the eldest surviving son of Chu Ch'ang-ying, the recently deceased Prince of Kuei. Having fled the Kuei princely estate in Heng-chou when Chang Hsien-chung invaded southern Hu-kuang in 1643, Chu Yu-ai and his father had taken refuge in Wu-chou, Kuang-hsi, where the latter died in 1644. Kuang-hsi Provincial Governor Ch'ü Shih-szu and others had regarded the Prince of T'ang as a presumptuous upstart whose claim to rulership obscured the principle of orderly succession; however, they had accepted his enthronement as a fait accompli. Moreover, Chu Yu-ai died suddenly not long after his investiture as the next Prince of Kuei. Of Chu Ch'ang-ying's progeny, there remained only the youngest, Chu Yu-lang, the Prince of Yung-ming. He had spent most of his twenty-two years in comfortable obscurity until the rebel horde had exposed him to the terrors of desperate flight, capture, and threatened execution. He had escaped only narrowly from southwestern Hu-kuang into Kuang-hsi and later had been housed and protected by Liang-Kuang Viceroy Ting K'uei-ch'u at his headquarters in

Kuang-tung. Now, by a process of rapid attrition among his elders, the Prince of Yung-ming suddenly had become the sole surviving grandson of the Wan-li emperor and next in line to become the emperor of Ming China.[17]

When news from Fu-chien had become ominous, Liang-Kuang officials had probed the prince's willingness to assume the throne, but they had received only steadfast refusals from his honorary mother, née Wang, the barren surviving wife of Chu Ch'ang-ying, who now dominated the affairs of her husband's only remaining son. She had objected, quite correctly as events bore out, that the Prince of Yung-ming was too young, inexperienced, and delicate of character to assume heavy responsibilities in chaotic times, and that Kuang-tung currently lacked enough officials, or even the semblance of an army, to constitute and defend a government.[18] The matter was not pressed until definite word was received of the Lung-wu emperor's demise. Then, stressing the urgency of the dynasty's plight, in mid-November Ch'ü Shih-szu and Ting K'uei-ch'u were able to persuade the prince to become Regent at Chao-ch'ing. Both Ch'ü and Ting became grand secretaries in the new court, concurrent ministerial posts were given to such officials as Viceroy Ho T'eng-chiao and Governor Tu Yin-hsi in Hu-kuang, and positions in the military hierarchy, generals' seals, and noble titles were bestowed on several dozen commanders in the southwestern provinces.[19] But no other governmental actions were taken at this time.

Kuang-tung previously had sent most of its organized armed forces to help defend southern Chiang-hsi, and only small, often mutinous local units had remained to deal with (or to join) the swarms of bandit and pirate groups that had been emerging ever more boldly in Kuang-tung since news had arrived there of the fall of Pei-ching in 1644. Consequently, when the regency at Chao-ch'ing learned in late November that the patriots at Kan-chou had been overwhelmed by Ch'ing forces, the new monarch and his family naturally felt insecure. And on November 24, they departed westward for Wu-chou, where they would be farther away from the Ch'ing threat and closer to the more reliable armies in Kuang-hsi.[20] They were unaware that another threat was emerging nearby on the Ming side—a stubbornly independent combination of prefectural localism and a rump Lung-wu court.

By this time a number of officials who had served directly under the Lung-wu emperor had begun arriving in the vicinity of the Kuang-tung provincial capital, Kuang-chou, the most prominent among them being three grand secretaries who were natives of Kuang-chou Prefecture. Several of these men had been in contact with supporters of the Prince of Yung-ming but had come to feel cool toward that group—some because of personal rebuffs and the failure of Chao-ch'ing to consult with anyone in Kuang-chou, others because they felt already excluded from the most desirable official positions in the new regency, and perhaps because of the Chao-ch'ing leaders' prejudice against the Lung-wu emperor and his regime. They and others in Kuang-chou also lacked confidence in the new regent, especially after he so lightly abandoned Kuang-tung when the first sign of danger appeared.[21] In any case, when the Lung-wu emperor's younger brother, Chu Yü-yüeh (who had been made Regent to oversee affairs in Fu-chou when the emperor left "on campaign"), arrived in Kuang-chou by sea on December 5, he was greeted with warm expectation. One week later he was enthroned there as Shao-wu emperor, on the principle of younger brother succeeding elder. His chief grand secretary, Su Kuan-sheng, and other important appointees almost uniformly were men of Kuang-chou.[22]

The regental party in Wu-chou soon learned of the Kuang-chou group's activities, but at first it was not known that enthronement ceremonies had been carried out. So it was decided that Regent Yung-ming should return promptly to Chao-ch'ing and assume the imperial throne himself, preempting any such move on the part of Chu Yü-yüeh, in hope that the greater prestige and wider range of the regent's appointees eventually would draw popular support solely to his court. Subsequently, Regent Yung-ming became the Yung-li emperor in Chao-ch'ing on December 24, 1646; and when he then learned of the Shao-wu enthronement, defenses hastily were set up to ward off any threat from Kuang-chou.[23] An attempt by the Yung-li court to initiate negotiations ended disastrously when the emissary was executed by Su Kuan-sheng, and armed hostilities between the two regimes became inevitable. Even though the Shao-wu forces consisted largely of untrustworthy local hill bandits and river pirates who had been persuaded to fight under official banners, still they were stronger militarily than the Yung-li side. Consequently, two battles that were fought between Yung-li and Shao-wu forces in the Kuang-chou delta in early January 1647 ended in the almost total annihilation of the Yung-li flotilla.[24]

Both courts allowed their attention to be absorbed, and precious military capability to be depleted, in this fratricidal competition, as the common enemy was forgotten. This situation, although more myopic and virulent, clearly is analogous to the earlier rivalry between Lu and Lung-wu. In both cases we can see not only the consequences of having many imperial princes roaming the land, but also the degree to which reliance on local solidarity could become paramount when the structures of national government cracked and swayed. In any case, this was the situation in central Kuang-tung as the Ch'ing began their invasion of that province in mid-January 1647. (For the following discussion, see maps 8 and 9.)

On January 20, the Shao-wu emperor was just celebrating the victory of his troops over those of Yung-li when Kuang-chou City suddenly was penetrated by a small unit of Ch'ing cavalry, which met only startled and disorganized

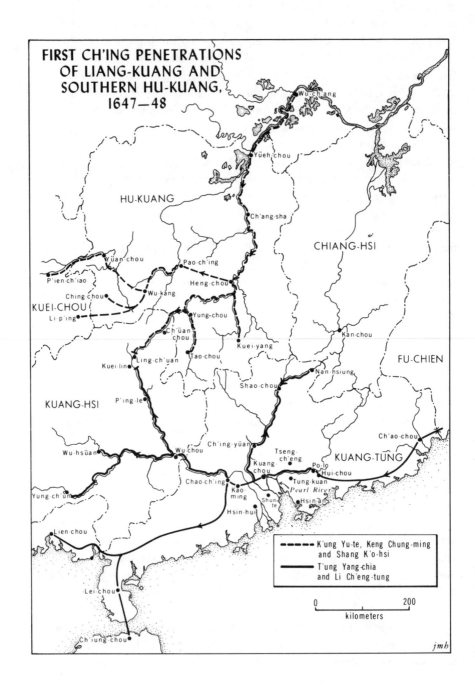

FIRST CH'ING PENETRATIONS
OF LIANG-KUANG AND
SOUTHERN HU-KUANG,
1647—48

Wu-ch'ang

Yüeh-chou

HU-KUANG

Ch'ang-sha

CHIANG-HSI

Yüan-chou
Pao-ch'ing
P'ien-ch'iao
Heng-chou
Ching-chou   Wu-kang
KUEI-CHOU   Kan-chou
Li-p'ing
Yung-chou
Ch'üan-
chou
Tao-chou   FU-CHIEN
Kuei-lin   Ling-ch'uan   Kuei-yang
Nan-hsiung
P'ing-le   Shao-chou
KUANG-HSI

Wu-hsüan   Ch'ing-yüan   Ch'ao-chou
Wu-chou   Tseng-
ch'eng
Kuang-   KUANG-TUNG
chou   Po-lo
Chao-ch'ing   Hui-chou
Tung-kuan
Kao-   Pearl River
Yung-ch'un   ming   Shun-   Hsin-an
te
Lien-chou   Hsin-hui

K'ung Yu-te, Keng Chung-ming
and Shang K'o-hsi
T'ung Yang-chia
and Li Ch'eng-tung

Lei-chou

0   200
kilometers
Ch'iung-chou

jmh

opposition. The Ch'ing had proceeded all the way through Ch'ao-chou and Hui-chou prefectures without being detected by the Shao-wu leadership. For one thing, they had used the captured seals of officials in those eastern prefectures to send false reports forward that nothing was amiss; but also, messengers who did try to warn Su Kuan-sheng were killed on suspicion of being subversives from Chao-ch'ing. Moreover, the Ch'ing in their final approach were thought to be just the Hua-shan outlaws, who had become dangerously unruly allies of the Shao-wu regime. Since no defense then was possible, Su Kuan-sheng committed suicide, whereas most of his colleagues submitted to the Ch'ing. The Shao-wu emperor attempted to flee but was captured and later executed for his refusal to cooperate, as were a large number of other Ming princes who had congregated in Kuang-chou.[25]

When news of this calamity reached Chao-ch'ing, the initial response of the Yung-li court was incredulity—surely it was a trick by the Shao-wu bunch to disrupt Yung-li ranks! But subsequent reports soon dispelled such illusions, and the Yung-li emperor hastily abandoned Chao-ch'ing in the last week of January, reaching Wu-chou again on February 5.[26] From there he soon continued on to Kuei-lin, establishing a pattern of sudden flight from confusedly perceived dangers which, in the long run, effectively precluded the development of true grassroots support anywhere in the South-Southwest and, from the start, permanently alienated the populace of Kuang-tung.

The Ch'ing forces that so swiftly captured Kuang-chou were a typical combination of disciplined and trustworthy Han Chinese from Liao-tung, who had long identified with the Ch'ing, and a larger number of less reliable, less disciplined troops who had surrendered with their erstwhile Ming commanders since the Ch'ing advance into China proper. In this case, the former were led by T'ung Yang-chia, who had been born under Manchu rule, had served as a court adviser to both Khungtaiji and the Shun-chih emperor, and who recently had accompanied Bolo in subduing Che-chiang and Fu-chien.[27] The latter were led by the aforementioned Li Ch'eng-tung, who, after bloodily pacifying the Yang-tzu delta for the Ch'ing, also had accompanied the campaign through Fu-chien.

After Kuang-chou was subdued, T'ung remained there with only a few hundred men while Li proceeded easily to seize Chao-ch'ing, the strategic nexus for all points in western Kuang-tung. From there contingents radiated in three directions: first, up the North River to make contact with other Ch'ing forces that had come southward from Kan-chou; second, southward through the Lei-chou Peninsula, easily reaching the far southwest of the province and later crossing to occupy Hai-nan Island; and, third, in pursuit of the Yung-li party up the West River to Wu-chou, where Li Ch'eng-tung arrived with his heaviest forces on March 5. Although Li was ordered not to proceed beyond that point, he sent probing missions into central Kuang-hsi and, more important, northwest-ward toward Kuei-lin, which almost was taken in a surprise attack by a small Ch'ing unit on April 15.[28]

All of Kuang-tung and half of Kuang-hsi had fallen before T'ung and Li with amazing speed, producing an extreme example of the initial overextension that marked each stage in the Ch'ing conquest. Numerous Ming officials submit-ted unresistingly, and the formal, physical trappings of Ming government—official seals, ya-men buildings, city walls, guard posts—were seized readily, but only because such things already had lost their effectiveness for the Ming. T'ung Yang-chia at first was very pleased at the smoothness with which his men established superficial control. But he soon found, as did Ch'ing officials else-where, that beyond occupying various ya-men it was a much more difficult matter to restore social order, especially when all kinds of disruptive elements now could cloak themselves in legitimacy by allying with Ming loyalists to oppose the invaders. And many communities, simply for self-preservation, armed and organized themselves to kill all intruders—Manchus, Northerners, loyalist bands, Ming regulars, bandits, pirates—what have you. T'ung soon realized that the true pacification of Kuang-tung depended on restoring the security of trade routes from Kuang-chou northward through Hu-kuang and Chiang-hsi to the Yang-tzu region, thus also restoring legitimate means of livelihood to the uncontrollably large number of men in Kuang-tung who now had to fight or steal to survive. But at this point, T'ung did not have enough men to accomplish the full task.[29]

4. Equally frustrating, in their continuing *initial penetration of southern Hu-kuang,* the Ch'ing command in that province even more narrowly failed to do what Li Ch'eng-tung almost had done from eastern Kuang-hsi: capture the surviving claimant to the Ming throne.

The Yung-li party had eschewed making a brave stand at Kuei-lin, the headquarters of Grand Secretary and Minister of War and Personnel Ch'ü Shih-szu. Instead they had moved on to Ch'üan-chou, the city that guarded the major pass between Kuang-hsi and Hu-kuang, there catching their breath and trying to ascertain which province offered the better prospects for safety.[30] Although Ch'ü and Regional Commander Chiao Lien almost miraculously repulsed a second Ch'ing challenge to Kuei-lin on June 27, the Yung-li emperor already had accepted refuge with the Ming general Liu Ch'eng-yin at Wu-kang, deep in the hills of southwestern Hu-kuang. Liu had gained preponderance there in 1643 by suppressing a popular uprising against the locally enfeoffed Prince of Min, and he now styled himself as a special protector of Ming royalty.[31]

This was the beginning of a chronic condition for the Yung-li emperor, that is, complete domination of his court by one ambitious militarist or another.

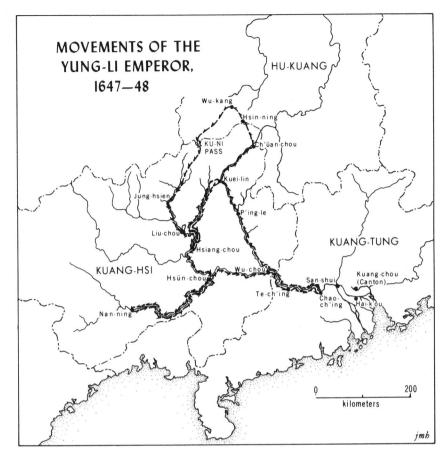

MOVEMENTS OF THE
YUNG-LI EMPEROR,
1647–48

Moreover, the emperor had just displayed a two-sided propensity which was to characterize his entire reign. On one hand, he disliked the urgings of high-minded civil officials such as Ch'ü Shih-szu that he be bold, courageous, and farsighted. He regarded with suspicion their roseate assessments of the strategic situation and their buoyant prophecies about how the people would rise up or stand firm when shown the imperial banners, and he felt that they too readily were willing to expose him to danger. On the other hand, he ran gratefully into the arms of any militarist who seemed capable of providing physical security for him and his family, only to chafe petulantly under the restrictions that such protection invariably imposed on him.

Liu Ch'eng-yin, the most recalcitrant of the long-time Ming commanders in Hu-kuang who had not fully submitted to the direction of Viceroy Ho T'eng-chiao (see chapter 2), is an example of the dissatisfaction among military men with their status in late Ming times. For many years at Wu-kang he had hosted officials traveling between Hu-kuang and points in the Southwestern provinces, and he always had impressed them with his knowledge of etiquette, his disciplined comportment, and his ability to speak like a cultured gentleman, even though he was wholly illiterate. Moreover, though he was known as "Iron Club" and loved to lead his big army in tough battles, he also had a taste for fineries such as jade and silk. Now, as the Yung-li imperial entourage came under his control, he remarked to some of them that

> he could not see why the nine categories [of meritorious military officers] always were regarded as the [side] wings on the [civil officials'] caps, and he put down two fingers [parallel], saying it would be better this way. Also, he said it was not good that a duke [i.e., a hereditary military noble such as himself] could die at no higher than the fifth rank, and that he would be glad to be called "Grand Secretary of the Eastern Hall."

Although that position was not directly within his grasp, Liu pressured the Yung-li court to appoint men whom he favored. Thus, Liu caused to be installed as a grand secretary of the Eastern Hall an old friend from his home province of Kuei-chou, who shared Liu's view that the merit of military leaders in the Southwest had gone unrecognized for too long.[32]

At Wu-kang, Liu kept the imperial family virtually under lock and key, isolating them from officials who were not of Liu's clique, and forcing the emperor secretly to appeal for help to Viceroy Ho T'eng-chiao elsewhere in southern Hu-kuang and to Ch'ü Shih-szu in Kuei-lin. Both Ho and Ch'ü, however, already were hard pressed to defend against Ch'ing drives from the north and south, and neither had sufficient control over the other Ming generals, nominally under their command, to challenge Liu's position in Wu-kang.[33] So eventually the emperor's release from this detention was effected not by Ming forces, but by the Ch'ing.

Like the campaign on Kuang-tung, since mid-March of 1647 the Ch'ing campaign on southern Hu-kuang, led by K'ung Yu-te commencing at Yüeh-chou, also had encountered little organized resistance, since the disunited Ming armies generally had collapsed and scattered when the enemy approached in force. Thus, while Tu Yin-hsi and the erstwhile Shun rebel armies under his charge were chased farther northwestward, into the rugged hills that surround the Yang-tzu where it flows out of Szu-ch'uan, Ho T'eng-chiao and Chang K'uang were forced to withdraw far up the Hsiang River into Yung-chou Prefecture (on the riverine route to Ch'üan-chou and Kuei-lin), where Chang subsequently died of bleeding stomach ulcers.[34] Concurrently, K'ung Yu-te in succession took over Ch'ang-sha, Hsiang-t'an, and Heng-chou, aiming to proceed all the way into Kuang-hsi and then Kuang-tung, to make the Ch'ing's two-armed invasion of the far South complete. But K'ung, like Ho T'eng-chiao, had found the situation in Hu-kuang to be frustratingly complex, and he was impeded by the same kinds of deceptive actions by quasi-independent militarists and the same severe shortages of provisions that had plagued the Ming side. Only belatedly did he learn the current location of the Ming claimant, so he was not able to lead a force through Pao-ch'ing toward Wu-kang until mid-September.[35]

When Ch'ing victory appeared imminent after several days of fighting over Wu-kang's outer defenses, Liu Ch'eng-yin prepared to surrender and, on September 23, passively allowed the Yung-li emperor and his family to escape by whatever means they could find. With a small and rapidly dwindling party, the emperor fled in great desperation by a circuitous route southwestward, through mountainous aboriginal territory, suffering dire travel conditions and harassment by native chieftains and renegade soldiers, until November when he arrived at Liu-chou in central Kuang-hsi.[36] There he was rejoined by a number of Ming officials and received protection from an ennobled general, Ch'en Pang-fu, who in the past few months had been instrumental in pushing Ch'ing forces from Kuang-tung back out of eastern Kuang-hsi. Subsequently it was decided that the empresses dowager, the empress, and other women in the imperial party should be removed to the relative security of Nan-ning farther to the southwest, while the emperor, responding to the appeals of Ch'ü Shih-szu to come and inspire the Ming forward guard, returned to Kuei-lin on December 30.[37]

Thus, the Yung-li emperor closed a nine-month-long circular odyssey of dreadful experiences; but his tribulations were far from over. Many frictions between "hosts" and "guests" had arisen as several Ming armies from southern Hu-kuang had fallen back and become crowded together in the far northeastern tip of Kuang-hsi. Consequently, when the Ch'ing command at Heng-chou resumed its southwestward drive in March of 1648, the Ming generals in charge of defending the corridor from Ch'üan-chou to Kuei-lin did not cooperate, and Kuei-lin was laid waste by the forces of a commander (the former Shun rebel, Heh Yao-ch'i) who constrained the emperor to retreat with him back into central Kuang-hsi. Subsequently, the emperor rejoined his family in Nan-ning, while Ch'ü Shih-szu was left to perform again the miracle of saving Kuei-lin. Ch'ü successfully repulsed the third Ch'ing attack on that city on April 14, and then, with the assistance of Ho T'eng-chiao, he managed to drive the overextended Ch'ing attack force out of northeastern Kuang-hsi, deeply back into Hu-kuang.[38] This was part of a general turn in the tide of events against the Ch'ing, which will be discussed more fully in chapter 5.

The most significant resistance generated by the Ch'ing drives into the far South and the Southeast arose in two areas: the southeastern maritime zone and central Kuang-tung. This was the beginning of a separation in overt Ming loyalist activity between the extreme Southeast and the Southwest. Although several attempts were made to link these theaters, no success ever was achieved on an operational level, and the centers of resistance in these two spheres gradually were forced farther and farther apart by the Ch'ing.

Although many unsubmitting Lu and Lung-wu officials had escaped into remote, mountainous parts of Eastern Che-chiang and Fu-chien, the most important among the survivors had sought the seacoast and the aid of various generals who commanded both land and naval forces. In maritime Che-chiang, the strongest of these was Chang Ming-chen, based at Shih-p'u and Nan-t'ien.[39] In maritime Fu-chien they were commanders in the now shaken and disintegrating organization of Cheng Chih-lung—mostly his relatives, but including such adjunct figures as Chou Ho-chih[40]—based in the coastal area between Ch'üan-chou and Chang-chou that includes the islands of Hsia-men (Amoy) and Chin-men (Quemoy). These were not the only armed forces on the seaboard. Pirates abounded, and indeed, many of these commanders and their lieutenants had begun their careers as freebooters. Now in the even more fluid coastal situation brought on by the collapse of Ming government in Che-chiang and Fu-chien, rivalry among these men—for good sailors, secure bases, trade advantages, reliable sources of food, fuel, and war materiel—became pandemic. Some undeniably were sincere Ming loyalists; nevertheless, nascent coastal warlordism unavoidably imbued the Lu maritime resistance effort and combined uneasily with the idealism of Regent Lu's scholar-official supporters.

In some developing coastal satraps we can see waterborne parallels to the semi-independent Ming generals in the peripheral hills of southern Hu-kuang who so frustrated Ho T'eng-chiao's attempt to recreate a unified command. The best example of this is Huang Pin-ch'ing, who in 1645 had begun in earnest to establish virtually a private colony on Chou-shan Island when he was charged by the Lung-wu emperor to coordinate counteroffensive activities in the Hang-chou Bay region. Subsequently, Huang had cooperated with other Ming naval commanders only guardedly, when such cooperation could be turned to his own advantage or to the disadvantage of his rivals. He soon gained a reputation for being more willing to reduce, subjugate, or eliminate his compatriots than to attack the Ch'ing.[41]

Two incidents, both involving Huang Pin-ch'ing, illustrate well the diverging interests of men who were inclined to build survival enclaves among the coastal islands, under the Ming aegis if possible, and loyalists who needed naval support to restore Ming control of major urban centers near the sea. First, in the spring of 1647 there was the planned reversion to Ming allegiance of Wu Sheng-chao, the Ch'ing regional naval commander at Sung-chiang southeast of Su-chou. Wu long had harbored in his ranks men who were known to have close contacts with the pro-Ming underground in urban areas and among the many lakes and waterways in the Su-chou region. When Huang was called on to provide the external naval catalyst for Wu's revolt, he demurred and left the task solely to Chang Ming-chen, instead. Unfortunately, Chang's fleet was broken up by typhoon winds when it reached the Ch'ung-ming channel in mid-May, and, having no backup fleet, it then was decimated by Ch'ing defense forces on the shore. Leaders of "righteous" volunteers in Wu's camp, who had been in conflict with Wu's more cautious regular officers, refused to abort their plans because of the naval failure and unsuccessfully attempted to carry off a coup on May 20.[42] The resulting executions of military and civilian conspirators in this incident were extensive, as the Ch'ing took special measures to break the seditious triangle of "lake bandits," traitors among Su-Sung military personnel, and coastal elements loyal to Regent Lu. Later that year, in December, Huang reluctantly agreed to take part in a planned overthrow of Ch'ing control in the nearby city of Ning-po, and he moved a fleet up the Yung River to await the loyalists' signal. But through a typical lack of circumspection, the "righteous" plotters were betrayed to the Ch'ing authorities, and Huang, unwilling to take the initiative or to battle against unfavorable odds, withdrew back into the sea.[43] After these incidents, Huang never again became involved in mainland offensives.

Given this disposition in Huang Pin-ch'ing, it is not surprising that when Regent Lu fled into coastal waters from T'ai-chou in the late summer of 1646, Huang refused to allow the reestablishment of his court on Chou-shan. So the regent's boats found temporary haven among the smaller islands around Chou-shan until the winter, when Cheng Ts'ai arrived and transported Regent Lu to the somewhat more secure Cheng base area in Fu-chien.[44]

Although Cheng Chih-lung's expectations had been betrayed and he had been removed from Fu-chien by the Ch'ing, the home of the Cheng clan at An-p'ing had not yet been violated. This was in accord with the principle of treating surrendered notables with respect. But the Ch'ing also felt that so long as Chih-lung remained alive and cooperative, it might be possible to obtain through him the submission of the other Chengs, thus saving a long, costly, and uncertain campaign against them. So for some time after the fall of the Lung-wu regime, the Chengs were able to maintain a strong presence in mainland areas of coastal Ch'üan-chou and Chang-chou prefectures, and also to develop bases on Hsia-men and Chin-men, as new leadership patterns emerged among them. The chief candidates to succeed the patriarch, Chih-lung, as effective head of the destabilized Cheng organization were the senior figures Cheng Hung-k'uei and Cheng Ts'ai, and the junior Cheng Ch'eng-kung, now just twenty-two years old.

Because of his especially close personal relationship with the Lung-wu emperor (see chapter 3), Ch'eng-kung for a time continued symbolically to use the Lung-wu calendar; and now, as in the future, he declined to acknowledge the regental status of the Prince of Lu, whose claims his dead father-ruler had denounced. Cheng Ts'ai, on the other hand, seems to have hoped to perform with Regent Lu a role similar to the one that Chih-lung had performed with the Lung-wu emperor, that is, that of chief provider to and protector of the throne, and chief recipient of the throne's delegated charismatic power. In any case, when Regent Lu was brought to Chung-tso-so on Hsia-men in December 1646, Cheng Ts'ai's noncombative rivalry with his clan-nephew gave Cheng Ch'eng-kung even greater reason to ignore the regent. But since Ch'eng-kung could not yet afford to definitely alienate his elder clansman, he made no attempt to drive the regent away.[45]

Through the spring and summer of 1647, Cheng Ts'ai aided his clansmen's first attacks on Ch'ing positions in Chang-chou and Ch'üan-chou; but also, with Chou Ho-chih and others, he fought northward from Hsia-men, concentrating especially on strategic points in Fu-chou Prefecture. And by September, Regent Lu himself had moved to the Ch'ang-yüan islands* to encourage his officials and generals who had seized the important garrison of Min-an, which guarded the waterway between Fu-chou City and the sea. Virtually the whole populace around Fu-chou was mobilized under Lu banners, and the city was starved under siege until Ch'ing relief forces arrived in the summer of the following year.[46] From this time on, Lu forces operated from Fu-chou Prefecture northeastward into Che-chiang, while Cheng Ch'eng-kung worked from Ch'üan-chou Prefecture southwestward into extreme eastern Kuang-tung.

This separation, which lasted until the effective demise of the Lu regime, should not be conceived as an extension of the earlier antagonism between the Lu and Lung-wu courts. In his enduring refusal to recognize Regent Lu, Cheng Ch'eng-kung was exceptional among erstwhile Lung-wu officials. Of those who rallied to the Lu standard, many formerly had served the Lung-wu court, were natives of Fu-chien, or previously had served as officials in that province.[47] Rather, the division was between a new Lu regime and the readjusting Cheng organization, which eventually was dominated by Ch'eng-kung. And more significant here, it was a division between a regime that still was burdened by rancor between scholar-officials and militarists, on one hand, and a regime that dispensed with that problem, on the other.

* Ch'ang-yüan was a collective term for a group of islands, the largest of which is present-day Ma-tsu. See Sheng Ch'eng, "Shen Kuang-wen," pp. 51–52.

In November at Ch'ang-yüan, Regent Lu began to reestablish the semblance of a legitimate court by again broadly appointing high civil ministers of
state. Former Lu and Lung-wu officials worked together harmoniously; and
spirits were buoyed when early successes in Fu-chou Prefecture were extended
into Fu-ning Prefecture to the northeast. (For this and the following discussion,
see map 10.) Also encouraging were the responses that Lu coastal attacks evoked
from loyalists in upland Fu-chien. A counterinsurgence began from Chien-ning
in late August and early September 1647 and soon spread to almost every district
in north-central Fu-chien.[48] But the Lu regime was not able to consolidate its
hold on the coastal areas it restored, nor could it link up or coordinate with the
inland resistance movement. This partly was due to a general lack of manpower
and the current, heavy reliance on naval forces, as well as to the fact that much of
the popular resistance in western Fu-chien, spurred by tenants, indentured
servants, transport workers, miners and ironworkers, not to mention the
ubiquitous bandits, was in opposition to all forms of upper-class control—Ming,
Ch'ing, or otherwise.[49] But the capacity of the Lu regime to constitute a viable
source of direction for the energies of genuine Ming loyalists also was weakened
by the enmity that grew between Cheng Ts'ai, the regime's predominant
military leader at this stage, and men of scholar-official background who now, as
in Eastern Che-chiang, had stridden forward to take up military functions.

For instance, the man most responsible for restoring Ming control in
northeastern Fu-chien was the Fu-ning native, and former Lung-wu Supervising
Secretary for War, Liu Chung-tsao. His rift with Cheng Ts'ai began when
numerous soldiers who had surrendered to the Ch'ing came to Lu officials
wishing to rejoin the Ming side. Liu regarded them all as traitors and forthwith
had them executed; Cheng, however, objected strenuously to the killing of
surrendered men and thereafter hated Liu for this act (as well as for the execution
of one of Cheng's own intermediaries). In part because of this enmity, Liu
received no help when he needed it, became isolated in Fu-ning, and committed
suicide in defeat in the spring of 1649.[50] Moreover, in spite of early attempts to
reinforce solidarity through marriage ties and fictive kinship relations, conflicts
also developed between Cheng Ts'ai and two stalwarts of the Lu regime from
Eastern Che-chiang, Hsiung Ju-lin and Cheng Tsun-ch'ien. Hsiung had criticized Cheng Ts'ai for appointing his own man (rather than a censorial official) as
troop supervisor; further, Hsiung continued his Che-chiang pattern of allowing
his men to attack at will, rather than subordinating them to general military
policies and strategies. Cheng Tsun-ch'ien, for his part, had betrayed the trust of
his "elder brother," Cheng Ts'ai, by cutting into the latter's provisions and
absconding with two of his richly loaded trading ships (presumably on the
principle that all goods were for the same cause). So in February 1648, when

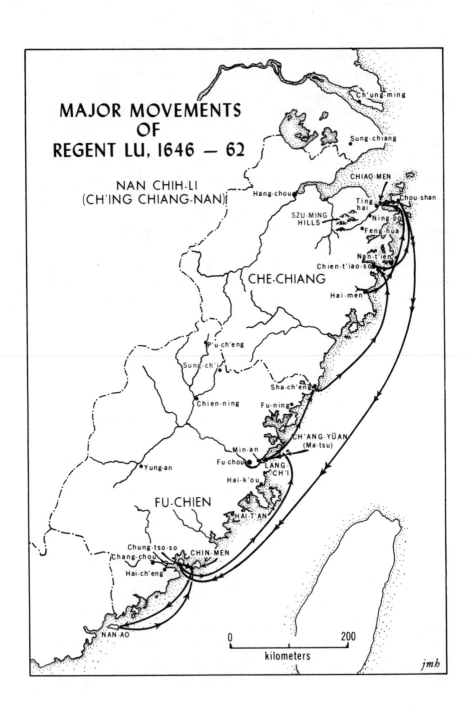

MAJOR MOVEMENTS
OF
REGENT LU, 1646 — 62

NAN CHIH-LI
(CH'ING CHIANG-NAN)

Ch'ung-ming

Sung-chiang

CHIAO-MEN

Hang-chou

Ting-hai

Chou-shan

SZU-MING
HILLS

Ning-po

Feng-hua

Nan-t'ien

Chien-t'iao-so

CHE-CHIANG

Hai-men

P'u-ch'eng

Sung-ch'i

Sha-ch'eng

Chien-ning

Fu-ning

CH'ANG-YÜAN
(Ma-tsu)

Min-an

Yung-an

Fu-chou

LANG-
CH'I

Hai-k'ou

FU-CHIEN

HAI-T'AN

Chung-tso-so

CHIN-MEN

Chang-chou

Hai-ch'eng

NAN-AO

0   200
kilometers

jmh

Cheng Ts'ai was given reason to think that Hsiung and Tsun-ch'ien were colluding in a plot against him, he probably engineered the circumstances whereby Hsiung died at the hands of some unruly toughs and Tsun-ch'ien committed suicide under shipboard detention.[51]

These deaths badly shook the Lu leadership and were followed by the departures of several important figures, including Grand Secretary Ch'ien Su-yüeh.[52]

> So in the end, [heroic] thoughts of tigers on the wind and dragons in the clouds turned to tragic feelings of sunken pearls and shattered jade,

and only a handful of ministers remained with the regent.[53] In large part because of this, beginning in the late spring of 1648 the Ch'ing were able to retake most of the three prefectures and twenty-seven districts that Lu forces had restored in northern Fu-chien, and in one year even the most stubborn locales, in Fu-ning, had succumbed.[54] At this point Cheng Ts'ai lost interest in maintaining the Lu regime and returned to Hsia-men hoping to mend fences with Cheng Ch'eng-kung. Regent Lu clung perilously to the seacoast until he was rescued again by the same Che-chiang naval commander who originally had taken him to sea, the perennial Chang Ming-chen. In July of 1649, Chang restored the coastal guard station of Chien-t'iao-so to Ming control and enabled Regent Lu to reestablish his court there,[55] thus beginning a new Che-chiang phase of the Lu resistance.

Sympathy for the Ming cause remained high in Che-chiang, and at Chien-t'iao-so Regent Lu's court was situated directly between the two areas that offered the best prospects for military support: the Szu-ming and T'ien-t'ai hills to the west, and the Chou-shan Islands to the east. Literally in the middle, with his home base at nearby Nan-t'ien, was Chang Ming-chen, now the central military figure in the Lu regime. The progressive course would have been for Chang to effect coordination between loyalist armies in the hills and naval forces on the islands, thereby to expand Lu-controlled territory in southeastern Che-chiang. He failed to do this, however, and instead the Ch'ing were able to defeat both sectors by driving them farther apart. The reasons for this lay not only in the considerable abilities and perseverance of the Ch'ing provincial officials, but, more germane here, in Chang's inability to establish the legitimacy of his leadership—this despite his unquestioned dedication to the Ming resistance.[56]

Like politically prominent commanders before him in the Southern Ming, Chang Ming-chen was criticized by civil officials, especially "righteous" ones, for overstepping his sphere of authority, for privatizing positions, and for ignoring established "standards of qualification" in offering high rank to men who, it was alleged, were skilled at inflating the political significance of their self-serving actions but had no proven merit in selflessly serving the dynasty.[57]

Morever, there appeared yet another manifestation of the old disharmony between volunteer forces and the regular military command.

The strongest and most conscientious of the stockade defenders in the Szu-ming Hills was Wang Yi, a boldly martial man of strong convictions who, in a typical marriage between the "knight-errant" and the "righteous" elements, had been collaborating closely with the indefatigable resistance leader and Fu She activist Feng Ching-ti.[58] Although these men had been set back by Ch'ing strikes in the spring of 1648, they had rebuilt their movement and reasserted control in virtually all of rural Szu-ming and adjacent areas. But when Regent Lu came to Chien-t'iao-so, Wang balked at accepting a military appointment from the Lu court if that would mean subordinating himself to the likes of Chang Ming-chen.[59] Consequently, no operational relation was worked out between the Lu court and the various stockade defenders in the hills. Moreover, the capacities of the latter were limited by the leadership style of Feng Ching-ti, who "was personally concerned about statecraft [as were many in 'righteous' circles] and tried to treat his soldiers according to forms and systems appropriate to peaceful times. He behaved in a superior manner, and it was not easy for his men to become close with him. This was a frequent cause of failure."[60]

On the island side, Chang became ever more ensnarled in the growing coastal warlordism which was most aptly represented by Huang Pin-ch'ing at Chou-shan. Although Chang had family relations with Huang, and for this reason had been allowed to maintain his own bases and activities near Huang's territory, still he could not induce Huang even to provide food when famine developed at Chien-t'iao-so, much less militarily support the Lu cause. Consequently, in a warlordistic countermove of his own, Chang joined in league with several other naval commanders (*cum* buccaneers) who held grudges against Huang to overthrow him and seize Chou-shan as a more secure site for Regent Lu's court. Facing defeat, Huang committed suicide at Chou-shan on October 29, 1649, and the Lu court moved there in November.[61] Although the regent's party thereby was relieved from Ch'ing pressures and starvation in its small mainland enclave, this move marked the end of any chance to effect a restoration in Che-chiang, and thereafter the court was completely on the defensive, concerned just to survive.

The Ch'ing strategy had been simultaneously to build their own seagoing naval fleet, with bases at Hai-men, Ting-hai,* and Ch'ung-ming, while also moving methodically to suppress stockade defenders in the mountains east and west of the Ch'ien-t'ang River. In October of 1650 they launched a concerted

---

*Ting-hai was the present-day Chen-hai, and the city of Chou-shan was what now is called Ting-hai, on Chou-shan Island.

attack on resisters in the Szu-ming Hills, destroying Wang Yi's organization and making hunted men of Wang and Feng Ching-ti.[62] Then in March 1651, Chang Ming-chen assassinated one of the commanders with whom he had conspired to overthrow Huang Pin-ch'ing; then, as happened repeatedly to the Southern Ming military, disgruntled subordinates defected to the Ch'ing and informed them about conditions on Chou-shan. Thus, by autumn the Ch'ing were prepared to attack the island with some confidence, especially when Wang Yi was captured and executed in front of the Ting-hai troops to raise their ardor.[63]

From October 4 through 15, the Ch'ing carried out what was to have been a three-pronged attack on Chou-shan. Both the southern contingent from Hai-men and the northern contingent from Wu-sung encountered resistance en route and were either forced back or delayed.[64] Consequently, the brunt of the fighting was borne by the Ch'ing contingent from Ting-hai alone. Largely by chance, this force caught the Ming side's most intrepid commander off guard and destroyed him with his fleet in the sea lane that separates Chou-shan from the mainland. Regent Lu was on shipboard, offshore with Chang Ming-chen, when the Ch'ing began their siege of stubbornly defended Chou-shan City. After ten days, the wall finally was penetrated by cannon fire, and all Lu relatives and officials who remained in or near the city went to martyr's deaths, many by self-immolation.[65]

Subsequently, Chang Ming-chen took Regent Lu southward along the coast, and probably in January of 1652 they, and a few other surviving members of the Lu regime, arrived at Cheng Ch'eng-kung's headquarters on Hsia-men. In the six years since Regent Lu last had been at Chung-tso-so, Cheng's power had increased steadily, whereas now the regent's official following had been almost totally annihilated, and his military supporters were so weakened that now they welcomed incorporation under Cheng's supreme command. Also in the interim, Cheng had been in contact with the Yung-li court in Liang-Kuang, which had bestowed on him the first in an ascending series of military and noble titles, and in the fall of 1648 he had changed from the Lung-wu to the Yung-li calendar.[66] Given these circumstances, it is likely that Cheng (or *Chu* Ch'eng-kung, as he had been named by the Lung-wu emperor) received Chu I-hai not as Regent Lu but, respectfully and cordially nevertheless, as the Prince of Lu, that is, as a senior fellow member of the Ming imperial clan. In any case, the prince was domiciled by Cheng on nearby Chin-men Island, and early in 1653 he renounced the regental title.[67]

Thus, although the Ming cause in southeastern Che-chiang had suffered a severe blow, new unity had been brought to the coastal resistance in two ways. First, the split between Lu and Cheng had been resolved, and all loyalists now were fighting under the same banners. Second, the Ming civil officialdom in the coastal resistance virtually had been wiped out. The few stalwart scholar-officials who remained soon received titular appointments from the Yung-li court, as had Cheng Ch'eng-kung himself; but to be effective they now had to serve in Cheng's organization, which had become wholly his own and (its mercantile aspect notwithstanding) was thoroughly military. So the chronic civil-military disunity on the Ming side disappeared in this particular theater, as did the problem of assistance for the emperor. (For further discussion of these two points, see chapter 6.)

Cheng Ch'eng-kung had been well educated as a boy in the traditional curriculum of Classics, histories, and belles lettres. But the times had not been conducive to stepping up the ladder of academic associations and civil service examinations into the ranks of scholar-officialdom. And after Fu-chien was invaded by the Ch'ing, he had explicitly renounced the civil vocation and dedicated himself to building and operating a military machine.[68] Ch'eng-kung's subsequent ascendance to become the undisputed leader of the Cheng organization can be explicated in three stages: (1) He began training his own core fighting units with just a few hundred men on a tiny island in the Hsia-men group early in 1646, and he soon recruited several thousand more men from the larger island of Nan-ao. With these forces, he first gained experience in amphibious warfare by joining with his uncles and other senior clansmen in attacks on Ch'ing positions in Chang-chou and Ch'üan-chou in 1647–48. The first Ch'ing action in retaliation for this, a raid on the Cheng family home at An-p'ing in the spring of 1647, resulted in the suicide of Ch'eng-kung's mother, making the son an even more implacable foe.[69] (2) Then in 1648–49 a famine in Fu-chien forced Ch'eng-kung to strike out on his own into Ch'ao-chou Prefecture in Kuang-tung, chiefly to obtain food but also to take advantage of the anarchic situation there, where dozens of local strongmen and stockade defenders were "neither Ch'ing nor Ming [or, literally, neither clean nor bright]."[70] This campaign had important formative effects on Ch'eng-kung's subsequently consistent pattern of operation, and he emerged so strengthened from it that he was able to return to Hsia-men in September of 1650 and simply seize control from his seniors.[71] (3) The following spring Ch'eng-kung enhanced his prestige, if not his fighting capability, by personally leading a campaign to assist the Yung-li regime in central Kuang-tung. As frequently occurred elsewhere, his fleet encountered rough weather along the eastern Kuang-tung coast and was not able to complete its mission.[72] What is worse, the Ch'ing had taken advantage of his absence from southern Fu-chien to carry out a very damaging raid on Hsia-men, which was countered only halfheartedly and ineffectually by two of Ch'eng-kung's uncles, whom he had left in charge. When Ch'eng-kung returned in May 1651, he was livid. Forthwith, one uncle was beheaded, and the other, Cheng Hung-k'uei, was forced to relinquish his command and retire.[73]

So in this instance, as well, a new unity emerged from adversity. Especially after he subordinated what remained of Regent Lu's forces the following winter, Ch'eng-kung had free rein to direct the southeastern coastal resistance as he saw fit. The Ch'ing, who thought they had conquered Fu-chien, were to be troubled a good deal more by this twenty-seven-year-old dynamo.

As we have seen, when the North was lost, the Ming was not able to fall back on well-constituted armies in the South. Now that the maritime provinces had been invaded, much less was the Ming, which largely had ignored the sea since early in its history, able to fall back on well-constituted navies. It was not just with the erosion of Ming authority on the seaboard that naval commanders began to recruit, consort with, and behave like pirate-traders. Many of them (Cheng Chih-lung being only the most outstanding case) had been pirate-traders in the past and had maintained their old associations and buccaneering dispositions. Even those who did not have such backgrounds nevertheless had been obliged to learn the ropes of a very tough and competitive seagoing environment in order to survive in their jobs. All of them were familiar with the lucrative trade that was flourishing then among entrepôts such as Macao, Manila, and Nagasaki, through way stations on T'ai-wan, the Liu-ch'iu (Ryūkyū) Islands, and along the pitted southeastern coast of China—this despite the fact that China officially had disallowed any direct trade with Japan outside the framework of the tributary system, in which that country had not participated for a century.[74]

Indeed, Japan's persistent need and desire for Chinese goods and the Ming government's persistent refusal to permit free commerce with Japan account to a considerable extent for the endemically piratical, smuggler-ridden character of East Asian maritime trade at this time, and for the presence of Japanese men among the freebooters. Moreover, the wars of elimination and consolidation that marked the gradual end of the Warring States (Sengoku) period and the concomitant establishment of the Tokugawa shogunate in Japan in the late sixteenth and early seventeenth centuries, had spilled some *rōnin* (masterless *samurai*) and other footloose Japanese swordsmen into the East Asian merchant marine.[75] Thus, the great prowess of Japanese fighters had become well known in the coastal sphere, even by men who never had personally sojourned in Japan.

Consequently, it is not surprising that many seaside bases and sources of recruits for the Lung-wu court, the regime of Regent Lu, and the coastal resistance of Cheng Ch'eng-kung had been notorious pirate lairs ever since the first wave of attacks by so-called Japanese raiders (*wo-k'ou*) in the sixteenth century,[76] nor that several attempts were made by various figures to obtain assistance—troops, ships, provisions, and other war materiel—from Japan.[77] The personnel involved in these solicitations reflect well the general composition of the loyalist resistance in the maritime zone, which was essentially the same as that inland. That is, an intriguing association of (1) idealistically Confucian scholar-officials and degree-holders, who felt they had to act on the principle of political loyalty to their state (such as the well-known expatriate Chu Chih-yü[78]); (2) Robin Hood-like "military specialists" (in this case, swashbuckling ship's captains), who at least affected some degree of adherence to standards of honor and social conscience, and who gravitated to any underdog's cause; and (3) remnants of the regular military establishment (here naval units), which by now were fluidly interchangeable with (4) outlaws, gangsters, and rebels (in this case, pirates and smugglers). As in the continental theaters of resistance, this was a friction-prone combination which showed few prospects of generating an effective Ming counterforce in time to thwart the Ch'ing. Inland, this induced attempts to incorporate ready-made fighting units from the large-scale rebel armies of Li Tzu-ch'eng and Chang Hsien-chung; whereas in the maritime theater, it produced a succession of attempts to borrow ready-made forces from Japan.

Men such as Cheng Chih-lung long had been in close contact with the lords (daimyō) and officials in southwestern Japan who profited from or were in charge of managing the China trade. Indeed, Cheng Ch'eng-kung had been born and reared to the age of six or seven in Hirado, his mother having been the daughter of a retainer to the Matsuura.[79] Most heavily involved in the southwestern overseas commerce at this time, however, were the Shimazu on their fief of Satsuma Island, from which they controlled the trade that passed through the Liu-ch'iu Islands.[80] The Tokugawa bakufu, also, was very interested in continuing advantageous aspects of the China trade, which it supervised carefully from its designated foreign-affairs port of Nagasaki.[81] This was in spite of the severance of official relations between Japan and China after Hideyoshi's abortive invasion of Korea in the 1590s and, in the 1630s, Japan's institution of an exclusion policy that strictly limited maritime contacts, mainly as a quarantine measure against European ships that might be infested with Christianity.[82]

Consequently, it is not surprising that the first to request soldiers from Japan to assist the Southern Ming was the mogul of the Japan-China trade, Cheng Chih-lung, whose representative appeared in Nagasaki in December 1645, after Cheng had become the military mainstay of the Lung-wu court. This was followed in January 1646 by a request for soldiers and armor from Chou Ho-chih, one of Cheng's most important collaborators, who had been assigned by the Lung-wu emperor to assist Huang Pin-ch'ing on Chou-shan. But the Japanese authorities backed away from these first appeals, citing the rupture of relations between the Ming and Japan, as well as a ban on the export of Japanese armaments.[83]

The next Lung-wu mission, however, seems to have been accorded more serious attention by the *bakufu* in Edo, that is, the *shōgun* Iemitsu and his advisers. On October 16, 1646, Huang Cheng-ming arrived in Nagasaki as concurrently the personal representative of Cheng Chih-lung and the official emissary of the Lung-wu court, again seeking crack troops to aid the resistance. This time the *bakufu* reply was only tentatively negative, since the Japanese leadership apparently was considering taking some military action in the Ming-Ch'ing conflict but needed more information about what was happening in China. Before this reply could be delivered to Huang, however, Edo learned that the Ming had lost Fu-chien and that Cheng Chih-lung had surrendered to the Ch'ing. Thus, all thoughts of rendering military assistance summarily were abandoned, and the various *daimyō* were informed of this decision.[84]

Formal efforts by followers of Regent Lu began with a mission initiated in the spring of 1647, again by Chou Ho-chih. This time Chou's adopted son, accompanied by a minor Ming prince, was refused formal reception by the Japanese on the excuse that neither man's name could be found on the lists that the Japanese kept of Ming civil service degree-holders, so their claim to official status could not be verified.[85]

Attempts also were made to circumvent the *bakufu* by appealing directly to the Shimazu clan leaders, who were sympathetic to the cause of their Chinese trade associates and may have had reasons of their own for wanting to engage in overseas military exploits. Chou Ho-chih is said to have arranged to receive 30,000 men, with provisions and armaments, from Satsuma early in 1646; but these plans allegedly were undercut by the cagey Huang Pin-ch'ing. In the summer of the following year, however, Huang sent his younger brother along with Feng Ching-ti to Satsuma, perhaps hoping to renew Ho's agreement. Eventually the Shimazu sent a large quantity of Chinese copper coins to Chou-shan, but no military aid was forthcoming.[86]

Cheng Ts'ai's early attempts to assume Cheng Chih-lung's mantle naturally extended to diplomacy. In December of 1648 he sent a letter to Nagasaki proposing to trade Chinese medicines and silks for Japanese weapons and war materiel; in addition, an accompanying letter from Cheng Ch'eng-kung pointed out his special affinity with Japan and asked for several ten-thousand troops to aid in resisting the "barbarians."[87] The following year Cheng Ts'ai also took advantage of the appearance in Fu-chien waters of a tributary mission (originally destined for the Lung-wu court) from the Liu-ch'iu Islands to request that the Liu-ch'iu authorities act as intermediaries with the Japanese, encouraging them to send muskets, swords, armor, and saltpeter in exchange for Chinese silver and other goods.[88]

In spite of repeated refusals by the Japanese to become involved militarily in the Southern Ming struggle by sending soldiers, hope persisted among loyalists that some other forms of aid could be gotten by fostering friendly relations with Japan. In December 1649, the Lu regime, newly established on Chou-shan, succumbed to the machinations of a Buddhist monk who claimed that the court could earn the gratitude of the Japanese by presenting to a temple in Nagasaki a statue of Kuan-yin and a sutra which then was owned by Regent Lu's mother. This mission came to naught when it was learned that this monk was persona non grata in Japan, having been expelled because of his undesirable proselytizing activities.[89] Nevertheless, the following summer Chou-shan is said to have received from Japan several hundred thousand liters of grain for famine relief. And in later years, after Cheng Ch'eng-kung ingratiated himself with the Japanese through extreme politeness and written expressions of admiration, he received metals and weapons—but no Japanese fighters—in return.[90]

Although we know very little of the specific responses to these appeals, it seems that in general the Japanese were unwilling to give direct military aid to the loyalists because of problems and concerns in stabilizing the young Tokugawa shogunate, and because of their low estimation of Southern Ming capabilities. The shoguns Iemitsu and Ietsuna still were grappling with many problems of consolidation, including enforcement of what later became referred to as the sakoku policies, which prohibited Japanese nationals from traveling abroad, and which subjected European traders either to complete exclusion (e.g., for the Spanish and Portuguese) or to restrictions (in the Dutch case) that many had been bellicosely unwilling to accept. Military ventures across the seas might have upset the delicate balance of daimyō power which the Tokugawa had forged. Moreover, such actions would have increased the possibility of attacks in the maritime zone by disgruntled Europeans—attacks which the Japanese, remembering the poor performance of their weak navy in the Korean campaign, feared they would not be able to counter.[91] Most evident in Japanese documents, however, is the glaring contrast between the grand portrayals of Ming strength and prospects by the loyalists, on one hand, and the Japanese perception— through Nagasaki, Korea, and Liu-ch'iu—of Ming disunity, ineffectuality, and poor prospects, on the other.[92] The Japanese were not at all sympathetic toward the Manchus (who, before invading China proper, had brought the buffer state of Korea to heel), nor did they see the Ch'ing conquest of China as inexorable. But they did see a China that no longer was controlled by the Ming, a dynasty toward which the current Japanese leadership hardly felt beholden, anyway; and they understandably were reluctant to leap into a fray the outcome of which seemed so uncertain.

In the other major theater of Ming loyalist resistance to the Ch'ing conquest of the Southeast and far South, central Kuang-tung, the action was less wide-ranging than in the southeastern maritime zone, but it was more intense. And in general configuration it was remarkably similar to the popular resistance that had flared earlier in southern Chiang-nan, the Pearl River delta virtually repeating the performance of the Yang-tzu delta in this respect. Ming officials temporarily withdrew as Ch'ing agents easily took over the symbols of authority in urban administrative centers. And even local notables who had loyalist inclinations also stepped to the sidelines, confused by recent events and needing time to find their bearings again. Anger was aroused among common people by the Manchu hair-and-dress decree and the cruel "pacification" measures of the same general who had bloodied the Su-Sung area, Li Ch'eng-tung. And resistance forces, when they eventually coalesced, were a hodgepodge of the same elements that constituted such forces in Chiang-nan and Eastern Che-chiang.

But there was one significant difference within this last point of similarity. The proportion of Ming regulars in the Kuang-chou resistance was much smaller—to the point of insignificance; and the proportion of bandit and pirate gangs (actually constituting sizable armies and navies) was much larger. In Chiang-nan the regional military commands had broken with the Ch'ing invasion, leaving regular military units with no central control or coordination; whereas in Kuang-tung the regular units themselves largely had disappeared, and those regional commanders who still were in the province had been left with few troops to command. Kuang-tung's standing armies previously had been siphoned off to aid the resistance in southern Chiang-hsi, and the few units that remained in Kuang-tung were so small and weak that their constituent soldiers either surrendered readily to the Ch'ing or disbanded, swelling the already sizable bandit and pirate organizations.

Moreover, rebelliousness and outlawry long had been more evident in Kuang-tung than in the lower Yang-tzu region. For instance, in 1640 officials of Hui-chou Prefecture were confronted with organized criminal control of roads and lands, as well as infiltration of military and administrative headquarters in copper-producing areas of Po-lo, a situation that led to the torture and murder of landlords and their agents, the harrowing of inspectors, and nonpayment of taxes. And 1643 is said to have marked the beginning of over forty years of continual bandit trouble in districts to the northeast and southwest of Kuang-chou. After the fall of Pei-ching, even before the transfers of Kuang-tung troops mentioned above, mutinies and independent actions among low-ranking military officers had become flagrant. For instance, in 1644–45 a military licentiate in Chieh-yang enlisted some "hill bandits" as the core of what became the extensively encamped "Nine Armies" insurgents, who proclaimed their own "Later Han" regime. And on the seacoast, minor officers cooperated with the Kuang-tung "boat people" (Tanka) and various brigands to take over naval installations and exert administrative control over maritime revenues. More threatening to the social leadership of central Kuang-tung were numerous revolts by local menials, generally called "servant bandits" (*p'u-tsei*) or "[secret] society bandits" (*she-tsei*). Unrest in this element began in the last years of the Ch'ung-chen reign, and it came to a head early in 1645 when the disgruntled servants of a magistrate's agent in Shun-te killed their master, burned his home, and went on a general rampage. This set off an epidemic of such incidents, which spread first through southwestern Kuang-chou and then into southern Chao-ch'ing Prefecture, some of the rebellious groups reportedly numbering in the thousands.[93]

Thus, we find that when prominent scholar-officials finally began to take overt action against the Ch'ing in Kuang-chou Prefecture, they did so chiefly in league with leaders of the river pirates, hill bandits, and roving mercenaries that T'ung Yang-chia (the "barbarian's" servitor from beyond the Wall) found startlingly ubiquitous in what he described as the wild, frontier atmosphere of Kuang-tung.[94] This may have caused fellow-gentry support to be withheld to a greater extent, or withdrawn more quickly, from the Kuang-tung loyalist leaders than from those in the Yang-tzu region.

During the late fall and winter of 1646, Ch'ing occupation forces had been sent radiating out from Kuang-chou in all directions, and Li Ch'eng-tung had taken his core army up the West River to Wu-chou, hoping to capture the Yung-li emperor in Kuang-hsi. Initially, things had gone so smoothly, and troops were in such short supply, that T'ung Yang-chia had kept only a small force of several hundred men with him in Kuang-chou City. It soon became apparent to both outlaws and loyalists in the delta region that the Ch'ing would be able to defend that city only weakly, and that they probably would be unable to deal with armed actions in other parts of Kuang-chou Prefecture. Consequently there ensued, from mid-March through November of 1647, a series of attacks and restorations led by the famous "Three Loyalists of Kuang-tung."[95]

Of the three, Ch'en Tzu-chuang of Nan-hai was the most senior and most distinguished for his literary accomplishments and participation in the "righteous" reform movements of the T'ien-ch'i and Ch'ung-chen reigns. He had declined appointments from both the Hung-kuang and Lung-wu regimes, in the former case probably because of partisan aversion, and in the latter case because in the 1630s he had been the most outspoken opponent of the Prince of T'ang's efforts to expand the governmental role of the imperial princes. Now he carried on resistance activities covertly, having submitted overtly to the Ch'ing.[96] Ch'en Pang-yen of Shun-te was a close political and literary associate of Tzu-chuang and had become a bureau secretary in the Ministry of War under the Lung-wu emperor. He had been transferring aboriginal troops from Liang-Kuang for service in Chiang-hsi when Fu-chien was lost, and subsequently he had tried but failed to reconcile the Yung-li and Shao-wu courts, thus losing credence with both of them.[97] Chang Chia-yü of Tung-kuan was the most fiery resister and the most able military leader of the three. He had been a Han-lin Bachelor in Pei-ching when that capital fell to Li Tzu-ch'eng, and subsequently he had been blacklisted by the Hung-kuang court on suspicion of collaborating with the rebels. Later he had served the Lung-wu emperor zealously by promoting the resistance in eastern Chiang-hsi, and he had been raising additional men in far eastern Kuang-tung when Fu-chien succumbed. His father having died, Chang then had returned home, hoping to protect his clan and locality by convincing the Ch'ing that they should respect harmless, retired Ming officials who wished to remain loyal to former rulers in their hearts.[98] It seems to have been the failure of this ploy, at least in part, that led Chang to reapply his impressive skills in military leadership to the resistance in Kuang-tung. Significantly, none of these men had identified closely with the Yung-li regime, and their efforts to undercut the Ch'ing presence in Kuang-tung, although they resulted in easing Ch'ing pressure from Kuang-hsi on the fugitive Yung-li party, were pursued independent of authorization or assistance from any Ming court.

Ch'en Tzu-chuang and Ch'en Pang-yen coordinated their activities to the west of the Pearl River estuary, beginning on the riverways of Shun-te District where they formed an alliance with the river pirate Yü Lung and his large following on several hundred boats. In the third week of March, Yü and other bandit groups unsuccessfully besieged Kuang-chou City, thus alerting T'ung Yang-chia to the danger in his situation and inducing him to recall Li Ch'eng-tung from Wu-chou.[99] After this initial failure, Tzu-chuang and Pang-yen then turned their attention to the recovery of such smaller cities as Shun-te, Kao-ming, and Hsin-hui, with the cooperation of assorted bandits, pirates, and volunteers, as well as displaced minor Ming officials and military officers.[100]

Meanwhile, Chang Chia-yü had opened his campaign east of the Pearl River estuary by restoring the seat of his home district, Tung-kuan, and executing the Ch'ing officials there. He then shifted southward and inflicted heavy losses on the pursuing Ch'ing forces before being beaten at Hsin-an, where he had allied with the private army of a local strongman.[101] Chang then escaped northeastward into Hui-chou Prefecture, where he rapidly rebuilt his base in Po-lo. From there he went on to restore several locales to the north and almost all of Hui-chou, displaying an amazing capacity to recruit outlaws, chivalric adventurers, self-defense forces, outraged commoners, et cetera, and forge them into large, effective fighting units within very short spans of time.[102] In the whole history of the Southern Ming, Chang was one of only a few scholar-officials who showed this kind of ability.[103]

Li Ch'eng-tung arrived back in the delta area in early April, and from then through the summer he was forced to run frantically from district to district, "like sweeping leaves in an autumn courtyard," suppressing one uprising after another. A turning point of sorts came in early August, however, when the two Ch'ens and their pirate allies made another larger and more concerted attempt to seize Kuang-chou City, utilizing inside agents and a two-pronged strategic approach. Because of the same kind of ineptitude, poor communication, failures in secrecy, and general amateurishness that characterized most gentry-led military actions, this undertaking ended in a debacle that put the resistance movement in western Kuang-chou and eastern Chao-ch'ing prefectures permanently on a defensive footing.[104] Ch'en Pang-yen then centered his resistance efforts in Ch'ing-yüan to the north, while Ch'en Tzu-chuang became isolated in Kao-ming. After persevering attacks by Li Ch'eng-tung, these two centers were penetrated and the two Ch'ens captured in October and November, respectively; and both men were publicly executed in Kuang-chou City by the most torturous of methods.[105] Also, in early November Chang Chia-yü was cornered in Tseng-ch'eng to the northeast and defeated in a furious battle with Li's men. Severely wounded, Chang committed suicide by casting himself into a canal.[106]

Thus, the cruelest blows against the Ming resistance in both Chiang-nan and Kuang-tung were inflicted by the same man, Li Ch'eng-tung. Ironically, however, Li also was about to give the Southern Ming its best new lease on life.

CHAPTER FIVE

Restoration and Third Stand:
The Yung-li Regime in Liang-Kuang

IN 1648–49 the soaring fortunes of the Ch'ing dynasty took a serious dip. And because dissatisfactions among military men on the Ming side had been one important factor in the Ch'ing success story, it is appropriate that events were turned against the latter and for the former by surrendered generals whose expectations of better conditions and opportunities with the Ch'ing had not been fulfilled.

The man who started it all was Chin Sheng-huan (see chapter 2), a prime example of the aspiration among military men for elevated status at the end of the Ming. Under the Hung-kuang court he had risen to the position of Military Assistant Commissioner-in-Chief and Regional Commander to Aid [the People] and Exterminate [Enemies] in Ho-nan and Hu-kuang.[1] And in June and July of 1645, when he surrendered and moved speedily to gain merit by taking over the P'o-yang Lake region for the Ch'ing, he is said to have behaved pompously and gloated over the deferential reception he received from the few minor degree-holders who came forth in places such as Chiu-chiang.[2] He had been disappointed when, after this, the Ch'ing initially appointed him to be Superintendent Regional Commander for Summoning [the Perspicacious] and Exterminating [the Benighted] in Chiang-hsi, at a rank even lower than he had held before.[3] But apparently Chin had hoped to gain promotion by further proving his merit in subjugating the remainder of Chiang-hsi; moreover, he had relished the general powers that he was able to exercise over both civil and military matters under the temporary, emergency charge to "summon and exterminate" (*chao-ch'ao*). So he had applied himself vigorously to the Chiang-hsi campaign for a year, seeking to elevate himself in the eyes of not only the

Manchus but also fellow turncoat commanders who disliked and saw little justification for his self-important airs.

The Ch'ing, for their part, did not stint to reward true merit, but they were very watchful, especially of Ming commanders who had surrendered in the Yang-tzu campaign, for signs of unwillingness to reform bad habits. Before long, they had become aware of Chin's tendency to inflate reports of his successes and the importance of the Chiang-hsi theater, while neglecting to mention (or covering up) both untoward conditions and his financial dealings in the province.[4] Moreover, a continuing reputation for pillage had marked for early removal Chin's closest subordinate general, Wang Te-jen.[5]

In view of these circumstances, the Ch'ing found Chin's self-praise and bold requests for additional rewards to be insufferably presumptuous. This was especially so in June of 1646 when Chin protested a change in his position to that of simply a defense commander, asserting that, rather, he should be retained in his former position with the additional prestige of a conferment from the throne and discretionary (*p'ien-i*) powers. The Ch'ing Ministry of War crisply replied that it was not Ch'ing practice to allow *p'ien-i*, and that the special civil-and-military powers that Chin had wielded as a general who "summons and exterminates" certainly would have to revert to the new provincial governor and regional inspector now that they had assumed their posts. But because Chiang-hsi remained volatile, and because the Ch'ing court was reminded that "civil officials cheating military officials was the downfall of the Ming," Chin was allowed to keep his position as Superintendent Regional Commander for Chiang-hsi, albeit without his former emergency powers.[6] This hardly satisfied him, especially since the new provincial governor and regional inspector both treated him and Wang Te-jen superciliously; nor was Chin at all happy when one of his subordinate generals was promoted to be a regional commander, thus further signaling the Ch'ing intention to undermine the semiprivate command structure that he had been nurturing in Chiang-hsi.[7]

Consequently, Chin Sheng-huan became resolved to revert and again declare allegiance to the Ming, but he delayed overt action until arrangements could be made secretly with Ming loyalists in Chiang-hsi and Yung-li officials in Hu-kuang. Wang Te-jen, however, learned that the regional inspector had memorialized indicting him for misdeeds in pacification; so, with the encouragement of loyalist infiltrators in his own ranks, Wang forced Chin's hand. In Nan-ch'ang on February 20–21, 1648, the Ch'ing provincial governor was imprisoned, the regional inspector was killed, and everyone else removed their queues. Chin and Wang arrogated to themselves titles as duke and marquis, initially proclaimed the Lung-wu calendar (best known among Ming loyalists in Chiang-hsi), and sent emissaries to find the Yung-li court and convey news of their "return to proper allegiance."[8] For added legitimacy, they persuaded the former Hung-kuang grand secretary Chiang Yüeh-kuang, a resident of Nan-ch'ang, to lend his support and prestige to their cause.[9]

Although Chin had acted out of self-interested pique and lacked any great vision or leadership ability, this reversion had wide repercussions. Not only were Chiang-hsi loyalists aroused, officials too in places as far away as western Hu-kuang and coastal Fu-chien began reverting from Ch'ing to Ming. Stockade defenders in northeastern Hu-kuang became active once more, sympathizers struck at Ch'ing positions as far down the Yang-tzu as Wu-wei, and Chin agents were caught fomenting insurrection in strategically important areas of north-eastern Ho-nan.[10] Moreover, the old Ch'ing trouble spots in the North flared again—central Shan-tung, the Han-chung area in southeastern Shen-hsi, and the Moslem-inhabited territory in what is now southeastern Kan-su.[11] What is worse, in January of 1649 the Ch'ing regional commander at Ta-t'ung, Chiang Hsiang, also rebelled in the name of Ming loyalism, and soon half the province of Shan-hsi and much of northern Shen-hsi, directly west of Pei-ching, were in revolt. While Manchu reinforcements were sent southward to help protect Nan-ching, Dorgon himself, among the other most able Manchu princes, went out to deal with Chiang's menace at their doorstep, and the Shan-Shen rebellion was not finally quelled until October of that year.[12] By no means were all the uprisings in the North inspired or led by genuine Ming loyalists, much less were any directly connected with the Yung-li court. Nevertheless, a perception of Ch'ing weakness seems to have pervaded the country following Chin Sheng-huan's reversion and turned a discrete, difficult situation into two years of crisis for the Ch'ing.[13]

Needless to say, the Ch'ing command in Hu-kuang, which was finding that province to be a huge bag of thorns anyway, contracted its operations markedly after word was received of Chin Sheng-huan's reversion to their east. The taxing campaign on Ch'üan-chou and Kuei-lin was called off; and only small, isolated (and doomed) garrison forces were left in Tao-chou and Yung-chou, while real Ch'ing control shrank back to include only the area from Ch'ang-sha to Wu-ch'ang. Ming forces were quick to take advantage of this situation, of course. Former rebel and renegade armies, which had holed up in the hills of northwest-ern Hu-kuang under the nominal control of Provincial Governor Tu Yin-hsi, moved back into the Tung-t'ing Lake region and occupied such major cities as Ch'ang-te and I-yang, inflicting some stunning defeats on the Ch'ing.[14] At the same time, Viceroy Ho T'eng-chiao and the various commanders under his authority were able to emerge from their confinement in far western Hu-kuang and northeastern Kuang-hsi to retake all their old positions back down to Hsiang-t'an through the fall and winter of 1648–49.[15] So within a year after

Chin's reversion, almost all of southern Hu-kuang had become Ming territory again.

The most important repercussion of Chin's action, however, was on Li Ch'eng-tung, another commander who had reason to be dissatisfied with his dispensation under the Ch'ing. Initially he had been appointed Military Vice Commissioner-in-Chief to serve as Regional Commander for the Wu-sung and Sung-chiang seaboard area, and as such he had played a large role in subjugating the Yang-tzu delta region. As a result of that service, he had been formally placed under investigation for alleged undue use of force; and even though he was absolved of those charges,[16] the Ch'ing apparently continued to have reservations about giving him any greater powers or responsibilities. As early as the completion of the Fu-chien campaign, at least, Li had suggested to Pei-ching that he and his men deserved better rewards. And having further carried out the initial pacification of Kuang-tung almost single-handedly, Li just had argued his own merits in the same vein when, in June and July of 1647, the Ch'ing court announced its regular appointments for Liang-Kuang.[17] To Li's disappointment, he was retained in a wholly military position, as Military Commissioner-in-Chief and Superintendent Regional Commander for Kuang-tung; whereas authority over both civil and military affairs in two provinces was given to T'ung Yang-chia, as Viceroy for Liang-Kuang.[18]

So Li definitely had reason to feel disgruntled. Some accounts say that during his initial drive through Kuang-tung into Kuang-hsi Li had captured and secretly kept the seal of the Ming viceroy for Liang-Kuang, and that in fighting to suppress the loyalist insurgents Li had been deeply impressed by their ardor. But there is no evidence that he contemplated revolt until after he learned of Chin Sheng-huan's reversion in the early spring of 1648.[19] Popular histories are fond of emphasizing the influence on Li of his favorite concubine, who committed suicide in late April as an ultimate recourse in persuading him to renew his allegiance to the Ming;[20] and, indeed, this may have poignantly affected Li's heart. But he probably was more affected in his brain by reports of Chin Sheng-huan's strength to his north[21] and by the likelihood that he would become even more isolated and vulnerable in Kuang-tung as Yung-li commanders regained the upper hand in Hu-kuang, as well.

Consequently, having conspired chiefly with his adopted son, Li Yüan-yin, and the new Kuang-tung education intendant, Yüan P'eng-nien, in the first week of May, 1648, Li Ch'eng-tung publicly proclaimed the Yung-li calendar in Kuang-chou. Stories of how he constrained T'ung Yang-chia to go along in this turnabout vary in detail, but he seems at first to have argued the need for an expedient to "allay the people's hearts." In any case, Li found a way to carry off this coup without killing T'ung, for whom he seems to have had a good deal of respect.[22] Manchu soldiers and others in Kuang-chou City who had adopted Ch'ing styles were not so fortunate, however, since a pogrom ensued against persons with queues and high collars, as Li Ch'eng-tung dispatched officials to convey his respects to the Yung-li court in Nan-ning.[23]

There the court had been in poor condition, as "all manner of betel-nut chewers, brine-well workers, and aborigine whorehouse owners had put on official robes," and native chieftains, whose favor the court thought it prudent to cultivate, had been elevated to become prefects and censorial officials.[24] The Yung-li emperor had learned from Chiang-hsi of Chin Sheng-huan's reversion only on May 2; and when news arrived of Li Ch'eng-tung's reversion just five weeks later, it all seemed too good to be true. Li's emissaries were received warily, and later personal missives and generous gifts from Li were required to overcome suspicions that he was luring the court into a trap. Subsequently, however, both Chin and Li were given ducal titles, and Li, in addition, was appointed Viceroy for the entire Southeast.[25] Then in late July and early August the Yung-li entourage moved through Hsün-chou and Wu-chou, picking up along the way scores of civil and military officials who had been scattered or hiding in Kuang-hsi, and finally arrived back in Chao-ch'ing on September 20, 1648. There the courtiers were pleased to find that Li Ch'eng-tung had provided handsomely for their dignified return after a year and a half of hardship and humiliation.[26]

The political configuration of the restored Yung-li regime was complex, but again it reflected well the two most debilitating problems of the Southern Ming: assistance for the emperor and the status of the military. Both of these problems were exacerbated in this context by, on the one hand, the realities of the preceding long period of imminent danger, desperate flight, and virtual hand-to-mouth existence, during which the Yung-li emperor had come to rely heavily on the services of his chief commander of the Embroidered Uniform Guard, Ma Chi-hsiang and, on the other hand, the current almost complete de facto reliance of the restored court on the military organization of Li Ch'eng-tung.

Ma Chi-hsiang had begun his career as a minor military officer in Kuang-tung and had been promoted to the Embroidered Uniform Guard for his special services to the Lung-wu regime. During the Yung-li emperor's perilous odyssey of 1647–48 through southwestern Hu-kuang and eastern Kuang-hsi, Ma had been especially solicitous for the safety and comfort of the imperial household, and had shown remarkable versatility in the things he was able to do for them. Having unusually high literacy for a military man, he came to handle official papers, himself drawing up edicts and conferments; and through his concubine, who waited on the appreciative senior empress dowager hand and foot, Ma even indirectly assumed the role of a head eunuch.[27]

> Ma [Chi-hsiang] was sharp-minded and capable in handling all sorts of matters. Inside the palace, everything down to needles and thread was gotten from him, and during the hardest times he never left the imperial family so far as an inch-long step. He performed all the functions of a grand secretary, minister, nobleman, and servant. But since everything had to be done by him, he could not see things in a wide perspective. He moved easily to take the advantage [in various circumstances], but he paid no attention to preserving the larger order. So Ma was like [a eunuch director of ceremonial] in this respect. He should not have been used, but ironically he proved very useful.[28]

When the Yung-li court was reestablished, Ma (then a marquis) properly eschewed becoming a grand secretary because of his military background. But he had "declined the office without declining the powers." By obtaining status as an assistant censor-in-chief and as acting head, or "signator," for various organs, he came to have a hand not only in the military affairs of the Embroidered Uniform Guard, but in the civil governmental affairs of the Six Ministries, the Censorate, the Transmission Office, and the Offices of Scrutiny, as well.[29]

Li Ch'eng-tung also was an interesting figure, though more darkly so. Outwardly hard and pitiless, he seems to have been fraught with sensitive, complex, and intense feelings, which he kept to himself.

> Li [Ch'eng-tung] lived simply, was slow of speech, tough and forbearing, self-restrained and humorless. He affected no manners and spoke few words, so all the civil and military officials inside and outside the court respected him but also feared him deeply.[30]

Li drank heavily and morosely, perhaps because of all the killing. He worked hard—if too harshly—for the governments that employed him, wanting not glory but just to be recognized and rewarded appropriately for his services. Instead, he repeatedly was stung by the mistrust of those whose interests he fought to protect—recently the Ch'ing and now the Yung-li court—even though he behaved toward the latter with utmost deference. His resentment toward civil officialdom having been reinforced by demeaning cuts from Chao-ch'ing, Li soon resolved to distance himself from the court by concentrating solely on fulfilling his military duty to the emperor. After declining to participate in a grand investiture ceremony that the Yung-li emperor had planned for him, Li shortly departed from his headquarters in Kuang-chou City to lead his army personally in the defense of Mei Pass and the recovery of southern Chiang-hsi, insisting only that no civil officials be assigned to his area of operation.[31]

However, the court was left under the watchful eye of Li Yüan-yin, who became Commander of the Capital Guard;[32] and although the two Lis, unlike Ma Chi-hsiang, were scrupulous about not directly meddling in the business of the court, in actuality little was done against their wishes.

The first business of the Yung-li court as it moved back into Kuang-tung was to reconstitute its official ranks. At first the chief difficulty in this was balancing the distribution of rewards and powers between, on the one hand, men who had loyally "accompanied the imperial carriage" during the court's recent tribulations and, on the other, those who had earned "merit in returning to correct allegiance" by joining Li Ch'eng-tung in reversion. The latter category included many who originally had supported the Shao-wu regime, and they initially were regarded by veteran Yung-li adherents with more resentment and suspicion than those who had supported the Ch'ing.[33] Ironically, those who had collaborated with the Manchus before coming to Kuang-tung now were considered more reliable, not only because the governmental and military organization of Li Ch'eng-tung and T'ung Yang-chia was superior to anything that the Yung-li court had developed, but also because, having served and now betrayed the conquerors, they would not be likely to seek Ch'ing mercy again.

Before long, however, the dichotomy between old and reverted officials gave way to more common bases for clique alignments in Ming government: place or region of origin, "teacher-student" (i.e., patron-client) relations, and positions held in certain key institutions. As we have seen in the case of the Hung-kuang regime, any clique, in order to survive and strive for predominant power, had to have effective members in (1) the so-called Inner Court near the emperor's person and the imperial family, (2) the Outer Court of ministries, commissions, and censorial offices, and (3) the provincial administration, which during the Southern Ming increasingly came to coincide with the organizations of the various regional commanders. The chief object of clique competition was to capture positions in the Grand Secretariat and thereby influence or control the official acts of the emperor, as well as appointments to other offices.

In the Yung-li court, two loose cliques developed: The core membership of the dominant "Ch'u" clique was in the Censorate. It had adherents or sympathizers among the eunuchs who served and the officers who guarded the imperial household. And it was favored by those in control of the most crucial Yung-li military forces, Li Ch'eng-tung and Ch'ü Shih-szu, as well as by Chief Grand Secretary Yen Ch'i-heng. The name of this clique derives from the regional origin (central Hu-kuang) of the clique heads, who occupied the two most important positions in the Censorate. They and three other censors became known as the "Tiger Five" for their political aggressiveness and stridence on court issues.[34]

The underdog "Wu" clique was based in the Inner Court, among the eunuchs and maternal in-laws of the emperor, but especially in the person of Ma Chi-hsiang who, in spite of the more formal structure that the court assumed, continued to act as an all-around Man Friday for the emperor. Its chief support outside central Kuang-tung was the unscrupulously ambitious commander Ch'en Pang-fu in central Kuang-hsi (who was despised for more than just factional reasons by both Ch'ü and Li). Its most important adherents in the Outer Court tended to be vice heads of ministries. Among the grand secretaries, two were considered to be Wu men. And the name of the clique probably derives from the circumstance that some of its leading members hailed from the Yang-tzu delta region.[35]

During the sixteen months of the restored court in Chao-ch'ing, the Ch'u clique remained ascendant. This in large part was because of the court's reliance on the organization of Li Ch'eng-tung, apart from which no real governmental network was instituted, and the fact that Li's subordinate generals and his adopted son continued to control Kuang-tung and the palace guard even after Ch'eng-tung's demise. But it also was because this clique, led by "righteous" figures and rooted in the watchdog organ of the Outer Court, the Censorate, established an identity by knowing and insisting on adherence to the proper, legal, and ethical Ming ways of doing things.[36]

> [As the court was moving back to Chao-ch'ing] an edict was sent down to hold examinations for "tribute students" [to serve in the temporary capital]. Village teachers, shamans, monks, and priests, anyone who could wield a brush and get a single character on paper submitted an application saying he was a licentiate from some district or prefecture in Shan-tung or Shan-hsi, always choosing a place far away so that the matter could not be verified. Robes dragging the ground, they filled the streets like ants.... Commoners falsely claimed to have been ministers or vice ministers, and within ten days they had lined up in great numbers, but none knew how to behave at court. Aside from one or two real degree-holders and two or three truly influential men who tried to hold themselves aloof, the rest were from the families of vegetable peddlers and butchers—common laborers, actors, and pimps. Although they actually [had dared to] come forth and don the caps of worthies, they moved furtively and bunched together, as though not wanting to show their faces.[37]

Though conditions may not have been quite as bad as in this derogatory account, certainly the Yung-li court needed a face-lift, so to speak. The Ch'u clique's emphasis on standards, qualifications, and propriety, especially when placed in the astringent, sarcastic style of the sharp-penned Supervising Secretary for Rites, Chin Pao, may have galled the emperor and many others (especially those in the Wu clique). But it was an emphasis that the court needed in order to attract large numbers of conscientious civil servants, through whom it might begin to reestablish a semblance of genuine government over the several provinces it then held only by military fiat. In other words, the Ch'u clique claimed to know how true Ming government should be run, and the Yung-li court needed at that time, more than ever, to look like a true Ming government.

But, being one variation on a recurrent pattern in Ming political history, the position of the Wu clique also was assured. During the previous period of constant danger and deprivation when the sheer survival of the imperial family, not rulership for an empire, had been of paramount concern, persons associated with the Inner Court naturally had been most influential. But the diffident character of the Yung-li emperor—who, though neither stupid, debauched, nor irresponsible, nevertheless disliked complexities and could not lead[38]—allowed Inner Court influence to remain high even after the court was reconstituted in 1648. Much like the Hung-kuang emperor before him, the Yung-li emperor's embarrassing ignorance of governmental forms and procedures, and his fear of being called on to make bold decisions, led him to maintain the screen provided by his eunuchs and Ma Chi-hsiang, and to recoil from the demands that "righteous" bureaucratic officials made of reigning emperors.

The vaunted aim of the Ch'u protagonists was to cleanse and rectify the court in order to attract all the "right men" to its service, win the hearts of the people, and reestablish the Ming order throughout the land. And in this they purported to be acting independently and selflessly for the greater good, not as a self-serving faction. But, as occurred repeatedly in the late Ming, arguments by men of "like mind" to uphold the "framework and mainstays" of proper government were the camouflage of collusive attempts to expel certain odious individuals. Granted that those individuals generally were tagged for removal because they were perceived to be undermining the fundamental principles of the state. But in the course of political struggle, so much emphasis was placed on the immoral character of the undesired figures, and so many expedients were seized and petty charges employed against them, that "righteous" figures tended to become blind not only to the damage that they themselves might be doing to the government's integrity, but also to the underlying conditions that gave rise to the behaviors they opposed. High-minded crusades took on the appearance of personal, self-interested vendettas; and in washing clean the "framework and mainstays," the baby often was thrown out with the bath.

In the case of the restored Yung-li court in Liang-Kuang, the attention of the Ch'u faction was almost wholly absorbed in combating the irregular powers (and clique network) of the undercover prime minister Ma Chi-hsiang and the self-aggrandizing regional satrap Ch'en Pang-fu, rather than in addressing the more fundamental problems of imperial consultation and leadership, and military support and rewards.[39] For instance, Ma was accused of accepting large bribes from his personal secretary, an imperial clansman, to have the latter appointed as an assistant censor-in-chief.[40] And he also was accused of conspiring with a drafter to change one character in a document of conferment so that Ch'en Pang-fu would be granted the right to "hereditarily" hold all of Kuang-hsi, thus officially condoning and extending Ch'en's gradual privatization of his territorial control in that province (for which he was most consistently and vigorously opposed by Minister of War Ch'ü Shih-szu at Kuei-lin).[41] When Ch'en Pang-fu memorialized in reply to Chin Pao's biting criticisms of him, concluding with the suggestion (a veiled murder threat) that Chin be dispatched to personally serve as his troop supervisor, a central figure in the Ch'u clique led all the officials in the Censorate to resign en masse. This demonstration was so stormy that the emperor, who was chatting with a guest in the adjacent chamber, is said to have spilled his tea in fright.[42]

Although the "righteous" censors all were called back, and two Wu-clique grand secretaries departed because of these and other controversies, the victories were hollow, since charges of corruption, favoritism, irregularities, and reliance on the outside power of a militarist could have been laid against most adherents of the Ch'u clique, as well.[43] Ma and Ch'en remained unscathed. And worse, virtually nothing was done, through the continual furors, to effect real governmental control in the regions that temporarily had been replaced on the Ming map.

One matter, which later had disastrous consequences for the Yung-li court, illustrates especially well the difference between the "righteous" stance of the Ch'u clique's spokesmen and the more accommodative "realism" of the Wu faction. In the late spring of 1649 two officials arrived in Chao-ch'ing acting as emissaries from Sun K'o-wang, the leader of a roving-rebel army which had occupied Yün-nan Province in the preceding year (see chapter 6). The emissaries presented gifts from Sun along with his request to be enfeoffed as a prince (*wang*) to confirm his newfound allegiance to the Ming dynasty.[44] A long debate then ensued over whether the court should comply. Those who favored catering to the vanity and even the territorial ambitions of military leaders, if such would enhance the physical security of the court, argued that the mere formality of issuing a seal and document of investiture could make a valuable ally of a man who otherwise might attack them.

However, guardians of the "framework and mainstays" of the dynasty (who also suspected that Sun might be in collusion with Ch'en Pang-fu) vigorously opposed such an act, and the cuttingly authoritative Chin Pao presented their summary arguments: In the first place, it was not permissible according to the Ancestor's Order to confer the title of Prince, whether of the first or second degree, on any living person who was not of the dynastic surname. More important, however, if the court submitted to such pressure, it surely would lose more in diminished respect and morale than it might gain perchance in military services from a notorious bandit. Whether the title were granted or not, the court would have no actual control over Sun; if the court staunchly held to its principles, however, then perhaps he would be sufficiently impressed to sincerely give his allegiance and be obedient. In any case, if the emperor, ministers, and generals would work together with singleness of purpose in opposing the archenemy, the Ch'ing, then the court would not need to concern itself about what rabble like Sun might do.[45]

This typical "righteous" emphasis on the suasive power of correctness and the efficacy of a common true spirit completely stopped open consideration of Sun's request until the Ch'u clique eventually fell from power. But to mollify Sun and perhaps satisfy his need to elevate himself above fellow rebel leaders in Yün-nan, the court offered him a ducal title, and the others marquisates. The emissaries finally departed Chao-ch'ing on their way back to Yün-nan in midautumn.[46] But the separate actions of two Wu-clique figures in Kuang-hsi soon altered their mission.

Ch'en Pang-fu, who had become wary of Sun's power to his northwest and wanted to form friendly relations with him, forged documents conferring on Sun the title "Prince[-of-the-Blood] of Ch'in," and had his own men deliver them.[47] Sun was overjoyed to receive this and had just been regaling in his new status, for the edification of all those around him, when his original team of emissaries returned with another title, "Prince[-of-the-Second-Degree] of P'ing-liao." The latter had been fabricated by the erstwhile provincial governor of Hu-kuang, Tu Yin-hsi, who had specialized, so to speak, in bringing former rebels under the Ming banner and resented having been berated for this by men like Chin Pao. Naturally, Sun was embarrassed and angered by these con-tradictory offers; and when his emissaries divulged under interrogation that the court actually had made him only a duke, Sun was completely enraged and forthwith sent agents back demanding clarification. In the meantime, the par-tisan complexion of the Yung-li court had changed, but in the spring of 1650, for different reasons than before, the court again unctuously refused to grant Sun's demand, and relations with him were set on a calamitous course.[48]

Disunity and mismanagement such as this, which arose to a large extent from differing views of the proper and potential role of military men in the state structure, also prevented the Yung-li court from responding effectively to oppor-tunities and dangers in closer and more crucial theaters than Yün-nan. In both Chiang-hsi and Hu-kuang the restoration failed because the court was not able to provide support to its commanders in those provinces. Consequently, they were not able to recover from strategic errors or setbacks, their men became unwilling to face the enemy, and the thick buffer zone they had created between the Ch'ing and the Yung-li court disappeared rapidly in mid-1649.

In Chiang-hsi, one command in particular had refused to go along with Chin Sheng-huan's reversion—fatefully, the one headquartered in Kan-chou. This not only blocked Chin from directly joining forces with Li Ch'eng-tung to the south, it also presented the possibility of attack from the rear if Chin proceeded northeastward from Nan-ch'ang and Chiu-chiang to attack Nan-ching. So Chin perhaps mistakenly placed the reconquest of Kan-chou for the Ming as his first priority, and thus gave the North ample time to respond.[49] Significantly, an army consisting wholly of elite banner troops, led by Manchu and Mongol (but no Han Chinese) lieutenant-generals, was sent all the way from Pei-ching to deal with Chin, and in mid-June 1648, this force proceeded from Tung-liu across far northeastern Chiang-hsi. Chin Sheng-huan and Wang Te-jen, having been unsuccessful in their siege of Kan-chou, dashed back northward and barely managed to reenter Nan-ch'ang before the Ch'ing made their first concerted attack on that city. Intensification of this siege in late August did not bring victory to the Ch'ing, however, so they settled in for a long vigil to starve the refractory city into submission.[50]

Nan-ch'ang remained surrounded and isolated for over half a year because no appreciable aid reached there from either Ho T'eng-chiao or Li Ch'eng-tung. In Hu-kuang the startling success of the Ming armies in reoccupying the province in 1648 was followed almost immediately, in January of 1649, by an extremely tumultuous falling out between the core of the former Shun rebel army—now called the "Loyal and True Battalion" under the supposed direction of Tu Yin-hsi—and a remnant of Tso Liang-yü's army, now supposedly under the direction of Ho T'eng-chiao.[51] Consequently, just as Ho was hoping to wrest Ch'ang-sha from the Ch'ing (and restore the land route between there and northern Chiang-hsi), the whole constellation of Ming forces south of Tung-t'ing Lake was thrown into complete disarray by the long, angry, desperate, and tortuous march of the "Loyal and True" all the way from the upper Yang-tzu into south-central Kuang-hsi (see map 11).[52] In their wake was left utter chaos among the other armies that were nominally answerable to Ho, so he never was able to give more than a token response to the urgent pleas of Chin and Wang in Nan-ch'ang.

In the border area between northern Kuang-tung and Kan-chou Prefecture in Chiang-hsi, Li Ch'eng-tung's army, which had seemed so invincible when backed up by Manchu cavalry and the efficient Ch'ing logistical system, now performed diffidently and balked when they encountered resistance from the

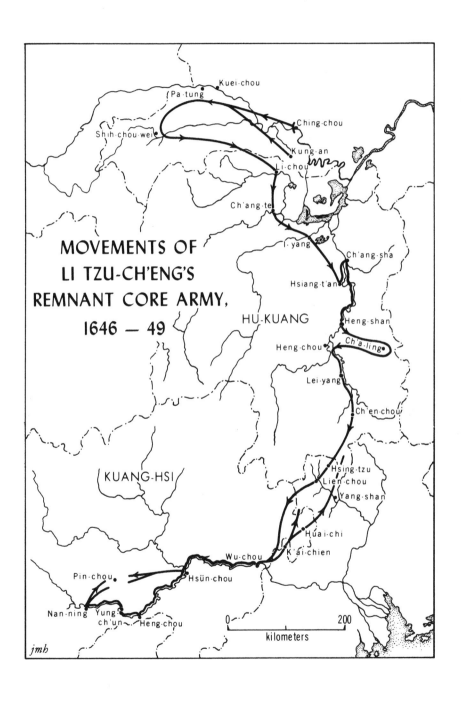

MOVEMENTS OF
LI TZU-CH'ENG'S
REMNANT CORE ARMY,
1646 — 49

HU-KUANG

KUANG-HSI

Kuei-chou
Pa-tung
Ching-chou
Shih-chou-wei
Kung-an
Li-chou
Ch'ang-te
I-yang
Ch'ang-sha
Hsiang-t'an
Heng-shan
Heng-chou
Ch'a-ling
Lei-yang
Ch'en-chou
Hsing-tzu
Lien-chou
Yang-shan
Huai-chi
Wu-chou
K'ai-chien
Pin-chou
Hsün-chou
Nan-ning
Yung-ch'un
Heng-chou

0   200
kilometers

jmb

hard-bitten people of South Kan. The latter now fought as tenaciously to preserve the Ch'ing-instituted order in their region as they had fought to preserve the Ming order there before. And Li Ch'eng-tung was forced to return to Kuang-chou in the winter of 1648–49 to reorganize and resupply for another campaign. By the time he crossed Mei Pass again the following February, the Ch'ing had been able to aid and reinforce Kan-chou from the north, however; so Li also was unable to rescue Nan-ch'ang.[53]

That city long since had been reduced to cannibalism when, after enduring over six months under heavy siege, some soldiers secretly agreed to capitulate and Ch'ing forces thus were able to scale the city wall on March 1, 1649. Chin Sheng-huan and Chiang Yüeh-kuang then both committed suicide, Wang Te-jen was killed after being captured in the fighting, and most of their loyalist supporters also, refusing to surrender, were slaughtered.[54] On this same day in Hu-kuang, Ho T'eng-chiao (who, in the hope of reconstituting some renegade forces, had gone forward without so much as a personal guard) was captured almost accidentally in Hsiang-t'an; several days later, still unsubmissive, he was executed in Ch'ang-sha.[55] Meanwhile Li Ch'eng-tung, still frustrated in his attempt to subdue Kan-chou, had become cornered in Hsin-feng by a Ch'ing relief force. Accounts of Li's final hours agree only that he drowned while trying to ford a rain-swollen river in the Hsin-feng area, probably in the second week of April 1649.[56] So within little more than a month's time, the three men who had been most responsible for the dramatic upturn in the Yung-li court's fortunes a year earlier—Chin, Ho, and Li—all had been removed from the scene. Southern Ming forces in Chiang-hsi and Hu-kuang then completely collapsed, and although the Ch'ing did not advance immediately, the stage was set for their second conquest of the far South.

CHAPTER SIX

Third Defeat and Standoff:
The Far Southwest and Southeast

THE Manchus ever were eager to promote their self-made image as saviors of China from the bandit scourge; and since the beginning of their invasion of China proper, they had placed high priority on breaking up and destroying part by part the large, roving-rebel armies of Li Tzu-ch'eng and Chang Hsien-chung. From the time in 1645 when most of Li's surviving forces joined in league with the Ming command in Hu-kuang, it became increasingly easier for the Ch'ing to identify their obligation to exterminate the bandits with their need, also, to defeat the armed forces of the various Southern Ming claimants. Whereas previously they had berated the Hung-kuang court for not lifting a finger against the Shun rebels in the northwest, now the Ch'ing could castigate the Southern Ming courts even more for having accepted as allies the very men who had destroyed the Ming dynasty in the North and caused the death of the (now grandly venerated) Ch'ung-chen emperor.

Thus, we find that in October 1648, as Yung-li armies under Ho T'eng-chiao and Tu Yin-hsi were recovering most of southern Hu-kuang, the Manchu prince Jirgalang was charged with the task of exterminating Li Tzu-ch'eng's successor, the "One-eyed Tiger" Li Chin, and the remaining core of the Shun rebel army. This was another way of saying that he was to lead a counter campaign against the Ming south of the Yang-tzu in Hu-kuang.[1] But when Jirgalang arrived the following spring to press his campaign, he found a chaotically fluid situation in which it was easy to advance, but difficult to obtain control, and impossible to find the real Li Chin (the "Loyal and True Battalion" having rampaged into Kuang-hsi). Through the summer of 1649, Ch'ing forces regained all major urban points in far southern Hu-kuang, but their hold on the

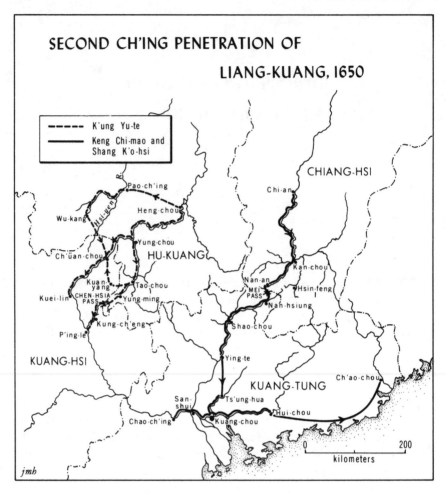

SECOND CH'ING PENETRATION OF
LIANG-KUANG, 1650

- - - - - K'ung Yu-te
———— Keng Chi-mao and
         Shang K'o-hsi

CHIANG-HSI

Pao-ch'ing
Chi-an
Heng-chou
Wu-kang
Yung-chou
Ch'üan-chou   HU-KUANG
Kan-chou
Kuan-yang   Tao-chou   Nan-an   Hsin-feng
Kuei-lin CHEN-HSIA   Yung-ming   MEI PASS
          PASS   Nan-hsiung
Kung-ch'eng
P'ing-le   Shao-chou

KUANG-HSI
Ying-te
                              KUANG-TUNG   Ch'ao-chou
San-shui   Ts'ung-hua
Chao-ch'ing   Kuang-chou   Hui-chou

0   200
kilometers

jmh

territory was tenuous, and no further concerted advance was undertaken at that
time. Anyway, Jirgalang had not been authorized to invade Liang-Kuang.[2]
Similarly in Chiang-hsi, Ch'ing generals had been charged only with recovering
Nan-ch'ang, saving Kan-chou, and squelching persistent Ming loyalist activity
in that province. So, after Li Ch'eng-tung's offensive units disintegrated near
Kan-chou, the Ch'ing victors simply scouted Mei Pass and, for the time being,
did not advance into Kuang-tung.[3]

As usual, the Ch'ing preferred to send fresh armies for major offensives. In
June of 1649 the court in Pei-ching again charged that famous threesome—the
veteran, ennobled commanders K'ung Yu-te, Keng Chung-ming, and
Shang K'o-hsi—with spearheading a renewed southward drive. This time,

however, Keng and Shang were to proceed through Chiang-hsi into Kuang-tung, while K'ung returned to Hu-kuang for a second try at penetrating Kuang-hsi (see map 12).[4] When these armies reached the field, there was a delay because some escaped fugitives were discovered among the troops in Keng Chung-ming's army, and Keng, dishonored by this revelation, committed suicide. But his eldest son, the equally able Chi-mao, was allowed to succeed to the elder Keng's command, and the campaign soon went on as planned.[5] Simultaneously, in January 1650, K'ung pressed southward from Ch'ang-sha and concentrated his full effort on retaking Yung-chou, while Keng and Shang moved southwest-ward across Mei Pass to Nan-hsiung.[6]

The Yung-li court had been thoroughly shaken by news of the deaths of Ho T'eng-chiao and Li Ch'eng-tung, not only because the court's defenses now were certain to deteriorate drastically, but also because those men's military capacity had underpinned the dominant faction in Yung-li politics. Efforts to reestablish effective leadership over the Kuang-tung and Hu-kuang armies were only partially successful,[7] and the only undamaged army on which the court immediately might rely became that of Ch'en Pang-fu, the chief military ally of the Wu clique, in Kuang-hsi. Consequently, in the first week of February 1650, when the court learned that Ming forces had abandoned their stations in north-ern Kuang-tung to the Ch'ing advance brigades, the imperial family departed hastily from Chao-ch'ing heading for Wu-chou, and in the course of this move the political constitution of the court changed cataclysmically. Although Li Yüan-yin and other commanders from Li Ch'eng-tung's army still performed the crucial tasks of holding Kuang-chou City and the West River,[8] nevertheless, the destabilization and frantic flight of the court into Ch'en Pang-fu's territory seems to have released a flood of pent-up hatred toward the Ch'u clique leaders, and an almost hysterical persecution of four of the Tiger Five ensued.[9]

In Wu-chou the four were arrested and interrogated by Ma Chi-hsiang's Embroidered Uniform Guard, and Chin Pao, in particular, was tortured so vengefully that he was permanently crippled. At the outset, the emperor, the senior empress dowager, and certain members of the Wu clique had wanted to have at least the most vituperative of the Ch'u clique executed, allegedly for seditious plotting but essentially for the crime of being loathsome in high places. But then the childishly excitable emperor calmed down somewhat, appeals poured in from numerous officials arguing the folly of becoming absorbed in punishing censors during a time of crisis, and Li Yüan-yin personally visited the court and challenged the emperor to punish him, too, for his close association with the imprisoned four.[10] But the persecution did not end until midsummer, when a portion of the Loyal and True Battalion, which now was in competition with Ch'en Pang-fu for territory in Kuang-hsi, moved to Wu-chou and, though cautioned not to commit "the error of interfering in court affairs," exerted pressure to blunt the sharp rise of the Wu clique and free the caged "Tiger." Eventually the four were variously sentenced to penal military servitude, exile, payment of fines, and removal of official status.[11] This sequence of events shows vividly the degree to which the tail had come to wag the dog—that is, despite the continuing rhetoric of civil-official authority over the military, the extent to which that rhetoric had become both false and self-destructive.

Meanwhile the Ch'ing had been encroaching steadily and more methodically this time than in 1647, concentrating on fewer points, avoiding overextension, and estimating the opposition more cautiously. Through the spring of 1650, K'ung Yu-te consolidated his hold on far southwestern Hu-kuang and positioned his units for a three-route penetration of the strategic corridor from Ch'üan-chou to Kuei-lin.[12] And in early March, Shang and Keng proceeded from northern Kuang-tung straight down to Kuang-chou City, avoiding the Ming forces at Chao-ch'ing and San-shui. When an initial attack failed to dislodge the city's stubborn defenders, the Ch'ing made preparations for a long and difficult siege, sparing only a few units to assist newly surrendered generals in pacifying volatile areas to the east. This siege was a miserable one for the Ch'ing, since both their men and their weapons performed poorly in the heat, humidity, mud, and malaria of the following Kuang-chou summer. And since the city was surrounded on three sides by water, conventional siege techniques were not wholly applicable. Although the mercurial river pirates of the area were enlisted by the Ch'ing, and a small flotilla was built, the battle turned mainly on the heavy use of cannon by both sides.[13]

After eight and one-half months under siege, the Ming commander at the West Gate of the Old City Wall was induced to defect, thus enabling the Ch'ing to position their cannon for bombardment of the inner wall.

It was upon the 24. of November, in the year 1650. when the Tartars upon this advantage rushed with their whole Army into the City, which was soon subdued by them, the Besieged not being in a condition to make any resistance; for no sooner was the Tartar horse got in, but they rid with great swiftness through all the Streets, to hinder the Chineses from gathering together; and though the Chineses were not inferior in number to the Tartars, yet they effected nothing, being in disorder, and surprized by the treachery of their Governour [sic]; so that the best course any could use, was to save himself by flight.

The whole Tartar Army being got into the City, the place was soon turned to a Map of misery, for every one began to tear, break, carry away whatsoever he could lay hands on: The cry of Women, Children, and Aged People, was so great, that it exceeded all noise of such loud distractions; so from the 26. of November, until the 15. of December, there was heard no other cry in the Streets, but Strike, Kill, and Destroy the Rebellious Barbarians [i.e., the Ming loyalists]; all places full of woful Lamentations, of Murder, and Rapine: Those that were able to ransom, bought their lives at dear rates, and so escaped the hands of these Inhumane Slaughterers. At last the Vice-Roys, and chief Commanders of the Army, upon the sixth of Winter month, did strictly forbid any such cruel Murder to be committed hereafter: And I was credibly informed, that during the space of eight[een] days, above eight[y] thousand were killed in cold blood by the Tartars:[14]

At this same time, K'ung Yu-te took advantage of a general breakdown in cooperation among the Ming generals defending northeastern Kuang-hsi—in particular, a mutiny at Ch'üan-chou—and thus was able to enter Kuei-lin (which three times before had fended off Ch'ing attacks) on November 27, 1650.[15] Ch'ü Shih-szu and one loyal aide were captured together and, after rejecting K'ung's attempts to obtain their submission, were executed in Kuei-lin the following January.[16]

As Ch'ing forces then converged on Wu-chou from both the north and east, the frightened imperial family departed in great haste on December 2, heading further up the West River.[17] En route the Yung-li flotilla was badly plundered by rampaging soldiers, and the emperor narrowly escaped being captured by generals who hoped to turn him over to the Ch'ing. Many followers who became scattered in the confusion fell victim to local bandits and aboriginal tribesmen, who robbed and otherwise harassed any scholars, officials, or merchants from outside the region. While Ch'en Pang-fu and his subordinates prepared to surrender to the Ch'ing from Wu-chou, the surviving members of the imperial party found temporary respite in Nan-ning, and the court subsequently entered a new phase in its history.[18]

The latter ten years of the Southern Ming, from 1651 through 1661, witnessed the almost total disappearance of the last vestiges of the regular Ming civil bureaucracy, as the Yung-li court became wholly dependent, for its physical existence and its political significance, on military organizations that originally had developed entirely outside the sphere of Ming institutions: in the Southwest, the strongest of the surviving late-Ming rebel armies, now led by Sun K'o-wang and Li Ting-kuo; and in the Southeast, the dominant quasi-piratical monopolizers of maritime trade, now led by Cheng Ch'eng-kung. Under such circumstances, "Ming" lost its theretofore heavily institutional meaning and came more to signify the persistence of a spirit to resist invasion and domination by a foreign power. But as we shall see, the very presence of a Ming emperor-figure in the southwestern theater assured the continuation there of friction between leaders with civil-administrative propensities and those whose forte was in waging military campaigns. By contrast, in the southeastern coastal theater, the absence of an actual Ming court ironically allowed greater unity and produced greater effectiveness in the resistance effort.

In order to understand the circumstances of the Yung-li court from 1651 onward, we must look back not only at events that had occurred in the southwestern provinces of Szu-ch'uan, Kuei-chou,* and Yün-nan since the fall of Pei-ching, but also to some extent at the place of the Southwest in the Ming governmental system.

Chang Hsien-chung, the one major rebel leader who had not been elim-inated or subordinated by Li Tzu-ch'eng during the Ch'ung-chen period, had begun to evince dynastic aspirations in 1643 when he first declared himself monarch of a "Great Western Kingdom" in central Hu-kuang. In 1644, how-ever, he moved his entire following into Szu-ch'uan and reestablished his kingdom there. From his capital at Ch'eng-tu, he asserted control over the most developed parts of that province and proceeded to institute what generally has been regarded as a blood-drenched reign of terror, which severely depleted Szu-ch'uan's population and resources. But in spite of the relative isolation of Ch'eng-tu, Chang never was secure there—from Ming generals who survived in outlying areas, from his old rival Li Tzu-ch'eng, or later from the Ch'ing in Shen-hsi—and he eventually exhausted Szu-ch'uan as a base area, anyway. So, late in 1646, Chang apparently embarked on the preliminary stage of a campaign to challenge Ch'ing control of Li Tzu-ch'eng's former stronghold, the region around Hsi-an in southeastern Shen-hsi. But while camping at a site in north-central Szu-ch'uan, he was attacked and killed by a special Manchu expe-ditionary force on January 2, 1647.[19]

In the month following Chang Hsien-chung's demise, his chief lieutenants, Sun K'o-wang, Li Ting-kuo, Liu Wen-hsiu, and Ai Neng-ch'i (all of whom had been "adopted" as sons by Chang)[20] strove desperately to regroup and lead the remnants of Chang's army to relative safety in Kuei-chou. They regained some strength after wresting Ch'ung-ch'ing from a Ming general there, and in the spring of 1647 they proceeded southward to take over defenseless Kuei-yang, encountering little resistance en route.[21] They did not remain long in Kuei-chou at this time, however, because the acknowledged "eldest brother" among them, Sun K'o-wang, soon was lured into Yün-nan by an extraordinary situation which had developed there.

Throughout the Ming dynasty, Yün-nan had been governed in a unique

---

*In Ming times Szu-ch'uan was much larger than it is now, including the northern third of present-day Kuei-chou, the northeastern arm of present-day Yün-nan, and approximately the eastern third of present-day Hsi-k'ang (the border there being unspecified). Kuei-chou correspond-ingly was smaller, until its present boundary with Szu-ch'uan was set in 1727.

manner. Like other provinces in the Southwest, Yün-nan employed a combination of the regular hierarchy of provincial, prefectural, and district civil offices common throughout the realm, and a network of hereditarily controlled "native" (*t'u*) local governments and "pacification offices" (*hsüan-wei szu*) common in regions that had large aboriginal populations.[22] Paralleling and, in effect, dominating these sectors in Yün-nan, however, was the military establishment (and extensive estate) of the hereditarily enfeoffed Mu family, descendants of Ming T'ai-tsu's most favored adopted son, Mu Ying. This revered ancestor virtually had created Yün-nan as a Ming province and made it a part of Han Chinese civilization. The prestige of the Mu family had remained high and its dominance unchallenged as successive dukes of Ch'ien-kuo carried on through the fifteenth and sixteenth centuries as the only Ming nobles to wield actual territorial powers.[23]

During the Ch'ung-chen period, however, Mu family control in Yün-nan had been weakened by two circumstances. First, the current Duke of Ch'ien-kuo, Mu T'ien-po, had allowed management of his affairs to fall into the hands of a corrupt subordinate, whose arrogant and extortionate behavior caused discontent among Mu's officers and the native military commissioners (*t'u-szu*) whose cooperation was essential in maintaining the security of the province.[24] Second, certain of Mu's officers, as well as native officials and commanders, had grown strong and ambitious as a result of their having been recruited in recent years to help suppress rebels outside of Yün-nan.[25] Note that in this particular context in the late Ming, it was the native (aboriginal) military leaders who had reason to be dissatisfied with their status in the Ming institutional structure; and they also had the means to act on that dissatisfaction vis-à-vis the organization that had controlled the regular civil and military governance of Yün-nan, i.e., that of the hereditary military noble Mu T'ien-po.

This situation eventually led to the revolt of an aggrandizing native pacification commissioner, Sha Ting-chou, who in January of 1646 took over Yün-nan Fu and tried to displace Mu T'ien-po as the hereditary military governor of the province. Sha usurped Mu's offices, defeated or subordinated most of his armed forces, and bullied most Ming civil officials and other *t'u-szu* into grudging acquiescence. But he was not able to eliminate Mu or the ranking censorial official for Yün-nan, who held out together with some loyal forces in the northwestern part of the province.[26] The resulting stalemate was broken when a native general (who previously had come to know Chang Hsien-chung's commanders in Hu-kuang) heard of Sun K'o-wang's presence in Kuei-chou and invited him to enter Yün-nan, assuring him preeminence in the province if he could stamp out Sha Ting-chou.[27]

Consequently, in April and May of 1647 the surviving armies of the Great

Western Kingdom invaded Yün-nan under the thin guise of taking revenge for
the Mu family and seeking to restore the Ming order. In doing so they not only
fought ruthlessly against Sha and his supporters but also bloodily suppressed
popular resistance to this new rebel takeover in eastern Yün-nan. Soon Sha was
chased out of Yün-nan Fu back southward to his home base in A-mi, and
negotiations were opened with Mu and other Ming officials to the northwest.
The latter were skeptical of Sun K'o-wang's claim that he had metamorphosed
from rebel into Ming loyalist, but they agreed to cooperate by lending their
prestige to his regime if he would refrain from committing atrocities and
completely eradicate Sha Ting-chou's movement. This was accomplished in the
fall of 1648 by Li Ting-kuo, who had done most of the hardest fighting since he
and his "brothers" entered Yün-nan.[28]

Meanwhile, Sun K'o-wang had proceeded to set up a government in Yün-
nan Fu. Demanding tax-like contributions from various localities, he constructed an imperial-style hall and other buildings, held examinations and appointed officials, including heads of the traditional Six Ministries, and received
important personages with a regal air. He had coins cast for a "newly risen"
dynasty, redistributed lands near Yün-nan Fu to provide ample "official fields,"
exerted control over brine wells, mines, and sources of fodder, and drafted the
services of craftsmen in the area.[29] Accounts differ as to the relative harshness or
humanity of Sun's regime, but generally speaking he seems to have pursued
orderly governance to a greater extent than his late leader, Chang Hsien-chung,
while also eschewing the worst of Chang's brutalities. It was because of Sun's
interest in rulership that he first sent emissaries to the Yung-li court in Chao-
ch'ing with his notorious request to be enfeoffed as a prince.* This title would
have officially confirmed Sun's superiority over his three "brothers," implied his
succession to Chang's patrimony, and partially legitimized any future move by
Sun to exercise regental or even imperial powers. However, Sun lacked a clear
mandate from his comrades to carry out this political maneuver. For this reason,
the dilatoriness of the Yung-li court and the contradictory signals that Sun
received on the enfeoffment issue frustrated and angered him greatly.

Indeed, it was because of Sun K'o-wang's pretensions that a rift began to
open between him and Li Ting-kuo, who had accepted Sun as the senior figure
among the four successors to Chang Hsien-chung, but who came to resent Sun's
attempts to elevate himself further through administrative and political manipu-
lations. Sun, on the other hand, became jealous and wary of Li's superior

* Upon entering Yün-nan, the four rebel leaders had assumed titles as "kings" (*wang*) that in the
Ming institutional context would have been appropriate for second-degree princes (*chün-wang*). The
title requested by Sun was that of a prince of the *first* degree, or prince of the blood (*ch'in-wang*).

generalship, inspirational qualities, and popularity among fighting men. In fact, because of what Sun saw as insubordination on Li's part, Sun had him flogged publicly in the spring of 1648. And although, when it was over, Sun tearfully embraced Li, helped him to rise, and entrusted him further with important pacification responsibilities, nevertheless, rancor persisted in Li's heart, conflicting with the sense of brotherhood that he apparently still felt toward Sun.[30] For the time being, however, this recrudescence of Ming civil-military friction even among Ming rebels was ameliorated by the demands of securing the Southwestern base area.

In the fall of 1650 Sun sent his armies back into Kuei-chou, where they easily defeated or absorbed Ming forces not encountered in their previous invasion of that province, and Sun proceeded to set up a second headquarters at the provincial capital, Kuei-yang.[31] From that central position he then launched campaigns to the north, south, and east. These began five years of offensive actions which forced the Ch'ing almost entirely out of the southwestern provinces and seriously challenged their hold on western Hu-kuang and western Kuang-tung (see map 13).

In western Szu-ch'uan, Sun's generals recovered most of the major urban centers and forced the army of Wu San-kuei to retreat back northward, relinquishing all positions in Szu-ch'uan south of Pao-ning. They had less success, however, in subduing various warlords in the southern part of the province, and they were unable to gain the cooperation of remnants of Li Tzu-ch'eng's forces that long since had occupied the border region near the Yang-tzu between Szu-ch'uan and Hu-kuang.[32] Sun K'o-wang himself participated in or oversaw the thrusts into southwestern Hu-kuang. He first recovered Yüan-chou, the "gateway" between that province and Kuei-chou, in 1651. Then in the winter of 1652–53 Sun sent one of his best generals to wrest Ch'en-chou from the Ch'ing, while he personally led an army into the Pao-ch'ing region. Although Sun was defeated in that campaign and returned to Kuei-yang, in the spring of 1655 another of his chief commanders descended rapidly down the Yüan River and very nearly captured Ch'ang-te.[33]

Much more spectacular, however, were Li Ting-kuo's campaigns to the southeast, which exhibited in sharp relief some of the most remarkable qualities of the late Ming "roving bandits": incredible speed and surprise attacks with large numbers of men (Li had learned to make excellent use of Southwestern war elephants and the aboriginal fighters' skill with firearms); a visceral, highly personal style of leadership; and a disinclination or inability to hold territorial bases. In June and July of 1652, Li first seized Pao-ch'ing and other key cities in west-southwestern Hu-kuang to protect his rear. Then he turned to personally lead a lightning-fast drive on Kuei-lin, which his forces overwhelmed on August 7.[34]

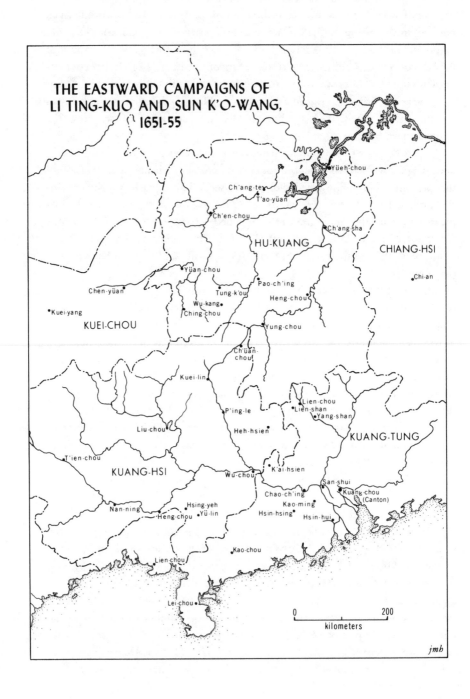

THE EASTWARD CAMPAIGNS OF
LI TING-KUO AND SUN K'O-WANG,
1651-55

Yüeh-chou

Ch'ang-te
T'ao-yüan
Ch'en-chou
Ch'ang-sha

HU-KUANG

CHIANG-HSI

Chi-an

Yüan-chou
Chen-yüan
Pao-ch'ing
Tung-k'ou
Heng-chou
Kuei-yang
Wu-kang
Ching-chou

KUEI-CHOU
Yung-chou

Ch'üan-
chou

Kuei-lin

Lien-chou
P'ing-le
Lien-shan
Yang-shan
Liu-chou
Heh-hsien

KUANG-TUNG

T'ien-chou

KUANG-HSI
Wu-chou
K'ai-hsien
San-shui
Chao-ch'ing
Kuang-chou
(Canton)
Nan-ning
Hsing-yeh
Kao-ming
Heng-chou
Yü-lin
Hsin-hsing
Hsin-hui

Kao-chou

Lien-chou

Lei-chou

0   200
kilometers

jmb

This remarkable accomplishment elicited a flood of reversions to the Ming side across Ch'ing-occupied parts of Kuang-hsi, leaving only Wu-chou in enemy hands. But Li did not remain in Kuei-lin. Rather, the next month he reentered Hu-kuang, sending a contingent to take over Lien-chou Prefecture in northern Kuang-tung and a vanguard to subdue Ch'ang-sha, while Li himself occupied Heng-chou. Despite these successes, however, Li was not able to hold the cities he restored, and in late March of 1653 he was forced to withdraw desultorily into northwestern Kuang-tung.[35]

Subsequently, Li Ting-kuo concentrated his offensive efforts on Kuang-tung. His first campaign there, in the early part of 1653, was little more than an extension of his retreat from Hu-kuang. Although the Ch'ing commands in northwestern Kuang-tung were caught unprepared and Li, thus, was able to attack Chao-ch'ing and threaten Kuang-chou City, this essentially was exploratory activity; and in the autumn of that year he sought respite in central Kuang-hsi, along the way failing to recover Kuei-lin, which had been reoccupied by the Ch'ing.[36]

Li's second campaign on Kuang-tung was much longer and more calculated. In the spring of 1654 he advanced through southern Kuang-hsi into the heart of Lei-chou Peninsula, which in the previous year had been the scene of some serious pro-Ming insurrections. Receiving a good degree of popular support, Li was able to establish a headquarters and remain in Kao-chou Prefecture unmolested by Ch'ing counterforces for over five months, during which he suffered through a debilitating illness.[37] By late September, however, Li had recovered sufficiently to advance into the southwestern part of the Pearl River delta region and begin a siege of Hsin-hui, the crucial stepping stone in his planned conquest of Kuang-chou City.[38] Hampered there by a lack of naval capability, Li twice appealed for assistance to Cheng Ch'eng-kung in Fu-chien, but for various reasons (discussed below) such help did not arrive in time. Hsin-hui held firm, and in late January 1655, Li's army was badly beaten there by Ch'ing reinforcements from Chiang-hsi. Li then was pursued, suffering severe losses, all the way back into southern Kuang-hsi; and when his men regrouped at Nan-ning, they numbered only several thousand.[39]

Through all of this, the rebels-cum-loyalists had not been able to *hold* any appreciable amount of Ch'ing territory. Nevertheless, the Ch'ing, who at this time seem to have had no good sources of intelligence on what was happening in the Southwest, were stunned by this burst of enemy activity, and their losses were very painful. The most celebrated of Ch'ing regional commanders, Hsü Yung, had been killed while trying to defend Ch'en-chou. The great generalissimo K'ung Yu-te had killed most of his family and immolated himself with his wife as Li Ting-kuo's men swarmed Kuei-lin. The Manchu prince Nikan, who had been specially deputed from Pei-ching to take the Hu-kuang situation in hand, had been killed in ambush by Li's men near Heng-chou. And the Ch'ing command in Kuang-chou had been thoroughly traumatized.[40] They came to realize more acutely how tenuous their control was in these regions. So for some time after this, the Ch'ing stuck mainly to consolidating their positions and truly pacifying the lands they held in Szu-ch'uan, Hu-kuang, and Liang-Kuang, adopting a wait-and-see attitude toward the even wilder far Southwest.[41]

Nor could Sun K'o-wang have been totally pleased by reports of Li Ting-kuo's startling victories, since each one further enhanced Li's glowing reputation among Sun's subordinate generals and made him a greater political liability. Indeed, during these years of the great "eastward campaigns," several movements made or directed by Sun in the western Hu-kuang theater may have been more threatening than reinforcing to Li Ting-kuo, and Sun allegedly tried to have Li assassinated on at least one occasion.[42] Moreover, Li remained in Liang-Kuang in 1653–54, rather than going back to Kuei-chou, probably because he could no longer bear Sun's jealous domination but did not want an open breach—whether because of his former brotherly relation with Sun and his adherents, or because he did not feel he could win a military contest against their combined armies.

Despite the now complete impotence of the Yung-li court, its very presence in the Southwest already had begun to widen the differences between Sun K'o-wang and some of his subordinates by providing an alternative source of legitimacy and object of loyalty. Those commanders who, like Li Ting-kuo, were unhappy with Sun's attempts to lord over them by instituting various aspects of traditional civil government could turn to the Yung-li court, which was more authentically Ming-imperial in background, and which also could not, in actuality, exert any constraint on them. (This is not to gainsay Li Ting-kuo's perhaps quite genuine feelings of newfound loyalty to the Ming dynasty.) Sun, of course, recognized the potential threat to his aggrandizement that the court posed. And he tried, unsuccessfully as it turned out, to carry through a delicate process of extracting from the court the last drops of power it could confer, while simultaneously reducing it gradually to a virtual nonentity—presumably so that his regime eventually could take its place as the imperial government of the Han Chinese people. Apparently he lacked both sufficient charisma and sufficient finesse to accomplish this. For the more Sun tried to feed his appetite for power by masticating and ingesting the now bite-sized court, the more Li and other commanders could cite this as the main cause of their alienation from him, and the more inclined they became to respond to appeals for help from the be-leaguered emperor and his remaining courtiers.

The Yung-li emperor's party had arrived in Nan-ning (southern Kuang-

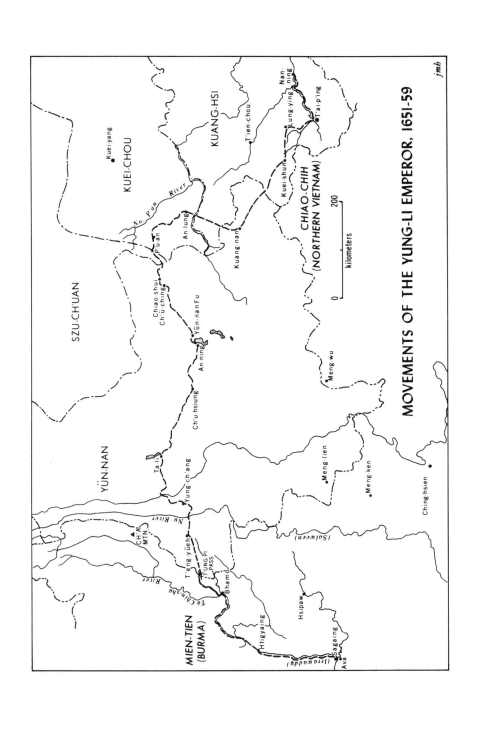

MOVEMENTS OF THE YUNG-LI EMPEROR, 1651-59

jmb

hsi) in December 1650, just after Sun had led his armies from Yün-nan back into Kuei-chou to establish a base for his subsequent fan-like array of campaigns. The following spring Sun sent an armed unit to "enter [the imperial] guard" in Nan-ning, suggesting that the emperor make his temporary capital in Sun's primary headquarters, Yün-nan Fu. Also, not incidentally, Sun's men murdered in cold blood several officials who were thought to have been the chief opponents of granting Sun the title "Prince of Ch'in." Under such intimidation, the emperor easily was led by more accommodating ministers such as Ma Chi-hsiang to formally grant Sun the title he wanted, and the imperial surname and a new given name, as well.[43] This came at just the right time to undergird Sun's ascent in power, as he launched offensives to the north and east from Kuei-yang.

Meanwhile the Ch'ing had been making steady progress in eastern Kuang-hsi, and in the fall of 1651 the Yung-li court was forced to flee Nan-ning. Although there was internal disagreement about where the court should go from there, actually, short of making a bid for the seacoast or Annam to the south, there were few options apart from trying to reach Sun K'o-wang's territory in Kuei-chou and Yün-nan. So through the winter of 1651–52, the again dwindling imperial party made its way largely overland, at one point with Ch'ing forces only a half day behind them, through the treacherous aboriginal territory of extreme southwestern Kuang-hsi. Eventually they were picked up by one of Sun's generals and taken to Kuang-nan, Yün-nan, where they arrived in late February 1652.[44] Then, however, rather than dignify the court and possibly detract from his own preeminence by reestablishing it in Yün-nan Fu (as he had suggested before), Sun K'o-wang had the emperor and his ragtag entourage of about fifty people taken to the isolated guard post of An-lung in the southwestern corner of Kuei-chou, as though tucking them into his back pocket. The sadly reduced court was to remain there for four years under conditions of worsening degradation, eating only local fare, deprived of menial help, and generally being treated by Sun's agents like so many head of livestock.

Meanwhile in Kuei-yang, Sun put on more imperial airs, issuing his own commentaries on the Classics to be used in further civil service examinations, casting his own official seals, setting up an imperial ancestral temple with Chu Yüan-chang in the center, Chang Hsien-chung to the left, and his own grandfather to the right, and allegedly planning to usurp the throne and begin a "Later Ming" dynasty.[45] But Sun seems to have done nothing to alleviate, and probably exacerbated, the ravaged condition of the people in Kuei-chou. A traveler who passed through the Kuei-yang area during this time observed:

> The bund guards in some places had been chased away by tigers, and the mountain slopes from top to bottom were strewn with human bones. There was not a sign of merchants or [other] travelers. All I saw were horsemen

flying back and forth [between] clashes. Also, I saw people whose ears and noses had been cut off and some whose two arms both were gone. But they still [were made to] bear heavy loads for long distances. It was terribly cruel. Even though the scenery was unusually interesting, I could not bear to watch it go by.[46]

Naturally, the Yung-li emperor sought to extricate himself from a bad and deteriorating situation. Gradually he came to know of Li Ting-kuo's military successes and of his alienation from Sun K'o-wang, so he made a series of secret appeals to Li for rescue, culminating in the early spring of 1654 with his offer to Li of status as a first-degree prince if he could liberate the court from Sun's tyranny.[47] Through agents in the field and collaborators in An-lung, however, Sun learned of these appeals; and in April his henchmen entered the court's quarters and began an inquisition, seeking to expose all those officials who had been involved in the plots to bring in Li Ting-kuo. True to his character, the Yung-li emperor declined to acknowledge his own responsibility for the matter, and on May 6 he allowed "Eighteen Gentlemen of An-lung" to be condemned to death as scapegoats.[48]

During the time of the Yung-li court's uncomfortable stay in An-lung, Li Ting-kuo had been deeply engaged in his Hu-kuang and Liang-Kuang campaigns and scarcely in a position, either geographically or politically vis-à-vis Sun K'o-wang, to do as the emperor begged. Moreover, he may have hoped to first regain Kuang-tung and then restore the court there, rather than in some more remote region. Anyway, in response to the first Yung-li appeals, Li demurred. Not until his campaign in Kuang-tung had completely failed, and he came under pressure from new Ch'ing advances in eastern Kuang-hsi, did Li turn his attention toward An-lung.[49]

Thus, Li began a risky political move during a time when his actual strength was at a low point. His subsequent success in defying Sun K'o-wang turned on his ability to co-opt Sun's other generals by treating them honorably and fairly, by showing sincerity in his concern for the Yung-li court, and by relying on his reputation for outstanding military leadership. The more Sun sent his lieutenants to harm, threaten, or counter Li, the more he lost them to Li's overt command or to his covert influence. Thus, as Li moved toward An-lung in the early spring of 1656, he received the quiet cooperation of certain soldiers and generals who had been dispatched by Sun to block him. On February 16 he arrived in An-lung and was assisted, rather than opposed, by one of Sun's most important generals, who had been sent to preemptively transfer the court elsewhere under Sun's closer control. Thus, four days later, Li was able to escort the Yung-li party away from An-lung toward Yün-nan. Li then made a rapid show of force at Yün-nan Fu and cowed Sun's generals there into accepting his coup. In late March, the Yung-li emperor was brought into that city, now called the "Tien Capital," and he began distributing appointments and titles, largely to Li's subordinates and allies, in an effort to recreate some semblance of a government.[50]

A long interval of suspense and uncertainty followed in the power struggle between Sun K'o-wang and Li Ting-kuo, neither man feeling secure enough in his own domain to move decisively against the other. Revolts, defections, and seditious plots occurred on both sides. Li tried several times to effect a reconciliation with Sun, first by sending to Kuei-yang members of Sun's family and personal guard who had been detained in Yün-nan, and later by deputing peace ambassadors. But Sun remained belligerent and would make no peace.[51]

Rather, by the summer of 1657 Sun had been persuaded to launch a punitive campaign against Li, not realizing that the very men who thus counseled him already had arranged to join Li's ranks at the crucial moment. In late September Sun's forces crossed western Kuei-chou, and one month later they clashed with those of Li Ting-kuo at Chiao-shui in eastern Yün-nan. As had been secretly planned, at that point Sun's key generals turned against him and, moreover, informed Li of another contingent that had been sent on a side route to attack him from the rear. Consequently, Sun's stratagems were foiled completely, and as he retreated back across Kuei-chou, even the commanders he had left there met him with hostility.[52] So incensed and weakened was Sun that he proceeded to retreat all the way into Hu-kuang, with only his family and a small guard totaling about four hundred people. On December 19, 1657, he surrendered to the Ch'ing authorities at Pao-ch'ing, spouting his hatred for those who had betrayed him and urging the Manchus to let him "take revenge and dispel his shame" by leading a Ch'ing campaign on Szu-ch'uan, Kuei-chou, and Yün-nan.[53] Although the Ch'ing distrusted Sun too much to place him in charge of any campaign, they did treat him very well and were delighted to have caught yet another windfall from the Ming side.

No such damaging split in leadership or civil-military conflicts occurred, however, in the regime that upheld the Ming banner in the coastal Southeast. There the power of Cheng Ch'eng-kung remained supreme for ten years, from 1651 until just before his death, and made him a national hero of legendary proportion, who has captivated the imaginations of historians, playwrights, and storytellers not only in China, but in Japan as well.[54] Although the administration of Cheng's wide-ranging mercantile and military operations was complex, employing hundreds of able men, and in effect constituted a special government for a special zone, Cheng never allowed any civil-military dichotomy to take form in his organization.

And it was *his* organization. The Yung-li court always was far away, and

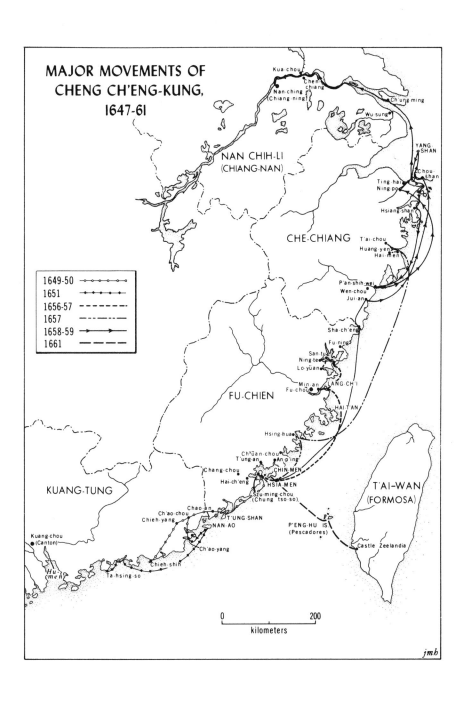

MAJOR MOVEMENTS OF
CHENG CH'ENG-KUNG,
1647-61

NAN CHIH-LI
(CHIANG-NAN)

Kua-chou
Chen-chiang
Nan-ching
(Chiang-ning)
Ch'ung-ming
Wu-sung

YANG-
SHAN
Chou-
shan
Ting-hai
Ning-po
Hsiang-shan

CHE-CHIANG   T'ai-chou
Huang-yen
Hai-men

P'an-shih-wei
Wen-chou
Jui-an

Sha-ch'eng
Fu-ning
San-tu
Ning-te
Lo-yüan
Min-an   LANG-CH'I
Fu-chou
HAI-T'AN

FU-CHIEN

Hsing-hua

Ch'üan-chou
T'ung-an   An-p'ing
CHIN-MEN
Chang-chou
Hai-ch'eng   HSIA-MEN
Szu-ming-chou
(Chung-tso-so)
Chao-an
Ch'ao-chou
Chieh-yang   T'UNG-SHAN
NAN-AO
Ch'ao-yang

T'AI-WAN
(FORMOSA)

KUANG-TUNG

Kuang-chou
(Canton)

Hu-
men
Chieh-shih
Ta-hsing-so

P'ENG-HU IS
(Pescadores)
Castle Zeelandia

1649-50	○—○—○—○
1651	●—●—●—●
1656-57	- - - -
1657	–·–·–
1658-59	→——→
1661	— — —

0   200
kilometers

jmb

communications between the emperor and Cheng were both slow and intermit-
tent. So although Cheng was faultlessly conscientious on a formal level about
remaining a loyal servant of the throne, to the point of abstemiousness in
declining to accept "undeserved" conferrals, actually he was free to do as he saw
fit and, in effect, was the king in his own sizable domain. After the spring of 1651,
when Cheng jeopardized his still fragile organization by going on a wild goose
chase hoping to aid Yung-li forces in Kuang-chou, he acted on occasional
directives from the Yung-li court only when it suited his own plans for the
southeastern theater. Similarly, although Cheng adopted many of the forms and
terms of standard Ming military organization, the overall composition and
modus operandi of his land and naval forces remained idiosyncratic.[55] Obviated
were the frustrations of dealing with emperors who were absolute in principle
but absolutely incompetent in practice, rivalries among Inner Court and Outer
Court figures (and their respective military allies) over who should "assist" the
emperor, and thumping censorial officials who partook of heaven's delegated
authority to find fault with every departure from the sacrosanct "framework and
mainstays" of imperial institutions. Thus, in the Southeast the symbolic presence
but actual absence of a Ming court gave Cheng Ch'eng-kung the flexibility and
independence that he needed to successfully conflate his own interests with those
of the Ming, and to perform at his best for the loyalist cause.

There were other elements, of course, in Cheng's rise to power, not the least
of which was the character of the man himself. Cheng Ch'eng-kung was cannily
intelligent, boundlessly energetic, obsessively hardworking, and exuded a charisma that enabled him to demand the utmost from other strong-willed men and
discipline them with an iron hand. Clearly—in his own mind, to be sure—he
was a man of destiny who would have stood out in any context. And his burning
sense of pride and honor, his desire to control but never be controlled, are
symptomatic of a deep-seated rebelliousness against constraint which, in the
peculiar circumstances of his time and location, became a potent political stance.

Of course, Cheng had followed a path that already had been cleared to some
extent by his equally remarkable father; but as we have seen, Ch'eng-kung did
not simply inherit a fully constituted, well-functioning regime when Chih-lung
was removed from Fu-chien. On the contrary, he had struggled for several years,
rebuilding and reinforcing the Cheng machine piece by piece and gradually
shunting aside his elder rivals for control. Through this process, Cheng Ch'eng-
kung had learned not only how to lead, but also how to nurture his flock, and he
hated for it to suffer injury unnecessarily. The tough cautiousness that this
induced, together with Cheng's strategic perspicacity and organizational ability,
made him a formidable foe, not only to the Ch'ing but also to independent
warlords along the seaboard. Especially during his campaigns in eastern Kuang-

tung in 1648–50, Cheng had learned hard lessons about conserving assets by avoiding direct assaults on enemy strongholds, building and protecting a secure home base, and systematically extracting and transporting "tribute" from local powerholders in designated resource areas. These lessons resulted in the formation of a highly efficient logistical system (for both regular supply and prompt merit rewards) and an affinity in Cheng for carrot-and-stick psychological warfare. That is, on the carrot side, obtaining the services of talented former adversaries by treating them generously and honorably; and, on the stick side, frightening enemies into submission with calculated threats and impressive sample demonstrations of force, rather than immediately, bluntly, and wastefully applying the fullest force available. Thus, by constantly attending to both the material and charismatic bases of his power, and by consummately practicing the arts of deception, Cheng Ch'eng-kung presented the Ch'ing with their greatest single challenge in conquest and pacification.

Cheng used his multiple capacities not only to thwart the Ch'ing but also to seize an organizational opportunity in the maritime sector, which had been left virtually stateless by the negative, indifferent, or merely self-defensive policies of the Ming government. In spite of lukewarm or obstructive official attitudes toward it, the volume and value of trade between the Chinese coast and various entrepôts in East and Southeast Asia had increased markedly in the latter part of the sixteenth century, especially with the appearance of aggressive mercantile enterprises sponsored by the dominant European maritime nations, Spain, Portugal, and the Netherlands.[56] A large segment of the populace in the southeastern coastal region of China thus had come to rely directly or indirectly on foreign commerce for its livelihood, in addition to carrying on the domestic coastal trade. Such people appear to have been amenable to regulation, taxation, and policing by any organization, official or unofficial, that would stabilize, perhaps facilitate, or at least not interfere grossly with their trades. The failure of Ming government to perform actively and positively in this sphere had left it open to men such as Cheng Chih-lung, his clansmen, and his progeny, who grew so successful as "protection" racketeers among people who had no other source of protection that they came to constitute a maritime government of sorts.

In resisting the Ch'ing, Cheng Ch'eng-kung used profits that he gained from maritime trade, as well as revenues that he derived from maritime police and "customs" control. And he also diverted a large portion of the manpower, manufacturing skill, and vessel tonnage of the maritime sector from the business of trade to the also profitable business of war.[57] There were limits to such substitution of hostility for utility in tapping the energies of the loosely associated maritime community. Many Chinese during this period sought to escape Cheng's exactions and involvement in his battle-strewn quest by emigrating to more remote lands such as T'ai-wan, Siam, Luzon, or even the coast of South America. But the size and vigor of Cheng's movement, and the high degree of collaboration with it by the coastal populace, testify that many others shared or could readily accommodate Cheng's interests—so long as he kept winning. And Cheng's excellent intelligence network throughout the region in which he dominated the coastal trade was an important aspect of his success.

Another element in Cheng Ch'eng-kung's rise to power was the special vulnerability of the Ch'ing, both attitudinally and geopolitically, to the tactics he used. Having descended from northern nomads, the Manchus took greatest pride in their tradition of superb skill in mounted combat, and thus they excelled in land-war operations. Although they adapted relatively well to riverine and lacustrine fighting, they were baffled and frightened by the sea. Invincibility on land, however, was sufficing for their conquest of the rest of China apart from the coastal strip. So it is understandable that the Manchus, reinforced by collaborating Chinese officials who also generally tended to ignore or disparage maritime affairs, did not place the eradication of Cheng Ch'eng-kung among their first priorities. Consequently, Cheng gained time to build his movement and to become more formidable than might have been the case if the Ch'ing had concentrated their efforts on Fu-chien earlier.

But even if the Ch'ing quickly had overcome their disinclination to deal with the seaboard, considerations of expense would have strongly inhibited any rapid, forceful Ch'ing response to the coastal resistance. The relative inaccessibility and limited agricultural resources of far southeastern Che-chiang, Fu-chien, and extreme eastern Kuang-tung made it especially difficult and costly to transport armies to and maintain large garrisons in those regions. If a stationary strategy were adopted, then huge numbers of soldiers would have been needed to guard every urban center on the pitted coastline from "pirate" attack. But meeting the seaborne rebels on their own ground, so to speak, would have required an unsustainably intense investment in building a Ch'ing navy from whole cloth (since the horse-heavy Manchus, terrified of the water anyway, had been sunk and capsized enough to grow very suspicious of requisitioned vessels and crews).

Thus, it is not surprising that the Ch'ing first sought assiduously to reach a negotiated settlement with Cheng Ch'eng-kung, and that even when they were able to turn their energies primarily to the maritime arena in 1661, they chose to strive for utter control of the land—that is, of a no-man's-land—by moving the entire coastal population a distance of several miles toward the interior,[58] rather than board ships and press the enemy on the high seas. In so doing the Ch'ing of course aimed to deprive Cheng's forces of any foothold or target of attack. But more important, they hoped to strike at Cheng's Achilles' heel, that is, his continual need for the products of the land—especially bulky commodities that could not be stored in long-lasting quantities on shipboard, such as grains and other staple foodstuffs, fresh water, metal ores, and wood for fires and repairs— and for the regular services of the best craftsmen in the construction and maintenance of large merchant vessels and battleships.[59]

Beginning in the spring of 1651, after he definitely asserted full control over the recently threatened Cheng operational headquarters on Hsia-men, Cheng Ch'eng-kung devoted even more attention to military preparedness, establishing a special training camp on Chin-men, creating a bureau to oversee the production of weapons and armor, and to a certain extent adopting the standard Ming quadripartite division for both his land and naval forces.[60] These had grown markedly in size as more fence-sitting militarists joined his increasingly successful organization, and as Cheng absorbed the units of his elder relatives; moreover, they expanded again the following winter when Cheng subordinated the surviving naval commanders from Regent Lu's decimated regime (see chapter 4). The most immediate aim of this preparation was a strong retaliatory attack on nearby Chang-chou Prefecture, which was carried out from the fall of 1651 into the fall of 1652. During this campaign, Cheng's forces blockaded Ch'üan-chou harbor, took over several district cities, very nearly starved the Chang-chou prefectural seat into submission, and collected the head of the Ch'ing viceroy for Che-chiang and Fu-chien, Ch'en Chin![61] The Ch'ing had been disturbed about Cheng's previous invasion of Ch'ao-chou Prefecture in Kuang-tung, but in that more remote case he mainly had attacked just a lot of other petty scoundrels. Now he really had become a thorn in their side, and something had to be done. But the Ch'ing also were finding that even a minimally credible response to the Chang-chou incursion could be awfully taxing—for their treasury, their troops, and the people of Fu-chien.[62]

Thus, in September of 1652 greater restrictions were politely placed on the movements and outside contacts of Cheng Chih-lung in Pei-ching, "for his own protection"; and in early November the Shun-chih emperor initiated the first of what became a two-year series of exchanges aimed at bringing Cheng Ch'eng-kung to heel by negotiation.[63] As the emperor explained in a directive to the new viceroy for Che-chiang and Fu-chien,

> Recently the pirates Cheng Ch'eng-kung et al. several times have disrupted districts and prefectures along the seaboard. They should have been cut out from the beginning, but I knew that in a previous year, when our Great Army had gone down into Fu-chien, [Ch'eng-kung's] father, Cheng Chih-lung, had led the way in returning to obedience. How could his son and younger brother bear to cast away their father and elder brother, willfully going into rebellion, if it were not that the local officials failed to understand

my meaning and handled matters wrongly? So Cheng Ch'eng-kung et al.,
though they have wished to reform, have not been able to find the path
upward. Moreover, they see [only] that [the late] Prince of Jui [i.e.,
Dorgon] ordered a guard placed around [Ch'eng-kung's] father and do not
consider how benevolently other relatives have been treated in their home
locale. Consequently, out of suspicion and fear they have turned and
rebelled. Also, I feel that since Cheng Chih-lung has been obedient to us for
some time now, I could not bear to attack and extirpate his son and brother,
who also are my naked babes. If Ch'eng-kung and the others come back [to
the proper allegiance], then they can be employed on the seas. Why should
it be necessary to have them come to the capital? Now I already have had
Cheng Chih-lung write a letter declaring my sincere intentions, and I have
sent a man forth to enjoin Ch'eng-kung, Hung-k'uei, and the others to take
cognizance of this. If they persist in delusion and do not come to their senses,
you should advance to exterminate them. But if Chih-lung's household
man brings a letter back to [Fu-chou, indicating that they], after all, have
developed goodness in their hearts and regret their transgressions, then you
... should allow them to return to their former locales of residence, not
requiring that they come to the capital. They should be given full authority
to rid Che-chiang, Fu-chien, and Kuang-tung of pirates, as well as to
manage the transit of all ocean-going vessels, collect and remit revenues,
and investigate nefarious characters. And if they can seize and behead at sea
the false prince [i.e., Regent Lu] and his pernicious ringleaders, then I will
not stint to bestow noble titles as rewards....[64]

Appropriately, the new viceroy investigated and had arrested those officials who
had been responsible for the 1651 raid on Hsia-men;[65] and Cheng Chih-lung's
letter, which first probed his son's willingness to begin negotiations, also con-
ceded that he had been justified in reacting forcefully to their reckless actions. But
Chih-lung warned that if hostilities continued, it would be "hard to dismount
from the tiger's back and disperse gathered troops."[66]

Cheng Ch'eng-kung seems to have been surprised by this communication,
but when he saw what was afoot, he entered the game with gusto and put on the
most cunningly deceptive performance of his career, alternately wooing the
Ch'ing representatives with goodwill gifts and expressions of false modesty and
contrition, then thumbing his nose at them and verily snorting implacability.
The remarkable documents from this interval present problems of interpretation
analogous to the frustrations of contemporaneous officials who strained to
discern what Ch'eng-kung really had in mind. Did he truly contemplate surrendering to the Ch'ing, or did he just shrewdly manipulate the negotiation
process to gain time for stuffing his war chest? Was he callously indifferent to the
fate of his father and other relatives on the Ch'ing side, or was he holding out in
an attempt to inhibit the Manchus from harming them? Below I will venture
some judgments, but from the evidence available, no unqualified answers to

these questions appear justifiable. It does seem clear, however, that Ch'eng-kung emerged much stronger at the end of this negotiation process than when it began, whereas the Ch'ing expended a good deal of time and energy only to lose actual ground. And it should be noted here, also, that no such process ever would have ensued if Cheng had been hampered by the presence of a Ming court in his sphere.

In early June of 1653 the Ch'ing court, stressing the desirability of father and son holding the same allegiance, pointed out to Ch'eng-kung that steps had been taken to right things that had angered him in the past. And they went on to make him an offer: a ducal title and the position of Regional Commander in Ch'üan-chou, with special powers to combat pirates, manage and inspect all seagoing vessels, and collect maritime tariffs along the Fu-chien coast. He would be allowed to keep all his own men, who would receive state salaries and pay. But ultimately he would be answerable to the Ch'ing viceroy and provincial governor.[67] Ch'eng-kung's reply to his father's missive in this exchange was as "boastfully preposterous" as before:

> Since [the Ch'ing] already have shown my father that they cannot be believed, how can I now believe my father's words? . . . You were among the first to surrender, but [much contrary to their promises] you have been among the last [in receiving rewards]. . . . Besides, I firmly hold the coastal area. The military revenues of the eastern and western seas I have produced and propagated myself. Whether I advance to fight or withdraw to hold, there is more than enough for my purposes. Why should I be willing, in such plenty, to submit to the control of others? That circumstances are favorable [to me] and unfavorable [to the Ch'ing] in Fu-chien and Kuang-tung is very clear. How is it that no one in the Ch'ing court recognizes this? Moreover, the far southeastern coast is several thousand li away from [their] capital, and the route is long with impediments. Their men and horses become exhausted and do not easily acclimate themselves to the [different] environments, so most of them die off. And with insufficient men, they find it hard to hold [the territory]. To build up troop strength, they then must recruit; and having recruited, they have difficulty delivering supplies. If unable to maintain supply, they surely will be unable to hold. To waste so much money and materiel in order to contest an area that cannot possibly be held—that is to suffer harm without [the prospect of] benefit. . . . If the Ch'ing dynasty cannot emulate the smart calculation of my dynasty, but insists on belaboring their troops to go back and forth, year after year, throwing away their resources to no good end, then how can they expect ever to rehabilitate the region?[68]

In spite of Ch'eng-kung's pugnacious attitude, the faults he found with their proposals were interpreted by the Ch'ing leaders as an encouraging willingness to dicker—surely he would need more than one measly prefecture to support his men, and higher status than a mere regional commander, also, to control them, et cetera. Though the Shun-chih emperor declined to cede the *three provinces* that Ch'eng-kung demanded, or to make him a prince on par with Wu San-kuei, he did soon offer him four prefectures instead of one and the title of Sea-quelling General to sweeten the deal. All Ch'ing forces would be withdrawn from the coastal area in Fu-chien to prepare for the transfer of authority to Cheng, and so that he need not feel wary about coming to make arrangements with the top Ch'ing officials there.[69] "So the Ch'ing court wants to cheat me, too!" Cheng said to his staff. "We'll use this in one way or another to get plenty of provisions for our soldiers."[70]

Indeed, knowing full well that it often took at least two months for exchanges to be completed between his headquarters and Pei-ching, Cheng took maximum advantage of the Ch'ing promise to withdraw from the coastal area during the negotiation stage. Claiming that he could not wait to "satisfy the hunger of his men," Cheng immediately sent his own forces into locales from Ch'ao-chou in the south to Fu-chou in the north, and virtually occupied the whole coast of Chang-chou and Ch'üan-chou prefectures. The Ch'ing authorities responded to these moves with gentle protestations, veiled threats, and some force—to little avail. Employing a variety of tactics, from simply trouncing petty satraps and bullying their ilk into client status to presenting gifts and greetings to gentry leaders who had taken refuge in the hills, Cheng easily raised in a short time, from the area of about one and one-half prefectures, sums that considerably surpassed the total revenues of the Lung-wu court from the whole province of Fu-chien.[71]

Moreover, consistent with Cheng's pattern of maintaining pressure on adversaries even while talking (to prove that he did not negotiate out of weakness), Cheng directed Chang Ming-chen to return to his camp on the sandbars southwest of Ch'ung-ming Island to maximally harass Ch'ing garrisons, cities, defense installations, and the Grand Canal traffic around the mouth of the Yang-tzu. This Chang did in three daring campaigns, one in the fall of 1653 and two in the early and late spring of 1654; he was not forced out of his island base until July of the latter year.[72] Moreover, during this same interval Cheng dispatched messages to Li Ting-kuo and the Yung-li court urging that they attack from the west so as to occupy the Ch'ing "at both head and tail."[73]

In the early spring of 1654, Ch'eng-kung was summoned to Fu-chou to formally receive investiture with his new titles and powers. But he only sent emissaries, who were not received because they refused to bow down like "guests" in what they considered to be their home territory. Then in the third week of March the Ch'ing representatives were induced to meet Cheng more than halfway in An-p'ing, where he put on a big banquet for them but would not accept the seal or documents they had brought. Declining to consider their offer of several prefectures, Cheng claimed that even several provinces would not be enough to support his armies and navies. Rather, he flagrantly suggested something on the order of Korea and urged the Ch'ing to "exhaust the treasures of [their suzerain polities?] outside the country" in gifting him.[74] Thus, the Ch'ing court's first attempt to "summon and soothe" Cheng Ch'eng-kung ended in perplexing failure.

Naturally, the opinion of many Ch'ing officials then hardened toward Cheng. The Ch'ing viceroy wrote warning him to deal realistically and castigating him for being absurd, duplicitous, and unfilial, wasting everyone's time and effort, endangering his father and family, and discrediting even the Ming cause.[75] And the Ch'ing censor-in-chief argued that Cheng must be made to take his place under regular Ch'ing authority and administrative structures.

> He is prideful and ambitious, with the courage and heart of a hero, so obviously he must be constrained and controlled. Even if he comes to submission, he will harbor a "second heart" and in the future will become a great scourge in the Southeast. Now that he has gained a foothold in the Chang-Ch'üan and Hui-Ch'ao areas, he uses our land to rear his people and uses our revenues to supply his troops. Later this sort of arrogation will become even more flagrant.[76]

But the Manchu leadership was persuaded by Cheng Chih-lung to try again, this time employing as emissaries two of Ch'eng-kung's younger brothers with whom he always had been on close terms. So in August the Shun-chih emperor sent a sternly worded edict to Ch'eng-kung, admonishing him to be reasonable and straightforward, and warning him to make the wise decision soon or face the consequences. At the same time, the Ch'ing equivalent of a grand secretary was deputed to Fu-chou to negotiate another meeting with Cheng. The chief ambassador then cautiously went down to Ch'üan-chou; and at Cheng's earnest invitation certain emissaries, accompanied by Ch'eng-kung's brothers and stepmother, even more nervously returned to An-p'ing on October 26.[77]

There followed a month-long melodrama in which the Ch'ing side insisted that Ch'eng-kung symbolically adopt the Manchu coiffure *before* receiving the imperial proclamation of his new status, responsibilities, and privileges; whereas Cheng objected that by all reason he could make such a commitment only *after* talking to the court's representatives to ascertain more clearly (that is, to bargain more toughly over) what his new status would be. By happenstance, during this time Ch'eng-kung received a return emissary from the Yung-li court, as well as a request from Li Ting-kuo that he come to assist him in attacking Kuang-chou. Although Cheng naturally did not openly acknowledge these contacts or act on Li's appeal at that time, the Ch'ing side knew something of this and became even more suspicious. In general, they found plenty of reason to throw back Cheng's accusations against them of trickery and belligerency.[78]

When the Ch'ing officials showed signs of losing patience, Cheng wrote in his own hand saying, "I want to receive the proclamation, and I want to shave my head!" but protesting that they had treated neither him nor the matter of negotiation with the appropriate degree of seriousness and dignity. On the other hand, when Ch'eng-kung's brothers and some men who long had served Cheng Chih-lung came to him crying that if the peace process failed again, their lives and that of Chih-lung would be worth little, Ch'eng-kung replied that they were not necessarily doomed, that his mind already was made up, and that he wanted to hear nothing more about it. And when Cheng Hung-k'uei acceded to Chih-lung's entreaty that he speak to their nephew-and-son in the same vein, Ch'eng-kung replied, "The greater honor is in extinguishing all [concern for one's own] clan. I have planned this for a long time and my calculations cannot be altered now."[79] Convinced that Cheng was not sincere about coming allegiance, the Ch'ing representatives pulled out quickly from southern Fu-chien in the first week of November, 1654, and the complete failure of their mission subsequently was reported to Pei-ching.[80]

In a parting letter to his favorite brother, Ch'eng-kung again complained about the Ch'ing emissaries' lack of statesmanship, their precipitous insistence that he and his men shave their heads, and the inadequacy of four prefectures to support his forces.

> In general, it simply was that if the Ch'ing court trusted my word, then I would [become] a man of the Ch'ing; and if they did not, then I would [remain] a servant of the Ming. . . . Tigers and leopards that live in the deep hills are feared by all things. But those that [fall] into barred traps and wag their tails for mercy [thereafter] are controlled by their own sense of impotence. Phoenixes, though, soar thousands of feet high—far, far into the universe, wherever they want to go, escaping way beyond [the realm of] worldly custom. The [Manchus] have known my reputation and fought against me for a long time. How could [they think that I] would leave behind [the life of] a phoenix for [that of a caged] tiger or leopard?[81]

And in a letter for his father, Ch'eng-kung summed up his view of the whole matter:

> The peace discussions were not my idea in the first place, . . . and I did not expect that the Ch'ing suddenly would order me to be the Duke of Hai-ch'eng with one prefecture. But I felt obligated to hold back my soldiers to show good faith. Then the order about four prefectures arrived, so again I could not but show good faith by accepting their proclamation. But when I asked for a larger territory in which to place my several hundred thousand troops and make firm the basis for rehabilitation [of the province], I

somehow was said to be "speaking very contrarily and arrogantly making insatiable demands." Little did I think that the territory would not be expanded, and that even the four prefectures would become "a picture of a cookie" [i.e., something inviting but insubstantial]. They wanted to devour me as before. This you well knew and I always had suspected. Then suddenly the order to shave heads came down, and the hair of [the soldiers in] my three divisions stood on end! . . . [If] the Ch'ing court [expects to] gather in men of talent to firm up the border regions, then they should not be niggardly in giving land; and [if] I am to settle my generals and troops and bring peace to the people's lives, then I surely must have land. . . . Who in the world ever heard of a man who would declare himself to be a loyal subject before receiving lands, or shave his head before making such a declaration? . . . And who in the world ever heard of placing more confidence in a man's hair than in his heart? . . . Simply put, if the Ch'ing had been able to believe my words, then I would be a man of the Ch'ing; but since they have not believed my words, I [remain] a servant of the Ming. . . . In truth, they have been courteous to you on the surface, but underneath they regard you as a rare commodity . . . that they clearly want to use to constrain me—in one way and then in limitless ways. But I surely am not a man who can be constrained! Moreover, when you, my father, went to see the Manchu noblemen, you put yourself into a shell, and that you have survived until today is a great good fortune. But if by some small chance you should meet with misfortune, that would be a matter of Heaven and Fate. Your son then could only in mourning garb take revenge out of loyalty and filiality. According to reports, the [Ch'ing] viceroy and governor have notified the various prefectures to make military preparations to deal with my great army. . . . Now I can only sharpen my weapons and await them. What more is there to say? What more is there to say?[82]

Ch'eng-kung may not have been happy that circumstances prevented the reconciliation of his obligations to both parents and nation, but having chosen political loyalty over family loyalty, he truly had to "extinguish his concern" for relatives on the Ch'ing side.

Clearly Cheng Ch'eng-kung and the Ch'ing authorities held very different views of what it meant to enter into negotiations. Cheng had been willing to "talk peace" in the sense of seeking an accommodation to alleviate hostilities. But the Ch'ing aim had been to "summon and soothe," that is, to help Cheng feel good about surrendering. With such cross-purposes and such profound mutual suspicion, the two sides could approach but never consummate an agreement. As for the question of what Cheng Ch'eng-kung really wanted, it seems to have been some sort of semiautonomous or suzerain realm, on the pattern of Korea or Chiao-chih (extreme northwestern Vietnam), composed most ideally of the three maritime provinces of Fu-chien, Che-chiang, and Kuang-tung. Through such an arrangement he could have kept his hair and possibly even his identification with the Ming. Whether he envisioned such a realm as permanently at peace with the Ch'ing, or as a place to wait and plot for a Ming restoration, it is impossible to say.

In any case, the Ch'ing court regarded such an idea as totally outrageous. Naturally, after their second sparring match with Cheng Ch'eng-kung had ended unfavorably, the Ch'ing provincial officials were quick to memorialize their bitter "I-told-you-so's," cursing Cheng's perfidy and urging that the court launch a chastisement campaign against him.[83] Consequently, on January 23, 1655, the Manchu princeling Jidu was appointed Generalissimo to lead an army to exterminate Cheng Ch'eng-kung,[84] as the latter energetically renewed his attempts to completely take over Chang-chou and Ch'üan-chou prefectures.[85] Both sides were preparing now for a fight to the finish.

CHAPTER SEVEN

Last Stands, Last Defeats

MAJOR organized support for the Ming dynasty ended at almost the same time in two areas that could not have been farther removed from one another or more different in geographical milieu: the barbarous border region between southwestern Yün-nan and Burma, on the one hand, and the equally hazardous oceanic frontier region between southern Fu-chien and the island of T'ai-wan (then inhabited largely by aborigines), on the other. In the extreme Southwest, things went steadily from bad to worse for the Yung-li emperor, whereas in the extreme Southeast, Cheng Ch'eng-kung was defeated only after he struck some stunning blows to the Ch'ing in a heroic climax. But in both arenas, some basic Ming problems persisted. Although the Yung-li party eventually became very small, and the persons in it had to struggle together ever more desperately for survival, wrangling and rancor over the question of assistance for the emperor continued until the ghastly end of the court itself. And one important element in Cheng Ch'eng-kung's failure to extend the range of his movement into the heartland of China was the lack of integration between civil and military modes of operation.

The Manchus had begun planning in December of 1656 for a large-scale campaign into Kuei-chou and Yün-nan, which was to be launched the following spring. But no such campaign materialized until over a year later, one month after the surrender of Sun K'o-wang. Then, in January 1658, marching orders were given to three generalissimos for a joint penetration of Kuei-chou: Wu San-kuei was to proceed from southern Szu-ch'uan, Loto from southwestern Hu-kuang, and Jobtei from northwestern Kuang-hsi. In late June 1658, the armies of these three converged on the Kuei-yang area (only Wu having encountered significant resistance en route); and they subsequently met with the grand

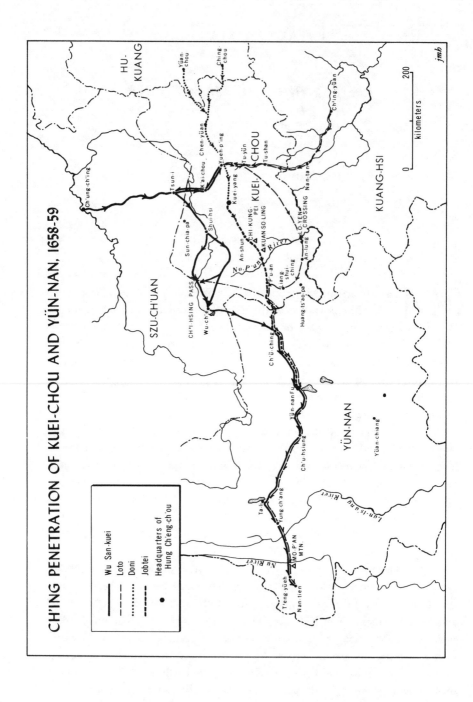

CH'ING PENETRATION OF KUEI-CHOU AND YÜN-NAN, 1658-59

Legend:

Wu San-kuei	
Loto	
Doni	
Jobtei	
Headquarters of Hung Ch'eng-ch'ou	●

HU-KUANG

Yüan-chou
Ching-chou

Ch'ung-ch'ing

Tsun-i
K'ai-chou
Chen-yüan
Yüeh-p'ing

Tu-yün
Tu-shan

KUEI-CHOU

KUEI-PEI
Shui-hsi
Kuei-yang
CHI KUNG

Ch'ing-yüan

Sun-chia-pa

An-shun
KUAN SO LING
O YEN CROSSING
Nan-tan

No Pan River
P'u-an
Liang
shui
ching
An-lung

SZU-CH'UAN

CH'I HSING PASS
Wu-ch'ê

KUANG-HSI

Chü-ching
Huang-ts'ao-pa

Yün-nan Fu

YÜN-NAN

Yüan-chiang

Ch'u-hsiung

Ta-li

Lan-ts'ang River

Yung-ch'ang

MO-P'AN MTN.

T'eng-yüeh
Nan-tien

Nu River

kilometers
0   200

jmb

overseer of all Ch'ing Southwestern affairs, Hung Ch'eng-ch'ou, at a military site near P'ing-yüeh to plan the next, more difficult stage of the campaign (see map 16).[1]

Meanwhile in Yün-nan Fu, the Yung-li court still was preoccupied with dispensing rewards and punishments, mending rifts, and "singing drunkenly in a leaky boat," floating in the wake of the previous year's triumph over Sun K'o-wang. And Li Ting-kuo, still not certain whom he could trust among Sun's former adherents, was fraught with disciplinary problems and inhibited in making troop deployments. Consequently, the Ming side was slow to field defenses against the Ch'ing in Kuei-chou, even though news of their presence there caused alarm at court.[2] In August, however, Li Ting-kuo designated three defensive areas in western Kuei-chou to guard the northern, central, and south-ern approaches from Kuei-yang to Yün-nan Fu. Li himself took the central position at Kuan-so-ling, to prevent any crossing of the North P'an River and to best oversee his commanders, among whom loyalties still were not firm.[3]

In late December and early January 1658–59, the Ch'ing moved again along three routes: Wu San-kuei, with the cooperation of certain aboriginal chieftains, was able to penetrate Ch'i-hsing Pass to the north; Doni (whose army had relieved that of Loto) took the center, seizing Kuan-so-ling and crossing the northern section of the North P'an River; while Jobtei swung to the south and executed the Lo-yen Crossing on the southern section of the North P'an River—all three aiming to converge at Ch'ü-ching in Yün-nan.[4] Li Ting-kuo registered some encouraging victories against the Ch'ing forward guard in this campaign, but as the full force of the enemy came to bear, his defenses began to disintegrate. Although he fought desperately to block the advances of both Doni and Jobtei, Li's situation steadily grew more bleak.[5]

So on August 7, as the Ch'ing went around or through Li's forces and crossed the border into eastern Yün-nan, the Yung-li court departed from Yün-nan Fu heading westward under the leadership of Mu T'ien-po, who had been militarily powerless since the rebellion of Sha Ting-chou, but who was the only member of the court who held influence among the native officials and chieftains through whose territories the court now would have to pass. At this point few wished to contemplate flight beyond China's southwestern borders, but it was hoped that a territorial line still might be drawn east of Ta-li. So as the imperial entourage (of about 4,000 persons) entered Yung-ch'ang on January 26, Li Ting-kuo and his strongest (though wounded) remaining general, Po Wen-hsüan, set up secondary lines of defense with about 20,000 men along the main route west of Yün-nan Fu, hoping to brake the next Ch'ing advance. Li then personally made an emotional visit to the court and, covered with shame, insisted that he be punished for his failings. The emperor had to go himself to Li's quarters and earnestly explain why he could not condemn such a loyal supporter before Li agreed to lift his self-indictment and carry on.[6]

On February 22, Wu San-kuei and Jobtei struck out from the Tien Lake region and defeated all opposition from there through the passes south of Ta-li. The Ch'ing forces then entered Yung-ch'ang on March 10 as the panic-stricken Yung-li party arrived in T'eng-yüeh, having been robbed repeatedly along the way by local toughs and its own escorting troops (the ladies long since had given away all their jewelry to support the armies, so now even several of the emperor's robes were stolen). There they lived encamped, with no white rice and only horseflesh for meat, not realizing how much worse things would become, as Li Ting-kuo prepared to make his last real stand against the Ch'ing along the tortuous trails of Mo-p'an Mountain, just west of the Nu River. There in mid-March Li's elaborate ambush belatedly was discovered by the Ch'ing vanguard, and a ferocious battle ensued, resulting in severe losses to both sides.[7]

Li previously had been at pains to persuade the reluctant emperor that, if defenses failed again, he should not surrender to the Ch'ing, making all Li's loyal efforts a waste, but should reside in Burma for one or two years "to observe what Heaven's mandate might be." So after the battle of Mo-p'an Mountain, as Li and his surviving men managed to escape southward toward the headwaters of the Salween River, the Yung-li party, plagued by mutinies among troops who refused to go any further, staggered breathlessly in great disarray through T'ung-pi Pass into Burmese territory in the third week of March.[8] The Ch'ing armies, on the other hand, having been weakened and unnerved by the Mo-p'an attack, and running short of provisions, merely scouted a short distance beyond T'eng-yüeh and did not pursue either the emperor or Li Ting-kuo before returning eastward.[9]

On the Burmese side of the border, the yung-li party of approximately 1,500, utterly destitute and already deserted by most of its escorting soldiers, was met by local officials who claimed that the simple people of that area would be afraid to come forth with essential supplies unless all the outsiders completely disarmed themselves. At this point a familiar threnody emerged again in the Yung-li story. That is the charge, repeatedly lodged by literati adherents of the court, that Ma Chi-hsiang (who formally had been appointed Chief Grand Secretary at Yün-nan Fu) monopolized the affairs of the emperor and, worse, was responsible for virtually every play-safe decision and compromising arrangement that led the emperor into situations that were even less favorable than before. Earlier Ma was said to have accommodated Sun K'o-wang to the point of encouraging his imperial pretensions and collaborating in Sun's persecution of the "Eighteen Gentlemen of An-lung." Then he was blamed in retrospect for the bad decision to enter Burma. And in this case, he was disparaged as the one who arbitrarily capitulated to the host officials' demands, which left the Yung-li party not only unarmed but "without so much as an inch of iron."[10] Subsequently, throughout the now minuscule court's ordeal in Burma, officials of the "Outer Court" found reason to criticize Ma Chi-hsiang for arrogating imperial powers to himself and leading the emperor to disaster—this in curious contrast to the memoir of a boy eunuch in the imperial household, which scarcely mentions Ma Chi-hsiang and generally portrays the emperor as making his own decisions.[11]

At the Burmese city of Bhamo, in the last week of March, the emperor with 646 members of his entourage boarded boats on the Irrawaddy River, while the remaining 900 or so followers set out by land southward, the two groups planning to meet later in the Burmese capital of Ava.[12] When the emperor's flotilla reached Htigyaing, however, the Burmese became threatening and obstructive. Claiming to need some verification of the party's identity, they asked questions about the protocol between Burma and China in late Ming times—questions that Ma Chi-hsiang, in his alleged ignorance of Ming institutions, was unable to answer—and they were not satisfied until they saw that the official seal of Duke Mu T'ien-po matched that on some documents they held from the Wan-li period.[13]

Fearing that they might be heading into an even less hospitable situation, several courtiers sought to take the emperor eastward to make contact with Li Ting-kuo in the upper Salween region. But this was blocked by Ma Chi-hsiang, who also is said to have written to a Chinese general in the Bhamo area, at the request of the Burmese, saying that the Yung-li emperor already had left for Fu-chien by sea and that he and other Chinese commanders should cease their incursions, lest their men and all the other Chinese in Burma be killed. Meanwhile, the overland group arrived in the Ava area unaware that the Burmese just had fought a bitter battle with Po Wen-hsüan, who had come seeking the Yung-li emperor. Perhaps because the Burmese took this party to be another Chinese renegade army, and perhaps simply for revenge, they attacked and slaughtered the group, killing over eight hundred while the remaining ninety or so escaped into the wilds, a few, it is said, eventually reaching Siam.[14]

But in the latter part of June 1659, the Burmese king sent two festive "dragon boats" to bring the smaller Yung-li party southward from Htigyaing, and they soon were settled at a site in Sagaing district across the river north of Ava. Accommodations were rustic—a large woven-grass dwelling with a bamboo fence for the emperor and his family, and do-it-yourself bamboo and wood housing for the rest—but the Burmese king had generous gifts presented very ceremoniously to the Yung-li emperor, and for the first time in months the harried followers of this Ming court in exile were able to relax and enjoy themselves a bit.[15]

The Chinese term for modern Burma, "Mien-tien," during the Ming dynasty denoted but one of several "barbarian" kingdoms and tribal states that existed within the geographical span of present-day Burma. In the Hung-wu and Yung-lo reigns, suzerainty had been established over these political entities by designating them as Ming "pacification offices" (but appointing no staffs), and by stipulating and receiving from them regular tributary missions. Since then relations among the various "Burmese" states and peoples had been as tumultuous as ever, and at one point the specific polity of Mien-tien had ceased even to exist. But by the middle of the sixteenth century, that state was reascendant, and in the Wan-li period Mien-tien's expansive campaigns to subjugate peoples to its north led to incursions across the loosely conceived border well into Yün-nan. With the weaker border states as pawns, attacks and counterattacks between Ming forces in Yün-nan and those of Mien-tien had marked the last three decades of the sixteenth century. By the turn of the seventeenth century, Mien-tien again was submissive to Chinese suzerain formalities, but relations were strained, and there had been no contact after the end of the Wan-li reign. In reality, the various states of upper Burma by this time had come to recognize Mien-tien as the dominant political power in their region and had accepted some administrative control from Ava, which was just beginning to function as the center of a protomodern national government.[16]

The current Burmese king, Pindale, weak and indecisive compared to his ground-breaking predecessor, had granted asylum to the Yung-li emperor on humanitarian grounds, but he was unprepared to deal with the trouble spawned by the Chinese military forces that fled into his country as the Ch'ing conquered Yün-nan. Such forces, mainly those of Li Ting-kuo and Po Wen-hsüan, not only caused considerable disruption and destruction to life and property in Burma's northeastern region, but also they threatened to rekindle latent hostilities against Mien-tien among outlying tribal peoples, such as the Shan.[17]

Worst of all, these forces approached Ava several times, separately and in joint campaigns from the spring of 1660 through the spring of 1661, demanding that the Yung-li emperor be released to them and thoroughly consternating the Burmese. Even if the Yung-li emperor were released, there was no assurance that he and his unruly supporters would or could leave Burmese soil voluntarily; and Ava, under Pindale, lacked the military might to drive them out. Ma Chi-hsiang complied with Burmese demands that imperial edicts be issued to send the marauders away. But Li and Po, who knew of previous official statements that the emperor had gone to the coast and out to sea, were even more angered and frustrated by this evidence that the court *was* in Ava, but for some reason was being kept from having contact with them. Mu T'ien-po and other members of the court plotted to kidnap the emperor and the heir-designate and take them to

Li Ting-kuo's camp. But this was discovered and an edict was issued (purportedly by Ma Chi-hsiang) to have some of the plotters seized and punished.[18]

The treatment accorded the Yung-li camp by the Burmese grew less hospitable as such armed incursions grew more distressing, and Mu T'ien-po was constrained to pay court to the Burmese king wearing white, knotting his hair, and going barefoot in the Burmese way. By midautumn of 1660, the court was in a state of utter destitution. Rice provisions from the Burmese had become meager, and every last valuable (including the jade imperial seal) was sacrificed to fend off starvation. Repeatedly under these circumstances, Ma Chi-hsiang was accused of arrogating to himself control over precious bits of sustenance and manipulating their distribution to his own advantage.[19]

But the court's fortunes were to plunge even deeper. In June of 1661 the exasperated Burmese council of state, the Hluttaw, deposed and executed Pindalè and placed on the throne his brother, Pye Min, a more vigorous leader who had won favor by taking initiatives to combat the intruders.[20] Shortly thereafter, all Yung-li officials were ordered to participate in a Buddhist investiture ceremony for the new king across the river in Ava proper, and at the same time to make new arrangements for the disposition of the court. Upon hearing this, Mu T'ien-po angrily charged the Burmese with being deceptive and unfeeling.

> What's more, [the status of] your place here as a pacification office originally was bestowed by my country. Now ruler and ministers have come as the Heavenly Court of the Superior Realm, but you have confined us here.... How is it that your king does not realize that his is the inferior realm? Now the August Emperor of the Heavenly Court has been here for three years. How contrary to reason it is that you show him no heartfelt concern, but [rather] practice this sort of treachery. You can go tell your king that the August Emperor of the Heavenly Court merely is following Heaven's command in coming as an ambassador to this lifeless place. Why should he take the trickery of you natives? Even though my ruler and [fellow] ministers currently are in straitened circumstances, I should think that your king would not dare to treat us discourteously. Bring on your million troops and thousand elephants! We, ruler and ministers, will simply follow Heaven's command in going to our deaths; but afterward others surely will come to settle accounts with you![21]

The next day, August 13, all the Yung-li officials were taken to the Burmese court in an indignant mood, and there they were slaughtered to the last man. Meanwhile, Burmese cavalry entered the Yung-li village in Sagaing and killed every able-bodied male over the age of fifteen, including those in the imperial household. Surviving this massacre were only about 340 widows and orphans of the hapless officials; and in the imperial household, only the emperor, empress dowager, empress, heir, two princesses, a few boy eunuchs, and one sick and

crippled guard were left alive. The survivors all were herded away from the scene
of carnage and kept confined for three days with no food, water, or sanitary
facilities. Then, in the gathering cold of autumn, they were allowed to return to
their former dwellings but still were provided with no food. The Burmese king
eventually sent gifts and apologies to the Yung-li emperor; but the latter,
surrounded by sick and dying women, just regarded those gestures in bitter
silence.[22] At that point he probably did not feel relieved that, institutionally
speaking, the problem of assistance for the emperor finally had been resolved.

These measures may have been more than a show of determination by the
new Burmese monarch; they also may have been preparatory to complying with
demands from the Ch'ing. In Yün-nan, under the general direction of Hung
Ch'eng-ch'ou, the Ch'ing had pursued the policies of gradual consolidation that
characterized Hung's career: restoring agriculture, learning to manage the native
officials, stationing troops in strategic areas, subduing recalcitrant aboriginal
chieftains and remnants of the rebel armies, and hoping that defeat, the hunger of
winter, and the malaria of summer eventually would disintegrate Li Ting-kuo's
forces.[23] At the same time, with the approval of the Ch'ing court, Hung had
begun to exert diplomatic pressure on the Burmese. In a proclamation to the
"soldiers, common people, and officials of the Mien-tien Pacification Office,"
Hung stated the Chinese position in midautumn of 1659:

> The cycle of the Ming came to an end, and crude bandits swarmed like
> bees.... [But now, after extermination by the long-suffering Ch'ing] only
> Li Ting-kuo, that bastard son of the rebel [Chang] Hsien-[chung], is left.
> Knowing that his awful crimes had incensed Heaven, the gods, and man
> alike, he scurried like a rat into Yün-nan and falsely used the illegitimate
> Yung-li reign title to bewitch the ignorant people. They do not consider
> that Ting-kuo, having ruined the country of the Ming at its height, now
> hardly could [wish to] support that scion of the Ming imperial house in his
> long trek, but merely wants to control [the Yung-li emperor to increase] his
> own power,...recklessly spread his cruelties, and poison all living
> things....If you can capture [Li] and turn him over to us, then it will be
> reported to the [Shun-chih] emperor, whose fine rewards and titles will be
> passed on to your sons and grandsons. But if you are not attentive to the
> trend of the times and, oblivious to this crucial matter, conceal that criminal
> against China, then not only will you deliver yourself into the jaws of tigers
> and wolves, but also, in pursuing their task of driving out evil, our troops
> necessarily will track [Li] down for extirpation, sweeping directly into your
> swampy region. At that time it will be hard to distinguish rock from jade,
> and you belatedly will regret [your error]. We have heard that Yung-li has
> followed Mu T'ien-po inside the boundaries of Mien-tien, and we think
> that he has been constrained and deceived into it against his will. When our
> Ch'ing emperor has eradicated Li Tzu-ch'eng, Chang Hsien-chung, and Li
> Ting-kuo, taking the revenge of countless ages for the Ming, if Yung-li can

feel [gratitude] for this virtuous [service] and can follow [Heaven's] command, then he surely will be treated by the emperor as in antiquity [when the Chou respectfully enfeoffed descendants of the Hsia and Shang royal lines] and receive beneficence without end....[24]

But Hung Ch'eng-ch'ou would not be present to see the result of this message to the Burmese. In the following month, at the age of sixty-six and having gone almost completely blind through years of extraordinarily conscientious service to the Ch'ing, he finally was allowed to retire. As Hung had suggested, all Yün-nan affairs then were placed in the hands of the Prince Who Pacifies the West, Wu San-kuei.[25]

Wu and his Manchu compatriots had been battling especially hard in the Yüan-chiang area of southern Yün-nan against native officials who had harbored some of Li Ting-kuo's family and who, at Li's instigation, had raised resistance forces against the Ch'ing.[26] Partly because of this hard experience, Wu was less of a gradualist than Hung Ch'eng-ch'ou had been; and in May of 1660 he memorialized arguing that Yün-nan would never have a day's respite from aboriginal rebelliousness, and that Ch'ing soldiers would face a perpetual seesaw struggle with pro-Ming guerrillas so long as Li Ting-kuo, Po Wen-hsüan, and the Yung-li emperor remained across the southwestern border in Burma. Provisioning the Ch'ing armies in Yün-nan already had become a critical problem. Wu further argued, therefore, that prolonged border hostilities would be unsustainable, and that it would be better to launch a final campaign to clear up the trouble as soon as possible.[27]

This proposal elicited extensive debate among Ch'ing officials. The government's finances in general were undergoing severe strain, and costs in the Southwestern campaign already had been colossal. Indeed, the Ministry of Revenue pointed out in alarm that military expenditures on Yün-nan in 1660 were running to 9 million taels—that is, 250,000 taels more than the anticipated military revenues from the whole country for that year! Moreover, officials in the maritime Southeast complained that they needed increased funding, too, in order to deal with Cheng Ch'eng-kung, and that their region generated a lot of revenue in return, whereas Yün-nan only consumed. Basically, the Ch'ing court seems to have acknowledged the need for a Burma campaign but, figuratively speaking, was not willing to write Wu a blank check for it. Various proposals were considered for pooling the resources of Pei-ching and Yün-nan Fu, both sides driving hard bargains, until September 22, 1660, when the Manchu duke Aisinga was appointed Generalissimo to join with Wu San-kuei in pursuing Li Ting-kuo beyond the Burmese border.[28]

In November of that year Wu reorganized his armies, and in March of 1661 the offensive got under way. Proceeding across the Lan-ts'ang River into the territory in northeastern Burma called Mu-pang, the Ch'ing drove a wedge between Li Ting-kuo, who escaped eastward, and Po Wen-hsüan, who retreated northward but subsequently was forced to surrender at Ch'a Mountain. And in late December and early January, 1661–62, they continued on toward Ava, sending a warning in advance to the Burmese king that if Yung-li were not turned over, they would attack the capital city.[29] The Yung-li emperor must have been aware of Wu San-kuei's approach, for during this time he sent a letter to Wu citing the honors he had received from the Ming, commending his past righteous action in defeating the rebels who had forced the death of the Ch'ung-chen emperor, but then wondering rhetorically why it was that Wu went on to turn his sword against the Ming. The emperor said that, although in the Southwest he and Li Ting-kuo had declared nonbelligerency, nevertheless,

> ... [you], General, forgot the great virtue in ruler-minister [relations] and, hoping to earn handsome rewards for merit in establishing [the Ch'ing], led troops into Yün-nan and overturned my nest. Because of this, I crossed over into the wilds and temporarily relied on the Burmese people to strengthen my [protective] fence. These hills and streams are so remote, no one has been happy enough to chat or laugh, and we only have sat and grown more sorrowful. Having already lost the rivers and mountains that my ancestors held, I fecklessly have sustained my insignificant life in this aboriginal land while feeling that I would be fortunate to die. Now [you], General, have shirked no danger and requested orders to come this long distance, leading several hundred thousand men in relentless pursuit of this solitary sojourner. Why is your view of the world so small that in all the space of heaven and earth you cannot tolerate the existence of this one person? Can it be that, having been enfeoffed as a prince, you still want to increase your merit by destroying me? ... Now my troops have dwindled and become weak. Standing here all alone, my minuscule life hangs in your hands. If you must have my head and neck, then I will not mind that, even if my body and bones are pulverized and my blood spatters the grassy weeds. I dare not hope that calamity might turn to good fortune and that you might cast off one square inch of ground to preserve [the ancient principle of respectfully providing lands to fallen royal lines]. But if perchance I could be allowed to live in peace and, like the grass and trees, be soaked in the rain and dew of [your new] sacred dynasty, then even if I had millions upon billions of people [as followers], I would entrust them [all] to you.[30]

At this point Wu San-kuei would have been foolish to be swayed by such appeals. And in any case, he did not have the authority to decide the eventual disposition of this piteous but problematical man and his now teenaged son.

Wu and Aisinga arrived in the vicinity of Ava on January 20. They were received courteously by the Burmese and immediately sent a special guard of one hundred men to Ava proper to take possession of what remained of the Yung-li

party.[31] That night the emperor and his family were brought in old carriages—
the rest of the women and children following on foot—from their village in
Sagaing to the shore of the Irrawaddy opposite Ava, where they were put in
boats and taken across the river.

> My emperor's asthmatic illness had flared again, and the empresses were full
> of anxiety. In the light of dawn they told [me], a boy eunuch named Yang
> Te-tse, to poke my head out the cabin door and take a look. I saw a lot of
> horses and men milling around, but no identifying banners. I heard the
> name of only Regional Commander Wang Hui and saw several large
> palanquins waiting on the shore.... [When she heard this] the empress
> dowager said, "These surely are Ch'ing soldiers. Otherwise Wang Hui
> would have come to greet us right away, rather than dallying around
> outside the boat."... I then told the empresses just to be calm, because in
> my opinion, if the [barbarian Manchus] already had received the world that
> had been the Ming's, then they naturally must treat people with decorum
> and conduct affairs of the nation and the Son of Heaven with propriety.

About eight o'clock that morning over a hundred men, none carrying any
weapons, came to the prow of the emperor's boat, and Wang Hui boarded,
saying he had been sent by Li Ting-kuo. But when the Yung-li emperor asked
him about news from Li, Wang could not reply at all, and the emperor knew
then that he actually was a representative of Wu San-kuei.

> My emperor then said in a loud voice, "What wrong has Our Great Ming
> done to you that makes you determined to trap the whole Ming court in
> one net? In my view, today you and the others [i.e., Wu San-kuei's
> organization] may be rewarded with a princedom for your merit in killing
> my mother and son; but in the future, to the [disgrace of] your ancestors,
> you will become criminals whose names will be vilified for a thousand
> years!"... And he went on to curse even Wu San-kuei. At that time the
> emperor's dragon visage [showed] great anger, as he pointed his finger at
> Wang Hui, berating him severely. "You cowardly character. Get out of
> here! This is a place where loyal ministers and fine generals kneel. How do
> *you* have the cheek to kneel here? Haven't you gone yet?!" Wang Hui,
> having been thoroughly shamed by this tongue-lashing from the emperor,
> and being advanced in years, then lost his footing as he got off the boat and
> fell down on the riverbank. A bunch of people dashed to lift him up and ask
> [what was wrong], but he already was speechless.[32]

Before long Generalissimo Aisinga himself boarded the emperor's boat and
addressed him very politely. "Today I heard that the sagely ruler of the Great
Ming had arrived, so I have come especially to see you and wish you 'peace for
ten-thousand years.'" The emperor replied, "I am a fallen nation's Son of
Heaven. Why does the Generalissimo [accord me] such great ceremony?"

Aisinga went on to compliment the Yung-li emperor on his truly imperial physiognomy, which everyone had heard about, but which he had not believed until seeing it for himself. And he further explained that the whole situation was a matter of Heaven's command and had nothing to do with them personally. "We received an edict dispatching us to invite Your Augustness to accompany us in your sacred chariot to the capital and together with [our ruler] enjoy [reigning over] the world. Moreover, we were told absolutely to alarm you in no way. Our ruler still wants personally to meet with you and to see your dragon form." [33]

One week later the Ch'ing task force, with the Yung-li emperor in custody, departed from Ava for the long journey back to Yün-nan Fu. As they arrived there three months later, the emperor's asthma took a very bad turn, and he literally was living from breath to breath. [34] But even less auspicious things were afoot. Perhaps it was because the Shun-chih emperor had died the year before, and the tough group of regents who then were acting for the new K'ang-hsi emperor, in his minority, sought to correct what they saw as some overly lenient policies of the previous reign. [35] Perhaps it was because, as several hearsay accounts claim, the presence of the Yung-li emperor was causing serious restlessness among the Ch'ing troops in Yün-nan, and the prospect of transporting him all the way across China to Pei-ching presented security problems that the Manchus preferred to avoid. In any case, in late May, 1662, the last claimant to the Ming throne and his son were executed in Yün-nan Fu, probably by strangulation. (The widowed empress later committed suicide in Pei-ching, but the empress dowager lived on to the age of ninety-one.) Tellingly, just one month later Wu San-kuei was recommended for elevation to Prince of the First Degree. [36]

Li Ting-kuo had been dismissed by Wu San-kuei as no longer worth pursuing. After being beaten by the Ch'ing in their drive through northeastern Burma, Li's army had entered its final stages of dissolution. As Li grew weak from despondency and illness, especially after hearing of the Yung-li emperor's capture, even his chief lieutenants began to defect, taking along members of Li's family as tokens of submission to the Ch'ing. Probably in August 1662, Li Ting-kuo died near the present-day border between Yün-nan and extreme north-western Laos. [37]

In the extreme Southeast, by contrast, every encounter with the Ch'ing, and every report or rumor about their fortunes in other regions of China, had reinforced Cheng Ch'eng-kung's perception of their growing weakness and ineffectuality. After "negotiations" broke down finally in the winter of 1655–56, Cheng sent a virtual manifesto to the Fu-chien provincial governor restating his complaints about that process and vowing to make the Ch'ing rue not having dealt on his terms.

Let the Ch'ing dynasty take the pick of their feeble, flock-of-crows eight-banner [forces] and transfer their worn-out soldiers from southern Che-chiang. I know already that their caliber will be no better than [what I have seen already]. I am just [sitting here] making military preparations. Who will have difficulty and who will have ease, who will win and who will lose—these [questions] have foregone conclusions. Moreover, the recent trend of events for the Ch'ing has differed increasingly from what it was ten years ago.

Regarding human affairs under the Ch'ing dynasty: Shen-hsi is the "head" of its world. But now the western [Moslem] barbarians have entered [the Lan-chou area*] and plan to cut away all of Shen-hsi. If the Ch'ing court allows this, then it will immediately break apart; but if it contests this, then the dynasty will collapse forthwith [anyway], its head having been severed and mutilated in this way. Hu-kuang is the "heart and abdomen" of the [Ch'ing] world. Previously your most elite forces, well trained and numerous, were completely annihilated [there]; so it is very fitting that Hung Ch'eng-ch'ou's big flock of crows also is being defeated, your heart and abdomen also having been cut out and mutilated like this. Kuang-tung constitutes the "hands and feet" of the [Ch'ing] world. But now the Prince of Hsi-ning [Li Ting-kuo] has attacked and any day now will penetrate Chao-ch'ing and Kuang-chou City; and the armored reinforcements that the Ch'ing court has sent in response number less than 3,000. This is like driving dogs and sheep into a pride of tigers just to fill their stomachs a bit—your hands and feet having been severed and mutilated to this extent.

Regarding natural occurrences under the Ch'ing dynasty: For several years now the common people north of the Yellow River have been consigned to a flooded country; and those in Chiang-nan mostly have become specters of drought. Rivers overflow, the earth quakes, and strange phenomena appear all year round. Mountains collapse and rivers run dry, showing signs that fit exactly with the miseries that attended the solar eclipses and stellar irregularities of the barbarian Yüan [dynasty]. As men of sagely wisdom have said, when a country is about to be lost, there always are supernatural indications. And such words clearly have proven true already [for the Ch'ing]....

For these reasons [I plan to] advance both northward and southward, driving all my land and naval forces, pinning down one place and then approaching from another side. Four regions will see my troops: When they reach [the Su-chou area], it will be laid waste; when they enter Che-chiang, it will be smashed; when they get to Kuang-tung, it will be broken; and when they move Fu-chien, it will [wag like a] tail. Understand that this is not [just] my boastful talk, but truly is a necessary development under these circumstances. Not only this. The revenues for [China] north of the Yang-tzu all are gotten from the Southeastern salt tax, and the Grand Canal transport [thus] is crucial to the life of the nation. My troops in particular will gain control of the Yang-tzu and Huai [effluences, and then] not only

* Kan-su Province, which later included Lan-chou, had not yet been created.

will South and North be cut apart, but also we will watch [your capital region] die straightway![38]

In reply, the governor said that all Cheng's arrogant claptrap about "Heaven, the times, and human affairs" had been nauseating, that Cheng had failed to see the broad scope and long range of the Ch'ing consolidation, in which the matters he mentioned were just minor problems to be cleared up, and that belief in omens and the supernatural significance of natural disasters was just "the talk of young boys."

> Crouching there on the seashore, you cannot see or hear very far. [So you have believed] one or two vagrant characters who like to stir things up and who fabricate stories to attract attention. [You are] like people who gather around the well and marketplace in rustic hill villages, exclaiming in astonishment at every rumor, not realizing that they are without substance.... You mistakenly have thought that your poor, seaswept, isolated islands actually are a ten-thousand-mile-long Great Wall, and that your ships and oars can be used as precious amulets [to guarantee] long life. As your attitude grows more vainglorious and your thoughts more extravagant, they hit even farther off the mark.[39]

For the time being, however, such words fell on deaf ears. Cheng already was busily engaged again in launching attacks and effecting other stratagems to seize major cities as well as small locales throughout coastal Ch'ao-chou, Chang-chou, and Ch'üan-chou prefectures.[40] At the same time he openly acknowledged receipt of the title Prince of Yen-p'ing from the Yung-li court and renamed Chung-tso-so on Hsia-men as Szu-Ming ("Think Ming") Prefecture. Besides expanding his personal guard and drilling it with new, more sophisticated methods, Cheng also, with his discretionary powers, instituted new categories of functionaries to handle surveillance, communications, and judicial matters, and to tighten up troop and logistical supervision. Eventually this might have evolved into a new civil bureaucracy, but under Cheng all men were employed wholly in military tasks.[41] For instance, troop supervisors were just that, at Cheng's personal behest, and not agents of a civil Censorate; and revenue officials actually were quartermasters who did not report to any Ministry of Revenues and had no other business than keeping track of military supplies and rewards. In seizing territories, Cheng seems to have been solely interested in obtaining sustenance for his military organization, and he never tried to institute any governmental administration for the general, largely agrarian populace.

The size, discipline, and elaborateness of Cheng's organization increased at this time commensurately with his ambitions, as did the sternness of his temperament. Literally whipping his units into shape, Cheng displayed with renewed intensity his obsession with unfailing success and unwavering obedience.

Throughout his career, the unreasonable severity with which he punished even minor infractions, regardless of the offender's rank or personal relation to himself, led to defections that unnecessarily weakened his movement and in some cases proved especially damaging to his interests. But for now, Cheng was riding high, his core Fu-chien forces numbering well over 100,000.[42]

The initial Ch'ing response to all this was threefold: First, in the capital, more ominous restrictions were placed on Cheng Chih-lung, who now had become more of a liability than an asset to the Ch'ing. It proved easy to charge that he and his household illicitly had been in contact with the enemy, and to argue that continued cordial treatment of them in Pei-ching would only encourage Cheng Ch'eng-kung to make more trouble, since he apparently thought that he would be handled delicately so long as his father and other family members were held in respect by the Ch'ing. By the end of 1656 Chih-lung had been arrested and incarcerated; but in response to his further appeals, Ch'eng-kung showed no sympathy, saying that his father had "cast himself into the tiger's mouth," and reiterating both his low estimation of the Ch'ing and his determination to remain outside their control.[43] Second, in the maritime provinces, the Ch'ing instituted their first prohibitions on trade with the "pirates," while also enhancing inducements for members of Cheng's organization to defect.[44] These were the first steps in what became, over several years' time, an increasingly successful dual policy of cutting off contact between people on the mainland and Cheng's men, so long as they remained rebellious, while welcoming them to surrender with demonstrations of good faith. Third, as Cheng anticipated, a chastisement campaign was launched against him for his stubborn refusal to be "summoned and soothed."

In spite of tremendous difficulties for the Ch'ing in supplying, reinforcing, and rotating units in and out of Fu-chien,[45] early in 1655 Manchu imperial clansman Jidu was appointed Generalissimo to lead the "extermination" of Cheng Ch'eng-kung. And for his part, from midsummer into the fall of that year, Cheng ordered torn down most of the city walls and other fortifications in mainland districts adjacent to Hsia-men, which itself was evacuated, thus delimiting a combat zone.[46] Jidu did not arrive in southern Fu-chien until October, his forces exhausted from the long journey. His offer of "forgiveness of sins" was rejected as "farcical" by the contemptuous Cheng Ch'eng-kung, and hostilities became inevitable. But not until May 9, 1656, was Jidu able to mount an assault on Chin-men, moving infantry through T'ung-an and sending a naval fleet from Ch'üan-chou. The ensuing battle, which was interrupted by a fierce storm, ended in the almost complete destruction of the dearly husbanded Ch'ing fleet and confirmed Cheng's view that the Ch'ing grip was infirm and slipping.[47]

In fact, by this time Cheng already had begun the first stage of his vaunted "northward campaign" into the Yang-tzu region, which he had been thinking about seriously since the spring of 1653, before "negotiations" with the Ch'ing intervened. For several reasons, he now was more determined than ever to carry out this plan. Most basic, perhaps, was Cheng's self-image as a man destined for national, not just regional, leadership and his image of the Ch'ing as a waning force in the country. But the increasing remoteness and isolation of the Yung-li court in the far Southwest made it imperative that the torch be kept burning near the more populous and politically important regions, if the fall of the Ch'ing were to be followed by a restoration of the Ming.[48] Moreover, the experience of negotiating with the Ch'ing had quickened Cheng's ambition for a northward campaign in three ways: First, Cheng stockpiles of provisions and war materiel had grown considerably during the moratorium on fighting, so in 1655 Cheng was better prepared materially to carry out a major campaign than he had been before. Second, Cheng knew that the Ch'ing would do their best to punish him in Fu-chien after their attempts to co-opt him had come to naught, and by striking at Che-chiang and Nan Chih-li he hoped to retard the movement of Ch'ing forces southward. Third, as is apparent from his statements quoted above, and others, he was determined to show the Ch'ing how truly formidable he could be and to make them regret having slighted him.

Actually, "the" northward campaign was not a single drive, but rather a series of halting, interrupted efforts which fall into four stages (again, see map 15):[49]

1. *Chou-shan and northeastern Fu-chien* from March 1655 to April 1657. Even before his victory over Jidu, Cheng Ch'eng-kung had assigned one of his best Fu-chien naval commanders to accompany Chang Ming-chen, the most experienced of his admirals in the more northerly waters, to probe the "heartland" of the Ch'ing by attacking coastal installations in Che-chiang and Nan Chih-li. This flotilla (of 5–6,000 ships with 60–70,000 men) had encountered stormy weather, however, and the expedition had stopped with the restoration of Chou-shan Island to Ming control on November 25, 1655.[50] To follow up on this advance action, to retaliate and recoup losses after the Ch'ing seized his main storage depot in Hai-ch'eng in August of 1656, and to put pressure on the provincial capital, Cheng then personally led a campaign with several thousand ships to coastal Fu-chou Prefecture in the fall of 1656, during which Cheng forces gained complete control of the Min River effluence.[51] And in the late fall and winter he moved further northward into coastal Fu-ning Prefecture, where, in February of 1657, Cheng troops annihilated a crack Ch'ing counterforce and killed in battle three renowned Ch'ing lieutenant-generals.[52]

The ease of these accomplishments certainly reinforced Cheng Ch'eng-kung's perception of Ch'ing incompetence and his determination to attack Chiang-nan. But things had continued to go awry farther north. Chang Ming-chen had died on Chou-shan in January of 1656; and then in mid-October of that year the other leading commanders from the former navy of Regent Lu either surrendered or were killed when the Ch'ing reconquered Chou-shan (which then was called a "useless place beyond the seas," devastated, evacuated, and not held).[53] So there remained no prominent figures to lead the way for Cheng through the unfamiliar waters north of Hang-chou Bay. Consequently, in the spring of 1657, while retaining his bases in northeastern Fu-chien, Cheng returned to Hsia-men and closed the first abortive phase of his northward campaign.[54]

2. *T'ai-chou Prefecture, Che-chiang,* in the autumn of 1657. After raiding Hsing-hua in southern Fu-chien for provisions in August of this year, Cheng sailed directly northward to enter the mouth of the Ling River in Che-chiang, first deactivating Ch'ing garrisons near the sea and then occupying the T'ai-chou prefectural seat on October 3.[55] But this time trouble cropped up to Cheng's south. By employing some extraordinary tactics, the Ch'ing in Fu-chou Prefecture managed to regain from Cheng's commanders the garrison town of Min-an, which guarded the mouth of the Min River and was the key position for Cheng's forces in northern Fu-chien. Cheng rushed there in an attempt to save the situation, but having arrived too late, he returned to Hsia-men and disbanded his expeditionary forces for the winter.[56] The following March, however, Cheng began a vigorous new training program, reorganized and strengthened his personal guard, and first created units of his famous "iron men," that is, of especially strong fighters who could bear the weight of being clothed in tunics made of iron plates.[57]

3. *Coastal southeastern Che-chiang,* June 1658 to June 1659. From the parting ceremonies on Hsia-men and Cheng's haranguing of his troops upon their embarkation, it was evident that this time Cheng intended to go all the way and not return for a very long time. To gather enough supplies for a seven-month drive, Cheng first invaded Wen-chou Prefecture, traveling overland across the border from Sha-ch'eng on the tip of northeastern Fu-chien.[58] Cheng then took his fleet to Chou-shan for more training exercises, and one month later they proceeded directly northward destined for Ch'ung-ming. As the fleet stopped midway among the Yang-shan islands, however, it was struck by an especially violent typhoon, resulting in disastrous losses. Six of Cheng's concubines and three of his sons, among 231 members of his household, drowned as their ship was destroyed by the three-day tempest; and of the luckier ones who were blown ashore on the mainland, the Ch'ing captured over 900. Cheng's men—as superstitious as any sailors—were seriously demoralized by this calamity. So

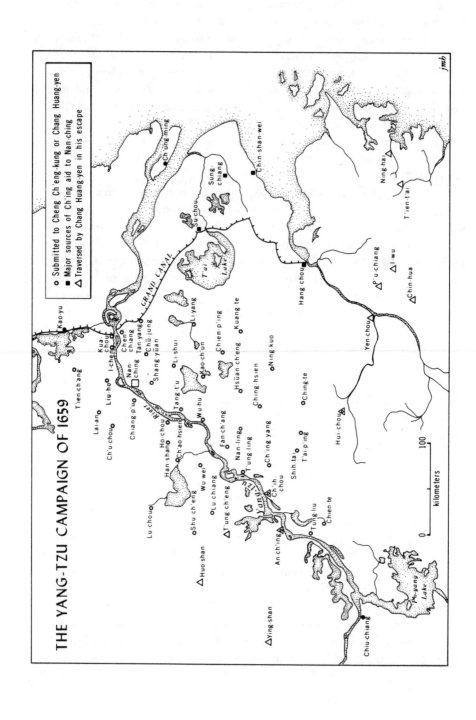

THE YANG-TZU CAMPAIGN OF 1659

Legend:
- ○ Submitted to Cheng Ch'eng-kung or Chang Huang-yen
- ■ Major sources of Ch'ing aid to Nan-ching
- △ Traversed by Chang Huang-yen in his escape

Map labels:
Ch'ung-ming, Sung-chiang, Su-chou, Chin-shan-wei, T'ai Lake, Hang-chou, Ning-hai, T'ien-t'ai, I-wu, P'u-chiang, Chin-hua, Yen-chou, GRAND CANAL, Kao-yu, Tien-ch'ang, Kua-chou, Liu-ho, I-cheng, Chen-chiang, Tan-yang, Chü-jung, Shang-yüan, Li-shui, Li-yang, Chien-p'ing, Kuang-te, Nan-ching, Chiang-p'u, Tang-t'u, Kao-ch'un, Hsüan-ch'eng, Ning-kuo, Lai-an, Chu-chou, Han-shan, Ho-chou, Chao-hsien, Wu-hu, Fan-ch'ang, Ch'ing-hsien, Lu-chou, Wu-wei, Nan-ling, Tung-ling, Ch'ing-yang, Ch'ing-te, Hui-chou, Shu-ch'eng, Lu-chiang, T'ung-ch'eng, Ch'ih-chou, Shih-t'a, T'ai-p'ing, Huo-shan, Ying-shan, An-ch'ing, T'ung-liu, Chien-te, Ch'iu-chiang, P'o-yang Lake, Yang-tzu River

0 ___ 100 kilometers

jmb

Cheng permitted the surviving portion of his fleet, still consisting of several thousand ships with well over 100,000 men, to return first to Chou-shan and then to T'ai-chou Prefecture to recover and reassess.[59] Cheng himself then occupied a garrison site at the mouth of the Ou River near Wen-chou City on December 1, 1658, and dispersed the various commands to spend the winter in numerous enclaves along the coast of northeastern Fu-chien and southeastern Che-chiang. In spite of Cheng's vulnerability at this time, the Ch'ing failed to dislodge him from Wen-chou early in 1659, and he was able to maintain his headquarters there until June of that year.[60]

4. *The Yang-tzu delta region*, June through September 1659 (see map 17). The climax of Cheng Ch'eng-kung's resistance career began with an invasion of Ning-po Prefecture via Ting-hai to further add men, ships, and supplies for the bigger task ahead, and to weaken the Ch'ing capacity to threaten Cheng's rear or block his route of retreat.[61] Then, after some additional training sessions on the nearby offshore islands, Cheng's fleet departed a second time for Ch'ung-ming and encamped on the notorious sandbars to the south of that island on July 7. Strictly restraining his men from their usual pillaging, Cheng kept his fleet in the broad outer mouth of the Yang-tzu for the rest of this month, allowing some foraging for such necessities as firewood but no attacks on urban centers to the more populous southern side of the effluence.[62]

Since Cheng ordinarily was quite secretive about his military plans and expeditionary destinations, it is significant that he at no point sought to make his Yang-tzu campaign a surprise to the enemy. Since 1655 he had told the Ch'ing flatly that he intended to attack the Nan-ching region. Then he had given them early warning by moving on Ning-po. Now he delayed three weeks before proceeding upriver (contacting potential defectors in the Ch'ing military ranks and probably gathering intelligence about conditions inland); at subsequent junctures he also adopted the slower course of action, seemingly unconcerned that the Ch'ing would be given time to amass their defense forces. The reason for this appears to be that the overconfident Cheng Ch'eng-kung wanted a maximally large battle so that he could win a maximally large victory and thus produce a correspondingly great psychological effect among the Han people and the Manchu leaders. This strategy was wholly consistent with his previous pattern in subduing smaller areas, that is, one of conserving manpower for a few key successes that would induce the enemy to capitulate. By overwhelming Kua-chou and Chen-chiang, he hoped that Nan-ching would be shaken into surrendering; failing that, once Nan-ching were taken by force, then the Ch'ing court in Pei-ching, having been dealt a dizzying blow, would not be able to maintain its footing.

In applying this strategy to Chiang-nan, however, Cheng overplayed his hand. For one thing, Ch'ing control in other parts of the country was not crumbling, as he imagined. Under any circumstances he would have found the Nan-ching region to be several times more heavily garrisoned than the coastal prefectures in which he had formed his opinion of Ch'ing capabilities. Moreover, repeated threats to the Yang-tzu delta area by Chang Ming-chen and others under Cheng's command in recent years had chastened the Ch'ing leadership and given them useful experience in defending the mouth of the Yang-tzu as a point of ingress to Chiang-nan. Garrison forces had been strengthened and a number of special measures had been taken—such as stretching a long cable across midchannel and placing fortified cannon barges at either end where ships, thus, were forced to sail—to prevent enemy navies from penetrating past Chen-chiang.[63] And Cheng had arrived late in another respect, too. If he had been able to carry out this phase of the northward campaign as he originally planned one year earlier, when Manchu forces were heavily committed to assist the invasion and pacification of the Southwest, then things might have been easier for him. But by the time Cheng arrived in the summer of 1659, Manchu units that previously had been dispatched to Kuei-chou and Hu-kuang already had returned, or were just returning, to Nan-ching.[64]

What is more, the pervasive intelligence network that always had served Cheng so well in the Southeastern maritime zone simply did not exist in Chiang-nan. And this factor, added to the geographical unfamiliarity of the region, caused Cheng's men to be ill at ease on this campaign, despite their thorough training and overwhelming numerical superiority. As mentioned above, all the leading commanders from Regent Lu's navy who were intimately familiar with the Yang-tzu effluence had already died or been killed. Consequently, for this stage of the campaign Cheng chose as one of his chief lieutenants a man of scholarly background who for several years had served as an aide-de-camp to the now deceased Chang Ming-chen. Steeped in the "righteous" tradition of Eastern Che-chiang, Chang Huang-yen had been a charter member of the Lu regime and since the fall of Shao-hsing had been an indefatigable supporter of the Ming cause, becoming involved in virtually every aspect of the coastal resistance.[65] In particular, he had accompanied Chang Ming-chen in three previous penetrations of the Yang-tzu mouth. So when Cheng finally proceeded into the channel of the Yang-tzu proper, Chang Huang-yen took the lead, and from this resulted the last significant civil-military disjunction in the history of the Ming.

For three days, from July 31 through August 2, 1659, Cheng Ch'eng-kung gathered forces from 2,300 ships on Chiao-shan in the middle of the Yang-tzu channel and conducted solemn ceremonies to impress the Ch'ing. The first day, in red uniforms, they sacrificed to Heaven; the second day, in black, they honored Earth; the third day, in white, they made obeisances to the Great

Ancestor of the Ming, Chu Yüan-chang.[66] And for the occasion, Cheng himself even composed a poem:

> In mourning garb I approach this stream and vow to
>   extinguish the [barbarous] Hu.
> A hundred thousand heroic troops have the stuff to
>   swallow the [region of] Wu.
> Let us see if my whip can lash across [this,] nature's
>   moat.
> I cannot believe that the Central Plain is not [still]
>   surnamed Chu.[67]

With tremendous fortitude, Chang Huang-yen then led his units to break through the midchannel "river-rolling dragon" and knock out several of the offshore cannon barges, thus enabling other Cheng forces to capture Kua-chou on August 4 and to block Ch'ing troop movements and official communications from that point northward along the Grand Canal. Chang then took a light naval unit to show the Ming flag upstream around Nan-ching and beyond, while Cheng soundly defeated Ch'ing shore defenses on the south side of the Yang-tzu and approached Chen-chiang with such force that the city surrendered on August 10.[68] From that point, because of unfavorable winds, ships could proceed up the Yang-tzu only slowly, by hauling from the shoreline. But Cheng did not take the advice of Chang and others that he save time by proceeding overland from Chen-chiang to Nan-ching. Because of Cheng's leisurely pace overall in this action, his main force did not arrive outside the walls of Nan-ching until two weeks later, on August 24, thus allowing eighty boatloads of Manchu troops returning from Kuei-chou to reach the city ahead of them. Again rejecting the counsel of his best strategists to attack the city preemptively, Cheng waited, hoping to avoid a costly siege by inducing certain key figures on the Ch'ing side to surrender. Moreover, he made no attempt to prevent the Ch'ing from bringing into Nan-ching reinforcements from other points, such as Sung-chiang, Su-chou, Chin-shan, and Hang-chou. Granted that a few hundred from here and a few thousand from there may not have seemed very threatening to Cheng, whose infantry alone at Nan-ching must have numbered about 85,000.[69] But the outcomes of battles depended more on the quality of the soldiers and generals than on their number, and Cheng soon was reminded sharply of this principle.

Even more significant here is that, although a startling number of localities in Chiang-nan surrendered or voluntarily sent representatives to Cheng or Chang Huang-yen proffering their allegiance—in all, seven prefectural seats, three subprefectures, and thirty-two districts[70]—no political plan had been laid nor any phalanx of officials made ready to respond in an organized manner to this popular upsurge. And although something like a Cheng mystique seems to have pervaded Chiang-nan by this time, Ch'eng-kung did not attempt to capitalize on that politically by addressing himself to the general populace in any way. Cheng sent out representatives, mostly military men, on a wholly ad hoc basis to locales that contacted him. But basically he seems to have regarded them in the same way that he always had regarded locales along the Southeastern seaboard—that is, as sources of men, animals, monies, food, and materiel for his war effort, and not as places to hold and govern in a general sense. The handful of literati whom he employed for liaison with various cities, including Chang Huang-yen, were completely overwhelmed by the demand for their services; however, Cheng did not respond to urgings that he devote more attention to this aspect of his campaign.[71] To the consternation of Chang, who believed ardently that the collective spirit of the local elite could change the course of events, Cheng placed his faith in the self-interest of military men and in affecting history primarily by winning battles. Consequently, when things went badly at Nan-ching, Cheng did not have any organized support to fall back on in the surrounding region and, feeling isolated in a strange environment, he beat a hasty retreat.

Cheng Ch'eng-kung's waiting strategy not only had allowed his men to become lax from idleness, it also had left the initiative for attack on the Ch'ing side.[72] Eventually, on September 8, they made a preliminary strike from I-feng Gate, a move which caused Cheng to redeploy his forces rapidly during that night. But with unanticipated speed, the following dawn the Ch'ing launched a general assault from Nan-ching's two northwestern gates. Having already been outmaneuvered, in the furious battle that ensued, Cheng's men also simply were outfought by the Ch'ing. Cheng lost several of his most able generals, including his closest adviser, Kan Hui, and his infantry was decimated. His navy, however, was virtually unscathed and was able quickly to transport Cheng and his few surviving infantrymen back to Chen-chiang.[73]

Chang Huang-yen sent a message to Cheng imploring him to stay at Chen-chiang and arguing that "to win the hearts of the people is more important than to lose a single battle." But Cheng was eager to withdraw, and on September 14 he led his forces back to Ch'ung-ming. Chang was was left stranded upstream near Ti-kang, where his small unit was defeated by a Ch'ing riverine fleet from Hu-kuang on September 23, as all the local support that had accrued to him and Cheng in Chiang-nan collapsed like a house of cards. At Ch'ung-ming, Cheng's main concern now was to inhibit the Ch'ing from proceeding directly to molest his home base in Fu-chien. So in his usual paradoxical manner, he on the one hand attacked the garrison town on Ch'ung-ming Island to show that his still was a force to be reckoned with, and on the other hand he asked the Wu-sung regional commander to intercede for him in reopening negotiations with the

Ch'ing court. But Cheng's men had become too dispirited to fight well, and the Ch'ing now flatly refused to talk. So while Chang Huang-yen, by a perilous odyssey, managed to escape overland from southwestern Nan Chih-li to the southeastern Che-chiang coast, Cheng returned southward with his fleet and arrived back at Hsia-men in late autumn 1659.[74]

Immediately Cheng began preparing for a major Ch'ing attack, which he knew would come soon. Indeed, while Cheng still was at Nan-ching, the Ch'ing court had appointed a chamberlain of the imperial bodyguard, Dasu, to lead a special expeditionary force against him, with the fullest backing of the Ch'ing treasury and other commands in the South. Dasu arrived in Fu-chou in February of 1660 and began to coordinate plans to concentrate the maximum Ch'ing naval resources of Ch'ao-chou in Kuang-tung, Wen-chou and T'ai-chou in Che-chiang, and Chang-chou and Ch'üan-chou in Fu-chien on the seizure of Cheng Ch'eng-kung's small cluster of islands in Hsia-men Bay.[75] Cheng, for his part, still had a core navy of over 2,000 ships—many more than the combined vessels of the Ch'ing side—and by recalling all his outlying units to the Hsia-men area, he made his defenses even more formidable.[76] But even though Cheng's forces were intact and strong, morale had been damaged and confidence shaken by the Nan-ching defeat. A military organization that not long before had reached a thousand kilometers to strike a body blow to the Ch'ing in unfamiliar territory now required special exhortations, reassurances, and disciplinary measures to get it to fight for the ground under foot.[77]

In the earlier part of June 1660, the principal Ch'ing naval contingent broke through the Cheng blockade of Ch'üan-chou Bay, and with the other contingent from Chang-chou they joined in battle with Cheng's forces on two fronts to the north and west of Hsia-men. As before, the Ch'ing fleets were almost completely vanquished, and to the thoroughly beaten Ch'ing commanders Cheng flagrantly sent a message penned on a woman's kerchief, challenging them to another fight.[78] But actually, this time Cheng had little cause for self-congratulation. He had been impressed by the Ch'ing preparations and dissatisfied with his own men's performance. Moreover, he knew now that the Ch'ing had triumphed in all other theaters, that subsequently they would be able to commit more resources to Fu-chien, and that they were capable of mounting such attacks again and again. Indeed, directly after this battle the Ch'ing demonstrated their seriousness by assigning to Fu-chien (rather than to Kuei-chou or Kuang-hsi) one of the three great princes in the South, Keng Chi-mao, and by appointing to assist him the veteran conquest general, imperial clansman Loto. It would have been impossible for Cheng indefinitely to maintain, in such a small area, sufficient forces to repulse successive assaults led by such figures.[79]

Consequently, in the early spring of 1661 Cheng pressed his commanders to accept a proposal about which theretofore they had been unenthusiastic, that is, to remove the Cheng main base to T'ai-wan. Again, few were happy about this, and one commander was punished for openly expressing what was on the others' minds: that T'ai-wan was a wild, inhospitable, disease-ridden place too far at sea. Cheng's mind was set, however, because he needed a territory that was larger and more secure from the Ch'ing, but which still was located proximate to the major East Asian maritime trade routes. Perhaps too credulously he now recalled the glowing description of T'ai-wan's resources and other advantages, and the ease with which these could be grasped, which previously had been painted for him by an ingratiating former Chinese employee of the Dutch East India Company.[80]

This state enterprise of the Netherlands had maintained a trading colony on the southwestern coast of T'ai-wan (which the Dutch called Formosa) since 1624. Company relations with Cheng Chih-lung had been less than uniformly amicable, but those with Cheng Ch'eng-kung had been worse because of his frequent interference with trade for the sake of pursuing "his war against the Tartars." Many of the officers of the company long had been concerned that Ch'eng-kung might suffer reverses on the China coast and try to occupy T'ai-wan; and in 1652 a revolt among the growing number of Chinese settlers near the Dutch colony there was thought to have been secretly instigated by Cheng agents. Since then, each spate of campaign preparation around Hsia-men had given rise to fresh rumors that Cheng was about to invade T'ai-wan, especially after his defeat at Nan-ching.[81]

But in Batavia (Jakarta), the East Asian headquarters of the Dutch East India Company, there was little inclination to invest further in the T'ai-wan outpost, and a corresponding inclination to expect that rumors of Cheng's impending invasion would "disappear like smoke before the wind." Moreover, some Dutch officers, whether from fatuity or from wishful thinking, apparently were taken in by Cheng's cordial reply to an inquiry that the Dutch governor of the T'ai-wan colony dispatched to him on October 31, 1660. Cheng opened with an expression of good will and affection for the Dutch people and then went on:

> You have received many false reports and accepted them as true. My father [Cheng Chih-lung] opened, directed, and successfully continued trade between China and the Hollanders who settled [on T'ai-wan]; and I have endeavored to increase, not diminish, that trade [*sic*]. But you remain in doubt regarding my good will because of the gossip of evil-minded people. I have been fully occupied with waging war for the recovery of territories [from the Ch'ing] and have had no reason to take hostile action against such a small, grass-producing country as [T'ai-wan]. My practice in waging war is to spread rumors that I am heading eastwards, when in fact I am preparing

to go west. My real intentions never are known to anyone. . . . I look to you for cessation of discord and jealousy, and for a renewal of friendship. Since the [Manchus] again are quiet, I shall order that trading be resumed.

Consequently, no steps were taken to significantly strengthen the colony's weak defenses.[82]

In March of 1661 Cheng made command assignments for the T'ai-wan campaign, and the following April his fleet departed from Chin-men. Midway, however, it was trapped for a week by inclement weather among the P'eng-hu Islands (the Pescadores). This was a serious matter, since Cheng had been assured that the sea passage would be fast and easy, and that food would be readily available in T'ai-wan, so the fleet had brought almost no provisions. Consequently, when Cheng's men finally reached shore near the Dutch colony on April 30, they already were very hungry and, first of all, dashed to impound grain stores in the Chinese settlement of Ch'ih-k'an (Sakkam). Nevertheless, to the several hundred Dutch soldiers and sailors who manned the two poorly constructed forts and two warships on T'ai Bay, Cheng's horde of several thousand men on several hundred ships—whether hungry or not—must have appeared threatening, indeed![83]

On May 1 Ch'eng-kung demanded the surrender of both the smaller Fort Provintia near Ch'ih-k'an and the larger Castle Zeelandia, which was situated on a sandbar near the narrow channel between T'ai Bay and the sea. He promised to let the Dutch leave safely, since he bore them no malice, but insisted that now he needed to repossess the territory that he and his father magnanimously had allowed them to use (sic). He rejected proposals from the company's Formosa Council and Governor Frederick Coyett for peaceful coexistence and for the preservation of Christianity on the island. Consequently, the Dutch surrendered the indefensible Fort Provintia forthwith, but they raised the "blood flag" over Castle Zeelandia, and battle lines with Cheng were drawn.[84]

Cheng did not immediately press the attack on Castle Zeelandia for several reasons. First, he always had disliked costly sieges. Moreover, he thought that (because of the northerly direction of the summer monsoon winds) many months would elapse before the Dutch could obtain help from Batavia, by which time the isolated castle defenders could be starved into capitulating. But equally important, Cheng also was facing a dire food shortage. Ships that Cheng ordered to bring foodstuffs from the mainland repeatedly failed to come, rice virtually disappeared, and the native corn and taro roots never were sufficient. Consequently, discontent spread among both Cheng's troops and the people of T'ai-wan—the Chinese and the aborigines who initially had accepted Cheng's authority with little qualm—and Cheng was forced to commit a large proportion of his men to the tasks of field-clearing and planting for the next harvest season. Moreover, many of his men had fallen ill or died from diseases prevalent in their new environment.[85] Surely Cheng had not expected to find the T'ai-wan Strait so difficult to cross or T'ai-wan so generally underdeveloped; and he might not have succeeded in this campaign if it had not been for some peculiar perfidies on the Dutch side.

In mid-August, to Cheng's surprise, a Dutch "succor fleet" arrived and managed to transfer needed men, food, and materiel to Castle Zeelandia. Thus, in September Cheng was forced to resume offensive action, in spite of his army's internal weakness. Oblivious to that, however, the captain of the succor fleet was discouraged by the size and skill of the enemy and the seemingly hopeless condition of the castle. Consequently, after Governor Coyett received from the Ch'ing authorities an offer to assist him in fighting Cheng, the fleet captain volunteered to carry the Dutch acceptance to Fu-chien. But instead, he abandoned his charge and went to Siam.[86] This naturally dampened the spirits of Castle Zeelandia's defenders (no more than 600 sick and starving men), and in mid-December some Dutch soldiers defected to the Cheng side and divulged valuable information on how most effectively to attack the castle. The vulnerable redoubt was bombarded and demolished on January 25, 1662; two days later Coyett and the Formosa Council decided to negotiate a surrender, which was formally concluded on February 1, ending a nine-month ordeal.[87]

Even before the Dutch departed, Cheng had changed the name of Ch'ih-k'an to the "Ming Eastern Capital," established a prefecture called "Receiving Heaven's [Command]," with two subordinate districts, promulgated the Yung-li calendar, and presumptuously demanded "tribute" from the Spanish governor of Luzon. And while still taking care not to appear usurpatious of imperial prerogatives, Cheng acted to establish the rudiments of civil government in his small realm—for instance, instituting a tax system, regulating hunting and fishing, and supervising land allocations.[88] But it is clear from circumstances that Cheng pursued these matters out of the dire necessity to prevent general revolt among his men and the populace. As a specialist in early T'ai-wan history has pointed out: "The government was mostly militarized; throughout the entire Cheng period [i.e., including the rule of Ch'eng-kung's heirs] there were at least 338 military officers, but only 56 civil officials. The island virtually was governed by martial law."[89] Thus, the problem of integrating *wen* and *wu* never was resolved in the Ming dynasty.

If Cheng really had intended to use T'ai-wan as a base for launching further attacks on the Ch'ing, the lack of supplies and especially of shipbuilding facilities there,[90] and the width and perilousness of the seaways between T'ai-wan and the mainland, simply made that unfeasible. And Cheng's men—those on T'ai-wan as well as those still stationed along the Fu-chien coast—surely knew that. The rate of defection to the Ch'ing side had increased directly after Cheng departed for T'ai-wan, partly because the "cat" had gone away, and partly because the intensification of Ch'ing efforts in removing the coastal population, interdicting maritime trade, and augmenting their own naval capabilities were having the intended effects.[91] And disciplinary problems grew worse when, in March of 1662, Cheng ordered his eldest son, Cheng Ching, and the commanders who had been left in charge on Hsia-men and Chin-men, to abandon those islands and move all their families to T'ai-wan. They effectively refused to obey this order by demurring; and, frustrated at all turns, Cheng now punished wrongdoing among his men on T'ai-wan with a harshness that bordered on madness.[92]

This situation became a crisis in May and June of 1662 when Cheng learned that his eldest son had fathered a baby boy by the wet-nurse to his youngest son (which, in the strict sense that characterized Cheng's thinking, constituted evidence of incest). Cheng promply ordered the executions of the eldest son, the mother and baby, and his own principal wife (for being remiss in governing her household). When his generals tried to placate him with just the heads of the mother and child, Cheng was even more enraged and ordered (futilely) the executions of all those who had disobeyed him, as well.[93] At this time Cheng also learned that the Yung-li emperor had been captured and probably killed in the far Southwest, and also that his father finally had been executed by the Ch'ing.[94] All this seems to have cast Cheng's mind into a state of turmoil so severe that he fell ill. And on June 23, 1662, he died on T'ai-wan, probably from a combination of insanity and some delirium-inducing disease, at the age of only thirty-seven.[95]

The last well-known symbols of Ming civil authority, Regent Lu and Chang Huang-yen, had been left to decline off the coasts of Fu-chien and Che-chiang, respectively, both in their health and in their circumstances. Chang, who had been pathetically unsuccessful in attempts to continue harassing Ch'ing positions with a small band of amphibious resistance fighters, had admonished Cheng not to abandon the mainland to contest with aboriginal and red-haired barbarians for a place far across the sea. Also, he pointed to the recent death of the Ch'ing emperor and the great unpopularity of Ch'ing coastal policies, arguing that if Cheng would campaign on the North again, "a million bravos would join and a thousand locales could be taken in."[96] When this persuasion failed, Chang pleaded earnestly several times with Regent Lu on Chin-men to actively take up the banner that Cheng had let fall, giving the Chinese masses one more chance to rise up in response to a Ming rallying cry.[97] But the former regent himself had become gravely ill from asthma, and he too died on December 23, 1662.[98] Thus, although people in T'ai-wan and elsewhere continued to use the Ming name as a symbol of resistance to conquest and political subjugation,[99] the Ming dynasty as such had come to an end.

Like a huge mountain of loose rock and soft soil, bombarded by heavy rains from above and shaken by tremors from below, the "Ming," as a functional entity and as a conception in the minds of people in seventeenth-century East Asia, gradually had lost one part, then another, and had been washed into obscurity. Since the Hung-kuang period, the Ming no longer had ruled over all of China proper or retained preponderance over China's neighboring peoples. After Nan-ching fell and the Lu and Lung-wu regimes were established, the Ming no longer had a single, central government located in one of China's traditional capital cities; and after these were defeated, the Ming had no capital to speak of, other than temporary sites on the peripheries of the polity.

The Hung-kuang government had been fully constituted with all the organs required by Ming precedent, including the Six Ministries, which had been basic to Chinese governance since T'ang times. Seriously undermined, however, had been the necessary capacity of those organs to affect and effect the conduct of public affairs in the various locales over which jurisdiction was claimed. Appointed officials could not, or would not, go to provincial posts; incumbents could not, or would not, do as they were instructed. Least of all were they able or willing to forward the revenues that were the lifeblood of the state. The Lung-wu emperor had struggled manfully to maintain the last, weak regular administrative relations between the capital and provincial locales. But after his government was destroyed, the Yung-li regime, even in its best days, never was able to restore such relations. Rather, it relied on the only organizations that then had supralocal power, the often rampant armies and largely arbitrary logistical systems of the various (and variegated) militarists.

Indeed, the history of this period also can be seen as the gradual remilitarization of the Ming, albeit in ways that certainly did not lead to restoration of the robustness of T'ai-tsu's day. In spite of the martial and populistic emphases in the dynasty's earliest reigns, by the middle of the fifteenth century the Ming had developed power and reward structures that definitely set *wen* over *wu* and the highly literate over all other classes of civilians. And later, when economic changes, political abuses, and military problems brought the status of the scholar-official elite into question, challenges to literati control—whether in the central government or in local communities—were regarded as challenges to the Ming order itself. Because of this, in the Southern Ming effective statesmanship and generalship seldom appeared in the same men, and statesmen and generals seldom were in accord. This contradiction did not disappear until virtually all Ming bureaucrats had disappeared—the early 1650s in both the Southeast and Southwest. But the regular Ming military establishment had not survived to enjoy even a Pyrrhic victory over civil officialdom. As militarization uncontrollably spread and deepened through the country, the military organizations that proved most hardy, and which represented the Ming in the end, were those born and nurtured illegitimately, outside the sphere of formal Ming government.

The last essential feature of the Ming to be lost was an emperor—a direct descendant of T'ai-tsu, ceremonially enthroned and entitled according to ancient tradition. Such a *person* survived until the execution of the Yung-li emperor in 1662. But the *institution* and its preferred qualities long since had died and been sloughed away. A Chinese emperor, in the Ming as well as in other dynasties, at least had to appear to rule as well as reign. In the Ming this appearance was supposed to be maintained through consultation with an informal, collegial group of senior statesmen and outstanding litterateurs. But for various reasons— the temperaments of certain Ming emperors, Chinese factional patterns, and some peculiar institutional ambiguities—this arrangement had been fraught with difficulties. And in the Southern Ming, when the very survival of the dynasty depended on achieving efficacious relations between the emperor and his top advisers, the successive rulers and their grand secretariats never truly were able to get together. Ignorance and faulty conceptions on the part of the imperial claimants regarding the use of the Secretariat, and continuing disagreement among officials regarding the proper role and constitution of that organ, per- petuated the Ming problem of providing assistance for the emperor.

In spite of all these difficulties, organized support for the Ming regimes, in opposition to Ch'ing conquest and rule, lasted for at least eighteen years. This is attributable in part to genuine pride and belief in basic Ming institutions, which were seen as having undergirded for almost three centuries a major, successful, *indigenous* ruling order. It was not, and still is not, clear that those institutions, even in their latter-day, distorted forms, were primarily to blame for the gross disorder that overwhelmed the East Asian subcontinent in the seventeenth century. But those institutions as handled, or mishandled, by the Ming ruling elites—with the habits and attitudes they had formed by the 1640s—clearly were not up to the task of dealing with such disorder. That the Ch'ing institutions and elites *were* up to it took considerably longer than the two decades of the Southern Ming to prove.

Abbreviations

CNW   *Chung-kuo nei-luan wai-huo li-shih ts'ung-shu* 中國內亂外禍歷史叢書. Comp. Chung-kuo li-shih yen-chiu she 中國歷史研究社. 17 vols. Shang-hai: Shen-chou kuo-kuang she, 1947. Repr. T'ai-pei: Kuang-wen shu-chü, 1964, under the title *Chung-kuo chin-tai nei-luan wai-huo li-shih ku-shih ts'ung-shu* 中國近代內亂外禍歷史故事叢書.

CYYY   *Chung-yang yen-chiu-yüan li-shih yü-yen yen-chiu-so chi-k'an* 中央研究院歷史語言研究所集刊 (Bulletin of the Institute of History and Philology of the Academia Sinica). Nan-kang, T'ai-pei.

KHSL   *Ta-Ch'ing Sheng-tsu Jen Huang-ti shih-lu* 大清聖祖仁皇帝實錄. In *Ta-Ch'ing li-ch'ao shih-lu* 大清歷朝實錄, vols. 8–13. Repr. T'ai-pei: Hua-wen shu-chü, 1964.

MCSL   *Ming-Ch'ing shih-liao* 明清史料. Comp. Institute of History and Philology of the Academia Sinica. 10 sets in 100 vols. Pei-p'ing, 1930–36; Shang-hai, 1951; T'ai-pei, 1953–75.

SCSL   *Ta-Ch'ing Shih-tsu Chang Huang-ti shih-lu* 大清世祖章皇帝實錄. In *Ta-Ch'ing li-ch'ao shih-lu*, vols. 5–7.

TW   *T'ai-wan wen-hsien ts'ung-k'an* 台灣文獻叢刊. 594 vols. Comp. T'ai-wan yin-hang ching-chi yen-chiu shih 台灣銀行經濟研究室. T'ai-pei: Bank of Taiwan, 1957–72.

NOTE: Many of the seventeenth-century texts cited below are available in more than the one edition or manuscript copy that I have used. Naturally, I have tried to avoid the worst of these editions or copies, but my choices often have been governed by personal convenience and should not uniformly be regarded as endorsements.

Notes

PREFACE

1. Ch'ien Ch'i, who died in the Hsien-feng reign period (1851–61), is said to have authored a work entitled *Nan-Ming shu*. See Hsieh Kuo-chen, *Wan-Ming shih-chi k'ao*, 2/55a.

2. "Uses of History in Traditional Chinese Society: The Southern Ming in Ch'ing Historiography," University of Michigan.

3. I especially regret having been unable to utilize the following important works: *Nan-tu lu* by Li Ch'ing, which has been discussed by several late Ch'ing and twentieth-century Chinese bibliophiles; *T'ien-nan chi-shih* by Hu Ch'in-hua, a manuscript copy of which is held in the National Library of Pei-ching; *Shou-Mien chi-shih* by Liu Chai and the pseudonymous *Tien-k'ou chi-lüeh*, both of which have been cited by the historian Kuo Ying-ch'iu; and the manuscript copy of Chi Liu-ch'i's *Ming-chi nan-lüeh* that was studied by the late Chang Yin (see *Ch'ing-shih lun-ts'ung*, 2 [1980]: 320–39).

4. *Tseng-ting wan-Ming shih-chi k'ao* (Shang-hai: Ku-chi ch'u-pan she, 1981).

5. John E. Wills, personal correspondence of January 11, 1983.

6. Frederic Wakeman's most recent book, *The Great Enterprise: The Manchu Reconstruction of Imperial Order in Seventeenth-Century China*, is forthcoming from the University of California Press; and Jerry Dennerline's chapter, "The Manchu Conquest and the Shun-chih Reign," will appear in the *Cambridge History of China*, vol. 9, book 1.

INTRODUCTION

1. The question of the parameters of the "Ming-Ch'ing transition" has been raised by editors Jonathan Spence and John E. Wills in their preface to *From Ming to Ch'ing: Conquest, Region, and Continuity in Seventeenth-century China* (New Haven, 1979), pp. xi–xii.

2. Frederic Wakeman, Jr., "The Shun Interregnum of 1644," in *From Ming to Ch'ing*, pp. 43–87. Also, see biogs. of the Ch'ung-chen emperor, Chu Yu-chien, and of Li Tzu-ch'eng in *Eminent Chinese of the Ch'ing Period*, ed. Arthur Hummel, 2 vols. (Washington, D.C., 1943), I: 191–92 and 491–92, resp.

3. Ch'en Sheng-hsi, "Ch'ing-ping ju-kuan yü Wu San-kuei hsiang-Ch'ing wen-t'i," in *Ming-Ch'ing shih kuo-chi hsüeh-shu t'ao-lun-hui lun-wen chi* (T'ien-chin, 1981), pp. 715–44. Angela Hsi, "Wu San-kuei in 1644: A Reappraisal," *Journal of Asian Studies*, 34.2 (Feb. 1975): 443–53. Li Kuang-t'ao, "Do-er-kun Shan-hai-kuan chan-i te chen-hsiang," in *Ming-Ch'ing shih lun-chi* (T'ai-pei, 1971), II: 443–48. Shang Hung-k'uei, "Ming-Ch'ing chih chi Shan-hai-kuan chan-i te chen-hsiang k'ao-ch'a," *Li-shih yen-chiu*, 1978, no. 5 (May), pp. 76–82. Also, see biogs. of Dorgon and of Wu San-kuei in Hummel, I: 215–19, and II: 877–80, resp.

4. Mitamura Taisuke, *Shinchō zenshi no kenkyū* (Kyoto, 1965). Franz Michael, *The Origin of Manchu Rule in China* (Baltimore, 1942). Wada Sei, "Some Problems Concerning the Rise of T'ai-tsu, Founder of the Manchu Dynasty," *Memoirs of the Research Department of the Tōyō Bunko*, 16 (1957): 35–73. Piero Corradini, "Civil Administration at the Beginning of the Manchu Dynasty: A Note on the Establishment of the Six Ministries (*Liu-pu*)," *Oriens Extremus*, 9 (1962): 133–38. Gertraude Roth, "The Manchu-Chinese Relationship, 1618–1636," in *From Ming to Ch'ing*, pp. 4–38. Also, see biogs. of Khungtaiji (Abahai) and of Nurhaci in Hummel, I: 1–3 and 594–99, resp.

5. Charles O. Hucker, "The Tunglin Movement of the Late Ming Period," in *Chinese Thought and Institutions*, ed. John K. Fairbank (Chicago, 1957), p. 156.

6. Li Kuang-t'ao, "Lun Chien-chou yü liu-tsei hsiang-yin wang Ming," CYYY, 12 (1947): 193–236. Three major works treat the large rebel movements that consumed Ming energies and resources internally just as the Manchus were rising in power: Li Wen-chih, *Wan-Ming min-pien* (Shang-hai, 1948); Li Kuang-t'ao, *Ming-chi liu-k'ou shih-mo* (T'ai-pei, 1965); and James B. Parsons, *Peasant Rebellions of the Late Ming Dynasty* (Tucson, 1970).

7. For an unusually sympathetic portrait of the Wan-li emperor, which does not, however, minimize the problems he caused, see Ray Huang, *1587: A Year of No Significance* (New Haven, 1981), chap. 1. For a more standard biography, see Chu I-chün in *A Dictionary of Ming Biography*, ed. L. C. Goodrich and Fang Chao-ying, 2 vols. (New York, 1976), I: 324–38. For more detail on the controversies of this reign, see Hsieh Kuo-chen, *Ming-Ch'ing chih chi tang-she yün-tung k'ao* (Shang-hai, 1934), pp. 14–45. And for a general description of various problems facing the Ming in its last decades, see Albert Chan, *The Glory and Fall of the Ming Dynasty* (Norman, Oklahoma, 1982), second part, "The Ming Empire in Decline."

8. Ray Huang, *Taxation and Governmental Finance in Sixteenth-Century Ming China* (Cambridge, 1974), passim. Idem, "Military Expenditures in Sixteenth Century Ming China," *Oriens Extremus*, 17 (1970): 39–62.

9. The origins of early Ming militarism in Yüan ethos and institutions, and the reassertion of civil dominance in the second quarter of the fifteenth century, is one of the main themes of Edward L. Dreyer's book, *Early Ming China: A Political History, 1355–1435* (Stanford, 1982). Other relevant works on the early Ming include: Frederick Mote, *The Poet Kao Ch'i, 1336–1374* (Princeton, 1962), chap. 1; Edward Dreyer, "The Poyang Lake Campaign, 1363: Inland Naval Warfare in the Founding of the Ming Dynasty," in *Chinese Ways in Warfare*, ed. Frank A. Kierman, Jr., Harvard East Asian Series, no. 74

(Cambridge, Mass., 1974), pp. 202−42; and David B. Chan, *The Usurpation of the Prince of Yen, 1398−1402* (San Francisco, 1976). Also see biogs. of Ch'eng-tsu (Chu Ti) and T'ai-tsu (Chu Yüan-chang) in Goodrich and Fang, I: 355−65 and 381−92, resp.

10. This twofold characterization does not include aboriginal chiefs, who also held hereditary military authority. Charles O. Hucker, "Governmental Organization of the Ming Dynasty," in *Studies of Governmental Institutions in Chinese History*, ed. John L. Bishop (Cambridge, Mass., 1968), pp. 67, 77−78, 114−21.

11. Wang Yü-ch'üan, *Ming-tai te chün-t'un* (Pei-ching, 1965), part 2. Wu Han, "Ming-tai te chün-ping," in *Tu-shih cha-chi* (Pei-ching, 1956), pp. 92−141. Shimizu Taiji, "Mindai gunton no hōkai," in *Mindai tochi seido shi kenkyū* (Tokyo, 1968), pp. 329−54. Huang, *Taxation*, pp. 66−68; and idem, "Military Expenditure," pp. 40−44.

12. Saeki Tomi, "Min-Shin jidai no minsō ni tsuite," *Tōyōshi kenkyū*, 15.4 (March 1957): 33−64. Iwami Hiroshi, "Mindai no minsō to hokuhen bōei," *Tōyōshi kenkyū*, 19.2 (Oct. 1960): 156−74. Sun Chin-ming, *Chung-kuo ping-chih shih* (T'ai-pei, 1960), pp. 173−76.

13. Wang Hsien-te, "Minmatsu dōran ki ni okeru gōson bōei," *Mindai shi kenkyū*, 2 (1975): 26−49.

14. Huang, "Military Expenditures," pp. 44−56, 59−62. Idem, "Fiscal Administration during the Ming Dynasty," in *Chinese Government in Ming Times: Seven Studies*, ed. Charles O. Hucker (New York, 1971), pp. 112−23. P'an Chen-ch'iu, "Ming-tai pei-pien chün-chen chi wei-so te peng-k'uei," *Ch'ung-chi hsüeh-pao*, 7.1 (Nov. 1966): 90−100.

15. Li, *Wan-Ming min-pien*, pp. 17−20, 99−100. Li, *Ming-mo liu-k'ou shih-mo*, pp. 11−21. Also, on government troops, see Parsons, *Peasant Rebellions*, pp. 49−50. The "floating" population of the metropolis of Nan-ching was especially great, and disciplinary problems among the soldiers there came to be correspondingly serious. See Kawakatsu Mamoru, "Minmatsu Nankin heishi no hanran—Minmatsu no toshi kōzō ni tsuite no ichi sobyō," in *Hoshi hakase taikan kinen Chūgokushi ronshū* (Yamagata, 1978), pp. 187−207.

16. Lo Hsiang-lin, "Lang-ping lang-t'ien k'ao," *Kuang-chou hsüeh-pao*, 1.2 (April 1937), not serially paginated.

17. Wu, "Ming-tai te chün-ping," p. 126, citing the *Ming-shih*, ch. 187, biog. of Hung Chung.

18. Tani Mitsutaka, "Mindai no kunshin ni kansuru ichi kōsatsu," *Tōyōshi kenkyū*, 29.4 (1971): 68.

19. Wu Chi-hua, "Ming-tai tsui kao chün-shih chi-kou te yen-pien," *Nan-yang ta-hsüeh hsüeh-pao*, 6.1 (1972): 149, 152−54. Tani, "Mindai no kunshin," pp. 92−103. Lung Wen-pin, *Ming hui-yao*, 2 vols. (Pei-ching, 1956), II: 745−46.

20. Tani, "Mindai no kunshin," p. 106. Hucker, "Governmental Organization," pp. 77−78.

21. See biogs. of Chu Ch'i-chen, Chu Ch'i-yü, Esen, and Wang Chen in Goodrich and Fang, I: 289−98, 416−20, and II: 1347−49, resp.

22. Frederick Mote, "The T'u-mu Incident of 1449," in *Chinese Ways in Warfare*, ed. Kierman, pp. 267−72.

23. For example: Wu Chi-hua, "Contraction of Forward Defenses on the North China Frontier during the Ming Dynasty," *Papers on Far Eastern History*, 17 (March 1978): 1−13. Jung-pang Lo, "Policy Formulation and Decision-making on Issues Respecting

Peace and War," in *Chinese Government in Ming Times*, ed. Hucker, pp. 56–60, 66–68. Ray Huang, "The Liao-tung Campaign of 1619," *Oriens Extremus*, 28.1 (1981): 30–54.

24. Bodo Weithoff, *Chinas dritte Grenze: Der traditionelle chinesische Staat und der küstennahe Seeraum* (Wiesbaden, 1969).

25. Jung-pang Lo, "The Decline of the Early Ming Navy," *Oriens Extremus*, 5 (1958): 158–62. For a thorough description of Ming naval defenses at the beginning of the dynasty, see Kawagoe Yasuhiro, "Mindai kaibō taisei no un'ei kōzō—sōsei ki o chūshin ni," *Shigaku zasshi*, 81.6 (1972): 28–53.

26. Huang, *1587*, chap. 6, esp. p. 159. Kwan-wai So, *Japanese Piracy in Ming China during the Sixteenth Century* ([East Lansing, Mich.], 1975), esp. pp. 135–40. Charles O. Hucker, "Hu Tsung-hsien's Campaign against Hsü Hai, 1556," in *Chinese Ways in Warfare*, ed. Kierman, esp. pp. 285–87. Merrilyn Fitzpatrick, "Local Interests and the Anti-pirate Administration in China's South-east," *Ch'ing-shih wen-t'i*, 4.2 (Dec. 1979): 1–33.

27. Introduction to *Chinese Ways in Warfare*, ed. Kierman, pp. 7–11.

28. Ray Huang's agreement with this interpretation is best expressed in his chapter on Ch'i Chi-kuang in *1587*, esp. pp. 157–58, 175–76.

29. Huang Tsung-hsi, *Ming-i tai-fang lu* (*Szu-pu pei-yao* ed.), "Ping-chih 3," 28b–29a.

30. Frederick Mote, "The Growth of Chinese Despotism: A Critique of Wittfogel's Theory of Oriental Despotism as Applied to China," *Oriens Extremus*, 8 (1961): 18–20, 26–29.

31. On the codependence of monarchy and bureaucracy, see Joseph R. Levenson, *Confucian China and Its Modern Fate: A Trilogy*, vol. II, *The Problem of Monarchical Decay* (Berkeley, 1968), part 2, chap. 5, esp. pp. 61–71.

32. My understanding of late Ming politics has been augmented by Andrew Nathan's writing on contemporary Chinese politics. In particular, see his article, "A Factionalism Model for CCP Politics," *China Quarterly*, 53 (Jan.–March 1973), esp. pp. 46–51.

33. Tu Nai-chi, *Ming-tai nei-ko chih-tu* (T'ai-pei, 1967), pp. 8–13. For a more condensed, general overview of the evolution of the Grand Secretariat, see Kuan Wen-fa, "Shih-lun Ming-ch'ao nei-ko chih-tu te hsing-ch'eng ho fa-chan," in *Ming-Ch'ing shih kuo-chi hsüeh-shu t'ao-lun-hui lun-wen chi*, pp. 45–65.

34. Robert B. Crawford, "Eunuch Power in the Ming Dynasty," *T'oung Pao*, 49.3 (1961): 117, 147.

35. Tu, *Ming-tai nei-ko chih-tu*, pp. 17–24, 138–40. Wu Chi-hua, "Ming Jen-Hsüan shih nei-ko chih-tu chih pien yü huan-kuan ch'ien-yüeh hsiang-ch'üan chih huo," CYYY, 31 (1960): 381–403. Idem, "Lun Ming-tai fei-hsiang yü hsiang-ch'üan chih chuan-i," *Ta-lu tsa-chih*, 34.1 (Jan. 1967): 6–8. Tilemann Grimm, "Das Neiko der Ming-Zeit von den Anfangen bis 1506," *Oriens Extremus*, 1 (1954): 139–77.

36. Jerry Dennerline, *The Chia-ting Loyalists: Confucian Leadership and Social Change in Seventeenth-Century China* (New Haven, 1981), pp. 16–23.

37. Charles O. Hucker, "Governmental Organization," pp. 88–89.

38. Idem, "The Tunglin Movement," p. 139. Huang Tsung-hsi also recognized the problem of the prime ministership. See W. T. de Bary, "Chinese Despotism and the Confucian Ideal: A Seventeenth-Century View," in *Chinese Thought and Institutions*, pp. 175–76.

39. For instance, see Ray Huang's chapter on Shen Shih-hsing in *1587*, pp. 42–74.

40. For the most notorious cases, see: Kwan-wai So, "Grand Secretary Yan Song (1480–1566?): A New Appraisal," in *Essays in the History of China and Chinese-American Relations* (East Lansing, Mich., 1982), pp. 1–40; and on Chang Chü-cheng, see Ray Huang, *1587*, chaps. 1 and 2, passim. Also, see biogs. of Chang Chü-cheng and of Yen Sung in Goodrich and Fang, I: 53–61, and II: 1586–91, resp.

41. Hucker, "The Tunglin Movement," pp. 139–41. Heinrich Busch, "The Tunglin Academy and Its Political and Philosophical Significance," *Monumenta Serica*, 14 (1949–55): 14–21. Robert Crawford, "Chang Chü-cheng's Confucian Legalism," in *Self and Society in Ming Thought*, pp. 367–413.

42. William S. Atwell, "From Education to Politics: The Fu She," in *The Unfolding of Neo-Confucianism*, ed. W. T. de Bary (New York, 1975), esp. pp. 339–41, 349–55. Hsieh, *Ming-Ch'ing chih chi tang-she*, pp. 46–98.

43. For instance, in *Self and Society in Ming Thought* see Robert Crawford's characterization of Chang Chü-cheng as a "Confucian Legalist" and Ray Huang's characterization of Ni Yüan-lu as a "realistic Confucian" (pp. 367–449).

44. Nunome Chōfū, "Minchō no shoō seisaku to sono eikyō," *Shigaku zasshi*, (1) 55.3 (March 1944): 1–32; (2) 55.4 (April 1944): 50–87. Hucker, "Governmental Organization," pp. 66–67. Chao I, *Nien-erh-shih cha-chi*, 2 vols. (T'ai-pei, 1965), II: 471–73. For a recent, general study of the Ming system for imperial clansmen, see Ku Ch'eng, "Ming-tai te tsung-shih," in *Ming-Ch'ing shih kuo-chi hsüeh-shu t'ao-lun-hui lun-wen chi*, pp. 89–111.

45. Nunome, "Minchō no shoō," (3) *Shigaku zasshi*, 55.5 (May 1944): esp. pp. 24, 33–34, 67–68. Wu Chi-hua, "Lun Ming-tai tsung-fan jen-k'ou," in *Ming-tai she-hui ching-chi shih lun-ts'ung* (T'ai-pei, 1970), II: 237–89. Lung, *Ming hui-yao*, II: 877. *Ming-shih*, 100/1a–b. For a study of the estate lands of the Prince of Luh, see Satō Fumitoshi, "Minmatsu shūhan ōfu no daitochi shoyū o meguru ni, san no mondai—Ro ōfu no baai," in (1) *Kimura Masao sensei taikan kinen tōyōshi ronshū* (Tokyo, 1976), pp. 325–57; (2) *Mindaishi kenkyū*, 3 (Dec. 1975): 23–41. For documents concerning the value of Ming princely estates that were confiscated by the Ch'ing, see Number I Historical Archive of China, *Ch'ing-tai tang-an shih-liao ts'ung-pien*, IV (Pei-ching, 1979): 149–255.

46. SCSL, 17/20a.

47. SCSL, 20/116; 25/18b–19a; 26/18b.

48. For pioneering studies, see: Fu I-ling, *Ming-Ch'ing nung-ts'un she-hui ching-chi* (Pei-ching, 1961), pp. 68–153 (also, see Fu's more recent findings in "Ming-mo nan-fang te 'tien-pien,' 'nu-pien',' " *Li-shih yen-chiu*, 1975, no. 5 [May]: 61–67); and Hsieh Kuo-chen, "Ming-chi nu-pien k'ao," appendix I to *Ming-Ch'ing chih chi tang-she* (originally published in *Ch'ing-hua hsüeh-pao*, 8.1 [1932]).

49. Mori Masao, "Minmatsu no shakai kankei ni okeru chitsujo no hendō ni tsuite," in *Nagoya daigaku bungakubu sanjisshūnen kinen ronshū* (Nagoya, 1979), pp. 135–59.

50. For a socio-historical analysis of one important area, see Jerry Dennerline, *The Chia-ting Loyalists*, pp. 71–103.

51. For a study of one region in the North, see I Songgyu, trans. Joshua Fogel, "Shantung in the Shun-chih Reign: The Establishment of Local Control and the Gentry Response," *Ch'ing-shih wen-t'i*, (1) 4.4 (Dec. 1980): 17–18; 4.5 (June 1981): 9–10, 15–16, 22.

CHAPTER ONE

1. T'an Ch'ien, *Kuo-ch'üeh* (Pei-ching, 1958), VI: 6035. Wu Wei-yeh, *Sui-k'ou chi-lüeh* (T'ai-pei repr., 1968), suppl. *chung*/6b.

2. Parsons, *Peasant Rebellions*, pp. 38–41, 58–60. Chu Wen-chang, *Shih K'o-fa chuan* (T'ai-pei, 1974), chap.2.

3. Ch'i Piao-chia, *Chia-i jih-li* (T'ai-pei, 1969), pp. 10, 18, 19. T'an, *Kuo-ch'üeh*, VI: 6033–34. [Wan Yen], *Ch'ung-chen ch'ang-pien* (*T'ung-shih* ed.), 2/23b. Wakeman, "The Shun Interregnum," pp. 47–49. William S. Atwell, "Ch'en Tzu-lung (1608–1647): A Scholar-Official of the Late Ming Dynasty," Ph.D. diss. (Princeton, 1974), p. 127.

4. Anon., *Huai-ch'eng chi-shih* (*T'ung-shih* ed.), 1a–2b. Chi Liu-ch'i, *Ming-chi nan-lüeh* (T'ai-pei, 1963), I: 66–67, 79.

5. Wakeman, "The Shun Interregnum," p. 50.

6. *Huai-ch'eng chi-shih*, 3a.

7. Chi, *Ming-chi nan-lüeh*, I: 115–18. Ch'en Chen-hui, *Kuo-chiang ch'i-shih* (*T'ung-shih* ed.), 1a. The call-to-arms also is recorded in Feng Meng-lung, comp., *Chia-shen chi-shih* (Shang-hai, 1941 repr. of Hung-kuang ed.), ch. 7; and in Shih K'o-fa, *Shih Chung-cheng Kung chi* (T'ai-pei, 1968), ch. 4.

8. Ch'en Chen-hui, "Shu-shih ch'i-tse," in *Ch'en Ting-sheng i-shu (1654)*, 3a.

9. T'an, *Kuo-ch'üeh*, VI: 6071, 6073. Confirmation of the Ch'ung-chen emperor's demise arrived on May 22. See Ch'en, "Shu-shih ch'i-tse," 3a. Three articles by Huang Yü-chai provide a general overview of the history of the Hung-kuang court: "Hung-kuang ch'ao te chien-li," "Hung-kuang ch'ao te shih-lüeh," and "Hung-kuang ch'ao te peng-k'uei," *T'ai-wan wen-hsien*, vol. 18, nos. 1, 3, and 4 (March, Sept., and Dec. 1967), pp. 88–115, 92–118, and 150–77, resp. Another helpful article on various problems of the court has been written by Yang Yün-p'ing, "Nan-Ming Hung-kuang shih-tai te chi-ke wen-t'i," *Chung-kuo li-shih hsüeh-hui shih-hsüeh chi-k'an*, 7 (May 1975): 157–78.

10. Other princes of the first degree who then were in the Huai and lower Yang-tzu area, having fled their estates because of rebel attacks, were the princes of Luh (from Wei-hui, northern Ho-nan), Lu (Yen-chou, Shan-tung), Chou (K'ai-feng, Ho-nan), and Hui (Ching-chou, northern Hu-kuang). See *Ming-shih*: 100/18a; 101/7a–b; 104/32a, 34a. Some consideration was given to the Prince of Kuei (*Ming-shih*, 104/34b), who had fled his estate in southern Hu-kuang and then was in Kuang-hsi Province, but then it was decided that he was too far away.

11. Chu Yu-sung: Hummel, I: 195–96. Cf. introduction, n. 7.

12. Hsia Yün-i and Hsia Wan-ch'un, *Hsing-ts'un lu* (*Ming-chi pai-shih ch'u-pien* ed., 1971), pp. 292–93.

13. Four of the Ch'ung-chen emperor's seven sons died in infancy. Surviving at the time of his suicide were: the heir-designate, Chu Tz'u-lang, who recently had turned sixteen years of age; the Prince of Ting, Chu Tz'u-ts'an, about twelve years old; and the Prince of Yung, Chu Tz'u-huan, in his tenth year. Standard sources are confused and mistaken regarding the names, titles, and relative positions of these princes. For a definitive study, see Meng Sen, "Ming Lieh Huang hsün-kuo hou-chi," in *Ming-Ch'ing shih lun-chu chi-k'an* (T'ai-pei repr., 1965), pp. 28–70.

14. Li Ch'ing, *San-yüan pi-chi* (*Ku-hsüeh hui-k'an* ed., 1964 repr.), suppl. *hsia*/7a–b. The Prince of Luh was fifth in the line of succession, whereas the Prince of Fu was first, after the emperor's own sons.

15. Ch'en, *Kuo-chiang ch'i-shih*, 1a–2b. Hsia, *Hsing-ts'un lu*, p. 292. T'an Ch'ien, *Tsao-lin tsa-tsu* (*Pi-chi hsiao-shuo ta-kuan* ed., T'ai-pei repr., 1960), *jen*/14a; and idem, *Kuo-ch'üeh*, VI: 6077. Chi, *Ming-chi nan-lüeh*, I: 47–48. Also, see biogs. of Liu Tse-ch'ing and of Ma Shih-ying in Hummel, I: 531–32 and 558–59, resp.

16. Ch'en, *Kuo-chiang ch'i-shih*, 2b–3a. Chi, *Ming-chi nan-lüeh*, I: 48. During the Ch'ung-chen years, Liu K'ung-chao had complained emotionally in court audience about the strictures imposed on the Commissioner-in-Chief for River Control by civil officials, so the censorial official who then was serving as the civil counterpart to Liu's position was removed, and authority for river control was given entirely to Liu. T'an, *Tsao-lin tsa-tsu*, *jen*/8a. Subsequently, as the Hung-kuang court was being established, two prominent Nan-ching officials were offered the post of civil Vice Commissioner for River Control, but both declined in order to avoid irritating Liu K'ung-chao. T'an, *Kuo-ch'üeh*, VI: 6098. Chi, *Ming-chi nan-lüeh*, I: 57. Ch'i, *Chia-i jih-li*, p. 29.

17. T'an, *Kuo-ch'üeh*, VI: 6077–79. Ch'en, *Kuo-chiang ch'i-shih*, 3a. Ch'i, *Chia-i jih-li*, p. 25. Anon., "Lung-fei chi-lüeh," in *Hsing-ch'ao chih-lüeh*, comp. Chou Shih-yung (1644), ch. 1, separate pagination 1b.

18. T'an, *Kuo-ch'üeh*, VI: 6081. Ch'i, *Chia-i jih-li*, p. 26. "Lung-fei chi-lüeh," 2b.

19. Ch'i, *Chia-i jih-li*, p. 26. "Lung-fei chi-lüeh," 2a. Chi, *Ming-chi nan-lüeh*, I: 49.

20. In Ming practice, the *chien-kuo* title had been used to elevate heir-designates to "acting emperor" status when the reigning emperor planned to be away from the capital for extended periods, on tours or campaigns (see *Ta-Ming hui-tien* [T'ai-pei repr., 1963], 54/1a–13b). In this case, however, officials were following the precedent of the Ching-t'ai emperor, who assumed the regency when his elder half-brother, the Cheng-t'ung emperor, was captured by the Mongols in 1449 (cf. introduction, nn. 21 and 22). On this point, see Ku Yen-wu, *Sheng-an pen-chi* (T'ai-pei, 1964), I: 2; and T'an, *Kuo-ch'üeh*, VI: 6083.

21. Chi, *Ming-chi nan-lüeh*, I: 49–50. Ch'i, *Chia-i jih-li*, pp. 28, 30.

22. Also called *t'ing-t'ui*. See Lung, *Ming hui-tien*, II: 901–04.

23. Chi, *Ming-chi nan-lüeh*, I: 56. Ch'i, *Chia-i jih-li*, pp. 28–29. "Lung-fei chi-lüeh," 4a. T'an, *Tsao-lin tsa-tsu*, *jen*/8b. Li, *San-yüan pi-chi*, *hsia*/22b. Liu's citation of a precedent for military nobles serving in the Secretariat revealed a natural confusion in his mind between chief councillors, which were abolished by T'ai-tsu, and grand secretaries, which later developed in their place (cf. introduction, nn. 33 and 35).

24. Chi, *Ming-chi nan-lüeh*, I: 49–50. Ch'i, *Chia-i jih-li*, pp. 25, 27. "Lung-fei chi-lüeh," 3a–b. He formally accepted the regental paraphernalia on the following day, June 7. T'an, *Kuo-ch'üeh*, VI: 6083. "Lung-fei chi-lüeh," 3b. Ch'i, *Chia-i jih-li*, p. 28.

25. T'an, *Kuo-ch'üeh*, VI: 6099–6100. Ku, *Sheng-an pen-chi*, I: 4.

26. The most complete texts of these proclamations are recorded in Chou, comp., *Hsing-ch'ao chih-lüeh*, 1/1a–17a.

27. T'an, *Kuo-ch'üeh*, VI: 6083, 6088, 6091, 6097–99. "Lung-fei chi-lüeh," 4a. Chi, *Ming-chi nan-lüeh*, I: 3, 57. Ku, *Sheng-an pen-chi*, I: 2–3.

28. Chi, *Ming-chi nan-lüeh*, I: 56–57. Ku, *Sheng-an pen-chi*, I: 3. T'an, *Kuo-ch'üeh*, VI: 6092. *Huai-ch'eng chi-shih*, 8a.

29. Ying T'ing-chi, *Ch'ing-lin hsieh* (*Ming-chi pai-shih hui-pien* ed.), *shang*/4a. "Kung-k'en liu tsai-ch'ao shu," in Shih, *Shih Chung-cheng Kung chi*, suppl., pp. 64–65.

30. Ku, *Sheng-an pen-chi*, I: 3. Chi, *Ming-chi nan-lüeh*, I: 58. Ch'i, *Chia-i jih-li*, p. 29. Shih, *Shih Chung-cheng Kung chi*, pp. 32–33.

31. A great deal has been written about Shih K'o-fa. His most widely cited chronological biography is by Yang Te-en, *Shih K'o-fa nien-p'u* (Ch'ang-sha, 1940); and his most popular biography is that by Chu Wen-chang, cited above. A doctoral dissertation by Joseph Liu, "She Ke-fa (1601–1645) et le contexte politique et social de la Chine au moment de l'invasion mandchoue" (Paris, 1969) is held in the Bibliothèque de la Sorbonne. For a Communist Chinese interpretation of his career, see Wei Hung-yün, *Shih K'o-fa* (Shang-hai, 1955); and on the controversy over Shih among mainland Chinese historians, see Liu Hui et al., comps., *Shih K'o-fa p'ing-chia wen-t'i hui-pien* (Hongkong, 1968).

32. The biography of Ma Shih-ying in the *Ming-shih*, ch. 308, has been translated and annotated by Robert B. Crawford, with a listing of many other biographical sources, in "The Biography of Juan Ta-ch'eng," *Chinese Culture*, 6.2 (March 1965): 36–48.

33. For complaints lodged against Ma for the wanton behavior of his troops in Hui-chou Prefecture, see Chin Sheng, *Chin T'ai-shih chi*, ch. 5, in *Ch'ien-k'un cheng-ch'i chi* (T'ai-pei repr., 1966), ch. 461.

34. Ch'en, *Kuo-chiang ch'i-shih*, 12a.

35. Ibid., 10b. Chi, *Ming-chi nan-lüeh*, I: 64–65. T'an, *Kuo-ch'üeh*, VI: 6155. Ying, *Ch'ing-lin hsieh, shang/8a, hsia/4a–b*. Hsia Wan-ch'un, *Hsü Hsing-ts'un lu* (*Ming-chi pai-shih ch'u-pien* ed.), p. 327.

36. Ch'en, *Kuo-chiang ch'i-shih*, 11b.

37. Ibid., 11a. Li, *San-yüan pi-chi, hsia/3a–b*.

38. Ch'en, *Kuo-chiang ch'i-shih*, 12a.

39. T'an, *Kuo-ch'üeh*, VI: 6090–91. Shih, *Shih Chung-cheng Kung chi*, pp. 2–3.

40. T'an, *Kuo-ch'üeh*, VI: 6096. Chi, *Ming-chi nan-lüeh*, I: 60. Chou, comp., *Hsing-ch'ao chih-lüeh*, 2/6a–9b. Shih, *Shih Chung-cheng Kung chi*, pp. 3–4. Though Shih later may have regretted setting up the four *chen* in this way, at the time he seems to have been fully behind the plan. See Ying, *Ch'ing-lin hsieh, shang/15a*, and Ch'en, *Kuo-chiang ch'i-shih*, 12a–b. The headquarters of the commanders were not fixed, but it was desired that they locate, temporarily at least, in or near the cities named.

41. Chi, *Ming-chi nan-lüeh*, I: 66.

42. Ch'en, *Kuo-chiang ch'i-shih*, 10b.

43. Lu Chen-fei, the able governor at Huai-an, who had successfully prevented harm to the area under his jurisdiction from both roving bandits and the rampant soldiers of Ma Shih-ying and Liu Tse-ch'ing, was simply removed from his post after Ma became Grand Secretary and Minister of War and Liu became Defense Commander for the Huai-an area. T'an, *Kuo-ch'üeh*, VI: 6110; *Huai-ch'eng chi-shih*, passim. Governor Ho T'eng-chiao, who later was made Viceroy for Hu-kuang, and Yüan Chi-hsien, Viceroy at Chiu-chiang, maintained good relations only tenuously with Tso Liang-yü in Wu-ch'ang, and then mainly through force of personality rather than by institutional means. Ultimately they both narrowly escaped death in failing to prevent Tso's fateful mutiny. Ho: Hummel, I: 290–91; T'an, *Kuo-ch'üeh*, VI: 6142, 6167; Li, *San-yüan pi-chi*, suppl. *hsia* for Hung-kuang, 1a–2b. Yüan: Hummel, II: 948–49; Li, *San-yüan pi-chi, hsia/1b–3b*, 34a–36a; Yüan Chi-hsien, *Hsün-yang chi-shih* (Hu, comp., *Yü-chang ts'ung-shu* ed.) passim. Ch'i Piao-chia, Governor for the Su-chou circuit, was chiefly concerned to prevent Kao Chieh and Liu Tse-ch'ing from coming southward across the Yang-tzu at Chen-chiang, to deal with agents of these generals and of Shih K'o-fa who upset the populace by arbitrarily demanding monies and supplies for use north of the Yang-tzu, and to keep

some of Shih's units from alienating the people of Chen-chiang and battling with forces transferred there from Che-chiang. Hummel, I: 126; *Chia-i jih-li*, passim.

44. Kao Chieh: Hummel, I: 410–11; Chi, *Ming-chi nan-lüeh*, I: 66–71.

45. Anon., *Yang-chou pien-lüeh* (*T'ung-shih* ed.), 1a, 2a–3a. Ying, *Ch'ing-lin hsieh*, *shang*/4b. The murdered mediator was a Fu She member, Cheng Yüan-hsün. On him, see Wu Shan-chia, *Fu She hsing-shih chuan-lüeh* (*Ming-Ch'ing shih-liao hui-pien* repr. ed.). 4/21a–b.

46. Ch'en, *Kuo-chiang ch'i-shih*, 10b.

47. Ying, *Ch'ing-lin hsieh*, *shang*/5a–b. Hsia, *Hsü Hsing-ts'un lu*, pp. 322, 325. *Yang-chou pien-lüeh*, 3b.

48. Ying, *Ch'ing-lin hsieh*, *shang*/5. *Yang-chou pien-lüeh*, 3b. For Shih's reports to the throne on these matters, see *Shih Chung-cheng Kung chi*, pp. 5–6.

49. The most outstanding examples are Li Ch'eng-tung, Chin Sheng-huan, and Chang T'ien-lu, to be discussed in chapters 2 and 5.

50. Ying, *Ch'ing-lin hsieh*, *hsia*/1a, 2a–3b. Ku, *Sheng-an pen-chi*, I: 21–23. Lu Ch'i, *Hsien-yen* (CNW ed.), p. 46. Chi, *Ming-chi nan-lüeh*, I: 68, 200. T'an, *Kuo-ch'üeh*, VI: 6180, 6183, 6184–86.

51. Liu Tsung-chou, *Liu Tzu ch'üan-shu* (*Chung-hua wen-shih ts'ung-shu* repr. of Tao-kuang ed.). 18/3a–5a, 8b–11a, 13a–16b. Yao Ming-ta, *Liu Chi-shan hsien-sheng nien-p'u* (Shang-hai, 1937), p. 320. Ku, *Sheng-an pen-chi*, I: 7. For a biographical sketch, see Hummel, I: 532–33. Because of his position, both as Censor-in-Chief and as the gray eminence of the "righteous" element, Liu's criticisms were the most earthshaking, but he was not alone in submitting such memorials. For similar ones by Ch'en Han-hui and Heh Shih-shou, see Feng, comp., *Chia-shen chi-shih*, ch. 7; T'an, *Kuo-ch'üeh*, VI: 6107; and Chi, *Ming-chi nan-lüeh*, I: 5, 118–19.

52. Chi, *Ming-chi nan-lüeh*, I: 88–92. Ch'en, *Kuo-chiang ch'i-shih*, 14a–15a. For a deprecatory biographical sketch of this meddlesome censor, Huang Shu, see T'an, *Tsao-lin tsa-tsu*, *jen*/10a–b.

53. On this point of interpretation, I agree with Hsia Wan-ch'un, *Hsü Hsing-ts'un lu*, p. 322. For testimony that Ma did not originally intend to make trouble for the Tung-lin but was forced to do so by Liu Tsung-chou and his cohort, see Ch'i, *Chia-i jih-li*, p. 73.

54. T'an, *Kuo-ch'üeh*, VI: 6129, 6131. Chi, *Ming-chi nan-lüeh*, I: 9.

55. T'an, *Kuo-ch'üeh*, VI: 6105; idem, *Tsao-lin tsa-tsu*, *jen*/8a–b. Ku, *Sheng-an pen-chi*, I: 5. Chi, *Ming-chi nan-lüeh*, I: 74–75.

56. T'an, *Kuo-ch'üeh*, VI: 6107, 6113. Ku, *Sheng-an pen-chi*, I: 6. Chi, *Ming-chi nan-lüeh*, I: 76–77.

57. Ch'en, *Kuo-chiang ch'i-shih*, 5a–6a.

58. Ibid., 10b.

59. T'an, *Kuo-ch'üeh*, VI: 6131–32. Chi, *Ming-chi nan-lüeh*, I: 73–74. Ku, *Sheng-an pen-chi*, I: 11.

60. Ku, *Sheng-an pen-chi*, I: 9. For Shih K'o-fa's memorial urging that the emperor take some initiative in resolving this conflict, see *Shih Chung-cheng Kung chi*, pp. 4–5.

61. Liu, *Liu Tzu ch'üan-shu*, 18/16b–17b.

62. On Tso Liang-yü, see Hummel, II: 761–62; and on the Tung-lin activist, Hou Hsün, and his son, the Fu She luminary Hou Fang-yü, see Hummel, I: 291–92. Also, see biographies that preface Hou Fang-yü's collected works, *Chuang-hui-t'ang chi* (T'ai-pei, 1968). And on both Hou Fang-yü and Tso as characters in the well-known historical play,

"The Peach Blossom Fan," see Chiang Yin-hsiang, *T'ao-hua-shan ming-jen hsiao-shih* (Hongkong, 1970), pp. 1–7 and 13–24, resp. Tso was not formally designated as the fifth *chen* until early September 1644. T'an, *Kuo-ch'üeh*, VI: 6136; Ku, *Sheng-an pen-chi*, I: 10.

63. T'an, *Kuo-ch'üeh*, VI: 6138, 6140, 6146. Chi, *Ming-chi nan-lüeh*, I: 93–95. Ku, *Sheng-an pen-chi*, I: 11. Li, *San-yüan pi-chi*, 7b.

64. Juan also was well known as one of the leading playwrights of the day. See Hummel, I: 398–99; Crawford, "The Biography of Juan Ta-ch'eng"; and Ch'ien Ping-teng, "Juan Ta-ch'eng pen-mo hsiao-chi," in *So-chih lu* (T'ai-pei repr., 1970), part 4.

65. For a discussion of this manifesto, see Atwell, "From Education to Politics: The Fu She," pp. 353–55. A list of signators is appended to Wu Ying-chi's *Ch'i-Chen liang-ch'ao p'o-fu lu*, ch. 10, in *Kuei-ch'ih hsien-che i-shu* (1920); and a narrative account by one of the signators is in Ch'en, "Shu-shih ch'i-tse," 4a–7b. Also, see Wu Ying-chi's vindication of this act in a collection of his writings, *Lou-shan-t'ang chi* (Shang-hai, 1935), ch. 15, pp. 176-77.

66. Ch'ien, "Juan Ta-ch'eng pen-mo," 4a–b.

67. T'an, *Kuo-ch'üeh*, VI: 6113–14, 6116–18, 6121. Chi, *Ming-chi nan-lüeh*, I: 6, 67, 85–88.

68. T'an, *Kuo-ch'üeh*, VI: 6133, 6141, 6143. Chi, *Ming-chi nan-lüeh*, I: 12, 88, 99–100. Ku, *Sheng-an pen-chi*, I: 9, 11. Most accounts simply assume that this direct edict was induced by Ma; but Ch'ien Ping-teng says that it was of Juan Ta-ch'eng's own doing and was unexpected by Ma ("Juan Ta-ch'eng pen-mo," 4a).

69. Charles O. Hucker, *The Censorial System of Ming China* (Stanford, 1966), pp. 209–10.

70. Yao, *Liu Chi-shan hsien-sheng nien-p'u*, pp. 324–25. T'an, *Kuo-ch'üeh*, VI: 6146, 6144, 6154. Chi, *Ming-chi nan-lüeh*, I: 144. Ku, *Sheng-an pen-chi*, I: 12, 14.

71. For instance, Lü Ta-ch'i already had stepped down as Senior Vice Minister of Rites on July 20, having been accused, among other things, of having harbored "different ideas" when the Prince of Fu was selected. T'an, *Kuo-ch'üeh*, VI: 6120; Ku, *Sheng-an pen-chi*, I: 7. Minister of Personnel Hsü Shih-ch'i was harassed by censors in Ma Shih-ying's clique and left office on October 30. T'an, *Kuo-ch'üeh*, VI: 6152–53, 6161; idem, *Tsao-lin tsa-tsu*, *jen*/15b–17b; Li, *San-yüan pi-chi*, *hsia*/9a–b. The influential governor of the Su-chou circuit, Ch'i Piao-chia, was permitted to resign in November after his loyalty and integrity were questioned by the same "Ma-Juan" censor who attacked many other "righteous" figures, Chang Sun-chen. Significantly, however, he received a personal letter from Ma Shih-ying asking him to stay on. Chi, *Ming-chi nan-lüeh*, I: 18–19; Ch'i, *Chia-i jih-li*, pp. 71, 74–76. The long-suffering Minister of Punishments, Hsieh Hsüeh-lung, finally succumbed to charges of letting traitors go free and was dismissed in February 1645. T'an, *Kuo-ch'üeh*, VI: 6178–80; Chi, *Ming-chi nan-lüeh*, I: 30. And Minister of Rites Ku Hsi-ch'ou lasted until March, when he resigned under retaliatory censure for trying to expose a corrupt official in Ma's clique. T'an, *Kuo-ch'üeh*, VI: 6146, 6148, 6185; Li, *San-yüan pi-chi*, *hsia*/8a. The most despised factional turncoat was the famed litterateur Ch'ien Ch'ien-i. See Hummel, I: 148–50; Li, *San-yüan pi-chi*, suppl. *hsia* on Hung-kuang, 4a; Hsia, *Hsü Hsing-ts'un lu*, p. 323; and T'an, *Kuo-ch'üeh*, VI: 6140, 6154.

72. T'an, *Kuo-ch'üeh*, VI: 6114, 6130–31, 6166, 6171. Chou, comp., *Hsing-ch'ao chih-lüeh*, 2/16a–17b. Ku, *Sheng-an pen-chi*, I: 8–9, 10, 13, 16, 28. Figures thus recognized fell into four categories (page numbers from Goodrich and Fang): (1) those unjustly killed or forced to commit suicide by Ming T'ai-tsu, such as Fu Yu-te (I: 466–70), Feng Sheng (I:

453–55), Liao Yung-chung (I: 909–10), and Keng Ping-wen (I: 713–18); (2) the Chien-wen emperor, Chu Yün-wen (I: 397-404), and his father, Chu Piao (I: 346–48), and those who died out of loyalty to them, such as Fang Hsiao-ju (I: 426–33); (3) the Ching-t'ai emperor, Chu Ch'i-yü (I: 294–97), and his adviser, Yü Ch'ien (II: 1608–11); and (4) those who resisted Wei Chung-hsien and either were killed under his tyranny or died later unrecognized, such as Li Ying-sheng (I: 708), Wen Chen-meng and Yao Hsi-meng (II: 1467–70), and Lü Wei-ch'i (I: 1014–17). On the belief that the calamities at the end of the Ming were being caused by the despondent spirits of the Chien-wen emperor and loyal supporters who died with him, see Wang Ch'ung-wu, *Ming ching-nan shih-shih k'ao-cheng kao* (Shang-hai, 1948), pp. 38–41.

73. T'an, *Kuo-ch'üeh*, VI: 6125–26, 6128. Chi, *Ming-chi nan-lüeh*, I: 6, 9, 37. Ku, *Sheng-an pen-chi*, I: 8, 16, 22, 24, 26.

74. For the best illustrations of this, peruse the public declarations in Feng, comp., *Chia-shen chi-shih*, ch. 7–8. Also, see Chi, *Ming-chi nan-lüeh*, I: 3; and Ku, *Sheng-an pen-chi*, I: 4.

75. T'an, *Kuo-ch'üeh*, VI: 6103, 6151–52. Chi, *Ming-chi nan-lüeh*, I: 16. Ku, *Sheng-an pen-chi*, I: 4. Shih, *Shih Chung-cheng Kung chi*, p. 11.

76. The court followed the pattern of prosecution of the T'ang dynasty in the aftermath of the An Lu-shan Rebellion by stipulating "six grades of criminality." T'an, *Kuo-ch'üeh*, VI: 6128, 6136, 6170, 6175. Chi, *Ming-chi nan-lüeh*, I: 9, 29, 124, 129. Ku, *Sheng-an pen-chi*, I: 12–13, 18. Also, see Chao, *Nien-erh-shih cha-chi*, pp. 756–59; and Szu-ma Kuang, *Tzu-chih t'ung-chien (Szu-pu ts'ung-k'an* ed.), 220/7b–12a.

77. Hsia, *Hsü Hsing-ts'un lu*, p. 328. Chi, *Ming-chi nan-lüeh*, I: 126. On the employment of turncoat officials, see T'an, *Kuo-ch'üeh*, VI: 6154, 6156; Chi, *Ming-chi nan-lüeh*, I: 17, 128; and Ku, *Sheng-an pen-chi*, I: 14, 18. The most egregious cases of unjust persecution were against prominent signators of the 1638 "Manifesto" against Juan Ta-ch'eng, especially Chou Piao. On this case, see Chi, *Ming-chi nan-lüeh*, I: 6, 11, 18, 19, 41, 126, 130; T'an, *Kuo-ch'üeh*, VI: 6116, 6140, 6156, 6212; idem, *Tsao-lin tsa-tsu, jen*/13b–14a; Li, *San-yüan pi-chi, hsia*/3b, 19b, 42b–43a; and Ku-ts'ang-shih Shih-ch'en [pseud.], *Hung-kuang shih-lu ch'ao* (CNW ed.), pp. 201, 255, 257–58. On the "Four Young Masters," Wu Ying-chi, Ch'en Chen-hui, Fang I-chih, and Hou Fang-yü, see Hummel, I: 52–53, 82–83, 232–33, and 291–92, resp.; T'an, *Kuo-ch'üeh*, VI: 6142; and Ku-ts'ang-shih, *Hung-kuang shih-lu ch'ao*, p. 258. For a general discussion of Hung-kuang partisan persecutions, especially the Chou Piao case, see Chao Ling-yang, "Lun Nan-Ming Hung-kuang ch'ao chih tang-huo," *Lien-ho shu-yüan hsüeh-pao*, 4 (1965): independently paginated.

78. Ch'en, *Kuo-chiang ch'i-shih*, 18a. Hsia, *Hsü Hsing-ts'un lu*, p. 326. Ch'ien, "Juan Ta-ch'eng pen-mo," 4a–b. T'an, *Kuo-ch'üeh*, VI: 6177.

79. Hsia, *Hsing-ts'un lu*, pp. 309–10; idem, *Hsü Hsing-ts'un lu*, p. 326. Li, *San-yüan pi-chi, hsia*/13a–b, 18b–20a, 23b. Chi, *Ming-chi nan-lüeh*, II: 173–76. T'an, *Tsao-lin tsa-tsu, jen*/17b–18a. Lu, *Hsien-yen*, p. 45. T'an, *Kuo-ch'üeh*, VI: 6195.

80. T'an, *Kuo-ch'üeh*, VI: 6168, 6179. Ku, *Sheng-an pen-chi*, I: 17. When others objected to this, the emperor, very irritated about the whole issue and again revealing his stupidity in politics, replied that it had nothing to do with incumbent officials and was solely a matter of his own family history. Ku, *Sheng-an pen-chi*, I: 23; Chi, *Ming-chi nan-lüeh*, II: 175. Yang and his allies also requested formal, imperial condolences for deceased *ni-an* figures and public absolution from guilt for others. T'an, *Kuo-ch'üeh*, VI: 6170, 6182; Chi, *Ming-chi nan-lüeh*, I: 34, and II: 174–75.

81. Hsia, *Hsing-ts'un lu*, p. 309.

82. One exception to this pattern was the reign of the Yung-lo emperor, Chu Ti, who became indebted to the court eunuchs in the course of his usurpation and subsequently made extensive use of their services. Crawford, "Eunuch Power," pp. 126–29.

83. Ch'ien, "Juan Ta-ch'eng pen-mo," 4a.

84. T'an, *Kuo-ch'üeh*, VI: 6126, 6179. Idem, *Tsao-lin tsa-tsu, jen/9a–b.* Hsia, *Hsing-ts'un lu*, p. 309. Chi, *Ming-chi nan-lüeh*, I: 29.

85. T'an, *Kuo-ch'üeh*, VI: 6136, 6140, 6145. Ch'i, *Chia-i jih-li*, p. 42. Chi, *Ming-chi nan-lüeh*, I: 104. Yao, *Liu Chi-shan hsien-sheng nien-p'u*, p. 323. Hucker, *Censorial System*, p. 44. Crawford, "Eunuch Power," pp. 131–33. Ch'i Piao-chia, *Ch'i Piao-chia chi* (Shanghai, 1960), pp. 21–22.

86. T'an, *Kuo-ch'üeh*, VI: 6106, 6110–11, 6150. Chi, *Ming-chi nan-lüeh*, I: 76. Ma was not formally designated Chief Grand Secretary until late January or early February 1645. Ku, *Sheng-an pen-chi*, I: 21; Chi, *Ming-chi nan-lüeh*, I: 27.

87. Li, *San-yüan pi-chi, hsia/44b.*

88. Chou, comp., *Hsing-ch'ao chih-lüeh*, 2/1a–3a. T'an, *Kuo-ch'üeh*, VI: 6103.

89. Ch'en, *Kuo-chiang ch'i-shih*, 8a–9b, 14a. Li, *San-yüan pi-chi, hsia/11a.* Ku, *Sheng-an pen-chi*, I: 6. T'an, *Kuo-ch'üeh*, VI: 6139.

90. T'an, *Kuo-ch'üeh*, VI: 6154.

91. Lu, *Hsien-yen*, p. 23.

92. T'an, *Kuo-ch'üeh*, VI: 6171, 6175. Chi, *Ming-chi nan-lüeh*, I: 149.

93. T'an, *Kuo-ch'üeh*, VI: 6141, 6155, 6157, 6203. Chi, *Ming-chi nan-lüeh*, I: 12, 42, and II: 172–73. Ku, *Sheng-an pen-chi*, I: 11, 14.

94. Li, *San-yüan pi-chi, hsia/15a.* T'an, *Kuo-ch'üeh*, VI: 6138–39, 6149, 6162. Chi, *Ming-chi nan-lüeh*, II: 153, 172.

95. T'an, *Kuo-ch'üeh*, VI: 6166. Chi, *Ming-chi nan-lüeh*, I: 148.

96. Ch'ien Ping-teng, "Nan-tu san i-an," in *So-chih lu*, part 3, 1a–b, 3a–6b. Chi, *Ming-chi nan-lüeh*, I: 24, 26, and II: 171. Hsia, *Hsü Hsing-ts'un lu*, p. 323. T'an, *Kuo-ch'üeh*, VI: 6168, 6191. Ku, *Sheng-an pen-chi*, I: 13, 18. Soon thereafter a leatherworker of Nan-ching, raving wildly that he was the father of the emperor, tried to enter the palace; but he immediately was beaten to death. Hsia, *Hsü Hsing-ts'un-lu*, pp. 327–28; Chi, *Ming-chi nan-lüeh*, I: 40.

97. T'an, *Kuo-ch'üeh*, VI: 6120, 6144, 6171. Chi, *Ming-chi nan-lüeh*, I: 8, and II: 166.

98. T'an, *Kuo-ch'üeh*, VI: 6190–94, 6196, 6198, 6200–01. Chi, *Ming-chi nan-lüeh*, I: 37, 39, and II: 153–57, 159–61. Ku, *Sheng-an pen-chi*, I: 24–25. Ch'ien, "Nan-tu san i-an," 5a–6b. Li, *San-yüan pi-chi, hsia/17a*, 27a–29b, 34a–b. Ying, *Ch'ing-lin hsieh, hsia/7b–8a.* Lu, *Hsien-yen*, pp. 34–38, 44. Lin Shih-tui, *Ho-cha ts'ung-t'an* (T'ai-pei, 1962), pp. 127–28.

99. SCSL, 12/14a–15a. MCSL, *chia*, I: 96a. Ch'ien Hsin, *Chia-shen ch'uan-hsin lu* (CNW ed.), pp. 149–53. Meng, "Ming Lieh Huang hsün-kuo hou-chi," pp. 29–43. On popular unrest in Ch'ing territory because of belief in the genuineness of the "Northern Heir," see T'an, *Kuo-ch'üeh*, VI: 6202–03; and Ch'ien, *Chia-shen ch'uan-hsin lu*, pp. 153–54.

100. T'an, *Kuo-ch'üeh*, VI: 6195–96. Chi, *Ming-chi nan-lüeh*, II: 167–70. Ku, *Sheng-an pen-chi*, I: 24. Ch'ien, "Nan-tu san i-an," 1b–6b. Li, *San-yüan pi-chi, hsia/30a–b.* Ying, *Ch'ing-lin hsieh, hsia/7b.* Lu, *Hsien-yen*, pp. 24–25. Lin Shih-tui even counts the true

identity of the purported Prince of Fu as one of the "Three Suspicious Cases of the Southern Capital"; see *Ho-cha ts'ung-t'an*, pp. 126–29.

101. For a history of how Nan-ching became the capital of the early Ming state, see Frederick Mote, "The Transformation of Nanking, 1350–1400," in *The City in Late Imperial China*, ed. G. Wm. Skinner (Stanford, 1977), pp. 101–53. On Nan-ching's subordination to the status of auxiliary capital, see Edward Farmer, *Early Ming Government: The Evolution of Dual Capitals* (Cambridge, Mass., 1976). On patterns of staffing in the course of the dynasty, see Huang K'ai-hua, *Ming-shih lun-chi* (Hongkong, 1972), chaps. 1 and 2. Nan-ching had come to serve the dynasty primarily as a military base for defending and policing the rich Chiang-nan region and, in effect, as provincial capital of the most important "province," Nan Chih-li, which fed and clothed, by production or transport, the Northern Metropolitan Area. Consequently, by the end of the Ming the most important officials there were the Nan-ching Minister of Revenues and a security triumvirate consisting of the Minister of War and (always concurrently) Grand Adjutant, a Grand Commandant, and a Commissioner-in-Chief for River Control. Lung, *Ming hui-tien*, I: 541, 566–67, and II: 1230–31.

102. T'an, *Kuo-ch'üeh*, VI: 6090–91, 6095, 6102, 6110, 6129, 6140, 6175. Chi, *Ming-chi nan-lüeh*, I: 5, 19, 29. Li, *San-yüan pi-chi, hsia*/14b–15a. Chou, comp., *Hsing-ch'ao chih-lüeh*, 2/13a–15a.

103. Liu, *Liu Tzu ch'üan-shu*, 18/3a–5a. Ku-ts'ang-shih, *Hung-kuang shih-lu ch'ao*, p. 185.

104. Ch'en, *Kuo-chiang ch'i-shih*, 1a. Shih, *Shih Chung-cheng Kung chi*, pp. 3–4. Chou, comp., *Hsing-ch'ao chih-lüeh*, 2/6a. T'an, *Kuo-ch'üeh*, VI: 6094–95.

105. T'an, *Kuo-ch'üeh*, VI: 6142. Chi, *Ming-chi nan-lüeh*, I: 73.

106. T'an, *Kuo-ch'üeh*, VI: 6110, 6134. Chi, *Ming-chi nan-lüeh*, I: 6, and II: 213, 216. Chou, comp., *Hsing-ch'ao chih-lüeh*, 2/4a. Ch'en Pang-yen, *Ch'en Yen-yeh hsien-sheng ch'üan-chi* (1805), 1/29b–30a.

107. *Huai-ch'eng chi-shih*, 1a–b, 3b, 4b–5a, 7b–8a. Yen Erh-mei, *Yen Ku-ku ch'üan-chi* (1911), 1/8a–b. T'an, *Kuo-ch'üeh*, VI: 6106, 6111. Chi, *Ming-chi nan-lüeh*, I: 115–26. Ku, *Sheng-an pen-chi*, I: 5.

108. In May and June the news seems only to have been of Wu's successes. See Ch'i, *Chia-i jih-li*, pp. 20, 34; *Huai-ch'eng chi-shih*, 9a; T'an, *Kuo-ch'üeh*, VI: 6017, 6106; and Chi, *Ming-chi nan-lüeh*, I: 4. On the receipt of the Manchus' first proclamation to the South in Nan-ching on July 9, and its publication on July 18, see T'an, *Kuo-ch'üeh*, VI: 6120; and Chi, *Ming-chi nan-lüeh*, II: 213–14.

109. Ch'en, *Ch'en Yen-yeh hsien-sheng ch'üan-chi*, 1/29a–30a.

110. T'an, *Kuo-ch'üeh*, VI: 6086, 6105, 6107–08, 6120, 6122, 6147. Chi, *Ming-chi nan-lüeh*, I: 9, 123, 133.

111. T'an, *Kuo-ch'üeh*, VI: 6127–28. Chi, *Ming-chi nan-lüeh*, I: 8, and II: 214–15. Ku, *Sheng-an pen-chi*, I: 7–9.

112. T'an, *Kuo-ch'üeh*, VI: 6127, 6131–32. Chi, *Ming-chi nan-lüeh*, II: 216. Ch'i, *Chia-i jih-li*, p. 54. Shih, *Shih Chung-cheng Kung chi*, pp. 6–7.

113. Li, *San-yüan pi-chi, hsia*/5b, 16a–b. Ch'ien Hsin, "Shih-ch'en pi-hsüeh," in *Chia-shen ch'uan-hsin lu*, ch. 10. T'an, *Tsao-lin tsa-tsu, jen*/13a. Wu, *Fu-She hsing-shih chuan-lüeh*, 10/3b–4a.

114. T'an, *Kuo-ch'üeh*, VI: 6130. Chi, *Ming-chi nan-lüeh*, II: 215. On Ma's role in

service to the Ch'ung-chen Minister of War, Ch'en Hsin-chia, who was executed for his peace-seeking efforts in 1642, see Chao, *Nien-erh shih cha-chi*, pp. 739–40; and Lo, "Policy Formulation and Decision-Making," pp. 68–69.

115. T'an, *Kuo-ch'üeh*, VI: 6111, 6114. SCSL, 5/17a, 23b.

116. Ch'en Hung-fan, *Pei-shih chi-lüeh* (*Ching-t'o i-shih* ed.), passim. Li Kuang-t'ao, ed. and annot., *Ming-Ch'ing tang-an ts'un-chen hsüan-chi* (T'ai-pei, 1959), I: 125–27. Chi, *Ming-chi nan-lüeh*, II: 219, 221. SCSL, 8/17a and 11/3b. Ch'ien, *Chia-shen ch'uan-hsin lu*, pp. 156–58. Various commentators assume that the Ch'ing decision to advance in force on the South was made on the basis of information divulged to them by Ch'en Hung-fan. Primary documents have shown that the Ch'ing had other informants before they contacted Ch'en. It does seem true, however, that Ch'en contributed to the final decision to begin the southward campaign, which was made during the time that the ambassadorial mission was in Pei-ching. Li, ed., *Ming-Ch'ing tang-an*, I: 115–16; SCSL, 10/10a–b, 12a–b, and 11/21a–b.

117. T'an, *Kuo-ch'üeh*, VI: 6161. Chi, *Ming-chi nan-lüeh*, I: 21, 23, and II: 217–18. Ku, *Sheng-an pen-chi*, I: 15–16. Ying, *Ch'ing-lin hsieh, shang*/14b.

118. Shih, *Shih Chung-cheng Kung chi*, pp. 11–13. Chi, *Ming-chi nan-lüeh*, I: 218. Ying, *Ch'ing-lin hsieh, shang*/15b.

119. T'an, *Kuo-ch'üeh*, VI: 6169. Chi, *Ming-chi nan-lüeh*, II: 220.

120. Jerry Dennerline, "Hsü Tu and the Lesson of Nanking: Political Integration and Local Defense in Chiang-nan, 1634–45," in *From Ming to Ch'ing*, pp. 118–22. Chi, *Ming-chi nan-lüeh*, I: 145–46. Atwell, "Ch'en Tzu-lung," pp. 114–21, 126.

121. T'an, *Kuo-ch'üeh*, VI: 6140. Ch'i, *Chia-i jih-li*, p. 32. Yao, *Liu Chi-shan hsien-sheng nien-p'u*, p. 319. On the fears aroused in southern Nan Chih-li by this militancy, see Ch'i, *Chia-i jih-li*, pp. 56–57.

122. T'an, *Kuo-ch'üeh*, VI: 6142, 6144. Chi, *Ming-chi nan-lüeh*, I: 145. Ch'i, *Chia-i jih-li*, pp. 54, 59. Ku-ts'ang-shih, *Hung-kuang shih-lu ch'ao*, p. 221.

123. Anon., *Ching-k'ou pien-lüeh* (*T'ung-shih* ed.), passim. Ch'i, *Chia-i jih-li*, pp. 32, 45, 47, 56, 63, 66, 69. T'an, *Kuo-ch'üeh*, VI: 6091, 6125. Ku, *Sheng-an pen-chi*, I: 8.

124. Ch'i, *Chia-i jih-li*, pp. 32, 47. Ku-ts'ang-shih, *Hung-kuang shih-lu ch'ao*, p. 198.

125. After Ch'i's departure, affairs at Chen-chiang were overseen by Juan Ta-ch'eng himself and by Ma Shih-ying's brother-in-law, the famous artist Yang Wen-ts'ung. Hummel, II: 895–96; Ch'i, *Chia-i jih-li*, p. 72.

126. Chi, *Ming-chi nan-lüeh*, I: 3. Ch'i, *Chia-i jih-li*, pp. 33, 37. Idem, *Ch'i Piao-chia chi*, pp. 18–19. Feng, comp., *Chia-shen chi-shih*, ch. 8.

127. T'an, *Kuo-ch'üeh*, VI: 6152, 6169, 6165, 6180–81, 6183, 6185, 6203. Chi, *Ming-chi nan-lüeh*, I: 15, 21, 24, 29, 32, 34, 36.

128. T'an, *Kuo-ch'üeh*, VI: 6130, 6132, 6143. Chi, *Ming-chi nan-lüeh*, I: 11, 24. Chou, comp., *Hsing-ch'ao chih-lüeh*, 2/11a–12b. Shih, *Shih Chung-cheng Kung chi*, pp. 9–11.

129. T'an, *Kuo-ch'üeh*, VI: 6150. Also, see Li, *San-yüan pi-chi, hsia*/20b.

130. Li, *San-yüan pi-chi, hsia*/13a–b, 19b–20a, 23b. T'an, *Kuo-ch'üeh*, VI: 6150. Chi, *Ming-chi nan-lüeh*, I: 20, 146. Ku, *Sheng-an pen-chi*, I: 16.

131. [Wan], *Ch'ung-chen ch'ang-pien*, 2/3a. T'an, *Kuo-ch'üeh*, VI: 6102.

132. Yasuno Shōzō, "'Kokō juku sureba tenka taru' kō," in *Kimura Masao sensei taikan kinen tōyōshi ronshū* (Tokyo, 1976), pp. 301–09. Shigeta Atsushi, "Shinsho ni okeru Konan bei shijō no ichi kōsatsu," in *Shindai shakai keizai shi kenkyū* (Tokyo, 1975), esp. pp.

10–13. Mark Elvin, "Market Towns and Waterways: The County of Shanghai from 1480 to 1910," in *The City in Late Imperial China*, ed. Skinner, pp. 441–73.

133. [Wan], *Ch'ung-chen ch'ang-pien*, 2/13a–b. T'an, *Kuo-ch'üeh*, VI: 6138. Ch'i, *Chia-i jih-li*, pp. 49, 52–53, 62–63, 66–67. Attempts were made, with limited success, to bring grain from Kuang-tung and Fu-chien. Ch'en, *Kuo-chiang ch'i-shih*, 1a; T'an, *Kuo-ch'üeh*, VI: 6150, 6120. Evelyn Rawski points out that, especially in the years 1643–44, various troops destroyed ten out of the twelve prefectural offices in Hu-kuang, and that the province did not regain its sixteenth-century agricultural yields until the eighteenth century, under a Ch'ing program to resettle abandoned land in that severely depopulated region (*Agricultural Change and the Peasant Economy of South China* [Cambridge, Mass., 1972], pp. 101–02). On Nan-ching's position as a service center to the Northern Metropolitan Area, see Wu Chi-hua, "Ming Ch'eng-tsu hsiang pei-fang te fa-chan yü nan-pei chuan-yün te chien-li," in *Ming-tai she-hui ching-chi shih lun-ts'ung*, I: 155–73.

134. Huang, *Taxation*, pp. 98–104. Jerry Dennerline, "Fiscal Reform and Local Control: The Gentry-Bureaucratic Alliance Survives the Conquest," in *Conflict and Control in Late Imperial China*, ed. Frederic Wakeman and Carolyn Grant (Berkeley, 1975), pp. 86–120. Wu Chi-hua, "Lun Ming-tai shui-liang chung-hsin chih ti-yü chi ch'i chung-shui chih yu-lai," in *Ming-tai she-hui ching-chi shih lun-ts'ung*, I: 33–73.

135. Ch'i, *Chia-i jih-li*, pp. 39, 60, 69–70, 76, 79. Idem, *Ch'i Piao-chia chi*, pp. 18–19. Ku, *Sheng-an pen-chi*, I: 16. Chi, *Ming-chi nan-lüeh*, I: 4.

136. T'an, *Kuo-ch'üeh*, VI: 6096, 6147. Li, *San-yüan pi-chi*, 13b–14b.

137. Over 7,800 taels were spent on cooking and dining utensils, and on kitchen staff uniforms. Chi, *Ming-chi nan-lüeh*, II: 153. The imperial wedding cost 20,000 taels; and a ceremonial crown encrusted with pearls ran to about 300,000 taels. Li, *San-yüan pi-chi*, hsia/15a. For complaints that soldiers had become too numerous and that they lacked provisions, see T'an, *Kuo-ch'üeh*, VI: 6142, 6151, 6161, 6163–64; Chi, *Ming-chi nan-lüeh*, I: 21, 28–29, 34; and Ying, *Ch'ing-lin hsieh*, hsia/1a.

138. T'an, *Kuo-ch'üeh*, VI: 6148, 6165, 6167, 6172, 6183, 6187, 6199, 6204. Chi, *Ming-chi nan-lüeh*, I: 15, 24. Ku, *Sheng-an pen-chi*, I: 13. On these and other common Ming miscellaneous taxes, see Huang, *Taxation*, chap. 6; and idem, "Ni Yüan-lu," p. 423. On the minting of coins by the Hung-kuang and other Southern Ming courts, see Yang Yün-p'ing, "Chi hsin-te Nan-Ming ch'ien-pi," *Ch'ien-pi t'ien-ti*, 2.1 (Jan. 1978): 3–7; and Shih Yang-sui, "Nan-Ming ch'ien-lu," *T'ai-wan feng-wu*, 11.4 (1962): 46–47.

139. T'an, *Kuo-ch'üeh*, VI: 6120, 6126, 6141, 6143, 6148, 6164, 6180, 6183. Chi, *Ming-chi nan-lüeh*, I: 13, 17. For an explanation of the beginnings and implications of the "gold floral silver," see Huang, *Taxation*, pp. 52–53.

140. T'an, *Kuo-ch'üeh*, VI: 6099–6100, 6106, 6136. Ku, *Sheng-an pen-chi*, I: 2, 4. Compare the taxation item in the *chien-kuo* proclamation with that in the enthronement proclamation (Chou, comp., *Hsing-ch'ao chih-lüeh*, 1a and 14a, resp.). On the various supernumerary taxes for "Liao-tung," "extermination," and "training" provisions, see Wu, "Ming-tai te chün-ping," pp. 138–41; Li, *Wan-Ming min-pien*, pp. 20–24; and Lung, *Ming hui-tien*, II: 1033–34.

141. Ying, *Ch'ing-lin hsieh*, hsia/17a. The Minister of Revenues under the Ch'ung-chen emperor also had urged that army commanders be given a free hand in raising funds in their own territories. See Huang, "Ni Yüan-lu," p. 423.

142. T'an, *Kuo-ch'üeh*, VI: 6200–02, 6204. Chi, *Ming-chi nan-lüeh*, I: 40–41, and II:

160–62, 192–97. Ku, *Sheng-an pen-chi*,I: 26–27. Li, *San-yüan pi-chi, hsia*/34b–36a, 37b–38b; suppl. *hsia* on Hung-kuang, 1a–2b. Yüan, *Hsün-yang chi-shih*, 11b, 13a–14a.

143. T'an, *Kuo-ch'üeh*, VI: 6200. Chi, *Ming-chi nan-lüeh*, I: 41, and II: 197–98. Ying, *Ch'ing-lin hsieh*, 10a–11b. Lin, *Ho-cha ts'ung-t'an*, pp. 124–26.

CHAPTER TWO

1. Li Kuang-t'ao, "Ch'ing-jen yü liu-tsei," in *Ming-Ch'ing shih lun-chi*, II: 349–50 (also see idem, "Lun Chien-chou yü liu-tsei," pp. 196–97).

2. Roth, "The Manchu-Chinese Relationship," pp. 7–10.

3. SCSL, 4/5a–7a, 8b, 11b.

4. Ibid., 13a–19b. Cf. introduction, n. 3.

5. Chi, *Ming-chi pei-lüeh*, III: 469. Wakeman, "The Shun Interregnum," p. 4. The date used here, however, follows SCSL, 5/1b–2a. Also, see biog. of the Shun-chih emperor (Fulin) in Hummel, I: 255–59. On the ease with which the Manchus entered Pei-ching, see MCSL, *chia*, I: 65a.

6. Slightly variant versions of this proclamation are recorded in Chi, *Ming-chi nan-lüeh*, II: 13–14 (dated June 5) and in T'an, *Kuo-ch'üeh*, VI: 6087 (dated June 9). However, it is not recorded in the SCSL.

7. SCSL, 5/2b, 4a–b, 10a–b. I Songgyu, "Shantung in the Shun-chih Reign," part 2, p. 7. On the policy, eventually enforced in both North and South, of requiring all men to adopt the Manchu hairstyle as a sign of political submission, see Nakayama Hachirō, "Hantō ni okeru bempatsu no mondai—Shinsho no bempatsu rei shikō o chūshin to shite," *Chūgokushi kenkyū*, 5 (1968): 1–24.

8. Roth, "The Manchu-Chinese Relationship," pp. 28–30.

9. According to Chaoying Fang ("A Technique for Estimating the Numerical Strength of the Early Manchu Military Forces," *Harvard Journal of Asiatic Studies*, 13.1–2 [June 1950]: 192–215), in 1644 there were 278 Manchu, 120 Mongol, and 563 Chinese companies (*niru*), each consisting of approximately 300 men. SCSL, 4/9a-b states that two-thirds of the Manchu and Mongol units and all of the Chinese units were used for the initial invasion of North China. This would mean roughly 248,500 men. Contemporary estimates of the size of Wu San-kuei's army, before its battles with Li Tzu-ch'eng, range from 20,000 to 50,000 (see Ch'en, "Ch'ing-ping ju-kuan," p. 738; and Hsi, "Wu San-kuei," pp. 448, 450).

10. Li, *San-yüan pi-chi, hsia*/14a.

11. Parsons, *Peasant Rebellions*, pp. 186–88.

12. T'an, *Kuo-ch'üeh*, VI: 6118–19.

13. SCSL, 5/15b–16a, 19b; 7/12b–13a.

14. This view is shared by Ku Ch'eng in his article, "Lun Ch'ing-ch'u she-hui mao-tun," *Ch'ing-shih lun-ts'ung* (Institute of History, Chinese Academy of Social Sciences), 2 (1980): 141–42.

15. Lai Chia-tu and Li Kuang-pi, "Shan-tung Yü-yüan ch'i-i chün k'ang-Ch'ing shih-chi ch'u-t'an," in *Chung-kuo nung-min ch'i-i lun-wen chi* (Pei-ching, 1958), pp. 288–94. Hsieh Kuo-chen, *Ch'ing-ch'u nung-min ch'i-i tzu-liao chi-lu* (Shang-hai: 1956), pp. 74–86. I Songgyu, "Shantung in the Shun-chih Reign," part 1, pp. 14–15. MCSL, *chia*, I: 69a, 74a–b. T'an, *Kuo-ch'üeh*, VI: 6143.

16. SCSL, 5/26a; 6/7a; 8/14a. MCSL, *chia*, I: 86a–b. Li, ed., *Ming-Ch'ing tang-an*, I:

118–19. Chi, *Ming-chi nan-lüeh*, II: 214, 216–17. T'an, *Kuo-ch'üeh*, VI: 6127, 6147, 6155. Ch'en, *Pei-shih chi-lüeh*, 1a.

17. SCSL, 6/2b–3a; 8/7a–b, 8b–9a; 10/12b–13a. MCSL, *chia*, I: 77a–b, 80a, 85a–b, 87a, 91a. Li, ed., *Ming-Ch'ing tang-an*, I: 128, 131.

18. SCSL, 5/17a–b, 23b; 11/4a, 21a–b. Li, ed., *Ming-Ch'ing tang-an*, II: 117 and note, p. 32. On the enigmatic case of Ling Chiung, who at times seems surely to have been aiding the Ch'ing, but who, in the end, died loyal to the Ming, see T'an, *Kuo-ch'üeh*, VI: 6139, 6141, 6163, 6167, 6198; Chi, *Ming-chi nan-lüeh*, I: 2, 23, 28, and II: 214–16, 223–26; MCSL, *chia*, I: 81a–b; and Li, ed., *Ming-Ch'ing tang-an*, I: 124 and note, p. 34.

19. Li, ed., *Ming-Ch'ing tang-an*, I: 122, 129–30, and note, p. 35. Ch'en, *Pei-shih chi-lüeh*, 2a–b, 4a. Another factor was that the mission arrived in the vicinity of Pei-ching just when security was tightened because of the simultaneous arrival of the "little khan," i.e., the Shun-chih emperor, and his installation in the imperial place. Ch'en, *Pei-shih chi-lüeh*, 2a. SCSL, 7/24a; 8/14a; MCSL, *chia*, I: 93a.

20. SCSL, 6/16b–19b. Of course, at this time such letters were written for the Manchu leaders by collaborating Chinese litterateurs.

21. Shih, *Shih Chung-cheng Kung chi*, pp. 23–25. Chi, *Ming-chi nan-lüeh*, II: 209. Also, see Hellmut Wilhelm, "Ein Briefwechsel zwischen Durgan und Schi Ko-Fa," *Sinica*, 8.5–6 (1933): 239–45. Shih is said to have softened the wording of a harsher draft which was prepared by one of his secretaries, Huang Jih-fang. So Huang had his draft published independently. T'an, *Tsao-lin tsa-tsu, jen*/18b. This latter version apparently is the one used by the K'ang-hsi scholar Wen Jui-lin in his history of the Southern Ming, *Nan-chiang i-shih* (Shang-hai, 1960), pp. 38–39.

22. Li, ed., *Ming-Ch'ing tang-an*, I: 115–16. MCSL, *chia*, I: 81a–b.

23. Ch'en, *Pei-shih chi-lüeh*, 1a–2a. SCSL, 8/17a.

24. SCSL, 10/12a–b. See biog. of Dodo in Hummel, I: 215.

25. For detailed accounts of this phase, see Li, *Ming-chi liu-k'ou shih-mo*, pp. 101–12; Li, *Wan-Ming min-pien*, pp. 156–59; and Parsons, *Peasant Rebellions*, pp. 163–66.

26. SCSL, 7/2a–3a; 8/11a–b; 10/7a–b.

27. Ibid., 7/2b; 10/10a–b, 12a–b, 14b–15b. See biog. of Ajige in Hummel, I: 4–5.

28. SCSL, 10/12a–b. MCSL, *chia*, I: 90. T'an, *Kuo-ch'üeh*, VI: 6158. Chi, *Ming-chi nan-lüeh*, I: 124, and II: 218. Hsieh, *Ch'ing-ch'u nung-min ch'i-i tzu-liao chi-lu*, pp. 117–19.

29. SCSL, 12/5a, 7a–b; 14/1b–3b. MCSL, *chia*, I: 99. T'an, *Kuo-ch'üeh*, VI: 6174.

30. T'an, *Kuo-ch'üeh*, VI: 6161. Chi, *Ming-chi nan-lüeh*, I: 20, and II: 218. Ku, *Sheng-an pen-chi*, I: 16. Ying, *Ch'ing-lin hsieh, shang*/15b. SCSL, 11/23b.

31. T'an, *Kuo-ch'üeh*, VI: 6162–64, 6171, 6174. Chi, *Ming-chi nan-lüeh*, II: 209–10, 218, 220. Ku, *Sheng-an pen-chi*, I: 18. Li, ed., *Ming-Ch'ing tang-an*, I: 131.

32. SCSL, 13/7b, 9b; 14/7b, 15a–b. MCSL, *chia*, II: 101 (also Li, ed., *Ming-Ch'ing tang-an*, I: 134). Moreover, I suspect that Ch'en Hung-fan was sent back to the South by the Ch'ing, with warning of their imminent advance, along the Grand Canal route precisely to reinforce the diversionary effect of this holding front.

33. T'an, *Kuo-ch'üeh*, VI: 6192. Chi, *Ming-chi nan-lüeh*, I: 37, 40. Li, ed., *Ming-Ch'ing tang-an*, III: 81.

34. Tai Li and Wu I, *Huai-ling liu-k'ou shih-chung lu* (*Hsüan-lan-t'ang ts'ung-shu* ed.), 18/5b–6a. Wang Fu-chih, *Yung-li shih-lu* (*Ch'uan-shan ch'üan-chi* ed., 1965), 13/1a. P'eng P'u-sheng, "Li Tzu-ch'eng pei-hai jih-ch'i t'an-k'ao," *Ku-kung po-wu-yüan yüan-k'an*, 1980, no. 3 (Aug.), p. 39. T'an, *Kuo-ch'üeh*, VI: 6206.

35. SCSL, 18/4a–6a.

36. SCSL, 14/7b–8a; 15/6b.

37. Chi, *Ming-chi nan-lüeh*, I: 28, and II: 199–201. Ying, *Ch'ing-lin hsieh, hsia*/1a, 2a–3b. Lu, *Hsien-yen*, p. 46. MCSL, *chia*, I: 100–01 (Li, ed., *Ming-Ch'ing tang-an*, I: 133–34).

38. Ku, *Sheng-an pen-chi*, I: 22–23, 26. T'an, *Kuo-ch'üeh*, VI: 6184–85, 6200. Ying, *Ch'ing-lin hsieh, hsia*/12a. Chi, *Ming-chi nan-lüeh*, I: 43. Shih, *Shih Chung-cheng Kung chi*, pp. 17–18. Hsia, *Hsü Hsing-ts'un lu*, pp. 328–29. Ch'i, *Chia-i jih-li*, p. 105.

39. SCSL, 15/6b, 11b–12a. The *shih-lu* mistakenly records "Nan-yang" for Lan-yang. This is typical of the many errors in proper names found in the Ch'ing *shih-lu* for the Southern Ming years, errors which may have resulted from the later translation of field reports from Manchu into Chinese. On this problem and others, see Huang Chang-chien, "Tu Ch'ing Shih-tsu shih-lu," in *Ming-Ch'ing shih yen-chiu ts'ung-kao* (T'ai-pei, 1977), pp. 594–612. Also, see T'an, *Kuo-ch'üeh*, VI: 6194, 6199, 6200; Chi, *Ming-chi nan-lüeh*, I: 37, and II: 227; and Ku, *Sheng-an pen-chi*, I: 24.

40. SCSL, 16/19b–20a. T'an, *Kuo-ch'üeh*, VI: 6201, 6203. Chi, *Ming-chi nan-lüeh*, I: 41, and II: 227; Ku, *Sheng-an pen-chi*, I: 24. The waterway at Huai-an then was called the Ch'ing River, and the strategic point at which the Huai and Yellow rivers intersected was called the "Ch'ing River Mouth."

41. Shih, *Shih Chung-cheng Kung chi*, pp. 21–22. Ying, *Ch'ing-lin hsieh, hsia*/10a. T'an, *Kuo-ch'üeh*, VI: 6200, 6202. Chi, *Ming-chi nan-lüeh*, I: 41, and II: 228. Ku, *Sheng-an pen-chi*, I: 26. Yüan, *Hsün-yang chi-shih*, 13a–14a.

42. T'an, *Kuo-ch'üeh*, VI: 6203–04, 6206. Chi, *Ming-chi nan-lüeh*, I: 42, 44, and II: 197–98, 227–28.

43. Ying, *Ch'ing-lin hsieh, hsia*/11a–12a. SCSL, 16/20a–b.

44. Ying, *Ch'ing-lin hsieh, hsia*/14a, 15b–16b.

45. SCSL, 16/20a. Ying, *Ch'ing-lin hsieh, hsia*/14a, 15b–16a. T'an, *Kuo-ch'üeh*, VI: 6205–06. Shu I, "Shih K'o-fa Yang-chou szu-nan k'ao," *Kuang-ming jih-pao*, History sec., Sept. 17, 1959.

46. From Wang Hsiu-ch'u, *Yang-chou shih-jih chi* (CNW, vol. 2), as translated by Lucien Mao, "A Memoir of a Ten Days' Massacre in Yangchow," *T'ien Hsia Monthly*, 4.5 (May 1937), pp. 520, 521–22, 527, 534. Also, see Chang Te-fang, "'Yang-chou shih jih-chi' pien-wu," in *Chung-hua wen-shih lun-ts'ung* (Shang-hai, 1964), V: 365–76.

47. MCSL, *chia*, II: 113a. SCSL, 16/20b; 17/9b–10b. Ying, *Ch'ing-lin hsieh, hsia*/16b. T'an, *Kuo-ch'üeh*, VI: 6206.

48. This is an interpretive summary of several disparate and somewhat garbled contemporaneous accounts. See SCSL, 16/20b–21a; Ying, *Ch'ing-lin hsieh, hsia*/17a; Chi, *Ming-chi nan-lüeh*, II: 233–34; Li, *San-yüan pi-chi*, suppl. *hsia* on Hung-kuang, 3a–b; and Ch'i, *Chia-i jih-li*, p. 106.

49. Martin Martinus, *Bellum Tartaricum*, English trans. (London, 1654), p. 115. The author was in Nan-ching at the time, but this work is cited more for its color than for its accuracy. Martinus, like other European missionary priests who wrote accounts of the conquest period in China, relied mainly on hearsay and imagination, and does not fully merit the praise he receives for veracity in two otherwise interesting works: Chen Min-sun, "Three Contemporary Western Sources on the History of the Late Ming and the Manchu Conquest of China," Ph.D. diss., University of Chicago, 1971; and Edwin J. Van Kley, "News from China: Seventeenth-Century Notices of the Manchu Conquest," *Journal of Modern History*, 45.4 (Dec. 1973): 561–82.

50. Chi, *Ming-chi nan-lüeh*, II: 234–36. Ku, *Sheng-an pen-chi*, I: 29. Li, *San-yüan pi-chi*, suppl. *hsia* on Hung-kuang, 3b.

51. T'an, *Kuo-ch'üeh*, VI: 6206(quotation)–07. Chi, *Ming-chi nan-lüeh*, II: 179.

52. T'an, *Kuo-ch'üeh*, VI: 6207–08.

53. Ibid., 6208–09. Chi, *Ming-chi nan-lüeh*, I: 44, and II: 231. Lu, *Hsien-yen*, p. 30. Accounts differ as to whether the empress dowager went with the emperor's party or with Ma; and some say that Ma attempted to pass off his own mother as the empress dowager (for instance, see Li, *San-yüan pi-chi*, suppl. *hsia* on Hung-kuang, 6b). But Ch'ing reports and the accounts of events in Hang-chou, where the Ma party went, confirm my statement here. See SCSL, 17/6b; Ch'i, *Chia-i jih-li*, p. 113; and Huang Tao-chou, *Huang Chang-p'u wen-hsüan* (T'ai-pei, 1962), II: 282–84.

54. T'an, *Kuo-ch'üeh*, VI: 6209–11. Chi, *Ming-chi nan-lüeh*, II: 180–82. Ku, *Sheng-an pen-chi*, I: 28–29. Lu, *Hsien-yen*, pp. 30–31, 38–40.

55. SCSL, 16/21a–22a. T'an, *Kuo-ch'üeh*, VI: 6212–13. Chi, *Ming-chi nan-lüeh*, II: 234–37.

56. Chi, *Ming-chi nan-lüeh*, II: 235. SCSL, 10/13b–14a. Dorgon's proclamation originally was issued at the outset of the southward campaign, on November 22 of the previous year.

57. T'an, *Kuo-ch'üeh*, VI: 6213, 6216. Chi, *Ming-chi nan-lüeh*, II: 237–38.

58. Lu, *Hsien-yen*, p. 50.

59. T'an, *Kuo-ch'üeh*, VI: 6216–17. Chi, *Ming-chi nan-lüeh*, II: 237–38. Ku-ts'ang-shih, *Hung-kuang shih-lu ch'ao*, pp. 260–61.

60. SCSL, 17/5b–6b. T'an, *Kuo-ch'üeh*, VI: 6213, places this action on June 14; Ku, *Sheng-an pen-chi*, I: 29, on June 15. Also, see Chi, *Ming-chi nan-lüeh*, II: 231–32.

61. T'an, *Kuo-ch'üeh*, VI: 6212, 6216. Chi, *Ming-chi nan-lüeh*, I: 45, and II: 323, 235. Ku, *Sheng-an pen-chi*, I: 29. Lu, *Hsien-yen*, p. 49.

62. SCSL, 18/19a–b. T'an, *Kuo-ch'üeh*, VI: 6217. Chi, *Ming-chi nan-lüeh*, II: 238. Ch'i, *Chia-i jih-li*, pp. 110, 113–17, 120. Huang, *Huang Chang-p'u wen-hsüan*, II: 282–84. Hsü Fang-lieh, *Che-tung chi-lüeh* (*T'ung-shih* ed.), 1a–2a. Min-jen [Ch'en Yen-i], *Szu-wen ta-chi* (T'ai-pei, 1967), p. 1. Also see biog. of Bolo in Hummel, I: 16–17.

63. The Prince of Luh probably was executed in a purge of Ming princes, ostensibly for seditious plotting, which occurred in Pei-ching in June and July of 1646 (SCSL, 26/10a–11a, uses the wrong character for "Luh"); and the "(false) heir" may have been put to death at this same time (Lu, *Hsien-yen*, p. 44). The Prince of Fu reportedly died in the spring of 1648 (T'an, *Kuo-ch'üeh*, VI: 6217), but others say that he was executed with the "heir" (Chi, *Ming-chi nan-lüeh*, II: 238).

64. The only important exceptions to this were the aforementioned Huang Te-kung and Ling Chiung, and the commander of a large confederacy of stockades in central Ho-nan, Liu Hung-ch'i. Chi, *Ming-chi nan-lüeh*, I: 22; Ku, *Sheng-an pen-chi*, I: 28; MCSL, *chia*, II: 142a–b; Li, ed., *Ming-Ch'ing tang-an*, I: 141–42. The only hereditary military noble who did not submit was Liu K'ung-chao. Chi, *Ming-chi nan-lüeh*, II: 238; T'an, *Kuo-ch'üeh*, VI: 6212.

65. SCSL, 16/22a.

66. Tso's army was led in surrender to Ajige by Liang-yü's son and chief deputy, Meng-keng, at a point between Chiu-chiang and Tung-liu. SCSL, 18/5a. From the seacoast, Liu Tse-ch'ing begged forgiveness and finally came in surrender back to Huai-an in August 1645. Li, ed., *Ming-Ch'ing tang-an*, I: 146–47; SCSL, 18/9a; 19/5b.

67. SCSL, 14/12a–b; 16/9b–10a, 15a; 17/4a–b; 18/2a–3b.

68. SCSL, 17/8a, 13a; 18/20a–21b, 24a; 19/2a–3b, 6a–b; 21/17a; 24/6a–7a. Li, ed., *Ming-Ch'ing tang-an*, I: 144–45. MCSL, *chi*, I: 8b.

69. SCSL, 18/15a, 22b. Li Kuang-t'ao, "Hung Ch'eng-ch'ou pei-Ming shih-mo," CYYY, 17 (April 1948): 227–301. Ch'en Tso-chien, "Lun Hung Ch'eng-ch'ou pien-chieh yü jen-ts'ai wai-liu," *Ch'ang-liu*, 27.11 (July 1963): 2–3; 27.12 (Aug. 1963): 12–13; 28.1 (Aug. 1963): 12–13.

70. SCSL, 6/9a–11a; 17/1b–2a, 15a–23b. Li, ed., *Ming-Ch'ing tang-an*, I: 11–13.

71. SCSL, 17/3a–b. Nakayama, "Hanto ni okeru bempatsu no mondai," pp. 13–16. Hai-wai San-jen [pseud.], *Jung-ch'eng chi-wen*, in *Ch'ing-shih tzu-liao*, vol. 1 (Pei-ching, 1980), p. 5.

72. T'an, *Kuo-ch'üeh*, VI: 6212. Chi, *Ming-chi nan-lüeh*, II: 236.

73. *Do-er-kun she-cheng jih-chi* (T'ai-pei, 1976), p. 1a. Earlier Dorgon had been irritated and indignant at the persistence of rumors around Pei-ching that the Manchus were about to do various weird and heinous things. SCSL, 9/2b–3a, 7b–8a. On August 29 the enforcement of the hair-and-dress policy in the North, also, was strengthened and accelerated. SCSL, 19/7a–b.

74. T'an, *Kuo-ch'üeh*, VI: 6216. Anon., *Su-ch'eng chi-pien* (*Ming-chi shih-liao ts'ung-shu* ed.), 4a. Cf. n. 80 below. On the phenomenon of riverine and lacustrine pirates during this period, see Wu Chih-ho, "Ming-tai te chiang-hu tao," *Ming-shih yen-chiu chuan-k'an*, 1 (July 1978): 107–37.

75. Cf. introduction, n. 48. Mori Masao, "1645-nen Taisōshū Sakeichin ni okeru Uryūkai no hanran ni tsuite," in *Nakayama Hachirō kyōju shōju kinen Min-Shin shi ronsō* (Tokyo, 1977), pp. 195–232. Huang Ch'un-yüeh, *Huang T'ao-an hsien-sheng ch'üan-chi* (preface 1761), 2/2b–3a. Ch'i, *Chia-i jih-li*, pp. 34–35, 41, 44, 46, 54, 56, 75, 95, 100. Chi, *Ming-chi nan-lüeh*, II: 255, 266–67. *Su-ch'eng chi-pien*, 1b–2b. Rootless men who, especially with the economic expansion of late Ming times, commonly found jobs in urban centers as guards and carriers, increasingly had formed gangs of thugs to engage in organized nefarious activities. They operated both independently and under the often covert employ of wealthy and influential local parties. See Ueda Noboru, "Minmatsu Shinsho Kōnan no toshi no 'burai' o meguru shakai kankei," *Shigaku zasshi*, 90.11 (Nov. 1981): 1–35.

76. For secondary studies, see: Frederic Wakeman, "Localism and Loyalism during the Ch'ing Conquest of Chiang-nan: The Tragedy of Chiang-yin," in *Conflict and Control in Late Imperial China*, pp. 43–85; Lai Chia-tu, "1645-nien Chiang-yin jen-min te k'ang-Ch'ing tou-cheng," and Yang K'uan, "1645-nien Chia-ting jen-min te k'ang-Ch'ing tou-cheng," in *Ming-Ch'ing shih lun-ts'ung*, ed. Li Kuang-pi (Wu-han, 1957), pp. 195–225; Jerry Dennerline, *The Chia-ting Loyalists*, pp. 261–301; Li T'ien-yu, *Ming-mo Chiang-yin Chia-ting jen-min te k'ang-Ch'ing tou-cheng* (Shang-hai, 1955); and Chang Mu, *Ku T'ing-lin hsien-sheng nien-p'u* (T'ai-pei repr., 1971), p. 17.

For contemporaneous sources, see: *Su-ch'eng chi-pien*; Chao Hsi-ming, *Chiang-shang ku-chung lu*; Hsü Ch'ung-hsi, *Chiang-yin shou-ch'eng chi* (often appended to a later, longer work by Han T'an, *Chiang-yin ch'eng-shou chi*); Lou-tung Wu-ming-shih [pseud.], *Yen-t'ang chien-wen tsa-chi*; Nan-yüan Hsiao-k'o [pseud.], *P'ing-Wu shih-lüeh*; Man-yu Yeh-shih [pseud.], *Hai-chiao i-pien*; Chu Tzu-su, *Tung-t'ang jih-cha* (also titled *Chia-ting t'u-ch'eng chi-lüeh*, and published in an abridged version, *Chia-ting hsien i-yu chi-shih*); Ch'en Tzu-lung, *Ch'en Chung-yü nien-p'u*, *chung*/31a–b; T'an, *Tsao-lin tsa-tsu*, *jen*/25a–b; Chi, *Ming-chi nan-lüeh*, II: 252–53, 255–56, 258–59, 262–63, 265, 279; MCSL, *chia*, II: 158a–b.

For a brief discussion of the behaviors that properly can be regarded as manifestations of Ming "loyalism," see my article, "Ambivalence and Action: Some Frustrated Scholars of the K'ang-hsi Period," in *From Ming to Ch'ing*, ed. Spence and Wills, pp. 326–28. Much attention has been devoted to discerning patterns in socioeconomic or scholarly-bureaucratic background among those who most vigorously resisted the Ch'ing, various authors implying that the best patriots were peasants, the ascendant bourgeoisie, or members of the often idealistically reform-minded politico-literacy societies of the late Ming. The first view derives from the circumstance that resistance lasted longest in remote areas, inhabited mainly by peasants; and the latter two views derive from the circumstance that resistance was sharpest in densely populated, highly urbanized areas, where city people and intellectual coteries were most numerous. The studies listed in the first paragraph above show that we are far from being able to generalize validly about the relative degrees of dedicated resistance (or passive surrender) in the multifarious social sectors and strata of seventeenth-century China. The picture is very complex even in discrete locales and is even more so when we scan the entire South. Future studies of this question, in positing patterns of resistance behavior, should examine incisively just what it was that various people were fighting for, or against, in the particular geographical situations and with the particular material resources of their communities, as well as the social statuses of the activists. And those who study the relation between resistance leadership and intellectual affiliation should be aware of the tendency of the historical record to inflate the roles played by prominent members of the late-Ming academies and societies. On this latter point, see my doctoral thesis, "Uses of History in Traditional Chinese Society: The Southern Ming in Ch'ing Historiography," pp. 105–08, as well as my article, "The Hsü Brothers and Semiofficial Patronage of Scholars in the K'ang-hsi Period," *Harvard Journal of Asiatic Studies*, 42.1 (June 1982), pp. 262–64.

77. MCSL, *chi*, I: 7a, 8a, 12a, 13b. SCSL, 22/18a.

78. MCSL, *ping*, VI: 502a–b; 516a–17b. SCSL, 21/4a–5a. Chi, *Ming-chi nan-lüeh*, II: 265–66, 268–69.

79. SCSL, 24/3a–b, 15a; 29/9a–b. MCSL, *chia*, II: 170a, 175a. Nan-yüan, *P'ing-Wu shih-lüeh*, p. 117. Another startling uprising, led by the Prince of Jui-ch'ang, swept the area just south of Nan-ching as late as midautumn 1646. MCSL, *chia*, II: 170a–b; SCSL, 28/2b.

80. MCSL, *chi*, I: 2b–3a, 12b, 14b, 17b–18b. Chi, *Ming-chi nan-lüeh*, II: 272–75. Nan-yüan, *P'ing-Wu shih-lüeh*, p. 112. Su-ch'eng chi-pien, 8a–9a. Liu Ya-tzu, *Huai-chiu chi* (Shang-hai, 1947), pp. 178–210.

81. P'eng Sun-i, *Hu-hsi i-shih* (Chang, comp., *Shih-yüan ts'ung-shu* ed.), 2b, 4a.

82. Ibid., 2b. Hsü Shih-p'u, *Chiang-pien chi-lüeh* (*Ching-t'o i-shih* ed.), 1a–b. T'an, *Kuo-ch'üeh*, VI: 6102, 6127, 6159. Chi, *Ming-chi nan-lüeh*, I: 78. Hummel, I: 166–67.

83. Most active were the princes of Yi (Chu Yu-pen), of Yung-ning (Chu Yu-che), of Jui-ch'ang (Chu I-le), and of Lo-ch'uan (name unknown). See biogs. of these princes in Hsü Ch'eng-li, *Hsiao-t'ien chi-chuan* (T'ai-pei, 1963), VI: 948–50, 957–60. SCSL, 20/11a, 23a; 23/6b. MCSL, *chi*, I: 5a. Huang, *Huang Chang-p'u wen-hsüan*, I: 105, 118, 126. Ch'en, *Szu-wen ta-chi*, p. 35. Huang Chang-chien, "Tu *Ming-shih* Yü Ying-kuei, Chieh Ch'ung-hsi, Fu Ting-ch'üan chuan," *Ming-shih yen-chiu chuan-k'an*, 1 (1978): 170–71.

84. Ch'ien Ping-teng, *Lung-wu chi-nien* (*So-chih lu*, part 1), 10b–11a, 16a, 17b. Wang, *Yung-li shih-lu*, 18/4a. Huang, *Huang Chang-p'u wen-hsüan*, I: 127.

85. Chang Chia-yü, *Chang Wen-lieh i-chi* (*Ts'ang-hai ts'ung-shu* ed.), 2 shang/17b–21b. SCSL, 24/9b–10a. MCSL, *chia*, II: 159a–b.

86. Li Chieh, *T'ien-hsiang-ko sui-pi* (in *Pi-chi hsiao-shuo ta-kuan*), 1/7a–b.

87. P'eng, *Hu-hsi i-shih*, 4a. Really fit troops in that area were estimated to number ten thousand. Chang, *Chang Wen-lieh i-chi*, 2 *shang*/17b.

88. Chang, *Chang Wen-lieh i-chi*, 2 *shang*/17a. On "slave revolts" in southern Chiang-hsi, see Fu, *Ming-Ch'ing nung-ts'un she-hui ching-chi*, pp. 109–10.

89. P'eng, *Hu-hsi i-shih*, 4a–b.

90. Ch'ien, *Lung-wu chi-nien*, 16a–b. P'eng, *Hu-hsi i-shih*, 5b. K'ang Fan-sheng, *Fang chih-nan lu* (*Ching-t'o i-shih* ed.), 1a–b. MCSL, *ping*, VI: 529a–b.

91. MCSL, *chia*, II: 156a–b.

92. Parsons, *Peasant Rebellions*, pp. 149–56.

93. See biogs. of the generals in Wang, *Yung-li shih-lu*, ch. 10.

94. Ho is said to have favored a proposal from a troop supervisor to break with precedent and completely combine civil and military government into one, but he was obstructed (by unstated circumstances) from doing so. Li, *San-yüan pi-chi*, suppl. *hsia* on Hung-kuang, 1a–2b. Wang, *Yung-li shih-lu*, 7/1b–2a. Biog. of Ho in Hummel, I: 290–91.

95. MCSL, *chia*, II: 121a–b; *ping*, VI: 511a, 512b, 513a, 515a. SCSL, 20/23a.

96. Tai and Wu, *Huai-ling liu-k'ou*, 18/5b–6b. Wang, *Yung-li shih-lu*, 7/2a, 5a–b; 13/1b. Chao Li-sheng and Kao Chao-i, " 'K'uei-tung shih-san chia' k'ao," in *Chung-kuo nung-min chan-cheng shih lun-wen chi*, ed. Chao (Shang-hai, 1955), pp. 156–57.

97. Wang, *Yung-li shih-lu*, 7/2a–b, 5b–6a; 13/2a–b.

98. MCSL, *chia*, II: 139a; *ping*, VI: 514a, 515a–b; *chi*, I: 22a.

99. MCSL, *chia*, II: 138a–b, 148a; VI: 503a–b; *ping*, VI: 606a, 607a–b, 614a–b. SCSL, 18/15a. Number I Archive, *Ch'ing-tai tang-an*, VI: 139–40.

100. MCSL, *chia*, II: 144a. SCSL, 21/14a–b; 25/7b. Biog. of Lekdehun in Hummel, I: 443–44.

101. Meng Cheng-fa, *San-Hsiang ts'ung-shih chi* (*Pi-chi hsiao-shuo ta-kuan* ed.), pp. 1310–13, 1316–19, 1324–25. Biog. of Chang K'uang in Wang, *Yung-li shih-lu*, 7/8a–10a. MCSL, *ping*, VI: 501a, 512b. SCSL, 28/9a. Number I Archive, *Ch'ing-tai tang-an*, VI: 145. Lei Liang-kung, *Kuei-lin t'ien-hai chi* (*Ming-chi shih-liao ts'ung-shu* ed.), 11b.

102. Wang, *Yung-li shih-lu*, 7/2b.

103. MCSL, *chia*, II: 139a, 172a; *ping*, VI: 511b–512a, 513a, 520–21a, 551a–b, 560a, 564a, 565a–b. SCSL, 22/8b–9a; 26/19a; 30/5b–6a. Wang Pao-hsin, *Ch'i-Huang szu-shih-pa chai chi-shih* (T'ai-pei repr., 1966), 1/24b–25a and passim. Districts in this region, such as Ma-ch'eng, had been the scenes of especially well organized "slave revolts," and of collaboration with the regimes of Li Tzu-ch'eng and Chang Hsien-chung, in the late Ch'ung-chen period. And social strife continued there under Ch'ing rule. See Fu, *Ming-Ch'ing nung-ts'un she-hui ching-chi*, pp. 101–03.

104. MCSL, *chia*, II: 147a; *ping*, VI: 514a. SCSL, 25/7b–8b, 14b. Lekdehun sought unsuccessfully to capture the "One-eyed Tiger," Li Chin, nephew and adopted son of Li Tzu-ch'eng. The man whom the Ch'ing called the "Two-eyed Tiger" was Liu T'i-ch'un, one of Tzu-ch'eng's chief lieutenants. On these identities, see Wang Tsung-yen, *Tu Ch'ing-shih kao cha-chi* (Hongkong, 1977), pp. 201–02.

105. MCSL, *chia*, II: 121b, 143a; *ping*, VI: 545a–48a. SCSL, 25/13b, 16a; 28/9b.

106. SCSL, 27/21b, 22b. See biogs. of Keng, K'ung, and Shang in Hummel, I: 416–17, 445–46, and II: 635–36, resp.

107. Meng, *San-Hsiang ts'ung-shih chi*, pp. 1321, 1327–29. MCSL, *ping*, VI: 593a–b.

108. MCSL, *ping*, VII: 608a.

CHAPTER THREE

1. Hsü, *Che-tung chi-lüeh*, 2a–b. Ch'i, *Chia-i jih-li*, p. 117. Yao, *Liu Chi-shan hsien-sheng nien-p'u*, p. 336.

2. Hsü, *Che-tung chi-lüeh*, 4a–5a. Anon., *Chien-kuo chi-nien* (*Ming-chi shih-liao ts'ung-shu* ed.), 1a. Ch'ien Su-yüeh, *Ch'ien Chung-chieh Kung chi* (*Szu-ming ts'ung-shu* ed.), 9/2a, 7a–9a. Cha Chi-tso, *Lu ch'un-ch'iu* (T'ai-pei, 1961), pp. 3–6. Ch'üan Tsu-wang, *Chi-ch'i-t'ing chi* (*Szu-pu ts'ung-k'an ch'u-pien* ed.), ch. 7, tomb inscription for Ch'ien Su-yüeh, pp. 85–95, and *Chi-ch'i-t'ing chi, wai-pien*, ch. 4, tomb inscription for Sun Chia-chi, pp. 681–85. Lin, *Ho-cha ts'ung-t'an*, pp. 131–32. Also, see SCSL, 19/7a.

3. *Chien-kuo chi-nien*, 1b–2a. Hsü, *Che-tung chi-lüeh*, 5b–6a, 7a. Ch'ien, *Ch'ien Chung-chieh Kung chi*, 9/2a. Weng-chou Lao-min [pseud.], *Hai-tung i-shih* (T'ai-pei, 1961), p. 2. Cha, *Lu ch'un-ch'iu*, p. 15. Anon., *Lung-wu i-shih* (*T'ung-shih* ed.), 12a. Ch'üan, *Chi-ch'i-t'ing chi*, ch. 7, tomb inscription for Ch'ien Su-yüeh, pp. 85–86. Lin, *Ho-cha ts'ung-t'an*, p. 133. Apparently the decision to establish the regency was made in T'ai-chou, whereas the formal ceremonies were carried out in Shao-hsing. The above sources differ widely regarding the dates when the prince left T'ai-chou and arrived in Shao-hsing. On these problems, see Yang Yün-p'ing, "Nan-Ming Lu chien-kuo shih-chi te yen-chiu," *Chung-kuo li-shih hsüeh-hui shih-hsüeh chi-k'an*, 8 (May 1976): 34–36. For a complete chronology of the career of Regent Lu, see Chuang Chin-te, "Ming chien-kuo Lu Wang I-hai chi-shih nien-piao," *T'ai-wan wen-hsien*, 11.1 (March 1951): 1–59. Also, see the biog. of Chu I-hai in Hummel, I: 180–81.

4. Hsü, *Che-tung chi-lüeh*, 5a–b, 6b, 7b. Ch'üan, *Chi-ch'i-t'ing chi*, ch. 26, pp. 321–23. Cha, *Lu ch'un-chiu*, pp. 6–14. MCSL, *ping*, VI: 524a–b. For a chart of the defensive stations and their commanders, see Sheng Ch'eng, "Shen Kuang-wen yü Ming Szu-tsung chi nan-tu chu-wang," *Hsüeh-shu chi-k'an*, 4.3 (March 1956): 46–47.

5. Ch'en, *Szu-wen ta-chi*, pp. 1–5.

6. Hsü, *Che-tung chi-lüeh*, 1b. See biog. of Cheng Hung-k'uei in Hummel, I: 112.

7. Ch'en, *Szu-wen ta-chi*, pp. 2–3, 5–17, 19–20. Hai-wai San-jen, *Jung-ch'eng chi-wen*, p. 4. Huang Yü-chai, "Ming Lung-wu Ti yung-li te ching-wei," *T'ai-wan wen-hsien*, 20.2 (June 1969): 128–55. For the text of the prince's regental proclamation, see Feng Meng-lung, comp., *Chung-hsing wei-lüeh* (*Min-Shin shiryō shū* ed.), 34a–44a. And for a general account of Lung-wu affairs, see Huang Yü-chai, "Ming Lung-wu Ti te cheng-lüeh," *T'ai-wan wen-hsien*, 20.4 (Dec. 1969): 142–70.

8. Ch'en, *Szu-wen ta-chi*, pp. 22, 24. Chang, *Chang Wen-lieh i-chi*, 1/1a–4a, 5b–7b, 8b; 2/3a–5a.

9. Huang, *Huang Chang-p'u wen-hsüan*, p. 111. Ch'en, *Szu-wen ta-chi*, pp. 33–34. Cha, *Lu ch'un-ch'iu*, pp. 17–18. Primary sources on diplomatic relations between the two courts are scattered and disparate. For studies, see Ch'en Han-kuang, "Lu-T'ang chiao-e chi Lu Wang chih szu," *T'ai-wan wen-hsien*, 11.1 (March 1960): 106–11; and Yang, "Nan-Ming Lu chien-kuo shih-chi te yen-chiu," pp. 38–46. As for the generational question, in the fall of 1645 the Prince of Lu was twenty-seven years old, and the Prince of T'ang was forty-three. According to surviving records of these two princes' own genealogical reckonings, their ancestors were the ninth and twenty-second sons of T'ai-tsu, respectively (see Richard C. Rudolph, "The Real Tomb of the Ming Regent, Prince of Lu," *Monumenta Serica*, 29 [1970–71]: 487–89; and Ch'en, *Szu-wen ta-chi*, pp. 21–22).

However, these appear to be imprecise. According to the tables of princely descent in the *Ming-shih* (*chu-wang shih-piao*, 2 and 3), Lu was the tenth-generation descendant of the tenth son of T'ai-tsu, and T'ang was the ninth-generation descendant of the twenty-third son. This latter reckoning is followed in the genealogical tables appended to Sheng Ch'eng's study, "Shen Kuang-wen yü Szu-tsung chi nan-tu chu-wang," pp. 66–73. In any case, the Prince of T'ang was acknowledged to be one generation senior to the Prince of Lu.

10. Chi, *Ming-chi nan-lüeh*, II: 294. Cha Chi-tso and Shen Ch'i, *Tung-shan kuo-yü* (T'ai-pei, 1963), pp. 8–10. Ch'ien, *Lung-wu chi-nien*, 9b–10a. Hsü, *Che-tung chi-lüeh*, 8b–9a.

11. Appended to *Lung-wu i-shih*, 11a–12b. Also, see Ch'en, *Szu-wen ta-chi*, p. 63.

12. Ch'en, *Szu-wen ta-chi*, pp. 60, 62, 86. Ch'ien, *Lung-wu chi-nien*, 14b. Hsü, *Che-tung chi-lüeh*, 14a–b. *Chien-kuo chi-nien*, 6a. Cha, *Lu ch'un-ch'iu*, p. 25. Another man, Chin Pao, who volunteered to act as liaison between Fu-chien and Che-chiang, also became an object of dispute among various Lu commanders and barely escaped with his life. See Chin, *Ling-hai fen-yü*, pp. 13–19.

13. Ch'en, *Szu-wen ta-chi*, p. 91. Ch'ien, *Lung-wu chi-nien*, 20b–21a.

14. *Chien-kuo chi-nien*, 2a, 6a. Cha, *Lu ch'un-ch'iu*, p. 24. Wang Kuang-fu, *Hang-hsieh i-wen* (*Ching-t'o i-shih* ed.), 1a.

15. *Chien-kuo chi-nien*, 2b, 3b. Weng-chou, *Hai-tung i-shih*, p. 2. Cha, *Lu ch'un-ch'iu*, p. 15. Hsü, *Che-tung chi-lüeh*, 7a–b. For the most complete list of Lu appointments see Lin, *Ho-cha ts'ung-t'an*, pp. 133–34.

16. The most regrettable case of this occurred when accusations from the camp of Fang Kuo-an, who surreptitiously had accepted a Lung-wu appointment, were made against Ch'ien Su-yüeh, who steadfastly had not. These charges, in part, brought about Ch'ien's resignation. Weng-chou, *Hai-tung i-shih*, p. 4. Ch'ien, *Ch'ien Chung-chieh Kung chi*, 10/14a. Ch'üan, *Chi-ch'i-t'ing chi*, ch. 7, p. 88.

17. Ch'ien, *Lung-wu chi-nien*, 1a–2a, 5a. Hummel, I: 196–98.

18. Chi, *Ming-chi nan-lüeh*, I: 7, 10. Ku, *Sheng-an pen-chi*, I: 9. There is some question about whether the Hung-kuang court restored Chu Yü-chien's princely title. Chi Liu-ch'i and Ch'ien Ping-teng say that his request for reinstatement was denied (*Ming-chi nan-lüeh*, I: 25; *Lung-wu chi-nien*, 2a); but Ch'en Yen-i, the official Lung-wu court historian, says it was granted (*Szu-wen ta-chi*, p. 3).

19. Ch'ien, *Lung-wu chi-nien*, 4b–5a, 10a, 14a. Ch'en, *Szu-wen ta-chi*, pp. 5–6, 14–15, 22, 24, 26, 30–31, 71. Feng, comp., *Chung-hsing wei-lüeh*, 34a–b, 39b, 41a, 42b–43a. The empress bore their first child (a boy, apparently defective) shortly before the demise of the Lung-wu regime (Ch'ien, *Lung-wu chi-nien*, 24a–b); but there is no evidence that the infant survived his parents.

20. Ch'en, *Szu-wen ta-chi*, pp. 44, 69, 78, 97, 114. Huang, *Huang Chang-p'u wen-hsüan*, pp. 105–06. Feng, comp., *Chung-hsing wei-lüeh*, 37a.

21. Lei, *Kuei-lin t'ien-hai chi*, 4a–8a. Ch'ien, *Lung-wu chi-nien*, 9a–b. Ch'en, *Szu-wen ta-chi*, pp. 26, 86. The Prince of Ching-chiang was Chu Heng-chia.

22. Ch'ien, *Lung-wu chi-nien*, 3a–4a, 5a, 6a, 10a–b. The emperor later realized and regretted his lack of prudence in making appointments. See Ch'en, *Szu-wen ta-chi*, pp. 104, 111, 118.

23. Ch'ien, *Lung-wu chi-nien*, 4b–5a. Wang, *Yung-li shih-lu*, 6/1b. For the names of most Lung-wu grand secretaries, see Ch'ien, 3a, and Ch'en, *Szu-wen ta-chi*, p. 13.

24. The emperor was explicitly criticized for this. See Ch'en, *Szu-wen ta-chi*, pp. 91–92.

25. Huang, *Huang Chang-p'u wen-hsüan*, I: 116–17, 130, 139, 149, 151, 155. Chang, *Chang Wen-lieh i-chi*, 2 *shang*/12a–b. Ch'en, *Szu-wen ta-chi*, pp. 61–62, 69, 71, 78, 81, 87.

26. Cha, *Lu ch'un-chiu*, pp. 17, 20; idem, *Tung-shan kuo-yü*, pp. 8–9. T'an, *Tsao-lin tsa-tsu, jen*/25b. Ch'en, *Szu-wen ta-chi*, p. 82.

27. Chang Lin-po, *Fu-hai chi* (T'ai-pei, 1972), p. 1. Ch'en, *Szu-wen ta-chi*, pp. 29, 34, 55, 83, 91. Cha, *Lu ch'un-ch'iu*, p. 22.

28. Ch'en, *Szu-wen ta-chi*, pp. 71, 74, 76, 84, 92, 96. Chang, *Chang Wen-lieh i-chi*, 2 *shang*/6b, 13a–b, 16a. Huang, *Huang Chang-p'u wen-hsüan*, I: 131–32.

29. Ch'en, *Szu-wen ta-chi*, pp. 32, 35, 59, 62–63, 87–88. Chang, *Chang Wen-lieh i-chi*, ch. 2 *shang* and *hsia*. For a study of Chang's full resistance career, see Mai Shao-lin, "Min-tsu ying-hsiung Chang Chia-yü," in *Kuang-tung wen-wu* (1941), II: 588–611.

30. Ch'en, *Szu-wen ta-chi*, pp. 35, 59–60, 63, 67, 74, 76–77, 88. Ch'ien, *Lung-wu chi-nien*, 11a. Li Chin (also known as Li Kuo) was given the personal name Ch'ih-hsin; Kao was named Pi-cheng, and Heh, Yung-chung. All of these names implied steadfast loyalty and correctness, thus symbolizing their conversion from being rebels to being devoted servants of the state.

31. Ch'en, *Szu-wen ta-chi*, pp. 59–60, 62, 77, 98, 103, 112. Ch'ien, *Lung-wu chi-nien*, 16b–17a, 23b. Chang, *Chang Wen-lieh i-chi*, 1/7b–8a. P'eng, *Hu-hsi i-shih*, 4b.

32. Ch'ien Ping-teng, *Ts'ang-shan-ko chi hsüan-chi* (T'ai-pei, 1966), I: 4–5. Idem, *Lung-wu chi-nien*, 14a. Ch'en, *Szu-wen ta-chi*, pp. 93–94, 101–02, 113–14. Chang, *Chang Wen-lieh i-chi*, 2 *hsia*/13b–14b.

33. Ch'en, *Szu-wen ta-chi*, pp. 23–24, 29, 67, 72–73, 81, 83–84, 96, 103–04, 107–08, 114, 140. Ch'ien, *Lung-wu chi-nien*, 17a–b. P'eng, *Hu-hsi i-shih*, 5a. Chang, *Chang Wen-lieh i-chi*, 2 *hsia*/31a. For a thorough study of both these problems in the late Ming and early Ch'ing, see Mori Masao, "Jūshichi seiki no Fukken Neikaken ni okeru Kō Tō no kōso hanran," *Nagoya daigaku bungakubu kenkyū ronshū*, Shigaku series, 20 (1973): 1–31; 21 (1974): 13–25; and 25 (1978): 25–65. For a primary account of various disturbances in southwestern Fu-chien from Ch'ung-chen to K'ang-hsi times, see Li Shih-hsiung, *K'ou-pien chi*, in *Ch'ing-shih tzu-liao* (Pei-ching, 1980), vol. 1. By no means were tenant uprisings new to the area during this period. Outbursts had occurred intermittently, at least twenty-five times, since the beginning of the sixteenth century. See Ng Chin-keong, "A Study of the Peasant Society of South Fukien, 1506–1644," *Nanyang University Journal*, 6 (1972): 204–05.

34. Ch'en, *Szu-wen ta-chi*, p. 22, 39–40, 54, 62, 64, 77, 81, 88, 90, 92–93, 98–99, 101–02, 108–09, 116. Ch'ien, *Lung-wu chi-nien*, 10b, 12b, 13a, 14a–b. Huang, *Huang Chang-p'u wen-hsüan*, I: 123. In late March, just as the emperor again was waxing enthusiastic about "going out along five routes" (Ch'en, *Szu-wen ta-chi*, p. 83), Chang Chia-yü memorialized warning that no route out of Fu-chien was safe and that he should stay and "secure the base" (*Chang Wen-lieh i-chi*, 2 *hsia*/12b–13a).

35. Ch'ien, *Lung-wu chi-nien*, 5b.

36. Ch'en, *Szu-wen ta-chi*, pp. 95–96. In their initial conquest of Fu-chien, the Manchus claimed to have received the surrender of over 68,500 troops (SCSL, 29/2b).

37. Ch'en, *Szu-wen ta-chi*, pp. 14, 108. Chin, *Ling-hai fen-yü*, p. 22.

38. Ch'en, *Szu-wen ta-chi*, pp. 95, 128–29, 136. Other amounts were ordered to be delivered directly from Liang-Kuang into Chiang-hsi and Hu-kuang. See, for instance,

Ch'en, *Szu-wen ta-chi*, p. 77. The emperor's lament sheds indirect light on the drastic decline in tax returns during these years of turmoil. After 1630, Fu-chien's yearly quota for just the late Ming land surtaxes was 161,069 taels, and this amount was 12 percent of the basic tax (Ng, "A Study on the Peasant Society of South Fukien," p. 196). Thus, Fu-chien's normal annual quota for the land tax alone must have been over 2 million taels.

39. Feng, comp., *Chung-hsing wei-lüeh*, 39b. Ch'en, *Szu-wen ta-chi*, pp. 59, 64, 70, 72, 82, 83–84, 100, 107, 110, 125. Ch'ien, *Lung-wu chi-nien*, 5b–6a.

40. *Lung-wu i-shih*, 5a. Ch'ien, *Lung-wu chi-nien*, 6a. Ch'en, *Szu-wen ta-chi*, pp. 122, 126.

41. Ch'en, *Szu-wen ta-chi*, pp. 35, 84, 96, 101, 125, 127, 129, 133. *Lung-wu i-shih*, 5a.

42. Rawski, *Agricultural Change*, chap. 4.

43. For general biographical treatments of Cheng Chih-lung, see Liao Han-ch'en, "Cheng Chih-lung k'ao," *T'ai-wan wen-hsien*, (1) 10.4 (Dec. 1959): 63–72, and (2) 11.3 (Sept. 1960): 1–15; Charles Boxer, "The Rise and Fall of Nicholas Iquan," *T'ien Hsia Monthly*, 11.5 (April–May 1941): 401–39; John E. Wills, "Maritime China from Wang Chih to Shih Lang: Themes in Peripheral History," in *From Ming to Ch'ing*, ed. Spence and Wills, pp. 216–19; and Hummel, I: 110–11. On his surrender and later service to the Ming authorities in Fu-chien, see: Ku Ying-t'ai, *Ming-shih chi-shih pen-mo* (T'ai-pei, 1968), vol. 375, pp. 39–42; and Maejima Shinji, "Tei Shiryū shōan no jijō ni tsuite," *Chūgoku gakushi*, 1 (1964): 141–70.

44. Ch'en, *Szu-wen ta-chi*, pp. 20, 60, 83. Ch'ien, *Lung-wu chi-nien*, 14a. *Lung-wu i-shih*, 1b.

45. Ch'en, *Szu-wen ta-chi*, pp. 31, 35. Ch'ien, *Lung-wu chi-nien*, 5b. *Lung-wu i-shih*, 5b. See biog. of Cheng Ch'eng-kung in Hummel, I: 108–10. Cheng Chih-lung's youngest brother, Chih-pao, was placed in charge of the palace guard. Ch'en, *Szu-wen ta-chi*, pp. 33–34. On the names and relative ages of Chih-lung's four younger brothers, see: Chang Tsung-hsia, "Cheng Chih-lung hsiung-ti chiu-hsi chi-jen," *Chung-kuo shih yen-chiu*, 1980, no. 3 (Sept.), pp. 167–68; and Cheng Hsi-wen, "Ming Cheng shih-shih wu-tse," *T'ai-pei wen-wu*, 10.1 (March 1961): 82. These supplement a general study of Cheng genealogy by Liao Han-ch'en, "Cheng Shih shih-hsi chi jen-wu k'ao," *Wen-hsien chuan-k'an*, 1.3 (1950): 54–64.

46. Ch'ien, *Lung-wu chi-nien*, 6a. *Lung-wu i-shih*, 5a.

47. Ch'en, *Szu-wen ta-chi*, pp. 68, 70, 78, 91, 104. Ch'ien, *Lung-wu chi-nien*, 6a. Hai-wai San-jen, *Jung-ch'eng chi-wen*, p. 4.

48. Ch'en, *Szu-wen ta-chi*, pp. 39–40, 59, 65, 68, 70, 83. Ch'ien, *Lung-wu chi-nien*, 7a, 12b. Chang, *Chang Wen-lieh i-chi*, 2 *shang*/7a, 24b–27a. On Cheng Ts'ai's career and his relation to Cheng Chih-lung's lineage, see Mao I-po, "Nan-Ming wu-ch'en Cheng Ts'ai te shih-chi," *Min-chu p'ing-lun*, 12.14 (July 1961): 14–18; and Cheng, "Ming Cheng shih-shih wu-tse," p. 83.

49. Ch'ien, *Ts'ang-shan-ko chi hsüan-chi*, I: 5.

50. *Lung-wu i-shih*, 6a. Huang Tsung-hsi, *Hai-wai t'ung-ch'i chi* (*Li-chou i-chu hui-k'an* ed.), 17a. Ch'ien, *Lung-wu chi-nien*, 14b–15a. As late as July 1646, one minister offered to contribute 10,000 taels of his own to help develop naval forces, which had been neglected. Ch'en, *Szu-wen ta-chi*, p. 135.

51. Ch'ien, *Lung-wu chi-nien*, 20b–21a. T'an, *Tsao-lin tsa-tsu*, *jen*/25a. Hua T'ing-hsien, *Min-shih chi-lüeh* (T'ai-pei, 1967), pp. 16–17.

52. Chuang Ch'i-ch'ou, "Chang-p'u Huang hsien-sheng nien-p'u," appendix 3 to

Huang Chang-p'u wen-hsüan, vol. 3. Hummel, I: 345–47. Huang Yü-chai, "Ming Lung-wu Ti yü shang-shu Huang Tao-chou," *T'ai-wan wen-hsien*, 21.1 (March 1970): 67–102.

53. Chi, *Ming-chi nan-lüeh*, I: 24–25. Ch'en, *Szu-wen ta-chi*, p. 22. Chang, *Chang Wen-lieh i-chi*, 2 *hsia*/20b–21a.

54. Huang, *Huang Chang-p'u wen-hsüan*, II: 161–63.

55. Ibid., I: 104–05.

56. Ibid., I: 108–09.

57. Ch'en, *Szu-wen ta-chi*, p. 25.

58. Huang, *Huang Chang-p'u wen-hsüan*, I: 107, 110–13, 117, 125–26, 143. Ch'ien, *Lung-wu chi-nien*, 7a–b.

59. Ch'ien, *Lung-wu chi-nien*, 7b.

60. Huang, *Huang Chang-p'u wen-hsüan*, I: 141–42, 144.

61. Ibid., I: 131–32, 151.

62. Ibid., I: 134–36, 141, 148–49, 155. Ch'en, *Szu-wen ta-chi*, pp. 56–57, 86–87. MCSL, *chia*, II: 145a, 146a. SCSL, 22/3b; 23/10b (which erroneously states that Huang was beheaded in Hui-chou shortly after his capture).

63. Huang, *Huang Chang-p'u wen-hsüan*, I: 142, 144.

64. Ch'ien, *Lung-wu chi-nien*, 6a–b.

65. Huang, *Huang Chang-p'u wen-hsüan*, I: 115, 141–42, 136.

66. Cheng Chih-lung is said to have favored admitting his old friend, Ma Shih-ying, into Fu-chien, but the emperor eventually disallowed it. Ch'en, *Szu-wen ta-chi*, pp. 22–24, 46. Huang Tao-chou's close associate and fellow "righteous" leader, Minister of Revenue Ho K'ai, angered the Chengs with his criticisms of such things as using fans at court sessions during the hot Indian summer. He soon resigned, was injured by an attacker (presumed to be a Cheng agent), and died not long after reaching his home. Ch'ien, *Lung-wu chi-nien*, 6b. The Lung-wu emperor repeatedly admonished against the sort of factionalism that had plagued Ming courts for over forty years. Feng, comp., *Chung-hsing wei-lüeh*, 42a; Ch'en, *Szu-wen ta-chi*, pp. 41–42, 60–61, 67, 93.

67. Ch'en, *Szu-wen ta-chi*, pp. 16–17, 72, 92–93, 99, 120, 129. Ch'ien, *Lung-wu chi-nien*, 11a. Idem, *Ts'ang-shan-ko chi hsüan-chi*, I: 3.

68. Ch'en, *Szu-wen ta-chi*, pp. 67, 90, 115–16, 123, 130–32, 138, 149, 151. Also, see Hsieh Hao, "Lung-wu 'Fu-ching' 'hsüan-chü' k'ao," *T'ai-pei wen-hsien*, 40 (June 1977): 105–92.

69. *Chien-kuo chi-nien*, 4a. Cha, *Lu ch'un-ch'iu*, p. 18.

70. Cf. nn. 2 and 4 above. On Hsiung, see: Huang, *Hai-wai t'ung-ch'i chi*, 9a; Chi, *Ming-chi nan-lüeh*, I: 94–95, 142–43, 188–89; and T'an, *Kuo-ch'üeh*, VI: 6134.

71. Fang: Cha, *Lu ch'un-ch'iu*, pp. 16, 20; T'an, *Tsao-lin tsa-tsu, jen*/25b–26a. Wang: Cha, *Lu ch'un-ch'iu*, pp. 16, 24; Hsü, *Che-tung chi-lüeh*, 11b (especially on his friction with civil officials); and Chi, *Ming-chi nan-lüeh*, II: 295–96. Cheng: Cha, *Lu ch'un-ch'iu*, p. 6; Lu, *Hsien-yen*, p. 52; and Chin, *Ling-hai fen-yü*, pp. 3–5, 14–15.

72. *Chien-kuo chi-nien*, 3b, 5a–b. Hsü, *Che-tung chi-lüeh*, 15b. Cha, *Lu ch'un-ch'iu*, pp. 23–24. Ch'ien, *Ch'ien Chung-chieh Kung chi*, 9/17a–b.

73. Hsü, *Che-tung chi-lüeh*, 8b, 13b–14a. Cha, *Lu ch'un-ch'iu*, pp. 19–20.

74. Lin, *Ho-cha ts'ung-t'an*, pp. 138–42.

75. *Chien-kuo chi-nien*, 3a–b. Ch'ien, *Ch'ien Chung-chieh Kung chi*, 9/21a–22a; 10/5b–7a, 12a–13a. Hsü, *Che-tung chi-lüeh*, 7b. Cha, *Lu ch'un-ch'iu*, p. 18. Lin, *Ho-cha ts'ung-t'an*, pp. 137–38.

76. Hsü, *Che-tung chi-lüeh*, 9b, 11b–12b, 14a, 15a. Ch'ien, *Ch'ien Chung-chieh Kung chi*, 10/9b–11b, 12a–13a. Cha, *Lu ch'un-ch'iu*, p. 25.

CHAPTER FOUR

1. MCSL, *chia*, VI: 501a; *ping*, VI: 509a, 553a–56a; *chi*, I: 4b–5a, 6a–b, 14a. SCSL, 20/17b; 21/6a–b; 22/18b; 25/15b. Also, see Hsü, *Che-tung chi-lüeh*, 8a, 13a.

2. The Eastern Che-chiang loyalists were crushed by news of the decimation of "righteous troops" to the south of T'ai Lake. Hsü, *Che-tung chi-lüeh*, 15a. The conquest of Hui-chou Prefecture had permitted the Ch'ing to send contingents further, into Kuang-hsin in Chiang-hsi and the T'ien-mu Mountains in southwestern Che-chiang. MCSL, *chia*, II: 145b, 153a, 159b. SCSL, 24/15b. And Chin Sheng-huan's chief deputy, Wang Te-jen, who had been campaigning successfully in northeastern Chiang-hsi, probed through Shan Pass into Lung-wu territory with ease. MCSL, *chia*, II: 156a–b. SCSL, 25/21b–22a.

3. SCSL, 24/16a–b; 26/22a.

4. Hsü, *Che-tung chi-lüeh*, 16a–b. Cha and Shen, *Tung-shan kuo-yü*, p. 10. *Chien-kuo chi-nien*, 6b. SCSL, 26/21b–22a. A travelogue from this year testifies to the shallow-ness of the river at T'ung-lu: "The water was clear to the very bottom, and one could count the swimming fish. My womenfolk vied to snatch varicolored pebbles, nearly capsizing our boat. At Seven-Mile Sandbank the channel gradually narrowed, and although it [still] was called a 'river,' actually it was [just] a mountain stream." Hua T'ing-hsien, *Min-yu yüeh-chi* (*Ching-t'o i-shih* ed.), 1/1b.

5. Hsü, *Che-tung chi-lüeh*, 16b. *Chien-kuo chi-nien*, 6b. Cha, *Lu ch'un-ch'iu*, p. 26. Wang, *Hang-hsieh i-wen*, 1a. The regent's concubine and his heir were kidnapped at sea by a renegade Ming naval commander who was bent on surrender, and both were killed by the Ch'ing. Huang, *Hai-wai t'ung-ch'i chi*, 2b. His wife had committed suicide in 1644 when rebels threatened the Lu estate in Shan-tung. Wang, *Hang-hsieh i-wen*, 1a.

6. Hsü, *Che-tung chi-lüeh*, 18a, 21b. Cha, *Lu ch'un-ch'iu*, pp. 30–31, 40–41. T'an, *Tsao-lin tsa-tsu*, *jen*/26a. SCSL, 27/21a.

7. Cha, *Lu ch'un-ch'iu*, pp. 27–28, 30–31. Chi, *Ming-chi nan-lüeh*, II: 297–300. Lin, *Ho-cha ts'ung-t'an*, p. 135. Huang Tsung-hsi, *Szu-ming shan-sai chi* (*Li-chou i-chu hui-k'an* ed.), 1a. For an inaccurate list of those who submitted, see MCSL, *chi*, I: 17a, which reports the surrender of only five hundred Ming cavalrymen and seven thousand infantrymen.

8. SCSL, 29/1b–2a. Hai-wai San-jen, *Jung-ch'eng chi-wen*, p. 5.

9. Ch'en, *Szu-wen ta-chi*, pp. 150–51.

10. Ch'ien, *Lung-wu chi-nien*, 25a–b.

11. Ch'ien, *Lung-wu chi-nien*, 26a. Ch'en, *Szu-wen ta-chi*, p. 15a. Hua, *Min-shih chi-lüeh*, p. 29. Stories of the ultimate fate of the Lung-wu emperor and empress vary considerably. For instance, see the note appended to a derivative work, also entitled *Lung-wu chi-nien* and attributed to Huang Tsung-hsi (*Li-chou i-chu hui-k'an* ed.), 4b. Here I follow the special testimony received by Chiang Jih-sheng, *T'ai-wan wai-chi* (T'ai-pei, 1960), I: 94, which is corroborated in SCSL, 29/2a.

12. Ch'en, *Szu-wen ta-chi*, pp. 152–54. Hai-wai San-jen, *Jung-ch'eng chi-wen*, p. 5.

13. Ch'en, *Szu-wen ta-chi*, p. 152. Ch'ien, *Lung-wu chi-nien*, 22b, 24a, 28a–b. SCSL, 29/2b. For texts of the Ch'ing pacification policies that were promulgated for Eastern

Che-chiang and Fu-chien, see: SCSL, 30/15a–21b; Li, ed., *Ming-Ch'ing tang-an*, I: 14–16; and MCSL, *ping*, VI: 583a–84b.

14. P'eng, *Hu-hsi i-shih*, 5b–6b. Ch'ien, *Lung-wu chi-nien*, 16b, 19b–20b, 29b. K'ang, *Fang chih-nan lu*, 1b–2a. SCSL, 26/6b; 27/20b–21a. MCSL, *chi*, I: 10a.

15. Ch'ien, *Lung-wu chi-nien*, 30a–b. K'ang, *Fang chih-nan lu*, 2a–b.

16. P'eng, *Hu-hsi i-shih*, 9b–10b. Ch'ien, *Lung-wu chi-nien*, 30b–31a. K'ang, *Fang chih-nan lu*, 2b–3a. SCSL, 28/10b. MCSL, *chia*, II: 171a; *ping*, VI: 573a–b.

17. Wang, *Yung-li shih-lu*, 1/1a–2a. Ch'ien Ping-teng, *Yung-li chi-nien* (*So-chih lu*, part 2), 1a. *Ming-shih*, 104/34b. Also, see biogs. of Chu Yu-lang, Ch'ü Shih-szu, and Ting K'uei-ch'u in Hummel, I: 193–95, 199–201, and II: 723, resp. Many Ch'ing and twentieth-century accounts refer to Chu Yu-lang as the Prince of Kuei; and even careful scholars have assumed, from reading materials of the late seventeenth and eighteenth centuries, that he formally succeeded to this title (for example, see [Liu Ya-tzu] "Chi-Ming szu-ti shih-fa k'ao," *Ta-feng pan-yüeh k'an*, 78 [Nov. 1940]: 2534–35). This assumption is ill-founded, however, because no primary source records such an investiture, and it does not appear possible that he could have been imperially confirmed as the next Prince of Kuei before the demise of the Lung-wu emperor.

18. [Lu K'o-tsao], *Ling-piao chi-nien* (manuscript copy, n.d.), 1/2a–b. Neither the prince's true mother, a concubine surnamed Ma, nor his own wife, also of the Wang family, had influence over him comparable to that of the future Senior Empress Dowager Wang. Lu, *Ling-piao chi-nien*, 1/1b; Wang, *Yung-li shih-lu*, 1/2a.

19. Wang, *Yung-li shih-lu*, 1/1b–2b. Lu, *Ling-piao chi-nien*, 1/2b–3a. Meng, *San-Hsiang ts'ung-shih chi*, pp. 1323–24. Ho Shih-fei, *Feng-tao wu-t'ung chi* (*Ching-t'o i-shih* ed.), 1/1a. Chao-ch'ing was the site of a former Ming princely estate and of special headquarters for the Kuang-tung provincial governor and the Liang-Kuang viceroy. Juan Yüan et al., comps., *Kuang-tung t'ung-chih* (1864), 18/1a–b; 83/28a. A doctoral dissertation has been written on the Yung-li period: David Shore, "Last Court of Ming China: The Reign of the Yung-li Emperor in the South (1647–1662)" (Princeton, 1976).

20. Lu, *Ling-piao chi-nien*, 1/3b. Ch'ien, *Yung-li chi-nien*, 2b.

21. Ch'ien, *Yung-li chi-nien*, 2b–3a. Lu, *Ling-piao chi-nien*, 1/3a, 4b. Ho, *Feng-tao wu-t'ung chi*, 1/1a. Ch'en, *Ch'en Yen-yeh hsien-sheng ch'üan-chi*, 2/1a. The three grand secretaries were: Su Kuan-sheng (Ch'en, *Szu-wen ta-chi*, pp. 24, 59–60; Ch'ien, *Lung-wu chi-nien*, 5b; Su Wei, *Ming Su chüeh-fu shih-lüeh* [Tung-kuan, 1919]); Ho Wu-tsou (Ch'en, *Szu-wen ta-chi*, p. 13; Wang, *Yung-li shih-lu*, 4/1b–2a; Li Lü-an, "Kuan-yü Ho Wu-tsou, Wu Jui-lung shih-chi chih yen-chiu," in *Kuang-tung wen-wu*, II: 612–44); and Huang Shih-chün (Ch'en, *Szu-wen ta-chi*, p. 146; Wang, *Yung-li shih-lu*, 4/2b).

22. Ch'en, *Szu-wen ta-chi*, p. 24. Ch'ien, *Yung-li chi-nien*, 2b–3a. Lu, *Ling-piao chi-nien*, 1/3b–4a. Also, see Yang Yün-p'ing, "Nan-Ming Yung-li shih-tai te yen-chiu," *Chung-kuo li-shih hsüeh-hui shih-hsüeh chi-k'an*, 9 (April 1977): 59–62; and Huang Yü-chai, "Ming Lung-wu Ti yü Shao-wu," *T'ai-wan wen-hsien*, 21.2 (June 1970): 102–05.

23. Ch'ien, *Yung-li chi-nien*, 3a. Lu, *Ling-piao chi-nien*, 1/4b. The intermediary between Kuang-chou and Wu-chou was Ch'en Pang-yen. See his collected works, *Ch'en Yen-yeh hsien-sheng ch'üan-chi*, 2/1b–2a, 4a–6a, and the appended *hsing-chuang* narrated by his son, Ch'en Kung-yin, esp. 28a. Also, see Ch'ü Ta-chün, *Huang-Ming szu-ch'ao ch'eng-jen lu* (*Kuang-tung ts'ung-shu* collated ed.), 10/355b; and Yen Hsü-hsin, "*Ming-shih* Ch'en Pang-yen chuan p'ang-cheng," in *Kuang-tung wen-wu*, II: 551–87.

24. Ch'ien, *Yung-li chi-nien*, 3b. Lu, *Ling-piao chi-nien*, 5b. Wang, *Yung-li shih-lu*, 1/2a. Shao-wu confidence was reinforced by the peculiar defensibility of Kuang-chou City, which until the recent troubles had garrisoned units of the Kuang-tung Regional Military Commission. Juan Yüan et al., comps., *Kuang-tung t'ung-chih*, 173/17b.

25. Ch'en Kung-yin, narr., *hsing-chuang* of Ch'en Pang-yen, in *Ch'en Yen-yeh hsien-sheng ch'üan-chi*, 4/28b. MCSL, *ping*, VII: 596a. SCSL, 30/24b. Chu Hsi-tsu, "Nan-Ming Kuang-chou hsün-kuo chu-wang k'ao," and T'i-hsien [pseud.], "Kung-yeh Nan-Ming Shao-wu chün-ch'en chung chi," *Wen-shih tsa-chih*, 2.7—8 (Aug. 1942): 51—54, and 55—57, resp. Ho, *Feng-tao wu-t'ung chi*, 2/5a.

26. Ch'ien, *Yung-li chi-nien*, 3b—4a, 5b. Lu, *Ling-piao chi-nien*, 1/6b—7a. Ho, *Feng-tao wu-t'ung chi*, 1/1b, 2b. Ch'ü Kung-mei, *Tung-Ming wen-chien lu* (*Ming-chi pai-shih ch'u-pien* ed.), p. 387.

27. T'ung Yang-chia: *Ch'ing-shih lieh-chuan* (Shang-hai, 1928), 4/27a—28b.

28. MCSL, *chia*, II: 190a—b; *ping*, VI: 581a—82a, 594a. SCSL, 30/14a; 31/9b, 13b. Ch'ien, *Yung-li chi-nien*, 6a—b. Lu, *Ling-piao chi-nien*, 1/11a, 14b, 17b. Wang, *Yung-li shih-lu*, 1/2b. Ch'ü, *Tung-Ming wen-chien lu*, p. 389. Ch'ü Shih-szu, *Ch'ü Chung-hsüan Kung chi* (*Ch'ien-k'un cheng-ch'i chi* ed.), 3/4b. Ting K'uei-ch'u surrendered to Li Ch'eng-tung at Wu-chou with a large load of valuables, but soon he was executed with his son. Lu, *Ling-piao chi-nien*, 1/8b—9a; Ho, *Feng-tao wu-t'ung chi*, 1/1b—2a.

29. MCSL, *chia*, II: 188a—b; *ping*, VI: 582a. Documents Committee of the National Palace Museum, comp., *Wen-hsien ts'ung-pien* (Pei-p'ing, 1930—43), vol. 24, 19a—20a. For the text of pacification policies for Kuang-tung, promulgated on August 25, 1647, see SCSL, 33/9a—14a. Li Ch'eng-tung had led less than 9,500 men into Kuang-tung, about half from southern Nan Chih-li and half from Fu-chien. Between Li and T'ung Yang-chia, they had been able to station only 700—800 soldiers in each prefecture, while still carrying on the campaign against "bandits" and Yung-li forces. MCSL, *ping*, VII: 601a—b.

30. Ch'ien, *Yung-li chi-nien*, 6a. Lu, *Ling-piao chi-nien*, 1/11a. Wang, *Yung-li shih-lu*, 1/2b—3a. Ch'ü, *Tung-Ming wen-chien lu*, pp. 388—89. Ch'ü, *Ch'ü Chung-hsüan Kung chi*, 3/3b.

31. Ch'ien, *Yung-li chi-nien*, 7b—8a. Lu, *Ling-piao chi-nien*, 1/13a, 21a—b, 23b—24b. Ho, *Feng-tao wu-t'ung chi*, 2b. Ch'ü, *Tung-Ming wen-chien lu*, p. 391. Ch'ü, *Ch'ü Chung-hsüan Kung chi*, 3/4a, 13b—14b. The uprising against the Prince of Min occurred in response to Chang Hsien-chung's invasion of Hu-kuang. The prince sought to reinforce the city walls in view of the rebel threat, whereas the people from whom labor and materials were demanded for this project were emboldened by the rebels to revolt against such exactions. See Ma Shao-ch'iao, "Ming-mo Wu-kang jen-min te fan fan-i tou-cheng," in *Ming-Ch'ing shih lun-ts'ung*, ed. Li Kuang-pi, pp. 135—44.

32. Lu, *Ling-piao chi-nien*, 1/10a—b, 15a—16a, 25b—26a (quotation). Ch'ü, *Tung-Ming wen-chien lu*, pp. 390, 392.

33. Meng, *San-Hsiang ts'ung-shih chi*, pp. 1331—34, 1336. Lu, *Ling-piao chi-nien*, 1/26a—b. Wang, *Yung-li shih-lu*, 1/3a—b; 7/4a. Ch'ü, *Tung-Ming wen-chien lu*, p. 390. Ch'ü, *Ch'ü Chung-hsüan Kung chi*, 3/15b—17b.

34. Meng, *San-Hsiang ts'ung-shih chi*, pp. 1327—32, 1334—35, 1341, 1346—47. Lu, *Ling-piao chi-nien*, 1/13a, 19a, 22b. Wang, *Yung-li shih-lu*, 1/2b—3a.

35. SCSL, 31/16a—b; 32/22b; 35/7a, 11a—15a. MCSL, *ping*, VI: 593. Significantly, the Ch'ing provincial governor for Hu-kuang complained that, although Ch'ing troops in the province had doubled in number (for the campaign), available supplies actually had

shrunk because of calls to use Hu-kuang resources to aid Ho-nan and Chiang-ning (Nan-ching). See Documents Committee, comp., *Wen-hsien ts'ung-pien*, vol. 25, 28b–29b.

36. Lu, *Ling-piao chi-nien*, 1/31b–32a, 34a–b. Meng, *San-Hsiang ts'ung-shih chi*, pp. 1345–46. Ch'ü, *Tung-Ming wen-chien lu*, p. 392. Ho, *Feng-tao wu-t'ung chi*, 1/2b. Ch'ien, *Yung-li chi-nien*, 9b–10a, 12a. Wang, *Yung-li shih-lu*, 1/3b.

37. Lu, *Ling-piao chi-nien*, 1/30a–32a, 33a–b, 38b, 40a–b; 2/4b–6b. Lei, *Kuei-lin t'ien-hai chi*, 10a–11b. Meng, *San-Hsiang ts'ung-shih chi*, pp. 1344–45, 1349–50. Ch'ü *Tung-Ming wen-chien lu*, pp. 394–95. Ch'ü, *Ch'ü Chung-hsüan Kung chi*, 4/3a–5a. Ch'ien, *Yung-li chi-nien*, 12a–13a, 14a. Ho, *Feng-tao wu-t'ung chi*, 1/3a. SCSL, 38/5a.

38. Meng, *San-Hsiang ts'ung-shih chi*, p. 1350. Lei, *Kuei-lin t'ien-hai chi*, 12a–b. Lu, *Ling-piao chi-nien*, 2/6a. Ch'ü, *Ch'ü Chung-hsüan Kung chi*, 4/18a. Ch'ien, *Yung-li chi-nien*, 13b–14a.

39. Chang Ming-chen: Hummel, I: 46–47.

40. Chou Ho-chih also used the name Ts'ui Chih. Because he changed his name in midcareer, and because of character variants and other confusions, he is referred to in different texts, and in different parts of the same texts, by several similar names. See Ishihara Michihiro, *Minmatsu Shinsho Nihon kisshi no kenkyū* (Tokyo, 1945), pp. 11–14; and Chang, *Fu-hai chi*, pp. 9–12.

41. Cha, *Lu ch'un-ch'iu*, p. 22. Ch'en, *Szu-wen ta-chi*, p. 34. Chang, *Fu-hai chi*, pp. 7–8. Wang, *Hang-hsieh i-wen*, 1b. Liu, *Huai-chiu chi*, pp. 178–210. Chang Chia-pi, *Nan-yu lu* (in *Ming-chi yeh-shih tsa-ch'ao*), unpaginated.

42. MCSL, *chia*, II: 185a, and III: 202a; *ting*, I: 6a–b; *chi*, I: 25a. SCSL, 31/19b–20a; 32/1b–2a, 4a–5b, 8a–b. Huang Tsung-hsi [attrib.], *Chou-shan hsing-fei (Li-chou i-chu hui-k'an* ed.), 1b–2a. Wang, *Hang-hsieh i-wen*, 1b–2a. Huang Tsung-hsi says that it was Ch'en Tzu-lung who carried Wu Sheng-chao's appeal to Huang Pin-ch'ing (*Hai-wai t'ung-ch'i chi*, 5a–b), but this appears questionable (see Atwell, "Ch'en Tzu-lung," pp. 139–40). More likely, Wu used some men from Chou-shan who were captured in the failure of another attempt to penetrate the Yang-tzu delta from Ch'ung-ming earlier that same year. MCSL, *chia*, II: 178a–b; *ting*, I: 4a–b; *chi*, I: 4a. Some accounts have assigned a leading role in this conspiracy to the ardent teenaged resister, Hsia Wan-ch'un. See Cha and Shen, *Tung-shan kuo-yü*, pp. 101–03; Liu, *Huai-chiu chi*, pp. 211–37; and the biographical preface to a modern edition of Hsia's collected works, *Hsia Wan-ch'un chi* (Pei-ching, 1959).

43. Cha, *Lu ch'un-ch'iu*, pp. 46, 65. Huang, *Hai-wai t'ung-ch'i chi*, 8b. Kao Yü-t'ai, *Hsüeh-chiao-t'ing cheng-ch'i lu* (T'ai-pei, 1970), II: 124. SCSL, 35/8b. Also, see Ch'üan, *Chi-ch'i-t'ing chi*, ch. 8, pp. 97–99, tomb inscription for Tung Chih-ning.

44. *Chien-kuo chi-nien*, 7b. Huang, *Chou-shan hsing-fei*, 1a. Wang, *Hang-hsieh i-wen*, 1b.

45. *Chien-kuo chi-nien*, 7b–8a. Huang, *Hai-wai t'ung-ch'i chi*, 3a.

46. *Chien-kuo chi-nien*, 8a–b. Huang, *Hai-wai t'ung-ch'i chi*, 3b–4a. MCSL, *ting*, I: 5a, 8a. Hai-wai San-jen, *Jung-ch'eng chi-wen*, pp. 7–8.

47. Listings of men who received appointments under Regent Lu can be found in Sheng Ch'eng, "Shen Kuang-wen," pp. 55–57, and in Mao I-po, "Lu Wang k'ang-Ch'ing yü Ming Cheng kuan-hsi," *T'ai-wan wen-hsien*, 11.1 (March 1960): 60–74. Both of these, however, understate the participation by men of Fu-chien, nor do they indicate that several figures from Che-chiang previously had been officials in Fu-chien.

48. *Chien-kuo chi-nien*, 8a–10a. Huang, *Hai-wai t'ung-ch'i chi*, 4b, 7a–8a, 9a. Wang,

Hang-hsieh i-wen, 2a. Cha, *Lu ch'un-ch'iu*, pp. 43–45, 48, 52. MCSL, *ting*, I: 8a–b. SCSL, 32/8b; 35/19a. Most threatening to Ch'ing control inland was a rebellion led by the Ming Prince of Yün-hsi and a monk named Wang Ch'i, who attacked the Ch'ing stronghold at P'u-ch'eng from bases in Chien-ning. Although the Ch'ing managed to retain P'u-ch'eng, Chien-ning was not pacified until the following April (1648) and suppression campaigns in the region continued at least into 1651. Through the winter of 1647–48, other Ming princes of the second degree and local loyalist groups also led uprisings throughout the length of Fu-chien's central, intermontane region, and they too were not fully suppressed for years. Huang, *Hai-wai t'ung-ch'i chi*, 10b. Cha, *Lu ch'un-ch'iu*, pp. 44, 53–54. MCSL, *chia*, III: 210a, 220a–b, 221a, 230a, 245a, 277a–b; *ting*, I: 10a–11a. SCSL, 33/8a–b; 36/2b–3a, 10b; 45/18a; 47/5b. The uprisings of August 1647 were well coordinated among insurrectionists in various locales of northern Fu-chien, including the provincial capital of Fu-chou, where the Ch'ing authorities resorted to draconian measures to maintain their tenuous control over the populace. Hai-wai San-jen, *Jung-ch'eng chi-wen*, pp. 6–7.

49. Indeed, the entire mountainous border region between Fu-chien and Chiang-hsi defied central governmental control into the late 1650s; and trouble flared there again when Ch'ing effectiveness in the far South was thrown into question by the "Rebellion of the Three Feudatories" in the 1670s. See Fu, *Ming-Ch'ing nung-ts'un she-hui ching-chi*, pp. 105–07, 112–15. The assertion that these people were especially resolute patriots because they fought so long against the Ch'ing authorities, however, is dubious.

50. *Chien-kuo chi-nien*, 11b. Cha, *Lu ch'un-ch'iu*, p. 56.

51. *Chien-kuo chi-nien*, 10a–b. Huang, *Hai-wai t'ung-ch'i chi*, 9a–10a. Wang, *Hang-hsieh i-wen*, 2a. Cha, *Lu ch'un-ch'iu*, pp. 47–48.

52. *Chien-kuo chi-nien*, 11a. Cha, *Lu ch'un-ch'iu*, pp. 53–54. Wang, *Hang-hsieh i-wen*, 2b. However, the charge that difficulties with Cheng Ts'ai caused Ch'ien Su-yüeh's congenital illness to become terminal is not substantiated in Ch'ien's collected memorials from this period. Rather, Ch'ien consistently supported Cheng as the best leader to unify and discipline Regent Lu's disparate military forces, and he was most frustrated by the reluctance of the various commanders, especially those of volunteer forces, to accept such direction. *Ch'ien Chung-chieh Kung chi*, 13/7b–10b, 14b–16a, 20b.

53. Wang, *Hang-hsieh i-wen*, 2b.

54. *Chien-kuo chi-nien*, 11a–b. Huang, *Hai-wai t'ung-ch'i chi*, 10b. Cha, *Lu ch'un-ch'iu*, pp. 56–57. SCSL, 42/1b–2a; 43/9a, 18b.

55. *Chien-kuo chi-nien*, 11b. Huang, *Hai-wai t'ung-ch'i chi*, 11b–12a. Cha, *Lu ch'un-ch'iu*, p. 54. Hayashi Shunsai, comp., *Ka'i hentai* (Tokyo, 1958–59), I: 31, 41, 43.

56. On Chang Ming-chen's full career, see Liao Han-ch'en, "Lu Wang k'ang-Ch'ing yü erh-Chang te wu-kung," *T'ai-wan wen-hsien*, 11.1 (March 1960): 81–102. Chang is said to have had his back scarred with characters that read "repay the country with true loyalty." Wang, *Hang-hsieh i-wen*, 5a.

57. The two most vocal critics of Chang's policies were Minister of Rites Wu Chung-luan and Senior Vice Censor-in-Chief Huang Tsung-hsi. Huang, *Szu-ming shan-sai chi*, 2a. Idem, *Hai-wai t'ung-ch'i chi*, 12b. Wu had voiced the same complaints when Cheng Ts'ai dominated the court's affairs. *Chien-kuo chi-nien*, 9b. On Wu, see *Hai-wai t'ung-ch'i chi*, 17a–b; and on Huang, see Hummel, I: 351–54.

58. Huang, *Hai-wai t'ung-ch'i chi*, 14b–15a, 16a. For biogs. of Wang Yi and Feng Ching-ti, see, respectively, Ch'üan, *Chi-ch'i-t'ing chi, wai-pien*, ch. 4, pp. 689–93; and Ch'en T'ien, comp., *Ming-shih chi-shih* (T'ai-pei, 1968), XXV: 2802–03.

59. Huang, *Szu-ming shan-sai chi*, 1a–b. Idem, *Hai-wai t'ung-ch'i chi*, 10b, 16a–b.

60. Huang, *Hai-wai t'ung-ch'i chi*, 15a.

61. *Chien-kuo chi-nien*, 12a–b. Chang, *Fu-hai chi*, p. 9. Wang, *Hang-hsieh i-wen*, 2b–3b. Huang, *Hai-wai t'ung-ch'i chi*, 13b–14a.

62. Huang, *Hai-wai t'ung-ch'i chi*, 14b–15a, 16a–b. Idem, *Szu-ming shan-sai chi*, 2a. MCSL, *chia*, III: 213a, 257a–b, 261a–b, 265a, 268a–b; *ting*, I: 7a; *chi*, I: 23a–24a. SCSL, 40/20b; 46/31a; 48/9b.

63. *Chien-kuo chi-nien*, 13a–b. Huang, *Hai-wai t'ung-ch'i chi*, 15b–16b. Idem, *Szu-ming shan-sai chi*, 2b. Wang, *Hang-hsieh i-wen*, 3b. Cha, *Lu ch'un-ch'iu*, p. 60.

64. *Chien-kuo chi-nien*, 13a. Wang, *Hang-hsieh i-wen*, 3b. MCSL, *chia*, III: 284a–85a; IV: 381b.

65. *Chien-kuo chi-nien*, 13b–15a. Wang, *Hang-hsieh i-wen*, 3b–4a. Chang, *Nan-yu lu*, unpaginated. Huang, *Hai-wai t'ung-ch'i chi*, 16b–17a, 19a. Cha, *Lu ch'un-ch'iu*, pp. 62–63. SCSL, 59/28b; 60/8a–b. Among those who died were Chang Ming-chen's elder brother and all fifty other members of his family, at least thirteen members of Regent Lu's household, and twenty-one ministers and other officials, many with their families. Regent Lu's eldest and second sons were taken captive, as was his concubine, whom he later secretly tried to ransom from the man who obtained her in Hang-chou. See Su T'ung-ping, "Lu Wang shih Liu Chung chih Hang-chou shu-ch'ü wang-fei chi ch'i tzu an," *T'ai-wan wen-hsien*, 20.3 (Sept. 1969): 111–17.

66. The history of Cheng Ch'eng-kung's titular elevation is complicated and problematical, especially regarding the title by which Cheng later became known most popularly, the Prince of Yen-p'ing. The most thorough study is by Chu Hsi-tsu, "Cheng Yen-p'ing Wang shou Ming kuan-chüeh k'ao," *Kuo-li Pei-p'ing ta-hsüeh kuo-hsüeh chi-k'an*, 3.1 (March 1932): 87–112. Also, see Huang Yü-chai, "Ming Yung-li Ti feng Chu Ch'eng-kung wei Yen-p'ing Wang k'ao," in *T'ai-wan wen-wu lun-chi* (T'ai-pei, 1966), pp. 87–94; Mao I-po, "Cheng Ch'eng-kung kuan-chüeh k'ao," *T'ai-wan feng-wu*, 23.4 (Dec. 1973): 5–6; and Su T'ung-ping, "Yen-p'ing wang yü Yen-p'ing chün-wang chih cheng p'ing-lun," *T'ai-wan wen-hsien*, 24.2 (June 1973): 10–13. For indications of contact between Cheng Ch'eng-kung and the Yung-li court in Chao-ch'ing, see Ch'ien, *Yung-li chi-nien*, 21a–b; and Lu, *Ling-piao chi-nien*, 2/18b.

67. No primary source satisfactorily records the date of Regent Lu's arrival or the circumstances of his reception on Hsia-men. Certain points here have been extrapolated from primary and secondary accounts, all of which are questionable in some aspect. On this problem, see Chuang Chin-te, "Ming chien-kuo Lu Wang I-hai chi-shih nien-piao," pp. 30–31, and notes, pp. 234–35; and Chang T'an, *Cheng Ch'eng-kung chi-shih pien-nien* (T'ai-pei, 1965), p. 46, note. Except for a three-year stay on the island of Nan-ao (1656–59), the Prince of Lu remained on Chin-men for the rest of his life (see his tomb inscription, translated by Richard Rudolph in "The Real Tomb of the Ming Regent, Prince of Lu," p. 490). The assertion, common in Ch'ing writings, that Cheng Ch'eng-kung had the prince drowned certainly is not true. Among Chinese scholars, Mao I-po has been most assiduous in pointing this out. See, for instance, his articles: "Shu Lu Wang chih szu yü Cheng Ch'eng-kung shou-wu shih," *Wen-hsien chuan-k'an*, 4.3–4 (Dec. 1953): 9–10; and "Che-Min kung-an yü Nan-ao kung-an," *T'ai-wan wen-hsien*, 11.1 (March 1960): 75–80 (reprinted in Mao's collected writings on the Southern Ming, *Nan-Ming shih-t'an* [Taipei, 1970], pp. 1–13).

68. The story that Cheng ceremonially burned his Confucian robes, however, probably is apocryphal. See Yang Yün-p'ing, "Cheng Ch'eng-kung fen ju-fu k'ao," *T'ai-*

wan yen-chiu, 1 (June 1956): 31–37; and Ch'en Pi-sheng, "1646-nien Cheng Ch'eng-kung hai-shang ch'i-ping ching-kuo," *Li-shih yen-chiu*, 1978, no. 8 (Aug.), pp. 92–93.

69. Juan Min-hsi [pseud. Lu-tao Tao-jen Meng-an], *Hai-shang chien-wen lu* (T'ai-pei, 1958), pp. 4–7. Yang Ying, *Yen-p'ing Wang hu-kuan Yang Ying ts'ung-cheng shih-lu* (Pei-p'ing, 1931), 1b–3b. Chiang, *T'ai-wan wai-chi*, I: 97–98, 100–03, 105–08. Ch'ien, *Lung-wu chi-nien*, 29a. SCSL, 43/15b; 46/15a; 49/6b. On this early stage of Cheng Ch'eng-kung's career in the coastal resistance, see Chin Ch'eng-ch'ien, "Cheng Ch'eng-kung ch'i-ping hou shih-wu-nien chien cheng-chan shih-lüeh," *T'ai-wan wen-hsien*, 23.4 (Dec. 1972): 80–82; and Ch'en Shih-ch'ing, "Ming Cheng ch'ien-hou chih Chin-men ping-shih," *T'ai-wan wen-hsien*, 6.1 (March 1955): 1–3.

70. Juan, *Hai-shang chien-wen lu*, pp. 7–9. Yang, *Yen-p'ing...shih-lu*, 3b–4b, 5b–9b. MCSL, *chia*, III: 276a. SCSL, 50/8b.

71. Juan, *Hai-shang chien-wen lu*, p. 9. Yang, *Yen-p'ing...shih-lu*, 9b–10a. Chiang, *T'ai-wan wai-chi*, I: 113–15.

72. Yang, *Yen-p'ing...shih-lu*, 10b–14b. Juan, *Hai-shang chien-wen lu*, p. 9. Wei Yung-chu, "Cheng Ch'eng-kung nan-hsia ch'in-wang chih t'an-t'ao," *T'ai-wan wen-hsien*, 33.1 (March 1982): 133–34.

73. Yang, *Yen-p'ing...shih-lu*, 13b, 14b–15a. Juan, *Hai-shang chien-wen lu*, pp. 10–11. Chiang, *T'ai-wan wai-chi*, I: 118–19.

74. Wang Yi-t'ung, *Official Relations between China and Japan, 1368–1549* (Cambridge, Mass., 1953), pp. 80–81. Wills, "Maritime China from Wang Chih to Shih-lang," pp. 210–15. Ng Chin-keong, "The Fukienese Maritime Trade in the Second Half of the Ming Period—Government Policy and Elite Groups' Attitudes," *Nanyang University Journal*, 5.2 (1971): 81–100.

75. Kwan-wai So, *Japanese Piracy in Ming China during the Sixteenth Century* (East Lansing, Mich., 1975), chap. 2.

76. Ibid., maps 1–4.

77. The classic studies in this area are by Ishihara Michihiro, *Minmatsu Shinsho Nihon kisshi no kenkyū*, pp. 1–130. Also see Yang Yün-p'ing, "Nan-Ming shih-tai yü Jih-pen te kuan-hsi," *Chung-kuo li-shih hsüeh-hui shih-hsüeh chi-k'an*, 6 (May 1974): 1–17; Huang Yü-chai, "Ming Cheng Ch'eng-kung teng te k'ang-Ch'ing yü Jih-pen," *T'ai-wan wen-hsien*, 9.4 (Dec. 1958): 90–126; and idem, "Cheng Ch'eng-kung shih-tai yü Jih-pen Te-ch'uan mu-fu," *T'ai-wan wen-hsien*, 13.1 (March 1962): 114–34. The number of Chinese ships that went to trade in Japan increased markedly from 1639 to 1646. This reflects the increased ability of the Japanese to pay for imported goods since the stabilization that attended the establishment of the Tokugawa *bakufu*, as well as the greater role that Chinese merchants were able to play after the Japanese government instituted its "seclusion" policies in 1639. Iwao Seiichi, "Japanese Foreign Trade in the 16th and 17th Centuries," *Acta Asiatica*, 30 (1976): 11. Moreover, it may reflect more flagrant disregard for Ming strictures on the part of Chinese seamen, as the dynasty's policing powers became even weaker.

78. Chu, better known by his style name, Shun-shui, eventually settled in Japan and became an influential teacher, founding the Mito School of Confucianism. See Julia Ching, "Chu Shun-shui, 1600–82: A Chinese Confucian Scholar in Tokugawa Japan," *Monumenta Nipponica*, 30.2 (Summer 1975): 177–91. For biographies, see: Hummel, I: 179–80; Wang Chin-hsiang, *Chu Shun-shui p'ing-chuan* (T'ai-pei, 1976); and Kuo Yüan, *Chu Shun-shui* (T'ai-pei, 1964 [1937]). Specifically regarding his involvement in the

coastal resistance, see Ishihara Michihiro, "Tei Seikō to Shu Shunsui," *T'ai-wan feng-wu,* 4.8–9 (Sept. 1954): 11–28. Liang Ch'i-ch'ao has disputed Ch'üan Tsu-wang's assertion that Huang Tsung-hsi accompanied Chu and Feng Ching-ti on at least one of their trips to Japan ("Huang Li-chou, Chu Shun-shui ch'i-shih Jih-pen pien," *Tung-fang tsa-chih,* 20.6 [March 1923]: 54–56), but his arguments are not convincing. For further consideration of this question, see Ishihara, *Minmatsu Shinsho,* pp. 20–21.

79. Liao Han-ch'en, "Cheng Chih-lung k'ao," (1) pp. 69–70, (2) pp. 1–2.

80. On the peculiar dual political status that the Liu-ch'iu princes maintained between China and Japan, see Robert K. Sakai, "The Ryukyu (Liu-ch'iu) Islands as a Fief of Satsuma," in *The Chinese World Order,* ed. John K. Fairbank (Cambridge, Mass., 1968), pp. 112–34.

81. On the Tokugawa supervision through Nagasaki of the "ships of T'ang," i.e., Chinese trading galleons, see Ura Ren'ichi, "Ka'i hentai kaisetsu—tōsen fusetsugaki no kenkyū," prefatory to Hayashi Shunsai, comp., *Ka'i hentai,* vol. 1.

82. Ronald P. Toby, "Reopening the Question of *Sakoku*: Diplomacy in the Legitimation of the Tokugawa Bakufu," *Journal of Japanese Studies,* 3.2 (Summer 1977): 323–63. On the hostilities between China and Japan because of the latter's invasion of Korea, see George Sansom, *A History of Japan, 1334–1615* (Stanford, 1961), pp. 358–60. On *sakoku,* see Sansom, *A History of Japan, 1615–1867* (Stanford, 1963), pp. 36–39; and Charles R. Boxer, *The Christian Century in Japan, 1549–1650* (Berkeley, 1951), chap. 8, esp. pp. 383–89. And on the anti-Christian campaign, see George Elison, *Deus Destroyed: The Image of Christianity in Early Modern Japan* (Cambridge, Mass., 1973).

83. Ishihara, *Minmatsu Shinsho,* pp. 9–10, 40. Hayashi, comp., *Ka'i hentai,* I: 11–13. [Nederlandsche Oost-Indische Compagnie], trans. Murakami Naojirō, *Deshima Rankan nisshi* (Tokyo, 1939), vol. 3, *daghregister* pp. 2, 6.

84. Ch'en, *Szu-wen ta-chi,* p. 144. Hayashi, comp., *Ka'i hentai,* I: 16–20, 22–25. Ishihara, *Minmatsu Shinsho,* pp. 31–35, 48. Further testimony to the interest of many Japanese leaders in sending armed forces to China is presented by Ronald Toby in "State and Diplomacy in Early Modern Japan," chap. 4, MS. (Dec. 1981) of a book forthcoming from Princeton University Press.

85. Huang Tsung-hsi [attrib.], *Jih-pen ch'i-shih chi (Li-chou i-chu hui-k'an* ed.), 1b. Cha, *Lu ch'un-ch'iu,* p. 61.

86. Huang, *Jih-pen ch'i-shih chi,* 1a. Idem, *Hai-wai t'ung-ch'i chi,* 4a–b, 6b–7a. Ishihara, *Minmatsu Shinsho,* pp. 2, 6–7, 16, 18–19. Chinese copper coins long had been standard currency in Japan, having been imported in especially large quantities during the early Ming reigns. See Wang, *Official Relations,* pp. 101–06. These particular coins were of Hung-wu vintage.

87. Hayashi, comp., *Ka'i hentai,* I: 25–29. Cheng Ch'eng-kung's letter, recorded here only in Japanese *katakana* translation, has been retranslated into Chinese by Kawaguchi Chōju in his *T'ai-wan Cheng Shih chi-shih* (T'ai-pei, 1958), *shang,* p. 25.

88. Hayashi, comp., *Ka'i hentai,* I: 30–32, 37–38, 40–41. On the place of Liu-ch'iu in the Ming-Ch'ing transition, see Ishihara, *Minmatsu Shinsho,* pp. 131–87; and Yang Yün-p'ing, "Nan-Ming shih-tai yü Liu-ch'iu chih kuan-hsi te yen-chiu," *Shih-hsüeh hui-k'an,* 2 (Aug. 1969): 173–87.

89. Huang, *Jih-pen ch'i-shih chi,* 2a–b. Wang, *Hang-hsieh i-wen,* 3b. Hayashi, comp., *Ka'i hentai,* I: 44.

90. Ishihara, *Minmatsu Shinsho,* pp. 51–52. Cha, *Lu Ch'un-ch'iu,* p. 61. Chiang,

T'ai-wan wai-chi, I: 123. Hayashi, comp., *Ka'i hentai*, I: 45–46. Juan, *Hai-shang chien-wen-lu*, p. 36.

91. Toby, "Reopening the Question of *Sakoku*," p. 358.

92. For reports to the *bakufu* on political conditions in China, see Hayashi, comp., *Ka'i hentai*, I: 33–35.

93. Lynn Struve, "A Sketch of Southern Ming Events Affecting the Canton Delta Area," paper presented to the Canton Delta Seminar, Hongkong University, 1973; pp. 1–4. The chief sources of information on these kinds of local disruptions are district, prefectural, and provincial gazetteers (*fang-chih*) of mid- or late-Ch'ing date. Here, for instance, see *Hui-chou fu-chih* (1688), ch. 5; *Kuang-chou fu-chih* (1879), ch. 79 and 80; *Chieh-yang hsien-chih* (1779), ch. 79; *Shun-te hsien-chih* (Hsien-feng period), ch. 31; *Hsin-hui hsien-chih* (1840), ch. 13; and *Kao-yao hsien-chih* (1826), ch. 10. Because gazetteers are not contemporaneous sources for this period, I have not employed them for research on the Southern Ming per se; but they are indispensable for any systematic research on social disruptions during this period. For an example of the latter, see Fu, *Ming-Ch'ing nung-ts'un she-hui ching-chi*, esp. pp. 120–22 on Kuang-tung.

94. MCSL, *chi*, I: 29b.

95. For the best composite study of the resistance activities of the *ling-piao san-chung*, see Li Chieh, "Nan-Ming Kuang-tung san-chung shih-chi k'ao," *Chu-hai hsüeh-pao*, 3 (June 1970): 162–73. For T'ung Yang-chia's summary report, see MCSL, *ping*, VI: 639a–40a. Also, see Hummel under the entry for Ch'en Tzu-chuang, I: 101–02.

96. Li Chien-erh, "Ch'en Tzu-chuang nien-p'u," in *Kuang-tung wen-wu*, II: 516–50. Ch'ü, *Huang-Ming szu-ch'ao*, 10/374a–77b. Wang, *Yung-li shih-lu*, 6/1a–b.

97. Yen Hsü-hsin, "*Ming-shih* Ch'en Pang-yen chuan p'ang-cheng," in *Kuang-tung wen-wu*, II: 551–87. Ch'ü, *Huang-Ming szu-ch'ao*, 10/355a–62a. Ch'en, *Ch'en Yen-yeh hsien-sheng chi*, 2/4a, 6a–b; 4/26a–32b (*hsing-chuang*).

98. Mai Shao-lin, "Min-tsu ying-hsiung Chang Chia-yü," in *Kuang-tung wen-wu*, II: 588–611. Ch'ü, *Huang-Ming szu-ch'ao*, 10/363b–69a. Chang, *Chang Wen-lieh i-chi*, 4/1a–b, 3a–7b.

99. Ch'ü, *Huang-Ming szu-ch'ao*, 10/356b–57a. Ch'en, *Ch'en Yen-yeh hsien-sheng chi*, 4/29a. MCSL, *chia*, II: 191a; *chi*, I: 29b.

100. Ch'ü, *Huang-Ming szu-ch'ao*, 10/357b. MCSL, *chi*, I: 30a. SCSL, 34/7a–b.

101. Ch'ü, *Huang-Ming szu-ch'ao*, 10/365b–66a. MCSL, *chi*, I: 29b. SCSL, 34/7b.

102. Ch'ü, *Huang-Ming szu-ch'ao*, 10/366b–67a. MCSL, *ping*, VI: 639b.

103. For other examples, see references to Chang Kuang in chap. 2, n. 101; and to Chang T'ung-ch'ang in chap. 6, n. 16.

104. Ch'ü, *Huang-Ming szu-ch'ao*, 10/357a–b. Ch'ien, *Yung-li chi-nien*, 10b. Ch'en, *Ch'en Yen-yeh hsien-sheng chi*, 4/29b–30b. MCSL, *ping*, VI: 619a.

105. Ch'ü, *Huang-Ming szu-ch'ao*, 10/358a–b, 376a–b. Ch'en, *Ch'en Yen-yeh hsien-sheng chi*, 4/31b. MCSL, *ping*, VI: 639a–b. SCSL, 35/2b.

106. Ch'ü, *Huang-Ming szu-ch'ao*, 10/367a–b. MCSL, *ping*, VI: 639a–b.

CHAPTER FIVE

1. T'an, *Kuo-ch'üeh*, VI: 6155, 6159.

2. Hsü, *Chiang-pien chi-lüeh*, 1a–b.

3. Hsü Shih-p'u's *Chiang-pien chi-lüeh* says that Chin's disappointment was in being made a regional *vice* commander (1b); but from various Ch'ing documents it is clear that

he was a full regional commander. The disparity actually was in his having lost status as an assistant commissioner-in-chief in one of the Ming Chief Military Commissions, which did not exist under the Ch'ing. Also, see P'eng, *Hu-hsi i-shih*, 2b; Hsü, *Chiang-pien chi-lüeh*, 3b; and Wang, *Yung-li shih-lu*, 11/1b.

4. MCSL, *chia*, II: 122b. Compare, for instance, Chin's glowing reports in SCSL, 22/6a–b, and MCSL, *ping*, VI: 552a–b, with later ones by the Ch'ing provincial governor for Chiang-hsi, who said that the province "truly has a worm-eaten belly." MCSL, *ping*, VII: 616a. Documents Committee, *Wen-hsien ts'ung-pien*, vol. 25, 33b–34a.

5. Wang had risen from the ranks of one Shun rebel army that had entered northern Chiang-hsi from Hu-kuang. Hsü, *Chiang-pien chi-lüeh*, 1a–2b. Wang, *Yung-li shih-lu*, 2b–3a.

6. SCSL, 26/9b–10a. MCSL, *chi*, I: 3b.

7. MCSL, *ping*, VI: 575a. Documents Committee, *Wen-hsien ts'ung-pien*, vol. 25, 34b, 36a. Wang, *Yung-li shih-lu*, 11/2a–b.

8. Wang, *Yung-li shih-lu*, 11/1a, 2b–3b. Hsü, *Chiang-pien chi-lüeh*, 2b–3a. Meng, *San-Hsiang ts'ung-shih chi*, p. 1351. Lu, *Ling-piao chi-nien*, 2/4a–b. Ch'ien, *Yung-li chi-nien*, 15a. SCSL, 36/9a–b. MCSL, *ping*, VII: 663a, 674a.

9. Wang, *Yung-li shih-lu*, 1/3b–4a; 6/4b.

10. SCSL, 36/10b; 37/20a; 38/4a–b, 8b–10a. MCSL, *ping*, VII: 663a, 674a; VIII: 701a–b. Ch'ien, *Chien-kuo chi-nien*, 10b. Huang, *Hai-wai t'ung-ch'i chi*, 10a–b.

11. On the relation of the northwestern Moslems to Li Tzu-ch'eng's movement and the trouble the Ch'ing had in subjugating them, see Morris Rossabi, "Muslim and Central Asian Revolts," in *From Ming to Ch'ing*, ed. Spence and Wills, pp. 185–92. Up to this time, the chief obstacle to Ch'ing pacification of Shen-hsi had been the former rebels and Ming army officers such as Heh Chen, Sun Shou-fa, and Wu Ta-ting, who (although they received noble titles from the various Southern Ming courts) operated independently in the extreme south of the province, around Han-chung and Hsing-an. SCSL, 23/2b–3a, 7b; 24/9b; 29/12a–b; 31/20b; 32/22b; 37/24b–25a. MCSL, *chia*, II: 103. Number I Archive, *Ch'ing-tai tang-an*, VI: 137–38. On both of these matters, see Hsieh Kuo-chen, *Ch'ing-ch'u nung-min ch'i-i tzu-liao chi-lu*, pp. 267–84.

12. SCSL, 41/17a, 19a, 20a–b, 21b; 42/2a, 4a, 6a–8b, 12b–13a, 17a; 43/1b–7a, 11a, 12a, 19a–b; 44/16b, 19b, 26b–27a; 45/1b, 3b, 6a–b, 9b–10a; 46/2a–b, 8a–b, 15a, 25a; 47/1b (citations for the Shan-hsi action only). On Chiang Hsiang see Hummel, I: 138.

13. Much of the unrest in the North during this time may have resulted from the reinstitution and vigorous enforcement of a prohibition that the Ch'ing had found it necessary to rescind two years earlier, i.e., against common people owning or trafficking in the sorts of weapons and animals that were used by bandits. SCSL, 28/14b; 34/16a–b; 40/7a–8b. This put pressure on the outlaw groups, who then had to openly attack and raid to get the things they needed; it also caused revolts among citizens, who were deprived of the means of defending themselves against outlaws. In May of 1649 the Ch'ing found it prudent to rescind this ban again, prohibiting only cannon and armor. SCSL, 43/9b.

The 1648–49 time of troubles for the Ch'ing was made worse by some losses in their leadership. Several important princes and noblemen were brought under indictment for various transgressions under Dorgon's heavy-handed rule (SCSL, 37/2a–15b); and in the midst of the Ta-t'ung campaign, an outbreak of smallpox in northern Pei Chih-li killed one of the Manchus' most talented leaders, Dorgon's brother Dodo, who then was only thirty-six (43/4b, 8b).

14. MCSL, *ping*, VII: 673a, 682a, 689a–b. Documents Committee, *Wen-hsien ts'ung-*

pien, vol. 13, Shun-chih *chieh-t'ieh*, 3b–4a. Number I Archive, *Ch'ing-tai tang-an*, VI: 152–53, 155–58, 159–60. Lu, *Ling-piao chi-nien*, 2/11a, 21a–b. Ch'ü, *Ch'ü Chung-hsüan Kung chi*, 4/19a–b. Ch'ien, *Yung-li chi-nien*, 22b, 24a. Wang, *Yung-li shih-lu*, 1/4a. Meng, *San-Hsiang ts'ung-shih chi*, p. 1359.

15. Lu, *Ling-piao chi-nien*, 12a, 21b–22a. Meng, *San-Hsiang ts'ung-shih chi*, pp. 1351, 1359. Wang, *Yung-li shih-lu*, 1/4b; 7/4a. Ch'ien, *Yung-li chi-nien*, 19b–20a, 21a–b. Ch'ü, *Ch'ü Chung-hsüan Kung chi*, 4/5a–7a, 18a, 19b–20a.

16. MCSL, *chi*, I: 8a, 12a, 13b.

17. MCSL, *ping*, VI: 596a–b; *ting*, I: 2a–b.

18. SCSL, 32/6b, 16a.

19. Wang, *Yung-li shih-lu*, 11/3b. Meng, *San-Hsiang ts'ung-shih chi*, p. 1352. At least one frequently cited account points to Li's having sent for some of his family members from Sung-chiang as an indication that he planned to revert (Ch'ien, *Yung-li chi-nien*, 15a–b, 16a–b). But this was consonant with the Ch'ing court's approval of T'ung Yang-chia's request that Li and his subordinate officers be allowed to bring their families to Kuang-tung (MCSL, *ping*, VI: 595a).

20. Ho, *Feng-tao wu-t'ung chi*, 1/3a–b. Ch'ien, *Yung-li chi-nien*, 16a. Wang, *Yung-li shih-lu*, 4a. This lady patriot subsequently became the heroine of numerous popular songs and plays. See Chien Yu-wen, "Nan-Ming min-tsu nü ying-hsiung Chang Yü-ch'iao k'ao-cheng," *Ta-lu tsa-chih*, 41.6 (Sept. 1970): 1–19.

21. Ch'ien, *Yung-li chi-nien*, 15a–b. Lu, *Ling-piao chi-nien*, 2/8a. Wang, *Yung-li shih-lu*, 11/5b.

22. Ch'ien, *Yung-li chi-nien*, 15b–17a. Wang, *Yung-li shih-lu*, 11/4a. Lu, *Ling-piao chi-nien*, 2/8a, 9a. Meng, *San-Hsiang ts'ung-shih chi*, p. 1352. T'ung was given an appointment by the Yung-li court, but he never actively supported the regime, and he remained loyal to the Manchus in sentiment. Later that year (1648) it was discovered that he had tried to communicate with Ch'ing compatriots to the north, so in December he was assassinated. Ch'ien, *Yung-li chi-nien*, 21a. Wang, *Yung-li shih-lu*, 1/4b, 11/5a–6b. Lu, *Ling-piao chi-nien*, 2/22a.

23. Lu, *Ling-piao chi-nien*, 2/8b–9b. Ch'ien, *Yung-li chi-nien*, 16a.

24. Ho, *Feng-tao wu-t'ung-chi*, 1/3a.

25. Ch'ien, *Yung-li chi-nien*, 14b, 16a. Wang, *Yung-li shih-lu*, 3b/4a. Lu, *Ling-piao chi-nien*, 2/10a–11a, 12b. Meng, *San-Hsiang ts'ung-shih chi*, p. 1353.

26. The date of the Yung-li emperor's return to Chao-ch'ing here follows Meng, *San-Hsiang ts'ung-shih chi*, p. 1354, as more reliable in this case than the frequently cited date given in Ch'ien, *Yung-li chi-nien*, 17b. Also, see Lu, *Ling-piao chi-nien*, 2/10a, 11a–12a, 15a, 16b, 17b; and Ho, *Feng-tao wu-t'ung chi*, 1/3b–4a.

Some consideration was given to renewed appeals from Ch'ü Shih-szu that the emperor return to Kuei-lin in preparation for an advance northward through Hu-kuang. But the court felt that since Chin and Li were responsible for so dramatically restoring the court's fortunes, the emperor should show them encouragement by moving back to Chao-ch'ing, close to Kuang-chou and on the principal communication route to Chiang-hsi. Moreover, it acceded to Li's claim that he could not calm agitation among the people of Kuang-tung and hold that province secure unless the court came there to validate his actions. See Wang, *Yung-li shih-lu*, 1/4a; 2/3a–b; Ch'ien, *Yung-li chi-nien*, 17a; Meng, *San-Hsiang ts'ung-shih chi*, p. 1353; and Ch'ü, *Ch'ü Chung-hsüan Kung chi*, 4/10b–11b. Ch'ü resisted the emperor's appeals that he come to Chao-ch'ing, stating that he still hoped the court would move into Hu-kuang via Kuei-lin. *Ch'ü Chung-hsüan Kung chi*, 4/12a–13a, 20a–b.

27. Lu, *Ling-piao chi-nien*, 1/10a; 2/15a, 23a. Meng, *San-Hsiang ts'ung-shih chi*, pp. 1356–57. Wang, *Yung-li shih-lu*, 1/3b, 4b. Ch'ien, *Lung-wu chi-nien*, 9a.

28. Lu, *Ling-piao chi-nien*, 2/2a.

29. Wang, *Yung-li shih-lu*, 11/6a. Chin, *Ling-hai fen-yü*, pp. 29–30.

30. Ho, *Feng-tao wu-t'ung chi*, 1/4a.

31. Wang, *Yung-li shih-lu*, 11/4b–5a. Ch'ien, *Yung-li chi-nien*, 17b–18a, 19a, 21b. Lu, *Ling-piao chi-nien*, 2/17b; 3/3b–4a. Ho, *Feng-tao wu-t'ung chi*, 1/4a–b.

32. Yüan-yin's surname originally was Chia. For a biography, see Wang, *Yung-li shih-lu*, 11/5b–8a.

33. The leading Shao-wu supporters Huang Shih-chün and Ho Wu-tsou, upon being recommended by Li Ch'eng-tung, were made grand secretaries under the Yung-li emperor; but they soon felt the disfavor of other officials, especially those of the Ch'u clique (see the following note) and resigned. Ch'ien, *Yung-li chi-nien*, 27a–28a, 36a. Wang, *Yung-li shih-lu*, 1/4a, 5a–b; 4/2a–3a; 19/2b. Lu, *Ling-piao chi-nien*, 2/13b, 19a–b. Li, "Kuan-yü Ho Wu-tsou," pp. 185–87. The most extensive list of Yung-li appointments at this time can be found in Meng, *San-Hsiang ts'ung-shih chi*, pp. 1355–56.

34. Yüan P'eng-nien, one of the leading figures in Li Ch'eng-tung's reversion (and nephew of the famous litterateur Yüan Hung-tao) was Censor-in-Chief; and Ting Shih-k'uei was Supervising Secretary (of the Office of Scrutiny) for Personnel. The other three of the Tiger Five (*wu-hu*) were Junior Vice Censor-in-Chief Liu Hsiang-k'o, Supervising Secretary for Revenues Meng Cheng-fa, and Supervising Secretary for War Chin Pao. Lu, *Ling-piao chi-nien*, 2/14b, 23b; 4/3a. Ch'ien, *Yung-li chi-nien*, 22a, 26a–b, 28a, 35a. Wang, *Yung-li shih-lu*, 11/6a; 21/2b. Ho, *Feng-tao wu-t'ung chi*, 1/4b. Further on Chin Pao, see Hummel, I: 166. These men were popularly caricatured as a tiger with five parts, each man constituting the head, fangs, hide, feet, and tail of the animal, respectively (Ho, *Feng-tao wu-t'ung chi*, 2/1a). Li Yüan-yin was the immediate power behind the Ch'u clique, and among the eunuchs, Director of Ceremonial P'ang T'ien-shou was their most important ally.

The famous intellectual Wang Fu-chih, who attended the Yung-li court for short periods, definitely favored the Ch'u clique, and this should be kept in mind when reading his history, the *Yung-li shih-lu*. The biography therein of Yen Ch'i-heng (2/4a–8a) is especially sympathetic. See Ian McMorran, "The Patriot and the Partisans: Wang Fu-chih's Involvement in the Politics of the Yung-li Court," in *From Ming to Ch'ing*, ed. Spence and Wills, pp. 136–66. Also, see Huang Yü-chai, "Ming-chi san ta-ju yü Yung-li Ti," *T'ai-wan wen-hsien*, 19.4 (Dec. 1968): 68–70.

35. For instance, Grand Secretary Chu T'ien-lin was from K'un-shan, and Vice Minister of Personnel Wu Chen-min was from I-hsing; but another group in the clique, including Grand Secretary Wang Hua-ch'eng (who did not always get along with Chu), hailed from northeastern Chiang-hsi. Ma Chi-hsiang, of course, was the power behind this clique; and among the eunuchs, Hsia Kuo-hsiang was his ally. Ch'ien, *Yung-li chi-nien*, 36a–b. Wang, *Yung-li shih-lu*, 2/2b–3a.

36. Wang, *Yung-li shih-lu*, 19/1a–2a; 21/2b.

37. Ho, *Feng-tao wu-t'ung chi*, 1/3b.

38. Lu, *Ling-piao chi-nien*, 1/1b, 6a–b; 4/24b–25a.

39. Chin Pao asserted that the absolute separation of military and civil functions was

fundamental to the Founder's Order, and that to have a hereditary military noble such as Ma Chi-hsiang behaving like a grand secretary and dabbling in the affairs of every office was unprecedented in the history of the dynasty (*Ling-hai fen-yü*, pp. 29–30).

Ch'ien Ping-teng had somewhat more positive suggestions for reform on both the central and provincial levels. But notably, he also argued that the emperor should surround himself with a *few dozen* worthy men, designating no one as prime minister, and that the first step in reinstituting district and prefectural government should be to *replace* military with civilian rule, and again to subordinate the military commands to the Ministry of War (*Ts'ang shan-ko chi hsüan-chi*, I: 12–15).

40. Wang, *Yung-li shih-lu*, 2/2b, 5b; 19/2b. Lu, *Ling-piao chi-nien*, 3/15b.

41. Ch'ien, *Yung-li chi-nien*, 20a–21a, 31a. Wang, *Yung-li shih-lu*, 1/4a; 21/2b. Lu, *Ling-piao chi-nien*, 1/9b; 2/12a–b, 19b–20a. Ho, *Feng-tao wu-t'ung chi*, 1/5b–6a.

42. Ch'ien, *Yung-li chi-nien*, 26a, 27a. Lu, *Ling-piao chi-nien*, 3/1a–b. Ho, *Feng-tao wu-t'ung chi*, 1/5b.

43. Wang, *Yung-li shih-lu*, 1/5a; 2/3a; 19/2b. Lu, *Ling-piao chi-nien*, 2/23a–24a; 3/3b; 4/3a. Ch'ien, *Yung-li chi-nien*, 34b–35a. Wang Hua-ch'eng was impeached for selling titles and civil service appointments to aboriginal chieftains and imperial clansmen. Ch'ien, *Yung-li chi-nien*, 47b. Wang, *Yung-li shih-lu*, 2/2a.

44. Lu, *Ling-piao chi-nien*, 3/8b, 22a–b. Wang, *Yung-li shih-lu*, 1/5b. Ho, *Feng-tao wu-t'ung chi*, 2/1a. Ch'ien, *Yung-li chi-nien*, 32a.

45. Chin, *Ling-hai fen-yü*, pp. 51–54. Wang, *Yung-li shih-lu*, 21/3a–4a. Ho, *Feng-tao wu-t'ung chi*, 2/1b.

46. Ch'ien, *Yung-li chi-nien*, 32b–33a. Wang, *Yung-li shih-lu*, 1/5b. Lu, *Ling-piao chi-nien*, 3/8b.

47. Lu, *Ling-piao chi-nien*, 3/5a. Wang, *Yung-li shih-lu*, 1/6a. K'un-ming-Wu-ming shih, *Tien-nan wai-shih*, 7b. Ch'en is said to have been urged into this and other aggrandizing schemes by a general who formerly had been his patron, and who now served as his special secretary and adviser, Hu Chih-kung. Hu had developed considerable literacy and knowledge of governmental affairs while serving as a quartermaster for the Ministry of War in Pei-ching, and he seems now to have tried to use both to create a quasilegitimate satrapy for Ch'en and himself in Kuang-hsi. Ch'ien, *Yung-li chi-nien*, 20a–21a; Lu, *Ling-piao chi-nien*, 2/5a–b. Sun's original request to the Yung-li court, as recorded in Ho, *Feng-tao wu-t'ung chi*, 2/1a–b, seems to imply that Chang Hsien-chung once called himself the "Prince of Ch'in." If that was so, then it would help to explain why Sun insisted on having that title and no other.

48. Ch'ien, *Yung-li chi-nien*, 33a–34a, 45b–46b. Meng, *San-Hsiang ts'ung-shih chi*, p. 1361. Ho, *Feng-tao wu-t'ung chi*, 2/1b.

49. Ch'ien, *Yung-li chi-nien*, 18b–19a. Wang, *Yung-li shih-lu*, 11/1b. Lu Shih-i, *Chiang-yu chi-pien* (*Shao-hsing hsien-cheng i-shu* ed.), 3a–4a.

50. Lu, *Chiang-yu chi-pien*, 4b–6a. Wang, *Yung-li shih-lu*, 1/4a–b. Lu, *Ling-piao chi-nien*, 2/13a. SCSL, 37/18b–19a; 38/17b; 40/1b. MCSL, *ping*, VII: 687a; VIII: 706a–07b, 713a–14b. The Ch'ing generalissimo for this campaign was Tantai, with Holohoi second in command.

51. Wang, *Yung-li shih-lu*, 1/4b; 7/4b, 6a–7a; 13/2b. Ch'ien, *Yung-li chi-nien*, 22b, 24a. Li Tzu-ch'eng's army, and remnants thereof, also commonly were called the "Thirteen Battalions." Contributing to suspicions and resentments among the disparate Ming armies in Hu-kuang was a noncooperative relationship between Ho T'eng-chiao

and Tu Yin-hsi, the latter feeling disparaged because of his close accommodation with the former rebels.

52. Wang, *Yung-li shih-lu*, 1/5a–b; 7/7a–b. Ch'ien, *Yung-li chi-nien*, 24b–25a, 30a. Lu, *Ling-piao chi-nien*, 2/21b–22a; 3/2b, 9b. Meng, *San-Hsiang ts'ung-shih chi*, pp. 1359, 1361. For an account of the disruption and destruction caused by this army when it moved through Wu-chou, see Ch'ü Ch'ang-wen, *Yüeh-hsing chi-wen* (in *Pi-chi hsiao-shuo ta-kuan*), 1/5a–b. Tu Yin-hsi followed after the "Loyal and True Battalion" and eventually was able to make contact with them again in Kuang-hsi. But many units of this once formidable army had dispersed in the triangular area midst Heng-chou, Pin-chou, and Nan-ning; others had split off and headed back into extreme southern Hu-kuang, eventually to surrender to the Ch'ing. Moreover, Li Chin soon died in Nan-ning, leaving command of the remaining "Loyal and True" in the hands of Kao I-kung. Wang, *Yung-li shih-lu*, 1/6a; 13/3b. Lu, *Ling-piao chi-nien*, 3/12a.

53. Ch'ien, *Yung-li chi-nien*, 19a, 21b. Wang, *Yung-li shih-lu*, 11/1b–2a. Lu, *Ling-piao chi-nien*, 2/24a. Ho, *Feng-tao wu-t'ung chi*, 1/5a, 6a. SCSL, 41/2a–b. For examples of the way in which Ch'ü Shih-szu frequently snatched at straws to compose overly optimistic reports for the Yung-li emperor, see his accounts of the situations in Chiang-hsi and Hu-kuang during this time in *Ch'ü Chung-hsüan Kung chi*, 4/16b–17a.

54. Lu, *Chiang-yu chi-pien*, 6b. Wang, *Yung-li shih-lu*, 1/5a; 6/4b–5a; 11/2b. SCSL, 42/12a–b. MCSL, *ping*, VIII: 706a. Tantai was instructed to leave only veteran Han Chinese units stationed in Chiang-hsi, and to transfer any that had surrendered since the Yang-tzu campaign to Pei-ching for redeployment. SCSL, 42/15a.

55. MCSL, *ping*, VIII: 712a. Wang, *Yung-li shih-lu*, 7/4b. Ch'ien, *Yung-li chi-nien*, 25a–b. Meng, *San-Hsiang ts'ung-shih chi*, pp. 1359–60. Lu, *Ling-piao chi-nien*, 3/2b. Lei, *Kuei-lin t'ien-hai chi*, 12b–13a.

56. Meng, *San-Hsiang ts'ung-shih chi*, pp. 1360–61. Ch'ien, *Yung-li chi-nien*, 28a. Ho, *Feng-tao wu-t'ung chi*, 1/6a–b. SCSL, 43/10b–11a. MCSL, *ping*, VIII: 727a–b. News of Li Ch'eng-tung's death reached Chao-ch'ing on April 18. Ch'ien, *Yung-li chi-nien*, 28a. Ho, *Feng-tao wu-t'ung chi*, 2/1a.

CHAPTER SIX

1. SCSL, 40/16a–b. Cf. chap. 2, n. 103.

2. SCSL, 45/13a–15a; 46/26a–27b. MCSL, *ping*, VIII: 768a–b. Wang, *Yung-li shih-lu*, 1/5a. Lu, *Ling-piao chi-nien*, 3/21b–22a. Ch'ien, *Yung-li chi-nien*, 39a.

3. SCSL, 45/7b. Meng, *San-Hsiang ts'ung-shih chi*, p. 1361.

4. SCSL, 44/6a, 9b–11a, 19b. Cf. chap. 2, p. 59, n. 106.

5. SCSL, 46/25a; 47/6a–b. Ch'ien, *Yung-li chi-nien*, 23a. The problem of runaways among the many Han Chinese whom the Manchus had enslaved in the North was a serious one for the Ch'ing, and prohibitions against harboring fugitives were severe. On this, see: Liu Chia-chü, "Shun-chih nien-chien te t'ao-jen wen-t'i," in *Ch'ing-chu Li Chi hsien-sheng ch'i-shih-sui lun-wen chi* (T'ai-pei, 1967), vol. 2, pp. 1049–80; Yang Hsüeh-ch'en, "Kuan-yü Ch'ing-ch'u te 't'ao-jen fa,'" *Li-shih yen-chiu*, 1979, no. 10 (Oct.): 46–55; and Ma Feng-ch'en, "Manchu-Chinese Social and Economic Conflicts in Early Ch'ing," in *Chinese Social History*, ed. Sun and deFrancis (Washington, D.C., 1956), pp. 343–47. On Keng Chi-mao, see Hummel, I: 415.

6. Lu, *Ling-piao chi-nien*, 3/22a; 4/5a. Ch'ien, *Yung-li chi-nien*, 42a–43a. MCSL, *ping*, VIII: 744a, 769a. SCSL, 47/2a. The advance of Shang and Keng into northern

Kuang-tung was facilitated by the prearranged surrender and collaboration of generals in Hui-chou and Ch'ao-chou prefectures. Ch'ien, *Yung-li chi-nien*, 44a–b. Lu, *Ling-piao chi-nien*, 4/6a.

7. Wang, *Yung-li shih-lu*, 1/5b, 6b–7a; 2/3b. Lu, *Ling-piao chi-nien*, 3/6a, 8a–b, 11a, 15b. Ch'ien, *Yung-li chi-nien*, 37a–b. Li Yüan-yin declined to accept command of his foster father's army, so it was given to one of Ch'eng-tung's subordinate generals, Tu Yung-ho. Because Tu formerly had been of equal status with the other generals, however, his authority was not readily accepted, and some violent measures had to be adopted to obtain a modicum of obedience. Ch'ien, *Yung-li chi-nien*, 29b, 47a. Wang, *Yung-li shih-lu*, 1/6a; 11/6a–7a. Lu, *Ling-piao chi-nien*, 3/13b. Ch'ü Shih-szu was given Ho T'eng-chiao's title as Viceroy for Hu-kuang, but his authority was undercut in other ways; and the armies from the Hu-kuang theater already were in such a state of disarray that the likelihood of Ch'ü's regaining even Ho's minimal control over them was small (cf. nn. 15 and 16 below). Even Ch'ü's ability to prevent and smooth over conflicts between Hu-kuang and eastern Kuang-hsi forces was failing. Lu, *Ling-piao chi-nien*, 3/12b–13a; 4/12a. Moreover, by Ch'ü's own admission, his forte was not as a commander, but as a coordinator; he put most of his efforts into raising and distributing provisions, not into field strategy and direction. *Ch'ü Chung-hsüan Kung chi*, 3/12b–13a. In the words of one Kuei-lin resident, "Ch'ü was from an old, established literary family in Ch'ang-shu [Nan Chih-li] and, thus, engaged a good deal in composing poetry and speaking of rites. In striking an imposing figure over cups of wine, however, he was no match for Ho T'eng-chiao. And in matters of military organization, tactics, and personal leadership, he really did exhibit the air of a young student [*shu-sheng*]." Lei, *Kuei-lin t'ien-hai chi*, 13a.

8. Wang, *Yung-li shih-lu*, 1/6b, 7b; 11/7a–8a. Lu, *Ling-piao chi-nien*, 4/1a, 2a. Ch'ien, *Yung-li chi-nien*, 43a–44a. Ho, *Feng-tao wu-t'ung chi*, 2/3b.

9. Wang, *Yung-li shih-lu*, 1/5b; 11/7a; 21/4a–b. Lu, *Ling-piao chi-nien*, 4/2a, 3b–4b. Ho, *Feng-tao wu-t'ung chi*, 2/1a. Yüan P'eng-nien, who previously had resigned his post, was spared because of his especially great "merit in returning to proper allegiance." Like Li Yüan-yin, he also visited the court to plead for the other four members of the Tiger Five. Wang, *Yung-li shih-lu*, 1/5b, 6b–7a; 19/3a. Lu, *Ling-piao chi-nien*, 4/2a.

10. Wang, *Yung-li shih-lu*, 1/6b; 11/7b; 18/2b; 21/4b. Ch'ien, *Yung-li chi-nien*, 44b–45b, 48a–b. Lu, *Ling-piao chi-nien*, 4/2a–3a, 6b–7b. One chronicler says that after three years on the throne, the first time the Yung-li emperor showed any enthusiasm was when the persecution of the Tiger Five began. Ho, *Feng-tao wu-t'ung chi*, 2/4a.

11. Wang, *Yung-li shih-lu*, 1/5b, 7a; 13/3b–4a; 21/4b. Ch'ien, *Yung-li chi-nien*, 45b, 47b–48a, 49a–b. Lu, *Ling-piao chi-nien*, 4/10a–b, 15b. Ch'ü, *Yüeh-hsing chi-shih*, 2/3a.

12. The three approaches were: (1) directly upriver from Yung-chou to Ch'üan-chou; (2) to the north, from Wu-kang across the Hsi-yen River; and (3) to the south, from Yung-ming through Chen-hsia Pass (also called Lung-hu Pass). Lu, *Ling-piao chi-nien*, 4/7b–8a, 26a. Ch'ien, *Yung-li chi-nien*, 51b–52a. Wang, *Yung-li shih-lu*, 1/7a–b. SCSL, 47/14b; 48/16b–17a.

13. MCSL, *ping*, VIII: 769a–70b. SCSL, 51/6b. Lu, *Ling-piao chi-nien*, 4/3a, 4b, 18b, 28a. Ho, *Feng-tao wu-t'ung chi*, 2/4b. Wang, *Yung-li shih-lu*, 1/7b. Ch'ien, *Yung-li chi-nien*, 55a. The commander-in-chief of the Ming defense of Kuang-chou City was Tu Yung-ho. The defecting commander was Fan Ch'eng-en. Tu fled out to sea when the city was penetrated.

Two Dutch gunners are said to have assisted the defense (see n. 14 below); and the

Yung-li court previously had received small amounts of military assistance from the Portuguese. See Charles R. Boxer, "Portuguese Military Expeditions in Aid of the Mings against the Manchus," *T'ien Hsia Monthly*, 7.1 [Aug. 1938]: 34. On the kind of cannon used in these battles, see Lo Hsiang-lin, "Hsiang-kang hsin fa-hsien Nan-Ming Yung-li szu-nien so-tsao ta-p'ao k'ao," *Wen-shih hui-k'an*, 1.1–2 (June 1959).

14. John Nieuhoff, trans. John Ogilby, *An Embassy from the East India Company of the United Provinces to the Grand Tartar Cham Emperor of China* (Menston, 1669), p. 39. This rare work is quoted more extensively in E. C. Bowra, "The Manchu Conquest of Canton," *The China Review*, 1 (1872–73): 92–93. On Ch'ing pacification measures in western Kuang-tung following this subjugation, see Ch'en Shun-hsi, *Luan-li chien-wen lu* (in *Kao-liang ch'i-chiu i-chi*), *chung*/14a–15a.

15. Ch'ien, *Yung-li chi-nien*, 52a–b. Wang, *Yung-li shih-lu*, 1/7b. Lu, *Ling-piao chi-nien*, 4/27a, 28b–29a. SCSL, 51/2b; 52/15b–16a; 53/25b.

16. Ch'ü Yüan-hsi, *Keng-yin shih-i-yüeh ch'u-wu-jih shih-an shih-lüeh* (in *Ching-t'o i-shih*), passim. Ch'ien, *Yung-li chi-nien*, 52b–54b. Wang, *Yung-li shih-lu*, 18/2b–3b. Lu, *Ling-piao chi-nien*, 4/29b. Lei, *Kuei-lin t'ien-hai chi*, 13b–14a. Fritz Jäger, "Die letzen Tage des Kü Schï-sï," *Sinica*, 8.5–6 (1933): 203. The loyal aide was Chang T'ung-ch'ang, a grandson of the controversial grand secretary to the Wan-li emperor, Chang Chü-cheng. He was another of the few Ming loyalists of literary background who came to exhibit genuine talent in military organization and leadership. After the death of Ho T'eng-chiao, Ch'ü Shih-szu attempted to have Chang appointed to lead the Hu-kuang armies; but this failed, probably for partisan reasons, and the Hu-kuang command continued to disintegrate. Wang, *Yung-li shih-lu*, 18/2a–b.

The date of this execution was January 8. To reconcile apparent differences on this point in the sources cited above, note that the insertion of intercalary months in the various Southern Ming calendars differs in several years from such insertions in the now standard Ch'ing calendar (specifically, 1648, 1650–51, 1653, 1659, and 1662). See Huang Tien-ch'üan, *Nan-Ming ta-t'ung li* (T'ai-nan, 1962); and Fu I-li, "Ts'an-Ming ta-t'ung li," in *Erh-shih-wu shih pu-pien* (Shang-hai, 1937), VI: 8841–45.

17. Ch'ü, *Yüeh-hsing chi-shih*, 2/4a–b. One interesting indication of the anxiety that afflicted the Inner Court at this time is the solicitation of spiritual (and possible political) assistance by Senior Empress Dowager Wang and eunuch Director of Ceremonial P'ang T'ien-shou from Pope Innocent X in Rome. P'ang, Ch'ü Shih-szu, and Ch'ü's most stalwart subordinate commander, Chiao Lien, previously had been baptized as Christians and probably had introduced the imperial family to the German Jesuit missionary Andreas Koffler. (This matter in general, and Ch'ü's degree of subscription to Christianity in particular, are discussed in Jäger, "Die letzen Tage des Kü Schï-sï," passim.) Subsequently, Koffler had baptized the senior and junior empresses dowager, the empress, and the heir-apparent. But apart from submitting a Western calendar for official use by the court, which later was rejected by conservative officials (Wang, *Yung-li shih-lu*, 1/5a, 6b), he exerted no discernible influence on Yung-li politics. Koffler's assistant, the Polish Jesuit Michael Boym, had accompanied the court in its 1650 flight from Chao-ch'ing to Wu-chou; it was he who subsequently agreed to carry two letters, dated November 1 and 4, from the senior empress dowager and P'ang to the Vatican. These letters begged the pope to pray for their souls and for restoration of the Ming dynasty, and to send more Catholic priests to China. See Kuwabara Jitsuzō, "Min no Hō Tenju yori Rōma hōō ni sōtei seshi bunsho," *Shigaku zasshi*, vol. 11 (1900), no. 3, pp. 338–39, and no. 5, pp. 617–30. And for

English translations of the letters, see Ignatius Ying-Ki, "The Last Emperor of the Ming Dynasty and Catholicity," *Bulletin of the Catholic University of Peking*, 1 [1925]: 25–27. By 1658, however, when Boym finally was able to return to the Tonkin Gulf with a spiritually uplifting but politically noncommittal letter from Pope Alexander VII, both the senior empress dowager and P'ang had died, and the Yung-li court had been forced deep into the Southwest beyond his reach. Paul Pelliot, "Michel Boym," *T'oung Pao*, ser. 2, 31.1–2 (1935): 95–151.

18. Ch'ien, *Yung-li chi-nien*, 55a. Wang, *Yung-li shih-lu*, 1/7b. Lu, *Ling-piao chi-nien*, 29a–b. Ho, *Feng-tao wu-t'ung chi*, 2/5b. For a general, chronological account of the Yung-li court in its later years, see Yang, "Nan-Ming Yung-li shih-tai te yen-chiu," pp. 62–84.

During this time the few remaining units of the Loyal and True Battalion, under the leadership of Kao Pi-cheng, avoided the Ch'ing offensive by moving into Kuei-chou. There they were attacked by Sun K'o-wang, however, and Kao was killed. The last remnants of this once formidable army then rejoined some other former commanders of Li Tzu-ch'eng's forces and some miscellaneous independent militarists in the rugged border region between eastern Szu-ch'uan and northwestern Hu-kuang. Wang, *Yung-li shih-lu*, 13/4a–b. Li Kuang-pi, "Nung-min ch'i-i-chün tsai Ch'uan-O ti-ch'ü te lien-Ming k'ang-Ch'ing tou-cheng," in *Chung-kuo nung-min ch'i-i lun-wen chi*, ed. Li et al. (Pei-ching, 1958), pp. 296–97, 300–05. Idem, "Chi Hou-Ming cheng-fu te k'ang-Ch'ing tou-cheng," *Li-shih chiao-hsüeh*, 2.3 (Sept. 1951): 26–28.

19. James B. Parsons, "The Culmination of a Chinese Peasant Rebellion: Chang Hsien-chung in Szechwan, 1644–46," *Journal of Asian Studies*, 6.3 (May 1957): 387–400. SCSL, 29/8b. Anon., *Shu chi* (*T'ung-shih* ed.), 14a. Tai and Wu, *Huai-ling liu-k'ou shih-chung lu*, suppl. 7a–b. Chang Hsien-chung was not the only affliction suffered by Szu-ch'uan in late Ming times, nor was this the first time Chang had invaded that province. See Li Kuang-ming, "Ming-mo Ch'ing-ch'u chih Szu-ch'uan," *Tung-fang tsa-chih*, 31.1 (Jan. 1934): 171–76.

20. The best recent treatment of these figures, especially the second, is Kuo Ying-ch'iu, *Li Ting-kuo chi-nien* (Shang-hai, 1960). Also, see Li Kuang-t'ao, "Li Ting-kuo yü Nan-Ming," in *Ming-Ch'ing shih lun-chi*, II: 591–614; and Hummel, I: 490, and II: 679. For a good early biography of Li, see Liu Pin, "Chin Wang Li Ting-kuo lieh-chuan," in *Tien-ts'ui* (Hang-chou repr., 1981), pp. 52a–58b.

21. *Shu chi*, 14b–16b. Kuo, *Li Ting-kuo chi-nien*, p. 78. On the Ming general at Ch'ung-ch'ing, Tseng Ying, see Parsons, *Peasant Rebellions*, p. 174.

22. Yü I-tse, *Chung-kuo t'u-szu chih-tu* (Ch'ung-ch'ing, 1944), chap. 2. Li Lung-wah, "The Control of the Szechwan-Kweichow Frontier Regions during the Late Ming: A Case Study of the Frontier Policy and Tribal Administration of the Ming Government," Ph.D. diss., Australian National University, 1978. Huang Kai-hua, "Ming-tai t'u-szu chih-tu she-shih yü hsi-nan k'ai-fa," in *Ming-shih lun-chi*, pp. 211–414. For a comparison of the Ming and Ch'ing systems of "native" control, see Hu Nai-an, "Ming-Ch'ing liang-tai t'u-szu," *Ta-lu tsa-chih*, 19.7 (Oct. 15, 1959): 1–8.

23. Peter R. Lighte, "The Mongols and Mu Ying in Yunnan—at the Empire's Edge," Ph.D. diss., Princeton University, 1981. Also see biogs. of Fu Yu-te, Lan Yü, and Mu Ying in Goodrich and Fang, I: 468–69, 789, and II: 1079–83, resp., as well as the *Ming-shih*, ch. 126.

24. K'un-ming Wu-ming-shih [pseud.], *Tien-nan wai-shih* (in *Ming-chi shih-liao ts'ung-shu*), 1b–2b. Ho, *Feng-tao wu-t'ung chi*, 2/1b–2b.

25. Feng Su, *Tien-k'ao* (*T'ai-chou ts'ung-shu*, part B), 2/91a–93b. On the use of Southwestern tribesmen for various campaigns throughout the Ming, see Li, "The Control of the Szechwan-Kweichow Border Regions," pp. 17–21, 31–32. On rebelliousness among native leaders in the late Ming, especially in Szu-ch'uan, see ibid., pp. 91–94; and Ku, *Ming-shih chi-shih pen-mo*, ch. 69.

26. K'un-ming, *Tien-nan wai-shih*, 3a–5b. Feng, *Tien-k'ao*, 2/94a.

27. Feng, *Tien-k'ao*, 2/93a–b, 95b.

28. K'un-ming, *Tien-nan wai-shih*, 5b–7a. Feng, *Tien-k'ao*, 2/95b–97a, 98a. P'eng Sun-i, *P'ing-k'ou chih* (1931 repr. of K'ang-hsi ed.), 12/11a. Kuo, *Li Ting-kuo chi-nien*, pp. 79–80, 88–89. The most important Ming civil official who resisted Sha and supported Mu was the circuit censor Yang Wei-chih, who later acted as one of Sun K'o-wang's emissaries to the Yung-li court.

29. K'un-ming, *Tien-nan wai-shih*, 6a, 7a–b. Feng, *Tien-k'ao*, 2/97b.

30. Feng, *Tien-k'ao*, 2/97b. K'un-ming, *Tien-nan wai-shih*, 8a. Ai Neng-ch'i soon was killed on a mission in Szu-ch'uan; and Liu Wen-hsiu willingly subordinated himself to Sun.

31. Fei Mi, *Huang-shu* (*I-lan-t'ang ts'ung-shu* ed.), 28b. Tai and Wu, *Huai-ling liu-k'ou shih-chung lu*, suppl. 10b.

32. Shen Hsün-wei, *Shu-nan hsü-lüeh*, 11b–12a. Fei, *Huang-shu*, 29a–31a. Tai and Wu, *Huai-ling liu-k'ou shih-chung lu*, suppl. 11a. P'eng, *P'ing-k'ou chih*, 12/11b. SCSL, 69/11b–12a.

33. MCSL, *chia*, IV: 247a; VI: 550a; *ping*, VIII: 785a–86a; IX: 822a, 833a. Number I Archive, *Ch'ing-tai tang-an*, VI: 165, 169–72, 182–84, 258–66. SCSL, 71/12b–13a; 76/7a–b; 92/8a; 93/2b–3b. Hung Ch'eng-ch'ou, *Hung Ch'eng-ch'ou chang-tsou wen-tz'u hui-chi* (Shang-hai, 1937), I: 112, 118.

34. MCSL, *chia*, IV: 306a, 333a; *ping*, IX: 812a, 813a, 828a. SCSL, 65/21a–b. Number I Archive, *Ch'ing-tai tang-an*, VI: 178–79. Li's army is said to have traveled 300 *li* in one day and night and to have approached Kuei-lin "like coming down from heaven and welling up out of the earth." Lei, *Kuei-lin t'ien-hai chi*, 16a.

35. MCSL, *ping*, IX: 812a, 813a, 823a, 856a, 877a–78b. SCSL, 76/7a. Lei, *Kuei-lin t'ien-hai chi*, 17a. Number I Archive, *Ch'ing-tai tang-an*, VI: 176–78, 187–88, 190.

36. MCSL, *chia*, III: 300a–b; *ping*, IX: 856a–b, 877a–78b. Number I Archive, *Ch'ing-tai tang-an*, VI: 195. SCSL, 77/20b; 81/9b. Lei, *Kuei-lin t'ien-hai chi*, 17a–18b.

37. MCSL, *ping*, IX: 884a. Ch'en, *Luan-li chien-wen lu*, *chung*/17b–18b, 21b–22a. Number I Archive, *Ch'ing-tai tang-an*, VI: 248, 289.

38. MCSL, *ping*, 887a. Number I Archive, *Ch'ing-tai tang-an*, VI: 243–45. SCSL, 86/20b–21a. Ch'en, *Luan-li chien-wen lu*, *chung*/22a–b. K'un-ming, *Tien-nan wai-shih*, 9b. At this same time, Li also sent contingents to again harass the Wu-chou region. MCSL, *ping*, II: 149a–50a.

39. MCSL, *ping*, IX: 885a–86a, 887a–b, 893a–b. Number I Archive, *Ch'ing-tai tang-an*, VI: 245–47, 272–74. Ch'en, *Luan-li chien-wen lu*, *chung*/22b–23a. SCSL, 84/6a; 87/16b–17a; 89/11b–12a; 91/6a–b. Yang, *Yen-p'ing ... shih-lu*, 45b–47b. Kuo, *Li Ting-kuo chi-nien*, pp. 133–35. Ch'ü Ta-chün, *An-lung i-shih* (*Chia-yeh-t'ang ts'ung-shu* ed.), *hsia*/10a. P'eng, *P'ing-k'ou chih*, 12/12a. For secondary writings on the failed alliance between Li Ting-kuo and Cheng Ch'eng-kung, see: Chu Feng, "Li Chin Wang yü Cheng Yen-p'ing," *T'ai-wan wen-hsien*, 12.3 (Sept. 1961): 155–58; Chin Ch'eng-ch'ien, "Cheng Ch'eng-kung, Li Ting-kuo hui-shih wei-ch'eng chih yüan-yin," *T'ai-wan wen-hsien*, 16.1

(March 1965): 115–27; Hsieh Hao, "Li, Cheng te shih-kung chi ch'i lien-chün yü lien-hun te yen-hsi," in *Nan-Ming chi Ch'ing-ling T'ai-wan shih k'ao-pien*, pp. 28–162; and Wei Yung-chu, "Cheng Ch'eng-kung nan-hsia ch'in-wang," pp. 134–36.

40. MCSL, *ping*, IX: 892a–b. Hsü Yung: SCSL, 67/5a; 68/31a; 69/3a; 70/10b. MCSL, *chia*, IV: 347a. K'ung Yu-te: SCSL, 66/2a. MCSL, *chia*, III: 300b; *ping*, IX: 874a–75b. Lei, *Kuei-lin t'ien-hai chi*, 16a. Nikan: SCSL, 66/9b–10b; 67/4b–5a. Wang, *Yung-li shih-lu*, 14/4b. Moreover, the whole Ch'ing leadership was still adjusting after the deaths of Dorgon (at age 39) on December 31, 1650 (SCSL, 51/10b–11a), of Bolo (age 40) and of Lekdehun (age 24) in April and May of 1652 (SCSL, 63/14a, 26a). Jirgalang also died (at age 57) in June of 1655 (SCSL, 91/14a–b).

41. SCSL, 67/6a. MCSL, *ping*, IX: 821a, 833a–b; X: 928a. Number I Archive, *Ch'ing-tai tang-an*, VI: 185–87. In recognition of the importance of the South-Southwest, and of applying both military and civil-administrative techniques in gaining genuine control, in June of 1653 the Ch'ing court transferred Viceroy Hung Ch'eng-ch'ou from Nan-ching to Wu-han, giving him broad authority to "plan and coordinate affairs in the five provinces" of Hu-kuang, Liang-Kuang, and Yün-Kuei. SCSL, 75/22b–23a; MCSL, *chia*, IV: 305a, 333a. Also, beginning in the fall of 1652, because of floods in the North and droughts in the South, the Ch'ing court began to be very concerned about supply shortages (SCSL, 67/25b–26a; 79/18a; 85/14b, 15b; 96/5b–6a), which Hung had proven most capable of handling. Although Hung initially was given the optimistic charge of "educating and transforming" Yün-Kuei, he soon saw the multiple problems and super-ficiality of Ch'ing control in Hu-kuang alone, and he subsequently adopted a more gradual approach to pacification. SCSL, 79/14b–15b, MCSL, *chia*, VI: 583a; *ping*, II: 157b. *Hung Ch'eng-ch'ou chang-tsou wen-tz'u hui-chi*, I: 68. For a vivid description of Ch'ing problems in Hu-kuang in 1652, see MCSL, *ping*, IX: 822a; and Number I Archive, *Ch'ing-tai tang-an*, VI: 180–81. And for further evidence that these were especially lean years for the Ch'ing, see Liu Ts'ui-jung, "Ch'ing-ch'u Shun-chih K'ang-hsi nien-chien chien-mien fu-shui te kuo-ch'eng," CYYY, 37.2 (1967), chart between pp. 760 and 761, which shows that the largest number of tax remissions for flood and drought in the whole early Ch'ing period clustered in the years 1652–54.

42. Wang, *Yung-li shih-lu*, 14/4a–5a. K'un-ming, *Tien-nan wai-shih*, 9a. Ch'ü, *An-lung i-shih*, *hsia*/6b–7a.

43. Wang, *Yung-li shih-lu*, 1/8a. K'un-ming, *Tien-nan wai-shih*, 8a. Ch'ü, *An-lung i-shih*, *shang*/20a. Ho, *Feng-tao wu-t'ung chi*, 2/5b–6a.

44. Ch'ü, *An-lung i-shih*, *shang*/22b–24a. SCSL, 59/12b; 64/6a–b. Chiang Chih-ch'un, *An-lung chi-shih* (CNW ed.), p. 311. Since late Wan-li times, Vietnam had been divided into mutually hostile northern and southern regimes and was in no position to resist pressure from the Ch'ing after the latter occupied Liang-Kuang in force. Although the Annamese did not formally submit to suzerain status under the Ch'ing until August of 1659, in practice they had favored the Ch'ing and thwarted the southern Ming cause for years before that. See P'eng Kuo-tung, "Nan-Ming Chung-Yüeh kuan-hsi shih-hua," in *Chung-Yüeh wen-hua lun-chi* (T'ai-pei, 1956), II: 256–58; Ch'en I-ling, "Ming-tai yü Yüeh-nan, Kao-mien, Liao-kuo te pang-chiao," in *Chung-kuo wai-chiao shih lun-chi* (T'ai-pei, 1957), I: 5; and Chang Hsiao-ch'ien, "Ming-Ch'ing liang-tai yü Yüeh-nan," *Ta-lu tsa-chih*, 35.3 (Aug. 1967): 19. For an account of an ambassadorial mission from Cheng Ch'eng-kung which was prevented from reaching the Yung-li court in Yün-nan by traveling through Annam, see Hsü Fu-yüan, *Chiao-hsing che-kao* (T'ai-pei, 1961).

45. Chiang, *An-lung chi-shih*, p. 313. K'un-ming, *Tien-nan wai-shih*, 8b. Ch'ü, *An-lung i-shih*, hsia/1a–2a. Shen, *Shu-nan hsü-lüeh*, 13b.

46. Huang Hsiang-chien, *Huang hsiao-tzu hsün-ch'in chi-ch'eng* (in *Pi-chi hsiao-shuo ta-kuan*), 3a.

47. The emperor's previous attempts to enlist Li's aid were in December of 1652 and the midsummer of 1653. Chiang, *An-lung chi-shih*, pp. 313–16.

48. Ibid., pp. 315–19. For a thorough study of this whole series of events, see Chu Hsi-tsu, "Yung-li ta-yü shih-pa hsien-sheng shih-liao p'ing," *Kuo-hsüeh chi-k'an*, 2.2 (Dec. 1929): 237–59.

49. The Ch'ing quickly moved into Li's former positions in Kuang-hsi and defeated his rear guard as he departed, leaving one of his concubines and her family behind. MCSL, *ping*, II: 157a–b; X: 912a–b. SCSL, 98/11a; 100/3b; 101/13b; 105/19a.

50. Ch'ü, *An-lung i-shih*, hsia/10b–15a, 17b–18a. K'un-ming, *Tien-nan wai-shih*, 9b.

51. Ch'ü, *An-lung i-shih*, hsia/16b–17a, 18b.

52. Ch'ü, *An-lung i-shih*, hsia/18b–21a. Yang Te-tse, *Yang chien pi-chi* (*Yü-chien-chai ts'ung-shu*, 1910), 3b, 4b, 7a–b. [Hu Ch'in-hua], *Ch'iu-yeh lu* (*Ming-chi pai-shih ch'u-pien* ed.), p. 331. K'un-ming, *Tien-nan wai-shih*, 9b.

53. MCSL, *chia*, III: 279a–b, VI: 582b–83a; *ping*, II: 176a. Number I Archive, *Ch'ing-tai tang-an*, VI: 296–97. SCSL, 103/7a–b; 117/2a–b, 6a. Ch'ü, *An-lung i-shih*, hsia/22a. Yang, *Yang chien pi-chi*, 6a.

54. Ralph C. Croizier, *Koxinga and Chinese Nationalism: History, Myth, and the Hero* (Cambridge, Mass., 1977). Donald Keene, *The Battles of Coxinga: Chikamatsu's Puppet Play, Its Background and Importance* (London, 1951), introduction and chaps. 3–4. Among Chinese scholars, Lou Tzu-k'uang has pioneered in studying Cheng Ch'eng-kung's life as folklore. For references to four of his articles, see the bibliography.

55. Shih Wan-shou, "Lun Cheng Ch'eng-kung pei-fa i-ch'ien te ping-chen," *Yu-shih hsüeh-chih*, 11.2 (June 1973): 10, 18; and idem, "Ming Cheng te chün-shih hsing-cheng tsu-chih," *T'ai-wan wen-hsien*, 26.4–27.1 (Dec. 1975–March 1976; double issue): 50–66.

56. Niels Steensgaard, *The Asian Trade Revolution of the Seventeenth Century* (Chicago, 1973), part I, chap. 3, and part 3, chap. 9. John E. Wills, *Pepper, Guns, and Parleys: The Dutch East India Company and China, 1662–1681* (Cambridge, Mass., 1974), esp. chap. 1. Chang T'ien-tse, *Sino-Portuguese Trade from 1514 to 1644* (Leiden, 1934). Han-sheng Chuan, "The Chinese Silk Trade with Spanish America from the Late Ming to the Mid-Ch'ing Period," in *Studia Asiatica*, ed. Lawrence Thompson (San Francisco, 1975), pp. 99–117. William S. Atwell, "International Bullion Flows and the Chinese Economy Circa 1530–1650," *Past and Present*, 95 (May 1982): 68–90.

57. Huang Yü-chai, "Ming Cheng k'ang-Ch'ing te ts'ai-cheng yü chün-hsü te lai-yüan," *T'ai-wan wen-hsien*, 9.2 (June 1958): 17–21. Yamawaki Teijirō, "The Great Trading Merchants, Cocksinja and His Son," *Acta Asiatica*, 30 (1976): 111–12. For a survey of the places and circumstances from which Cheng Ch'eng-kung obtained fighting men throughout his career, see Shih Wan-shou, "Lun Ming Cheng te ping-yüan," *Ta-lu tsa-chih*, 41.6 (Sept. 1970): 20–29.

58. Hsieh Kuo-chen, "Ch'ing-ch'u tung-nan yen-hai ch'ien-chieh k'ao," appendix II to *Ming-Ch'ing chih chi tang-she yün-tung k'ao*, pp. 290–329. Su Mei-fang, "Ch'ing-ch'u ch'ien-chieh shih-chien chih yen-chiu," *Li-shih hsüeh-pao*, 5 (July 1978): 367–425.

59. Chuang Chin-te, "Cheng Shih chün-liang wen-t'i te yen-t'ao," *T'ai-wan wen-

hsien, 12.1 (March 1961): 55–66. Fang Hao, "Yu Shun-chih pa-nien Fu-chien wu-wei shih-t'i lun Cheng Shih k'ang-Ch'ing te chu-li," *Ta-lu tsa-chih*, 22.6 (March 1961): 1–20. Huang Yü-chai, "Ming Cheng k'ang-Ch'ing te ts'ai-cheng," pp. 21–32.

60. Yang, *Yen-p'ing . . . shih-lu*, 17a–b. Chiang, *T'ai-wan wai-chi*, p. 119. Shih, "Lun Cheng Ch'eng-kung pei-fa i-ch'ien te ping-chen," pp. 5–6.

61. Yang, *Yen-p'ing . . . shih-lu*, 18b–26b. Hai-wai San-jen, *Jung-ch'eng chi-wen*, p. 8. Wang, *Hang-hsieh i-wen*, 5a–b. SCSL, 66/4b. Cheng first was contacted by a representative of Li Ting-kuo from Kuang-hsi just as he withdrew from this campaign. Cheng sent one of his own men back to negotiate possible joint actions in the future (Yang, *Yen-p'ing . . . shih-lu*, 28a–b).

62. MCSL, *chia*, III: 276a; *ting*, II: 166a–67b. SCSL, 70/26b–27a. Yang, *Yen-p'ing . . . shih-lu*, 28b, 30a–32b. Many officials were eager to confiscate the Cheng lands, which were thought to be worth several hundred thousand taels, to help pay military expenses. MCSL, *ting*, II: 164a. For vivid accounts of what befell Fu-chou each time the Manchus had to billet an expeditionary force there, see Hai-wai San-jen, *Jung-ch'eng chi-wen*, pp. 5–6, 10–11, and 13–14.

63. SCSL, 69/6b–7b. Chuang Chin-te, "Cheng-Ch'ing ho-i shih-mo," *T'ai-wan wen-hsien*, 12.4 (Dec. 1961): 1–40.

64. SCSL, 72/17b–18a.

65. SCSL, 66/18b; 67/1b–2a. Hai-wai San-jen, *Jung-ch'eng chi-wen*, p. 8.

66. Yang, *Yen-p'ing . . . shih-lu*, 28a–29a.

67. SCSL, 75/8b–10b. MCSL, *ting*, I: 84a–87a.

68. Yang, *Yen-p'ing . . . shih-lu*, 34a–35b.

69. MCSL, *ting*, I: 91a–b. SCSL, 75/20a–21a; 78/13b; 79/3a–7a.

70. Yang, *Yen-p'ing . . . shih-lu*, 34a.

71. Ibid., 36a–38a, 41a–42b, 43a, 44b–45a, 57a. MCSL, *ting*, II: 107a; *chi*, II: 197a–b. In inland Fu-chien, also during the 1650s, the Ch'ing tried to "summon and soothe" lawless elements as a recourse in view of their military weakness in the province; and there the policy yielded similar results.

> Ever since the orders to summon and soothe were issued in 1656–57, the hill bandits have become *more* numerous. Those who want to become officials first become bandits and, at year's end, use what they have stolen to bribe the summoning and pacifying authorities to designate them "sincerely surrendered officials." Then when they swagger through the streets and markets, no one dares say anything [about it], and their enemies dare not finger them. . . . In Yung-pei Ward [for instance], the bandits having surrendered, people were off their guard; [but the bandits] continued their depredations as before, saying, "Our expenses in surrendering were a certain amount, so now we're taking compensation from you." The locale reported this to the authorities, but [pursuit of the case] was not permitted. Those in the offices of the viceroy and provincial governor who summon and pacify the most are given promotions and noble titles, so both [these officials and the bandits] benefit. [Hai-wai San-jen, *Jung-ch'eng chi-wen*, p. 12.]

72. Yang, *Yen-p'ing . . . shih-lu*, 29a, 39a–40a. MCSL, *chia*, IV: 337a, 341a–b, 346a; *ting*, II: 109a. Documents Committee, *Wen-hsien ts'ung-pien*, vol. 13, 11a–12b, 13a, 14a, 15a, 16b–17a. SCSL, 79/22b; 80/9b, 10b; 81/12b–13a; 83/6a. Wang, *Hang-hsieh i-wen*, 5b. Also see Li Hsüeh-chih, "Ch'ung-k'ao Li Chen-hua hsien-sheng 'Ming-mo hai-shih san-

cheng Ch'ang-chiang k'ao,'" *Ta-lu tsa-chih*, 7.11 (Dec. 15, 1953): 7–8; and 7.12 (Dec. 30, 1953): 21–27; as well as Liao Han-ch'en, "Lu Wang k'ang-Ch'ing yü erh-Chang te ch'eng-kung," pp. 93–100.

73. Yang, *Yen-p'ing . . . shih-lu*, 41a–b. Messages sent previously, in the fifth month of 1653, apparently were lost (ibid., 32b–33a).

74. Yang, *Yen-p'ing . . . shih-lu*, 38a–39a. SCSL, 83/9b, 17b–18a.

75. Yang, *Yen-p'ing . . . shih-lu*, 43a–44b. SCSL, 85/6a–b. MCSL, *chia*, VI: 544a.

76. MCSL, *ting*, I: 97.

77. SCSL, 84/25b–26a; 85/3a–4a. MCSL, *ting*, II: 106b. Yang, *Yen-p'ing . . . shih-lu*, 45a–b, 48a.

78. Yang, *Yen-p'ing . . . shih-lu*, 45a–49b, 53b. MCSL, *ting*, II: 106a–b. Chu, "Yen-p'ing Wang shou Ming kuan-chüeh k'ao," p. 102. Cheng began preparations to aid Li in late November, after this second round of "negotiations" had broken up. Yang, *Yen-p'ing . . . shih-lu*, 55a–56a. But the contingent that he sent in the winter trade winds returned the following summer without having made contact with Li. Hsia Lin, *Hai-chi chi-yao* (T'ai-pei, 1958), pp. 14–15. Yang, *Yen-p'ing . . . shih-lu*, 68b. Cf. n. 39 above.

79. Yang, *Yen-p'ing . . . shih-lu*, 48a, 49b, 51a–52b, 53b.

80. Yang, *Yen-p'ing . . . shih-lu*, 49b, 53b–54a. MCSL, *ting*, II: 106a–07a. SCSL, 87/4a, 6b–7a.

81. Yang, *Yen-p'ing . . . shih-lu*, 50a–b.

82. Ibid., 52b–53a, 54b.

83. MCSL, *ting*, II: 106a–07a.

84. SCSL, 87/15a–16a. Biog. of Jidu in Hummel, I: 397, gives the wrong date for this appointment.

85. Yang, *Yen-p'ing . . . shih-lu*, 56a–57a. MCSL, *chia*, IV: 545a–b.

CHAPTER SEVEN

1. Feng Su, *Chien-wen sui-pi* (in *T'ai-chou ts'ung-shu*, part A), *hsia*/19b–20a. SCSL, 104/13b; 113/11b, 12a–b, 15b–18b; 116/5b–6a; 117/23a; 118/2b–3a; 120/7a. Former roving rebels, still active in the Nan-ning, Heng-chou, and Pin-chou area, were either defeated or forced out of Kuang-hsi into the Chiao-chih (northwestern Vietnam) border region during this time. MCSL, *ping*, X: 955a. SCSL, 115/13a–b; 117/22a.

2. Hu, *Ch'iu-yeh lu*, pp. 331–32. Ch'ü, *An-lung i-shih*, *hsia*/23a–24a. Yang, *Yang chien pi-chi*, 10a–b. Feng, *Chien-wen sui-pi*, *hsia*/19b. Especially lamentable was the distrust that lingered between Li Ting-kuo and his former rebel "brother" Liu Wen-hsiu, who died in despair in May of 1658.

3. Hu, *Ch'iu-yeh lu*, p. 333. Ch'ü, *An-lung i-shih*, *hsia*/25b–26a. Yang, *Yang-chien pi-chi*, 7b. K'un-ming, *Tien-nan wai-shih*, 9b–10a. The possibility of betrayal by aboriginal chieftains also was a problem (see the following note).

4. SCSL, 114/7a–b; 123/2a–4a. Wang Hsien-ch'ien et al., comps., *Shih-erh-ch'ao tung-hua lu* (T'ai-pei, 1963), SC15/8/11. Wu successfully executed the northern route, but he defeated Li's generals there only with the amply rewarded cooperation of aboriginal leaders in that region. SCSL, 120/7a. Tai and Wu, *Huai-ling liu-k'ou shih-chung lu*, suppl., 12a. Kuo, *Li Ting-kuo chi-nien*, p. 160. He and the other Ch'ing commanders were given explicit instructions to avoid disrupting or irritating the aboriginal peoples, and to treat their leaders generously if they came in submission. SCSL, 115/14b–15a; 122/15b–16a.

5. Yang, *Yang chien pi-chi*, 10b–14b, 15b. Hu, *Ch'iu-yeh lu*, p. 333. Ch'ü, *An-lung i-shih*, hsia/26b–27a. Feng, *Chien-wen sui-pi*, hsia/20a.

6. Yang, *Yang chien pi-chi*, 11b–12a, 15a, 17a–26b. Ch'ü, *An-lung i-shih*, hsia/27b–28b. Hu, *Ch'iu-yeh lu*, pp. 333–34. Teng K'ai, *Yeh-shih lu (Ming-chi pai-shih ch'u-pien* ed.), p. 345. Feng, *Chien-wen sui-pi*, hsia/20b.

7. Yang, *Yang chien pi-chi*, 8b–10a, 29a–36b. Ch'ü, *An-lung i-shih*, hsia/28b–29b. Teng, *Yeh-shih lu*, p. 345. SCSL, 137/12a–13a. Yeh Meng-chu, *Hsü-pien sui-k'ou chi-lüeh*, ch. 4; and [Liu Chai], *Shou-Mien chi-shih*, both as cited in Kuo, *Li Ting-kuo chi-nien*, p. 165. Also see Kuo, p. 171.

8. Yang, *Yang chien pi-chi*, 33a–34a. Hu, *Ch'iu-yeh lu*, p. 335. Teng, *Yeh-shih lu*, p. 345. Liu, *Shou-Mien chi-shih*, as cited in Kuo, *Li Ting-kuo chi-nien*, p. 165. Tai and Wu, *Huai-ling liu-k'ou shih-chung lu*, suppl., 12a–b. Teng K'ai records that the Yung-li party went through T'ieh-pi Pass; but the more specific geographical information given by Liu Chai indicates that, as his work records, it must have been the more northerly T'ung-pi Pass.

The dating of Yung-li events during the flight into Burma is complicated by the chronological inaccuracy of the *Yang chien pi-chi* (a memoir), differences at this point between the Yung-li and Ch'ing calendars (discussed above in chap. 6, n. 16), and the circumstance that both the *Ch'iu-yeh lu* and the *Shou-Mien chi-shih* lump together events of the Yung-li calendar's first and intercalary first months of this year.

9. SCSL, 125/28a–b. MCSL, *chia*, VI: 595a.

10. Chiang, *An-lung chi-shih*, pp. 311–14. Liu, *Shou-Mien chi-shih*, as cited in Kuo, *Li Ting-kuo chi-nien*, p. 165. Teng, *Yeh-shih lu*, p. 345. Yang, *Yang chien pi-chi*, 37b–38a.

11. Yang Te-tse, author of the *Yang chien pi-chi*, was orphaned by Moslem rebels in the Northwest and subsequently was reared by a man who fought in Sun K'o-wang's army. At the age of eight *sui* he was sent to Yün-nan Fu to be a study companion for the Yung-li heir-designate, and subsequently he was castrated and kept in the imperial household as a eunuch. Because of his youth and closeness to the emperor, he was among only a handful of male survivors of the court's tribulations in Burma. See his preface to the *Yang chien pi-chi*. Liu Chai, author of the *Shou-Mien chi-shih*, held titles as a Han-lin Academician and Classics Banquet Lecturer in the Yung-li court. He survived by becoming separated from the court after it reached Ava. See Chu Hsi-tsu, *Ming-chi shih-liao t'i-pa* (Pei-ching, 1961), p. 62. Teng K'ai, author of the *Yeh-shih lu*, was a native of Chi-an, Chiang-hsi, and earlier had served under the "righteous" resistance leaders in that province, Yang T'ing-lin and Liu T'ung-sheng. He joined the Yung-li court in Yün-nan Fu and thereafter served as head of the guard that immediately protected the imperial household. In that capacity he held military titles, but from his writings and his later life it is clear that he was a literary man. Ironically, he survived the general slaughter of all adult males in the Yung-li party because he had been crippled in a previous altercation with Ma Chi-hsiang. See Hsü Tzu, *Hsiao-t'ien chi-nien* (T'ai-pei, 1962), V: 914–15; Shao T'ing-ts'ai, *Szu-fu-t'ang wen-chi*, "I-min so-chih chuan," 73a–b; and *Yeh-shih lu*, p. 348.

12. See Victor B. Lieberman, "The Transfer of the Burmese Capital from Pegu to Ava," *Journal of the Royal Asiatic Society of Great Britain and Ireland*, 1980, no. 1, pp. 64–83.

13. Teng, *Yeh-shih lu*, pp. 345–46. Liu, *Shou-Mien chi-shih*, as cited in Kuo, *Li Ting-kuo chi-nien*, p. 165. Hu, *Ch'iu-yeh lu*, pp. 335–36.

14. Teng, *Yeh-shih lu*, p. 347. Liu, *Shou-Mien chi-shih*, as cited in Kuo, *Li Ting-kuo chi-nien*, pp. 166–67.

15. Teng, *Yeh-shih lu*, p. 347. Liu, *Shou-Mien chi-shih*, as cited in Kuo, *Li Ting-kuo chi-nien*, p. 167. Hu, *Ch'iu-yeh lu*, p. 336.

16. Chang Ch'eng-sun, *Chung-Ying Tien-Mien chiang-chieh wen-t'i* (Pei-p'ing, 1937), pp. 19–23. Victor B. Lieberman, "Provincial Reforms in Toung-ngu Burma," *Bulletin of the School of Oriental and African Studies*, 43.3 (1980): 548–69. Idem, "Europeans, Trade, and the Unification of Burma, 1540–1620," *Oriens Extremus*, 27.2 (1980): 203–26. Biog. of Szu Jen-fa in Goodrich and Fang, II: 1209–14.

17. Maung Htin Aung, *A History of Burma* (New York, 1967), pp. 147–48. Number I Archive, *Ch'ing-tai tang-an*, VI: 351–52.

18. Teng, *Yeh-shih lu*, pp. 347–49. Hu, *Ch'iu-yeh lu*, pp. 337–39. Liu, *Shou-Mien chi-shih*, as cited in Kuo, *Li Ting-kuo chi-nien*, p. 180.

19. Teng, *Yeh-shih lu*, p. 348. Hu, *Ch'iu-yeh lu*, p. 337.

20. Htin Aung, pp. 149–50. Teng, *Yeh-shih lu*, p. 349. Hu, *Ch'iu-yeh lu*, p. 339.

21. Yang, *Yang chien pi-chi*, 40a–b.

22. Yang, *Yang chien pi-chi*, 40b–41b. Teng, *Yeh-shih lu*, pp. 349–50. Hu, *Ch'iu-yeh lu*, pp. 339–40.

23. MCSL, *chia*, VI: 595a–96a. SCSL, 125/30a; 126/22a–b. Number I Archive, *Ch'ing-tai tang-an*, VI: 335–38.

24. Documents Committee, *Wen-hsien ts'ung-pien*, vol. 24, prefatory photograph of archival document (printed in Number I Archive, *Ch'ing-tai tang-an*, VI: 338–39). Also, for the Ch'ing court's instructions to Hung, see MCSL, *chia*, VI: 597a.

25. SCSL, 124/14b–15a; 129/9b–10b. MCSL, *chia*, VI: 598a. This, of course, was the beginning of Wu's kingdom-building in the Southwest, which led to the "Rebellion of the Three Feudatories" in the 1670s. On Wu's mature organization in Yün-nan, see Kanda Nobuo, *Heiseiō Go Sankei no kenkyū* (Tokyo, 1952); on the *san-fan chih-luan*, see Tsao Kai-fu, "K'ang-hsi and the San-fan War," *Monumenta Serica*, 31 (1974–75): 108–30.

26. MCSL, *ping*, II: 193a; *ting*, VIII: 701b. SCSL, 130/11b; 132/2a. Li, "Hung Ch'eng-ch'ou," p. 292. Liu Chien, *T'ing-wen lu* (T'ai-pei, 1968), pp. 20–22.

27. SCSL, 134/18b–20a. MCSL, *ping*, II: 199a–200a. Liu, *T'ing-wen lu*, pp. 23–25. The Mu family estate holdings were given to laborers to cultivate in order to relieve the severe rice shortage in Yün-nan. SCSL, 135/6b–7a.

28. SCSL, 134/22a–b; 136/21a–22b; 137/9a–10a, 11a–12a; 139/16a–17a.

29. SCSL, 141/11a–b. KHSL, 6/9a–10a. MCSL, *ting*, VIII: 702a. Wang et al., comps., *Shih-erh-ch'ao tung-hua lu*, KH1/2/keng-wu. P'eng, *P'ing-k'ou chih*, 12/13a.

30. Recorded in the original *Tung-hua lu*, compiled by Chiang Liang-ch'i (under the month SC18/11), and reprinted in Wang Ch'ung-wu, "Pa Yung-li Ti chih Wu San-kuei shu," *Tung-fang tsa-chih*, 43.9 (May 1947): 37. Also, see Yin [pseud.], "Ming Kuei Wang chih Wu San-kuei shu," *T'ien-chin i-shih pao*, Shuo-yüan sec., April 24–26, 1937.

31. Wang et al., comps., *Shih-erh-ch'ao tung-hua lu*, KH1/2/keng-wu. P'eng, *P'ing-k'ou chih*, 12/13a.

32. Yang, *Yang chien pi-chi*, 43b–45a. Also, see Teng, *Yeh-shih lu*, pp. 350–51.

33. Yang, *Yang chien pi-chi*, 45b–46a. The Ch'ing throne was exultant in reporting the Yung-li emperor's capture to the Ministry of Rites on April 18; and on the 29th, formal ceremonies were conducted and a public proclamation issued to mark and celebrate the event. KHSL, 6/11a–b, 13b–14a. Number I Archive, *Ch'ing-tai tang-an*, VI: 353.

34. Teng, *Yeh-shih lu*, p. 351. Hu, *Ch'iu-yeh lu*, p. 340. Yang, *Yang chien pi-chi*, 46a–b. Wang et al., comps., *Shih-erh-ch'ao tung-hua lu*, KH1/2/keng-wu.

35. Robert B. Oxnam, *Ruling from Horseback: Manchu Politics and the Oboi Regency, 1661–1669* (Chicago, 1975). SCSL, 144/2a–b. KHSL, 1/6b.

36. No official source so much as alludes to this matter. An execution date of May 25 is given in the *Yeh-shih lu* (p. 351) by Teng K'ai, whom the emperor had sent away several days earlier, sensing that the end was near for his household. A manuscript copy of Yang Te-tse's memoir, the *Yang chien pi-chi*, held in the Pei-ching Library, which retains certain lines that have been expunged from printed copies (page 46b), gives a date of May 19 but indicates the wrong year. For a composite rendering and critical discussion of several early Ch'ing accounts, none of which is wholly acceptable, see [Ch'en Ch'ü-ping], "Yung-ming Huang-ti hsün-kuo shih-chi," *Min-pao*, 23 (Aug. 1908), T'an-ts'ung sec., pp. 89–96. On Wu San-kuei's elevation, see KHSL, 6/21b–22a; and MCSL, *ting*, VIII: 702a.

37. Yang, *Yang chien pi-chi*, 39a–b. KHSL, 7/17a. Kuo, *Li Ting-kuo chi-nien*, pp. 184–86. For a special study on the place of Li's death, see the introduction to Kuo's work, pp. 27–30.

38. Yang, *Yen-p'ing . . . shih-lu*, 58a–59a.

39. Ibid., 59b–60b.

40. SCSL, 87/17a. MCSL, *chia*, VI: 545a; *ting*, II: 138a–40b, 152a–53a. Yang, *Yen-p'ing . . . shih-lu*, 61a–64b, 71b–72a, 76a. Hsia, *Hai-chi chi-yao*, p. 16. Juan, *Hai-shang chien-wen lu*, p. 20.

41. In many cases, the titles and actual duties of these functionaries differed from standard Ming usage, partly because they were idiosyncratically established by Cheng, and partly to avoid the appearance of usurping imperial forms. However, Cheng requested and obtained permission from the Yung-li court to assign high ranks to positions that in Ming nomenclature were of lower status. Yang, *Yen-p'ing . . . shih-lu*, 66a–67b. Hsia, *Hai-chi chi-yao*, p. 13. Chu, "Cheng Yen-p'ing Wang," p. 105. Cheng also set up special quarters to accommodate "worthies" who had passed the Ming civil service examinations, and to rear the progeny of military leaders who had died in service. But when one general complained that such men were just "fancy pants" and incompetent in the field, Cheng personally made certain that only experienced men were assigned to duty as troop supervisors. Juan, *Hai-shang chien-wen lu*, p. 17. For an exhaustive listing of men who held noble, civil, and military titles under Cheng, see Lai Yung-hsiang, "Ming Cheng fan-hsia kuan-chüeh piao," *T'ai-wan yen-chiu*, 1 (1956): 79–101; and 2 (1957): 47–78.

42. Yang, *Yen-p'ing . . . shih-lu*, 68b–69a, 72b–73a. The most important men whom Cheng alienated with his severe disciplinary measures were Shih Lang and Huang Wu. Shih escaped execution on Hsia-men in the spring of 1651. Subsequently he was employed by the Ch'ing only in minor naval capacities until after Cheng Ch'eng-kung's death, when he became the principal architect of Ch'ing plans to conquer T'ai-wan. Yang, *Yen-p'ing . . . shih-lu*, 15b–16b. Chiang, *T'ai-wan wai-chi*, pp. 121–22. Chu Wei-ching, "Shih Lang yü Cheng Yen-p'ing te en-yüan," *Wen-shih hui-k'an*, 1 (June 1959): 88–95. Hummel, II: 653. Huang, having felt the sting of Cheng's harsh punishments after the failure of a campaign on Chieh-yang in Ch'ao-chou Prefecture in the early spring of 1656, the following August defected to the Ch'ing, turning over to them Cheng's most important supply depot in Hai-ch'eng. For this he was given the title Duke of Hai-ch'eng,

which previously had been spurned by Cheng Ch'eng-kung, and otherwise was generously rewarded. Subsequently he served the Ch'ing avidly, arguing for the elimination of Cheng Chih-lung and becoming the chief advocate of coastal control measures that eventually forced the Cheng regime to abandon the Fu-chien coast entirely for T'ai-wan. Yang, *Yen-p'ing . . . shih-lu*, 76b, 78b. Hsia, *Hai-chi chi-yao*, p. 17. Juan, *Hai-shang chien-wen lu*, p. 21. MCSL, *chia*, VI: 400a–b, 406a, 414a; *ting*, III: 159a–60a. SCSL, 102/22b; 103/10b, 13b; 108/21a–22a. Hummel, I: 355. On Shih, Huang, and other commanders who defected from or rebelled against Cheng, see Chin Ch'eng-ch'ien, "Ming Cheng chung-yao chiang-ling shih-shih fen-shu," *T'ai-wan wen-hsien*, 24.4 (Dec. 1973): 74–78, 81–83; and idem, "Shih Lang, Huang Wu hsiang-Ch'ing tui Ming-Cheng chih ying-hsiang," *T'ai-wan wen-hsien*, 17.3 (Sept. 1966): 151–66.

43. SCSL, 88/16a; 90/21a; 108/18b–19a. MCSL, *chia*, IV: 355a–b. Yang, *Yen-p'ing . . . shih-lu*, 81b, 83a–84b. After receipt of Ch'eng-kung's final reply to Chih-lung in early May of 1657, the Ch'ing had the latter, his younger brother Chih-pao, and his four other sons formally indicted by the Ministry of Punishments. The emperor magnanimously lifted the death penalty from Chih-lung but ordered him exiled to Ninguta in the far Northeast and had all his properties confiscated. SCSL, 108/19b–20a; 109/3b–4a. Further, because it was feared that Chih-lung might escape from exile and rejoin his son by sea in the Southeast, it was ordered that his hands and feet be chained and that he be kept under especially heavy guard. SCSL, 110/4a; 111/3a–b.

44. SCSL, 92/10b; 102/10a–12a. MCSL, *ting*, II: 155a. Ch'in Shih-chen, *Fu-Che chiao-ts'ao* (*Ch'ing-shih tzu-liao*, vol. 2, 1981), pp. 171–72.

45. SCSL, 102/18b–20b. MCSL, *chi*, III: 236a.

46. SCSL, 87/15a–16a. Yang, *Yen-p'ing . . . shih-lu*, 70b, 72a, 73b. Hsia, *Hai-chi chi-yao*, p. 15.

47. Yang, *Yen-p'ing . . . shih-lu*, 69a–70b. 77a–b. Hai-wai San-jen, *Jung-ch'eng chi-wen*, p. 15. Jidu had been prodded on by the court in Pei-ching, which had not anticipated that he would take so long. SCSL, 100/8a.

48. Cheng Ch'eng-kung last exchanged letters with Li Ting-kuo around this time. Again he urged Li to attack from the west, since "there are opportunities to be seized on the North China Plain during this time when the luck of the barbarians is just about exhausted. So it would be best to rise with the tide of circumstances and combine forces in simultaneous action. . . . Responding from both inside and outside, we could straightway wash out their rank-smelling lair, and then sweep clean the palaces and conclude a pact between us in the capital." Scholars agree that this letter is misdated in the *Yen-p'ing . . . shih-lu*, 41a–b, as having been sent in the early spring of 1654; but they do not agree on whether it should be placed in the midsummer of 1656 or the early spring of 1657. See Chang, *Cheng Ch'eng-kung chi-shih pien-nien*, p. 87; and Kuo, *Li Ting-kuo chi-nien*, p. 148, resp.

49. The stages delineated below generally correspond to those seen by Liao Han-ch'en in "Yen-p'ing Wang pei-cheng k'ao-p'ing," *T'ai-wan wen-hsien*, 15.2 (June 1964): 47–74.

50. Yang, *Yen-p'ing . . . shih-lu*, 71a–72a, 73b–75b. Wang, *Hang-hsieh i-wen*, 6a. The Ch'ing had assigned only 240 cavalry and 3,000 infantry to the Chou-shan garrison, and only half of these actually had come. Moreover, their whole naval defense force for the island was undergoing repairs in Ting-hai at the time. MCSL, *ting*, II: 123a–b. From Chou-shan the Ming forces proceeded to raid deep into Che-chiang, and it was this

mainland activity that forced the Ch'ing to reconquer the "pirates'" island base. MCSL, *chia*, IV: 388a; *ting*, II: 142a–43a; *chi*, III: 294a–95a, 299b.

51. Yang, *Yen-p'ing . . . shih-lu*, 78a, 79a–81a. SCSL, 103/12a. MCSL, *ting*, II: 181a. Hai-wai San-jen, *Jung-ch'eng chi-wen*, p. 10.

52. Yang, *Yen-p'ing . . . shih-lu*, 81a–82b, 84b–85b. Hai-wai San-jen, *Jung-ch'eng chi-wen*, pp. 10–11. SCSL, 106/9a–10b. MCSL, *chia*, V: 409a–b; *chi*, IV: 395a. From Fu-ning, Cheng sent contingents into Wen-chou Prefecture in extreme southeastern Che-chiang, as well. Yang, *Yen-p'ing . . . shih-lu*, 85a. MCSL, *chi*, V: 403a.

53. Chang Ming-chen died some time between January 12 and 25, 1656. See Liao, "Lu Wang k'ang-Ch'ing yü erh-Chang te wu-kung," p. 102; and MCSL, *chia*, IV: 576b. The Manchu generalissimo for the reconquest of Chou-shan was Irdei. On that campaign, see MCSL, *chia*, IV: 376a–b, 381a–83b; *ting*, II: 161a, 163a, 165a–b; *chi*, III: 270a–b. SCSL, 96/11a–b; 97/9b–10a; 103/21b–22a, 27b. Yang, *Yen-p'ing . . . shih-lu*, 76b, 80b. Wang, *Hang-hsieh i-wen*, 6a.

54. Yang, *Yen-p'ing . . . shih-lu*, 85a–b.

55. Yang, *Yen-p'ing . . . shih-lu*, 88a–90b. SCSL, 111/13a–b. The nearest Ch'ing relief forces were less than eight hundred men in T'ien-t'ai, but they were sent to Ning-po and Ting-hai (where naval defenses still were ludicrously undermanned) for fear that Cheng would go on to attack there. MCSL, *ting*, II: 179a–b.

56. MCSL, *ting*, II: 181a. SCSL, 111/22b–23a. Yang, *Yen-p'ing . . . shih-lu*, 90b–92b, 94b. Juan, *Hai-shang chien-wen lu*, p. 26. Hai-wai San-jen, *Jung-ch'eng chi-wen*, p. 11. Probably during this winter Cheng received but declined the title Prince [of the First Degree] of Ch'ao from the Yung-li court. Chu, "Cheng Yen-p'ing Wang," pp. 107–09.

57. Yang, *Yen-p'ing . . . shih-lu*, 95a–96a. Juan, *Hai-shang chien-wen lu*, p. 25. On Cheng's iron men, see Huang Yü-chai, "Ming Cheng k'ang-Ch'ing te ts'ai-cheng," pp. 21–24.

58. Yang, *Yen-p'ing . . . shih-lu*, 97b–101b. Juan, *Hai-shang chien-wen lu*, p. 27. MCSL, *chia*, V: 421a–23b. SCSL, 118/15a.

59. Yang, *Yen-p'ing . . . shih-lu*, 102b–04a, 105a–06a. Juan, *Hai-shang chien-wen lu*, p. 28. MCSL, *chia*, V: 429a–31a; *ting*, III: 201a–04a; *chi*, V: 428b, 433a–b, 435a–b. SCSL, 120/11b.

60. Yang, *Yen-p'ing . . . shih-lu*, 106a–09a. MCSL, *chia*, V: 443a–44a, 465b–66a; *ting*, III: 206a, 217a–19b; *chi*, V: 452a. SCSL, 123/15b; 124/13a–b; 126/9a. Reports of great victories over the coastal invaders by some Ch'ing authorities in Che-chiang were specious. See Chang, *Cheng Ch'eng-kung chi-shih pien-nien*, p. 106.

61. Yang, *Yen-p'ing . . . shih-lu*, 109a–10b, 112a. SCSL, 126/10b.

62. Yang, *Yen-p'ing . . . shih-lu*, 112b–13a, 114a–15b. Chang Huang-yen, *Pei-cheng te-shih chi-lüeh*, in *Chang Ts'ang-shui shih-wen chi* (T'ai-pei, 1962), vol. 1, p. 1. MCSL, *ting*, III: 233b. Cheng tried unsuccessfully at least three times to co-opt the commander-in-chief of Ch'ing naval forces at Wu-sung, Ma Chin-pao, whose name under the Ch'ing was changed to Ma Feng-chih.

63. On measures taken to strengthen naval defenses in Chiang-nan since the incursions of Chang Ming-chen, see SCSL, 83/4a–b; 91/15a; 112/15a. MCSL, *chia*, IV: 341a–b. Chi, *Ming-chi nan-lüeh*, II: 330. Of course, after Cheng Ch'eng-kung's attack the Ch'ing realized that they still had not done enough. See SCSL, 127/8b–10a, 14b, 17b–18b.

64. SCSL, 127/11a–b, 21a–b. MCSL, *ting*, III: 226a. For a complementary view of the reasons for Cheng's failure at Nan-ching, see Chin Ch'eng-ch'ien, "Cheng Ch'eng-

kung Nan-ching chan-pai yü cheng-T'ai chih i," *T'ai-wan wen-hsien*, 25.1 (March 1974): 45–53.

65. Li Chen-hua, *Chang Ts'ang-shui chuan* (T'ai-pei, 1967). Ishihara Michihiro, "Chō Kōgen no kōnan kōhoku keiryaku," *T'ai-wan feng-wu*, 5.11–12 (1955): 7–53. Hummel, I: 41–42.

66. Chi, *Ming-chi nan-lüeh*, II: 329–30. Yang, *Yen-p'ing ... shih-lu*, 115b.

67. Cheng Ch'eng-kung and Cheng Ching [attrib.], *Yen-p'ing erh-wang i-chi*, in *Tseng-ting Chung-kuo hsüeh-shu ming-chu*, ser. 1, vol. 8 (T'ai-pei, 1965), unpaginated.

68. Yang, *Yen-p'ing ... shih-lu*, 116b–21b. Chang, *Pei-cheng te-shih chi-lüeh*, pp. 2–3. Chi, *Ming-chi nan-lüeh*, II: 330–32. MCSL, *chi*, V: 491b–92a, 541a–42a, VI: 539a; *ting*, III: 238a. SCSL, 126/22a.

69. Yang, *Yen-p'ing ... shih-lu*, 121b–27b. SCSL, 127/6b, 11b–12a. The Ch'ing counted 83 *ying* encamped around Nan-ching, which at the standard level of 1,025 men per *ying* would have been 85,075 soldiers. Of course, this does not include Cheng's naval force moored nearby, or the others that he left stationed at Ch'ung-ming, Kua-chou, and Chen-chiang.

70. This count is my own, based on scattered evidence in both Ming and Ch'ing sources, and thus is not the same as the numbers that are frequently cited in Chang Huang-yen's *Pei-cheng te-shih chi-lüeh*, pp. 2–3. An important Ch'ing source is MCSL, *chia*, V: 465b–57a.

71. Yang, *Yen-p'ing ... shih-lu*, 121b–22a, 124b–25b, 127b–28a. Cheng, *Pei-cheng te-shih chi-lüeh*, pp. 2, 5.

72. The leading figures on the Ch'ing side were Viceroy Lang T'ing-tso, Chiang-nan Provincial Governor Chiang Kuo-chu, Regional Commander-in-Chief Kuan Hsiao-chung, Su-Sung Regional Naval Commander Liang Hua-feng, and the Manchu lieutenant-generals Gachuha and Kakamu. In spite of these men's stunning victory over Cheng, afterward the Ch'ing court was in a very bad mood and, figuratively speaking, a lot of heads rolled in Chiang-nan. Chiang Kuo-chu and Kuan Hsiao-chung, in particular, were enslaved, and all their family properties were confiscated. SCSL, 127/30a; 133/16b–17a.

73. Yang, *Yen-p'ing ... shih-lu*, 128b–30b. SCSL, 127/12b–13a. MCSL, *chi*, V: 490a. On Kan Hui and other generals who were lost in this action, see Chin Ch'eng-ch'ien, "Kan Hui, Chou Ch'üan-pin, Liu Kuo-hsüan yü Ming Cheng san-shih," *T'ai-wan wen-hsien*, 16.4 (Dec. 1965): 133–43; and idem, "Ming Cheng chung-yao chiang-ling," pp. 67–73.

74. Yang, *Yen-p'ing ... shih-lu*, 130b–34a. Chang, *Pei-cheng te-shih chi-lüeh*, pp. 4–6. Chi, *Ming-chi nan-lüeh*, II: 306–10. SCSL, 127/13a, 21a–b, 22b. MCSL, *ting*, II: 233a. For secondary writings on Cheng's northward campaign, in addition to that by Liao Han-ch'en, cited in n. 49 above, see Huang Yü-chai, "Ming Cheng Ch'eng-kung pei-fa san-pai chou-nien te chi-nien," *T'ai-pei wen-wu*, 7.4 (Dec. 1958): 123–28; 8.1 (Apr. 1959): 122–28; 8.2 (June 1959): 116–24; and 8.3 (Oct. 1959): 146–52; as well as Chin Ch'eng-ch'ien, "Cheng Ch'eng-kung ch'i-ping hou," pp. 88–92.

75. SCSL, 127/3b–4b. MCSL, *chia*, V: 462a–b; *ting*, III: 243a, 265a; *chi*, V: 500a, 524b. Yang, *Yen-p'ing ... shih-lu*, 140a–41a. Chang, *Cheng Ch'eng-kung chi-shih pien-nien*, p. 123. Debate then was renewed among Ch'ing officials over whether to maintain a garrison on Chou-shan, at great trouble and expense, on the chance that Cheng might occupy that island if he were forced out of Hsia-men. In December of 1661 Chou-shan

was ordered evacuated again, this time as part of the general coastal removal policy. MCSL, *chia*, V: 464a; *ting*, III: 243b, 250a–b. SCSL, 139/2b–3a, 7b; 143/11b–12a. KHSL, 1/18b; 5/4b.

76. Yang, *Yen-p'ing … shih-lu*, 134b, 136b, 138a–b. MCSL, *chia*, V: 462a; *ting*, III: 243a–b.

77. Yang, *Yen-p'ing … shih-lu*, 135b, 138a–42a.

78. Yang, *Yen-p'ing … shih-lu*, 140a, 146b–47a. Yang Ying's account of this battle is somewhat garbled and is inaccurate concerning the positions of leaders on the Ch'ing side. For a coherent reconstruction, see Chang, *Ch'eng-kung chi-shih pien-nien*, pp. 127–28.

79. Yang, *Yen-p'ing … shih-lu*, 146a–b. SCSL, 138/14a–15a, 22a–23a. Hai-wai San-jen, *Jung-ch'eng chi-wen*, pp. 15, 19.

80. Yang, *Yen-p'ing … shih-lu*, 134b, 148b–49a. Wu Mi-ch'a, "Cheng Ch'eng-kung cheng-T'ai chih pei-ching," *Shih-i*, 15 (Sept. 1978): 24–44. Liao Han-ch'en, "Yen-ping Wang tung-cheng shih-mo," *T'ai-wan wen-hsien*, 12.2 (June 1961): 57–84. Ho T'ing-pin, called Pincqua by the Dutch, had been sent by them to negotiate a deal with Cheng Ch'eng-kung in the summer of 1657. Subsequently he had colluded with one of Cheng's chief revenue officials to levy taxes in T'ai-wan on Chinese vessels bound for points in Cheng's territory. When this was discovered by the Dutch in 1659, Ho was dismissed and charged a heavy fine, which he escaped by fleeing to Cheng's organization. C.E.S. [Frederic Coyett], trans. and ed. Inez de Beauclair et al., *Neglected Formosa* (San Francisco, 1975), pp. 19–20, 108, 111–12. On general conditions in T'ai-wan during this time, see Wen-hsiung Hsu, "From Aboriginal Island to Chinese Frontier: The Development of Taiwan before 1683," in *China's Island Frontier*, ed. Ronald Knapp (Honolulu, 1980), pp. 12–23; and Ts'ao Yung-ho, "Ho-lan yü Hsi-pan-ya chan-chü shih-ch'i te T'ai-wan," in *Ta'i-wan wen-hua lun-chi* (T'ai-pei, 1954): 105–22. For works on Dutch mercantile enterprises in all of Asia during this period, see Charles R. Boxer, *The Dutch Seaborne Empire, 1600–1800* (London, 1965); and M. A. P. Meilink-Roelofsz, "Aspects of Dutch Colonial Development in Asia in the Seventeenth Century," in *Britain and the Netherlands in Europe and Asia*, vol. 3 (New York, 1968), pp. 56–82.

81. C.E.S., *Neglected Formosa*, pp. 16, 19, 21–23, 25, 30, 32, 105–07, 109–13. Lin Ch'ao-tung, "Cheng Ch'eng-kung k'o-T'ai chien T'ai-Hsia chih-chien te ching-wei," *T'ai-nan wen-hua*, 5.2 (July 1956): 91–98. Su T'ung-ping, "Yu Ch'ung-chen liu-nien te Liao-lo hai-chan t'ao-lun tang-shih te Min-hai ch'ing-shih chi Ho-Cheng kuan-hsi," *T'ai-pei wen-hsien*, 42 (Dec. 1977): 1–39. Wills, *Pepper, Guns, and Parleys*, pp. 23–24. On friction between the Dutch and the Chengs, see Yamawaki, "The Great Trading Merchants," pp. 107–10.

82. C.E.S., *Neglected Formosa*, pp. 27–29; quotation, pp. 34–36. In June of 1661 the Dutch East India Company office in Siam dispatched to their fellow officers in T'ai-wan a report of Cheng's preparations to launch a major campaign "on Luzon or Formosa," but by this time Cheng already had brought Castle Zeelandia under siege (ibid., p. 114).

83. Yang, *Yen-p'ing … shih-lu*, 149a–50b. C.E.S., *Neglected Formosa*, p. 44. Conflicting dates in the Yang and Coyett accounts have been puzzling. For solutions to this problem, see: Tada Ōkuma, trans. Shih Wan-shou, "Kuo-hsing-yeh te teng-lu T'ai-wan," *T'ai-pei wen-hsien*, 44 (June 1978): 111–21; and Ch'en Kuo-ch'iang, "Cheng Ch'eng-kung shou-fu T'ai-wan te shih-chien wen-t'i," *Hsia-men ta-hsüeh hsüeh-pao*, 1962, no. 1 (April): 161. For general accounts of the Cheng conquest of the Dutch colony on T'ai-Bay, see: Chang T'an, "Cheng-Ho ho-yüeh te ch'ien-ting jih-ch'i chih

k'ao-ting chi Cheng Ch'eng-kung fu-T'ai chih chan kai-shu," *T'ai-wan wen-hsien*, 18.3 (Sept. 1956): 1–18; and Charles R. Boxer, "The Seige of Fort Zeelandia and the Capture of Formosa from the Dutch, 1661–1662," *Transactions and Proceedings of the Japan Society of London*, 24 (1926–27): 16–47; and Wills, *Pepper, Guns, and Parleys*, pp. 25–27. On the forces that Cheng took to T'ai-wan, see Shih Wan-shou, "Lun Cheng Ch'eng-kung pei-fa i-hou te ping-chen," *T'ai-wan wen-hsien*, 24.4 (Dec. 1973): 15–26.

84. C.E.S., *Neglected Formosa*, pp. 49–53, 57–58, 128–30. Yang, *Yen-p'ing . . . shih-lu*, 151a.

85. Yang, *Yen-p'ing . . . shih-lu*, 151b–52b, 154b–55a. Juan, *Hai-shang chien-wen lu*, p. 39. C.E.S., *Neglected Formosa*, pp. 59, 64, 75.

86. C.E.S., *Neglected Formosa*, pp. 70, 71–73, 75, 77–78, 131–32, 134.

87. Ibid., pp. 80–86, 134–37.

88. Yang, *Yen-p'ing . . . shih-lu*, 152b–54a. Chu Feng, "Cheng Shih tsai-T'ai ch'uang-chien cheng-chih jih-ch'i k'ao," *T'ai-nan wen-hua*, 2.2 (April 1952): 50–54. On Cheng's missive to Luzon's governor, Don Sabiniano Manrique de Tara, and its consequences, see: Chang, *Cheng Ch'eng-kung chi-shih pien-nien*, pp. 145–46; Emma Blair and James Robertson, *The Philippine Islands, 1493–1898* (Cleveland, 1903–09), vol. 36, "Events in Manila, 1662–63"; and Francisco Combés, *Historia de Mindanao y Joló* (Madrid, 1897 [1667]), pt. 8, chap. 13. Also, see chaps. 2 and 3 by Milagros Guerrero and Rafael Bernal, resp., in *The Chinese in the Philippines, 1570–1770*, ed. Alfonso Felix (Manila, 1966).

89. Wen-hsiung Hsu, "From Aboriginal Island to Chinese Frontier," p. 22.

90. Fang Hao, "Yü Shun-chih pa-nien Fu-chien wu-wei shih-t'i lun Cheng Shih k'ang-Ch'ing te chu-li," part 2, pp. 18–19.

91. On defections, see: KHSL, 3/13a; 4/2b; 6/6a; and Yang, *Yen-p'ing . . . shih-lu*, 154a–b. On the intensification of Ch'ing coastal policies, see: SCSL, 136/4b–6a; 140/2b–3a, 6a–b; 141/4a; and KHSL, 2/21b; 4/10b. Chuang Chin-te, "Cheng Shih chün-liang wen-t'i te yen-t'ao," pp. 59–60. Hai-wai San-jen, *Jung-ch'eng chi-wen*, p. 23.

92. Juan, *Hai-shang chien-wen lu*, p. 40.

93. Ibid.

94. Chiang, *T'ai-wan wai-chi*, II: 210. KHSL, 5/2a. It was publicly announced in Fuchou on February 1, 1662, that Cheng Chih-lung had been executed by the slow-slicing method. Hai-wai san-jen, *Jung-ch'eng chi-wen*, p. 24.

95. Li T'eng-yüeh, "Cheng Ch'eng-kung te szu-yin k'ao," *Wen-hsien chuan-k'an*, 1.3 (1950): 54–64. Also, see KHSL, 6/27b–28a; and Wang, *Hang-hsieh i-wen*, 5a.

96. Chang, *Chang Ts'ang-shui shih-wen chi*, pp. 29–31. Also, see Mao I-po, "Cheng Ch'eng-kung yü Chang Ts'ang-shui," *T'ai-wan feng-wu*, 4.4 (April 1954): 4–10.

97. Chang, *Chang Ts'ang-shui shih-wen chi*, pp. 42–44. Chang was captured by the Ch'ing on a small island near Nan-t'ien and executed in 1664. Cf. n. 65 above.

98. Wang, *Hang-hsieh i-wen*, 5a. Ch'en Han-kuang, "Lu-T'ang chiao-e chi Lu Wang chih szu," pp. 113–14. Tomb inscription as recorded in the following articles: Rudolph, "The Real Tomb of the Ming Regent, Prince of Lu," pp. 486–87; Ch'en Han-kuang and Liao Han-ch'en, "Lu Wang shih-chi k'ao-ch'a chi," *T'ai-wan wen-hsien*, 11.1 (March 1960): 119; and Chu Feng, "Chin-men fa-hsien te Nan-Ming pei-chieh erh-chien," *Wen-shih hui-k'an*, 2 (Dec. 1960): 100. For other research on this tomb, see Huang Chung-ch'in and Hsia T'ing-yü, "Chin-men Ming chien-kuo Lu Wang mu," *Kuo-li Chung-shan ta-hsüeh yü-yen li-shih hsüeh yen-chiu-so chou-k'an*, 6.69 (Feb. 1929): 2805–08.

99. The veteran rebel leader Li Lai-heng survived for several years with the last remnants of Li Tzu-ch'eng's "Great Shun" army in the remote, mountainous locale of Fang-hsien in northwestern Hu-kuang. This group declared a "Later Ming" regime and supported a man who claimed to be the Ming Prince of Han from Shen-hsi. But this claim is unverifiable, especially since this claimant, too, apparently died before Ch'ing forces finally stormed the rebels' last bastion and eliminated their regime in the fall of 1664. Cf. the writings of Li Kuang-pi cited in chap. 6, n. 18. Also, see Cha Chi-tso, *Tsui-wei lu hsüan-chi* (TW, no. 136), II: 74–75.

After Cheng Ch'eng-kung's death, leadership of the Cheng organization was maintained by his son, Ching, until the latter's death in 1681, and nominally by his grandson, K'o-shuang, who surrendered to the Ch'ing when they finally conquered T'ai-wan in 1683. Although these heirs of Cheng Ch'eng-kung paid lip service to Ming symbols, and although Cheng Ching collaborated loosely with Keng Ching-chung, the Ch'ing over-lord of Fu-chien, and thus aided the Revolt of the Three Feudatories against Manchu rule during the years 1674–80, no Ming imperial figure was elevated to succeed the Yung-li emperor or Regent Lu. Numerous articles have been written on this phase of T'ai-wan and early Ch'ing history. For a reliable, general account, see Sheng Ch'ing-i et al., *T'ai-wan shih* (T'ai-chung, 1977), pp. 152–240. One Ming imperial clansman, the Prince of Ning-ching, who accompanied the Cheng army in its move to T'ai-wan, was treated with due respect by Cheng Ch'eng-kung but was disregarded and deprived of any stipend by Cheng Ching. He lived in straitened circumstances in Chu-hu Village, south of present-day T'ai-nan, until 1683 when, as the Ch'ing fleet approached T'ai-wan, he ceremonially committed suicide with his two surviving concubines and three maidservants (all four of his children having died previously). See Ch'en Han-kuang, "Ming Ning-ching Wang chi wu-fei wen-hsien," *T'ai-wan wen-hsien*, 20.3 (Sept. 1969): 45–64.

The youngest male heir of the Ch'ung-chen emperor, Chu Tz'u-huan, managed to survive the Ch'ing conquest and lived quietly, under assumed names, until the first years of the eighteenth century, when his true identity as the "Third Chu Crown Prince" became known to others. Subsequently, in 1707, two anti-Ch'ing uprisings in Che-chiang and Chiang-su were inspired by this news. As a result, Chu was discovered by the Ch'ing authorities and was executed, under disguised circumstances, early in 1709. This case is considered by many to be the progenitor of the T'ien-ti Hui, the most important of the secret societies that harbored ideas of "overthrowing the Ch'ing and restoring the Ming" through the rest of the Ch'ing era. For documents of the "Third Chu Crown Prince Case," see *Ko-ming yüan-yüan* (T'ai-pei, 1963), II: 298–308; and for elucidation of the case, as well as an introduction to literature on the T'ien-ti Hui issue, see Chikusa Masaaki, "Shu San Taishi an ni tsuite," *Shirin*, 62.4 (1979): 1–21.

Bibliography of Works Cited

Anonymous. *Chien-kuo chi-nien* 監國紀年. In *Ming-chi shih-liao ts'ung-shu*, vol. 9.

Anonymous. *Ching-k'ou pien-lüeh* 京口變略. In *Chia-shen chi-shih*, ch. 6. Comp. Feng Meng-lung.

Anonymous. *Huai-ch'eng chi-shih* 淮城紀事. In *T'ung-shih*, vol. 8.

Anonymous. "Lung-fei chi-lüeh" 龍飛紀略. In *Hsing-ch'ao chih-lüeh*, ch. 1. Comp. Chou Shih-yung.

Anonymous. *Lung-wu i-shih* 隆武遺事 In *T'ung-shih*, vol. 9.

Anonymous. *Shao-wu cheng-li chi* 紹武爭立記. Among several works of obscure origin that have been grouped under the heading *Hsing-ch'ao lu* 行朝錄 and commonly are published as the writings of Huang Tsung-hsi 黃宗羲. The edition cited here, for instance, is from a collection of Huang's works, *Li-chou i-chu hui-k'an* 梨洲遺著彙刊, vol. 2. T'ai-pei: Lung-yen ch'u-pan she, 1969.

Anonymous. *Shu chi* 蜀記. In *T'ung-shih*, vol. 9.

Anonymous. *Su-ch'eng chi-pien* 蘇城記變. In *Ming-chi shih-liao ts'ung-shu*, vol. 8.

Anonymous. *Tien-k'ou chi-lüeh* 滇寇紀略. (Manuscript in the Pei-ching Library.)

Anonymous. *Yang-chou pien-lüeh* 揚州變略. In *Chia-shen chi-shih*, ch. 6. Comp. Feng Meng-lung.

Atwell, William S. "Ch'en Tzu-lung (1608–1647): A Scholar-Official of the Late Ming Dynasty." Ph.D. diss., Princeton University, 1974.

———. "From Education to Politics: The Fu She." In *The Unfolding of Neo-Confucianism*, pp. 333–67. Ed. W. T. de Bary. New York: Columbia University Press, 1975.

———. "International Bullion Flows and the Chinese Economy *Circa* 1530–1650," *Past and Present*, 95 (May 1982): 68–90.

Blair, Emma H., and James A. Robertson. *The Philippine Islands, 1493–1898.*

55 vols. Notes and introduction by Edward G. Bourne. Cleveland: A. H. Clark Co., 1903–09.

Boxer, Charles R. "The Siege of Fort Zeelandia and the Capture of Formosa from the Dutch, 1661–1662," *Transactions and Proceedings of the Japan Society of London*, 24 (1926–27): 16–47.

———. "Portuguese Military Expeditions in Aid of the Mings against the Manchus," *T'ien Hsia Monthly*, 7.1 (August 1938): 24–36.

———. "The Rise and Fall of Nicholas Iquan," *T'ien Hsia Monthly*, 11.5 (Apr.–May 1941): 401–39.

———. *The Christian Century in Japan, 1549–1650*. Berkeley: University of California Press, 1951.

———. *The Dutch Seaborne Empire, 1600–1800*. London: Hutchinson, 1965.

Bowra, E. C. "The Manchu Conquest of Canton," *The China Review*, 1 (1872–73): 86–96, 228–37.

Busch, Heinrich. "The Tunglin Academy and Its Political and Philosophical Significance," *Monumenta Serica*, 14 (1949–55): 1–163.

C. E. S. [Frederic Coyett]. *Neglected Formosa*. Trans. and ed. Inez de Beauclair, Pierre Martin Lambach, William Campbell, and A. Blusse. Chinese Materials and Research Aids Service Center, Occasional Series no. 21. T'ai-pei: Chinese Materials Center, 1975. Original Dutch version, *t'Verwaerloosde Formosa*. Amsterdam, 1675.

Cha Chi-tso 查繼佐. *Lu ch'un-ch'iu* 魯春秋. TW, no. 118. 1961.

———. *Tsui-wei lu hsüan-chi* 罪惟錄選輯. Ed. T'ai-wan yin-hang ching-chi yen-chiu shih 台灣銀行經濟研究室. TW, no. 136, in 2 vols. 1962.

———. *Tung-shan kuo-yü* 東山國語. Rev. and suppl. Shen Ch'i 沈起. TW, no. 163. 1963.

Chan, Albert. *The Glory and Fall of the Ming Dynasty*. Norman, Oklahoma: University of Oklahoma Press, 1982.

Chan, David B. *The Usurpation of the Prince of Yen, 1398–1402*. San Francisco: Chinese Materials Center, 1976.

Chang Ch'eng-sun 張城孫. *Chung-Ying Tien-Mien chiang-chieh wen-t'i* 中英滇緬疆界問題. Special issue of *Yen-ching hsüeh-pao* 燕京學報, no. 15. Pei-p'ing: Harvard-Yenching Institute, 1937.

Chang Chia-pi 張家璧. *Nan-yu lu* 難遊錄. In *Ming-chi yeh-shih tsa-ch'ao* 明季野史雜鈔. Microfilm of undated manuscript. National Library of Pei-ching.

Chang Chia-yü 張家玉. *Chang Wen-lieh i-chi* 張文烈遺集. Ed. Chang Po-chen 張伯楨. In *Ts'ang-hai ts'ung-shu* 滄海叢書, sec. 1, vols. 4–6. Repr. *Ming-Ch'ing shih-liao hui-pien*, sec. 8, vol. 74.

Chang Hsiao-ch'ien 張效乾. "Ming-Ch'ing liang-tai yü Yüeh-nan" 明清兩代與越南, *Ta-lu tsa-chih* 大陸雜誌, 35.3 (Aug. 1967): 18–21.

Chang Huang-yen 張煌言. *Pei-cheng te-shih chi-lüeh* 北征得佚紀略. In *Chang Ts'ang-shui chi* 張蒼水集. Ed. Chang Shou-yung 張壽鏞. Excerpts republished as *Chang Ts'ang-shui shih-wen* 詩文 *chi*. TW, no. 142, in 2 vols. 1962.

Chang Lin-po 張麟白. *Fu-hai chi* 浮海記. Appended to Ch'ien Ping-teng, *So-chih lu*. T'ai-pei: Shih-chieh shu-chü, 1971.

Chang Mu 張穆. *Ku T'ing-lin hsien-sheng nien-p'u* 顧亭林先生年譜. T'ai-pei: Kuang-wen shu-chü, 1971; repr. of *Yüeh-ya-t'ang ts'ung-shu* 粵雅堂叢書 edition of 1851–61.

Chang T'an 張菼. "Cheng-Ho ho-yüeh ch'ien-ting jih-ch'i chih k'ao-ting chi Cheng Ch'eng-kung fu-T'ai chih chan kai-shu" 鄭荷和約簽訂日期之考訂及鄭成功復台之戰概述, *T'ai-wan wen-hsien* 台灣文獻, 18.3 (Sept. 1956): 1–18.

———. *Cheng Ch'eng-kung chi-shih pien-nien* 鄭成功紀事編年. *T'ai-wan yen-chiu ts'ung-k'an* 台灣研究叢刊, no. 79. T'ai-pei: Bank of T'ai-wan Economic Research Office, 1965.

Chang Te-fang 張德芳. "'Yang-chou shih-jih chi' pien-wu" 「揚州十日記」辨誤. In *Chung-hua wen-shih lun-ts'ung* 中華文史論叢, vol. 5, pp. 365–76. Shanghai: Chung-hua shu-chü, 1964.

Chang T'ien-tse. *Sino-Portuguese Trade from 1514 to 1644: A Synthesis of Portuguese and Chinese Sources*. Leiden: E. J. Brill, 1934.

Chang Tsung-hsia 張宗洽. "Cheng Chih-lung hsiung-ti chiu-hsi chi-jen" 鄭芝龍兄弟究系幾人, *Chung-kuo shih yen-chiu* 中國史研究, 1980, no. 3 (Sept.): 167–68.

Chang Yin 張岙 [posth.]. "Chi Liu-ch'i yü 'Ming-chi nan-/pei-lüeh'" 計六奇與「明季南北略」, *Ch'ing-shih lun-ts'ung* 清史論叢, 2 (1980): 320–39.

Chao Hsi-ming 趙曦明. *Chiang-shang ku-chung lu* 江上孤忠錄. In TW, no. 258. 1968. Some other editions give Huang Ming-hsi 黃明曦 as author.

Chao I 趙翼. *Nien-erh-shih cha-chi* 廿二史箚記. 2 vols. T'ai-pei: Shih-chieh shu-chü, 1965.

Chao Ling-yang 趙令揚. "Lun Nan-Ming Hung-kuang ch'ao chih tang-huo" 論南明弘光朝之黨禍, *Lien-ho shu-yüan hsüeh-pao* 聯合書院學報, 4 (1965): independently paginated.

Chao Li-sheng 趙儷生 and Kao Chao-i 高昭一. "'K'uei-tung shih-san chia' k'ao" 「夔東十三家」考. In *Chung-kuo nung-min chan-cheng shih lun-wen chi* 中國農民戰爭史論文集, pp. 154–62. Shang-hai: Hsin chih-shih ch'u-pan she, 1955.

Chen Min-sun. "Three Contemporary Western Sources on the History of Late Ming and the Manchu Conquest of China." Ph.D. diss., University of Chicago, 1971.

Ch'en Chen-hui 陳貞慧. "Shu-shih ch'i-tse" 書事七則, *Ch'en Ting-sheng i-shu* 陳定生遺書. In *Ch'ang-chou hsien-che i-shu* 常州先哲遺書, vol. 5. 1895–98.

———. *Kuo-chiang ch'i-shih* 過江七事. In *T'ung-shih*, vol. 11.

[Ch'en Ch'ü-ping 陳去病], pseud. Yu-kuei Hsüeh-yin 有嬀血胤. "Yung-ming Huang-ti hsün-kuo shih-chi" 永明皇帝殉國實紀, *Min-pao* 民報, 23 (Aug. 1908), T'an-ts'ung 譚叢 sec., pp. 89–96.

Ch'en Han-kuang 陳漢光. "Lu-T'ang chiao-e chi Lu Wang chih szu" 魯唐交惡
    及魯王之死, *T'ai-wan wen-hsien* 台灣文獻, 11.1 (March 1980): 106–14.
———. "Ming Ning-ching Wang chi wu-fei wen-hsien" 明寧靖王及五妃
    文獻, *T'ai-wan wen-hsien*, 20.3 (Sept. 1969): 45–64.
Ch'en Han-kuang and Liao Han-ch'en 廖漢臣. "Lu Wang shih-chi k'ao-ch'a
    chi" 魯王史蹟考察記, *T'ai-wan wen-hsien*, 11.1 (March 1960): 115–25; and
    "Lu Wang shih-chi k'ao-ch'a hsü-chi" 續記, *T'ai-wan wen-hsien*, 15.4 (Dec.
    1964): 135–42.
Ch'en Hung-fan 陳洪範. *Pei-shih chi-lüeh* 北使紀略. In *Ching-t'o i-shih*,
    unnumbered volume.
Ch'en I-ling 陳以令. "Ming-tai yü Yüeh-nan, Kao-mien, Liao-kuo te pang-
    chiao" 明代與越南, 高棉, 寮國的邦交. In *Chung-kuo wai-chiao shih lun-chi*
    中國外交史論集, vol. 1, separate pagination. T'ai-pei: Chung-hua wen-
    hua ch'u-pan shih-yeh wei-yüan hui, 1957.
Ch'en Kuo-ch'iang 陳國强, "Cheng Ch'eng-kung shou-fu T'ai-wan te shih-
    chien wen-t'i" 鄭成功收復台灣的時間問題, *Hsia-men ta-hsüeh hsüeh-pao*
    廈門大學學報, 1962, no. 1 (April): 158–64.
Ch'en Pang-yen 陳邦彥. *Ch'en Yen-yeh hsien-sheng ch'üan-chi* 陳巖野先生全集.
    Ed. Wen Ju-neng 溫汝能. N.p.: Ting-sung-ko, 1805.
Ch'en Pi-sheng 陳碧笙. "1646-nien Cheng Ch'eng-kung hai-shang ch'i-ping
    ching-kuo" 一六四六年鄭成功海上起兵經過, *Li-shih yen-chiu* 歷史研究,
    1978, no. 8 (Aug.), pp. 92–93.
Ch'en Sheng-hsi 陳生璽. "Ch'ing-ping ju-kuan yü Wu San-kuei hsiang-Ch'ing
    wen-t'i" 清兵入關與吳三桂降清問題. In *Ming-Ch'ing shih kuo-chi hsüeh-
    shu t'ao-lun hui lun-wen chi*, pp. 715–44.
Ch'en Shih-ch'ing 陳世慶. "Ming Cheng ch'ien-hou chih Chin-men ping-
    shih" 明鄭前後之金門兵事, *T'ai-wan wen-hsien* 台灣文獻, 6.1 (March
    1955): 1–5.
Ch'en Shun-hsi 陳舜系. *Luan-li chien-wen lu* 亂離見聞錄. In *Kao-liang ch'i-chiu
    i-chi* 高涼耆舊遺集. Comp. Wu Hsüan-ch'ung 吳宣崇. Microfilm from
    the National Library of Pei-ching.
Ch'en T'ien 陳田. *Ming-shih chi-shih* 明詩紀事, 185 ch. Repr. in 30 vols. T'ai-
    pei: Commercial Press, 1968.
Ch'en Tso-chien 陳作鑑. "Lun Hung Ch'eng-ch'ou pien-chieh yü jen-ts'ai wai-liu"
    論洪承疇變節與人才外流, *Ch'ang-liu* 暢流, (1) 27.11 (July 1963): 2–3; (2)
    27.12 (Aug. 1963): 2–3; (3) 28.1 (Aug. 1963): 12–13.
Ch'en Tzu-lung 陳子龍. *Ch'en Chung-yü nien-p'u* 陳忠裕年譜. In *Ch'en Chung-
    yü ch'üan-chi* 陳忠裕全集. Ed. Wang Yün 王澐. N.p., 1803.
[Ch'en Yen-i 陳燕翼], pseud. Min-jen 閩人. *Szu-wen ta-chi* 思文大紀. TW,
    no. 111. 1967.
Cheng Ch'eng-kung 鄭成功 and Cheng Ching 鄭經 [attrib.]. *Yen-p'ing erh-wang
    i-chi* 延平二王遺集. In *Tseng-ting Chung-kuo hsüeh-shu ming-chu* 增訂中國
    學術名著, ser. 1, vol. 8. T'ai-pei: Shih-chieh shu-chü, 1965.

Cheng Hsi-wen 鄭喜文. "Ming Cheng shih-shih wu-tse" 明鄭史事五則, *T'ai-pei wen-wu* 台北文物, 10.1 (March 1961): 74–84.

Chi Liu-ch'i 計六奇. *Ming-chi nan-lüeh* 明季南略. TW, no. 148, in 3 vols. 1963.

———. *Ming-chi pei-lüeh* 明季北略. TW, no. 275, in 4 vols. 1969.

Ch'i Piao-chia 祁彪佳. *Ch'i Piao-chia chi* 集. Shang-hai: Chung-hua shu-chü, 1960.

———. *Chia-i jih-li* 甲乙日曆. TW, no. 279. 1969.

Chiang Chih-ch'un 江之春. *An-lung chi-shih* 安隆紀事. In CNW, vol. 14.

Chiang Jih-sheng 江日升. *T'ai-wan wai-chi* 台灣外記. Coll. and ed. Fang Hao 方豪. TW, no. 60, in 3 vols. 1960.

Chiang Yin-hsiang 江蔭香. *T'ao-hua-shan ming-jen hsiao-shih* 桃花扇名人小史. Hongkong: Han-wen t'u-shu kung-szu, 1970.

Chien Yu-wen 簡友文. "Nan-Ming min-tsu nü ying-hsiung Chang Yü-ch'iao k'ao-cheng" 南明民族女英雄張玉橋考證, *Ta-lu tsa-chih* 大陸雜誌, 41.6 (Sept. 1970): 1–19.

Ch'ien Ch'i 錢綺. *Nan-Ming shu* 南明書. (Probably not extant.)

Ch'ien Hsin 錢馹. *Chia-shen ch'uan-hsin lu* 甲申傳信錄. In CNW, vol. 8.

Ch'ien Ping-teng 錢秉鐙. *So-chih lu* 所知錄, 4 ch.: (1) *Lung-wu chi-nien* 隆武紀年; (2) *Yung-li chi-nien* 永曆紀年; (3) *Nan-tu san i an* 南渡三疑案; (4) *Juan Ta-ch'eng pen-mo hsiao-chi* 阮大鋮本末小紀. T'ai-pei: Shih-chieh shu-chü, 1971. Facsimile reproduction of rare ms.

———. *Ts'ang-shan-ko chi hsüan-chi* 藏山閣集選輯. TW, no. 225, in 2 vols. 1966.

Ch'ien Su-yüeh 錢肅樂. *Ch'ien Chung-chieh Kung chi* 錢忠介公集. In *Szu-ming ts'ung-shu* 四明叢書, sec. 2, vol. 2. Ed. Chang Shou-yung 張壽鏞. Szu-ming, 1932–48.

Ch'ien-k'un cheng-ch'i chi 乾坤正氣集. Ed. Yao Ying 姚瑩 and Ku Yüan 顧沅. Repr. T'ai-pei: Huan-ch'iu shu-chü, 1966.

Chikusa Masaaki 竺沙雅章. "Shu San Taishi an ni tsuite—Shinsho Kōnan no himitsu kessha ni kansuru ichi kōsatsu" 朱三太子案について—清初江南の秘密結社に関する一考察, *Shirin* 史林, 62.4 (1979): 1–21.

Chin Ch'eng-ch'ien 金成前. "Cheng Ch'eng-kung, Li Ting-kuo hui-shih wei-ch'eng chih yüan-yin" 鄭成功李定國會師未成之原因, *T'ai-wan wen-hsien* 台灣文獻, 16.1 (March 1965): 115–27.

———. "Kan Hui, Chou Ch'üan-pin, Liu Kuo-hsüan yü Ming Cheng san-shih" 甘輝周全斌劉國軒與明鄭三世, *T'ai-wan wen-hsien*, 16.4 (Dec. 1965): 133–43.

———. "Shih Lang, Huang Wu hsiang-Ch'ing tui Ming-Cheng chih ying-hsiang" 施琅黃梧降清對明鄭之影響, *T'ai-wan wen-hsien*, 17.3 (Sept. 1966): 151–66.

———. "Cheng Ch'eng-kung ch'i-ping hou shih-wu-nien chien cheng-chan shih-lüeh" 鄭成功起兵後十五年間征戰事略, *T'ai-wan wen-hsien*, 23.4 (Dec. 1972): 80–99.

———. "Ming Cheng chung-yao chiang-ling shih-shih fen-shu" 明鄭重要將領史事分述, *T'ai-wan wen-hsien*, 24.4 (Dec. 1973): 67–85.

———. "Cheng Ch'eng-kung Nan-ching chan-pai yü cheng-T'ai chih i" 鄭成功南京戰敗與征台之役, *T'ai-wan wen-hsien*, 25.1 (March 1974): 44–58.

Chin Pao 金堡. *Ling-hai fen-yü* 嶺海焚餘. TW, no. 302. 1972.

Chin Sheng 金聲. *Chin T'ai-shih chi* 金大史集. In *Ch'ien-k'un cheng-ch'i chi*, ch. 457–65.

Ch'in Shih-chen 秦世禎. *Fu-Che chiao-ts'ao* 撫浙檄草. In *Ch'ing-shih tzu-liao* 清史資料, vol. 2. Comp. Ch'ing History Section, Institute of History, Chinese Academy of Social Sciences 中國社會科學院歷史研究所清史研究室. Pei-ching: Chung-hua shu-chü, 1981.

Ching, Julia. "Chu Shun-shui, 1600–82: A Chinese Confucian Scholar in Tokugawa Japan," *Monumenta Nipponica*, 30.2 (Summer 1975): 177–91.

Ch'ing-shih lieh-chuan 清史列傳. Shang-hai: Chung-hua shu-chü, 1928.

Ching-t'o i-shih 荊駝逸史. Comp. Ch'en-hu I-shih 陳湖逸士 [pseud.]. N.p.: Chin-chang t'u-shu chü, n.d.

Chi-tsai hui-pien 紀載彙編. In *Shen-pao kuan ts'ung-shu* 申報館叢書, *hsü-chi* 續集. N.p.: Tsun-wen-ko, 1878.

Chou Shih-yung 周昔雍, comp. *Hsing-ch'ao chih-lüeh* 興朝治略. 1644. Rare book in the Fu Szu-nien Memorial Library, Academia Sinica, T'ai-pei.

Chu Feng 朱鋒, "Cheng Shih tsai-T'ai ch'uang-chien cheng-chih jih-ch'i k'ao" 鄭氏在臺創建政制日期考, *T'ai-nan wen-hua* 台南文化, 2.2 (April 1952): 50–54.

———. "Chin-men fa-hsien te Nan-Ming pei-chieh erh-chien" 金門發現的南明碑碣二件, *Wen-shih hui-k'an* 文史薈刊, 2 (Dec. 1960): 97–100.

———. "Li Chin Wang yü Cheng Yen-p'ing" 李晉王與鄭延平, *T'ai-wan wen-hsien* 台灣文獻, 12.3 (Sept. 1961): 155–58.

Chu Hsi-tsu 朱希祖. "Yung-li ta-yü shih-pa hsien-sheng shih-liao p'ing" 永曆大獄十八先生史料評, *Kuo-hsüeh chi-k'an* 國學季刊, 2.2 (Dec. 1929): 237–59.

———. "Cheng Yen-p'ing Wang shou Ming kuan-chüeh k'ao" 鄭延平王受明官爵考, *Kuo-li Pei-p'ing ta-hsüeh kuo-hsüeh chi-k'an* 國立北平大學國學季刊, 3.1 (March 1932): 87–112.

———, pseud. T'i-hsien 逷先. "Nan-Ming Kuang-chou hsün-kuo chu-wang k'ao" 南明廣州殉國諸王考, and "Kung-yeh Nan-Ming Shao-wu chün-ch'en chung chi" 恭謁南明紹武君臣塚記, *Wen-shih tsa-chih* 文史雜誌, 2.7–8 (Aug. 1942): 51–54 and 55–57, resp.

———. *Ming-chi shih-liao t'i-pa* 明季史料題跋. Pei-ching: Chung-hua shu-chü, 1961.

Chu Tzu-su 朱子素. *Tung-t'ang jih-cha* 東堂日箚, 2 ch. By this title in *Chi-tsai hui-pien* and *Ching-t'o i-shih*. Titled *Chia-ting t'u-cheng chi-lüeh* 嘉定屠城紀略 in *Ming-chi pai-shih ch'u-pien*, ch. 13, and in CNW, vol. 2. Shortened, altered version, *Chia-ting hsien i-yu chi-shih* 嘉定縣乙酉紀事, in *T'ung-shih*, vol. 8.

Chu Wei-ching 朱維靜. "Shih Lang yü Cheng Yen-p'ing te en-yüan" 施琅與鄭延平的恩怨, *Wen-shih hui-k'an* 文史薈刊, 1 (June 1959): 88–95.

Chu Wen-chang 朱文長. *Shih K'o-fa chuan* 史可法傳. T'ai-pei: Commercial Press, 1974.

Ch'ü Ch'ang-wen 瞿昌文. *Yüeh-hsing chi-shih* 粵行紀事. In *Pi-chi hsiao-shuo ta-kuan*, orig. vol. 220.

[Ch'ü Kung-mei 瞿共美], pseud. I-shih Shih 逸史氏. *Tung-Ming wen-chien lu* 東明聞見錄. In *Ming-chi pai-shih ch'u-pien*, ch. 23.

———. *Yüeh-yu chien-wen* 粵游見聞. In *Ming-chi pai-shih ch'u-pien*, ch. 20.

Ch'ü Shih-szu 瞿式耜. *Ch'ü Chung-hsüan Kung chi* 瞿忠宣公集. In *Ch'ien-k'un cheng-ch'i chi*, ch. 557–64.

Ch'ü Ta-chün 屈大均. *An-lung i-shih* 安龍逸史. In *Chia-yeh-t'ang ts'ung-shu* 嘉業堂叢書, vol. 70. Wu-hsing, 1918.

———. *Huang-Ming szu-ch'ao ch'eng-jen lu* 皇明四朝成仁錄. Coll. and ed. Yeh Kung-ch'o 葉恭綽. In *Kuang-tung ts'ung-shu* 廣東叢書, part 2, vols. 1–6. Shang-hai: Commercial Press, 1948.

Ch'ü Yüan-hsi 瞿元錫. *Keng-yin shih-i-yüeh ch'u-wu-jih shih-an shih-lüeh* 庚寅十一月初五日始安事略. In *Ching-t'o i-shih*, unnumbered volume.

Chuan, Han-sheng. "The Chinese Silk Trade with Spanish America from the Late Ming to the Mid-Ch'ing Period." In *Studia Asiatica*, pp. 99–117. Ed. Lawrence Thompson. San Francisco: Chinese Materials Center, 1975.

Ch'üan Tsu-wang 全祖望. *Chi-ch'i-t'ing chi* 鮚埼亭集, and *Chi-ch'i-t'ing chi wai-pien* 外編. In *Szu-pu ts'ung-k'an* 四部叢刊, vol. 95. Repr. in 2 vols. T'ai-pei: Hua-shih ch'u-pan she, 1977.

Chuang Ch'i-ch'ou 莊起儔. "Chang-p'u Huang hsien-sheng nien-p'u" 漳浦黃先生年譜. Appended to Huang Tao-chou, *Huang Chang-p'u wen-hsüan*, vol. 3.

Chuang Chin-te 莊金德. "Ming chien-kuo Lu Wang I-hai chi-shih nien-piao" 明監國魯王以海紀事年表, *T'ai-wan wen-hsien* 台灣文獻, 11.1 (March 1951): 1–59.

———. "Cheng Shih chün-liang wen-t'i te yen-t'ao" 鄭氏軍糧問題的研討, *T'ai-wan wen-hsien*, 12.1 (March 1961): 55–66.

———. "Cheng-Ch'ing ho-i shih-mo" 鄭清和議始末, *T'ai-wan wen-hsien*, 12.4 (Dec. 1961): 1–40.

Combés, Francisco, collab. Pablo Pastells. *Historia de Mindanao y Joló*. Rev. ed. W. E. Retana. Madrid: [Viuda de M. Mineusa de los Ríos], 1897 [1667].

Corradini, Piero. "Civil Administration at the Beginning of the Manchu Dynasty: A Note on the Establishment of the Six Ministries (*Liu-pu*)," *Oriens Extremus*, 9 (Dec. 1962): 133–38.

Crawford, Robert B. "Eunuch Power in the Ming Dynasty," *T'oung Pao*, 49.3 (1961): 115–48.

————. "The Biography of Juan Ta-ch'eng," *Chinese Culture*, 6.2 (March 1965): 28–105.

————. "Chang Chü-cheng's Confucian Legalism." In *Self and Society in Ming Thought*. Ed. W. T. de Bary. New York: Columbia University Press, 1970.

Croizier, Ralph C. *Koxinga and Chinese Nationalism: History, Myth, and the Hero.* Harvard East Asian Monographs, no. 67. Cambridge, Mass.: Harvard University Press, 1977.

De Bary, W. T. "Chinese Despotism and the Confucian Ideal: A Seventeenth-Century View." In *Chinese Thought and Institutions*, pp. 163–203. Ed. John K. Fairbank. Chicago: University of Chicago Press, 1957.

Dennerline, Jerry. "Fiscal Reform and Local Control: The Gentry-Bureaucratic Alliance Survives the Conquest." In *Conflict and Control in Late Imperial China*, pp. 86–120. Ed. Frederic Wakeman and Carolyn Grant. Berkeley: University of California Press, 1975.

————. "Hsü Tu and the Lesson of Nanking: Political Integration and Local Defense in Chiang-nan, 1634–1645." In *From Ming to Ch'ing*, pp. 92–132. Ed. Jonathan Spence and John E. Wills, Jr.

————. *The Chia-ting Loyalists: Confucian Leadership and Social Change in Seventeenth-Century China.* New Haven: Yale University Press, 1981.

————. "The Manchu Conquest and the Shun-chih Reign." 1982 draft of chapter for the *Cambridge History of China*, vol. 9.

Documents Committee of the National Palace Museum 故宮博物院文獻委員會, comp. *Wen-hsien ts'ung-pien* 文獻叢編. 51 vols. Pei-p'ing: 1930–37.

Dorgon. *Do-er-kun she-cheng jih-chi* 多爾袞攝政日記. Repr. *Pi-chi wu-pien* 筆記五編 series, vol. 13. T'ai-pei: Kuang-wen shu-chü, 1976.

Dreyer, Edward L. "The Poyang Lake Campaign, 1363: Inland Naval Warfare in the Founding of the Ming Dynasty." In *Chinese Ways in Warfare*, pp. 202–42. Ed. Frank Kierman, Jr.

————. *Early Ming Government: A Political History, 1355–1435.* Stanford: Stanford University Press, 1982.

Elison, George. *Deus Destroyed: The Image of Christianity in Early Modern Japan.* Cambridge, Mass.: Harvard University Press, 1973.

Elvin, Mark. "Market Towns and Waterways: The County of Shanghai from 1480 to 1910." In *The City in Late Imperial China*, pp. 441–73. Ed. G. Wm. Skinner. Stanford: Stanford University Press, 1977.

Fang Chao-ying. "A Technique for Estimating the Numerical Strength of the Early Manchu Military Forces," *Harvard Journal of Asiatic Studies*, 13.1–2 (June 1950): 192–215.

Fang Hao 方豪. "Yu Shun-chih pa-nien Fu-chien wu-wei shih-t'i lun Cheng Shih k'ang-Ch'ing te chu-li" 由順治八年福建武闈試題論鄭氏抗清的主力, *Ta-lu tsa-chih* 大陸雜誌, 22.6 (March 1961): 1–20.

Farmer, Edward. *Early Ming Government: The Evolution of Dual Capitals.*

Harvard East Asian Monograph, no. 66. Cambridge, Mass.: Harvard University Press, 1976.

Fei Mi 費密. *Huang-shu* 荒書. Author's preface, 1669. In *I-lan-t'ang ts'ung-shu* 怡蘭堂叢書, vol. 7. Ed. T'ang Hung-hsüeh 唐鴻學. Ch'eng-tu, 1922.

Felix, Alfonso, Jr., ed. *The Chinese in the Philippines, 1570–1770*. Manila: Solidaridad Publishing House, 1966.

Feng Meng-lung 馮夢龍, comp. *Chia-shen chi-shih* 甲申紀事. In *Hsüan-lan-t'ang ts'ung-shu, ch'u-chi* 玄覽堂叢書初集, vols. 107–18. Ed. Cheng Chen-to 鄭振鐸. Shang-hai, 1941.

―――, comp. *Chung-hsing wei-lüeh* 中興偉略. In *Min-Shin shiryō shū* 明清史料集. Annot. Nagasawa Kikuya 長澤規矩也. Tokyo: Iwanami shoten, 1974.

Feng Su 馮甦. *Tien-k'ao* 滇考. In *T'ai-chou ts'ung-shu* 台州叢書, part B. Ed. Sung Shih-lo 宋世犖. Lin-hai, 1817–21.

―――. *Chien-wen sui-pi* 見聞隨筆. In *T'ai-chou ts'ung-shu*, part A, vols. 7–8.

Fitzpatrick, Merrilyn. "Local Interests and the Anti-pirate Administration in China's South-east," *Ch'ing-shih wen-t'i*, 4.2 (Dec. 1979): 1–33.

Fu I-li 傅以禮. "Ts'an-Ming ta-t'ung li" 殘明大統曆. In *Erh-shih-wu shih pu-pien* 二十五史補編, VI: 8841–45. Shang-hai: K'ai-ming shu-tien, 1937.

Fu I-ling 傅衣凌. *Ming-Ch'ing nung-ts'un she-hui ching-chi* 明清農村社會經濟. Pei-ching: San-lien shu-tien, 1961.

―――. "Ming-mo nan-fang te 'tien-pien,' 'nu-pien'" 明末南方的「佃變」,「奴變」, *Li-shih yen-chiu* 歷史研究, 1975, no. 5 (May): 61–67.

Goodrich, L. C., and Fang Chao-ying, eds. *A Dictionary of Ming Biography*. 2 vols. New York: Columbia University Press, 1976.

Grimm, Tilemann. "Das Neiko der Ming-Zeit von den Anfangen bis 1506," *Oriens Extremus*, 1 (1954): 139–77.

Hai-wai San-jen 海外散人 [pseud.]. *Jung-ch'eng chi-wen* 榕城紀聞. In *Ch'ing-shih tzu-liao* 清史資料, vol. 1. Comp. Ch'ing History Section, Institute of History, Chinese Academy of Social Sciences 中國社會科學院歷史研究所清史研究室. Pei-ching: Chung-hua shu-chü, 1980.

Han T'an 韓菼. *Chiang-yin ch'eng-shou chi* 江陰城守記. In CNW, vol. 3.

Hayashi Shunsai 林春勝, comp. *Ka'i hentai* 華夷變態. 3 vols. Tokyo: Tōyō Bunko, 1958–59.

Ho Shih-fei 何是非 [pseud.]. *Feng-tao wu-t'ung chi* 風倒梧桐記. In *Ching-t'o i-shih*, unnumbered volume.

Hou Fang-yü 侯方域. *Chuang-hui-t'ang chi* 壯悔堂集. T'ai-pei: Commercial Press, 1968.

Hsi, Angela. "Wu San-kuei in 1644: A Reappraisal," *Journal of Asian Studies*, 34.2 (Feb. 1975): 443–53.

Hsia Lin 夏琳. *Hai-chi chi-yao* 海紀輯要. TW, no. 22. 1958.

Hsia Wan-ch'un 夏完淳. *Hsia Wan-ch'un chi* 集. Pei-ching: Chung-hua shu-chü, 1959.

Hsia Yün-i 夏允彝 and Hsia Wan-ch'un. *Hsing-ts'un lu* 幸存錄, and *Hsü* 續 *Hsing-ts'un lu*. In *Ming-chi pai-shih ch'u-pien*, ch. 14–16.

Hsieh Hao 謝浩. "Li, Cheng te shih-kung chi ch'i lien-chün yü lien-hun te yen-hsi" 李鄭的事功及其聯軍與聯婚的研析. In *Nan-Ming chi Ch'ing-ling T'ai-wan shih k'ao-pien* 南明暨清領台灣史考辨, pp. 28–162. T'ai-pei: author. 1976.

———. "Lung-wu 'Fu-ching' 'hsüan-chü' k'ao" 隆武「福京」「選舉」考, *T'ai-pei wen-hsien* 台北文獻, 40 (June 1977): 105–92.

Hsieh Kuo-chen 謝國楨. *Wan-Ming shih-chi k'ao* 晚明史籍考. National Pei-p'ing Library, 1932. Revised and expanded. *Tseng-ting wan-Ming shih-chi k'ao* 增訂晚明史籍考. Shang-hai: Ku-chi ch'u-pan she, 1981.

———. "Ming-chi nu-pien" 明季奴變, *Ch'ing-hua hsüeh-pao* 清華學報, 8.1 (1932): not serially paginated.

———. *Ming-Ch'ing chih chi tang-she yün-tung k'ao* 明清之際黨社運動考. Shang-hai: Commercial Press, 1934.

———. *Ch'ing-ch'u nung-min ch'i-i tzu-liao chi-lu* 清初農民起義資料輯錄 Shang-hai: Jen-min ch'u-pan she, 1957.

Hsu, Wen-hsiung. "From Aboriginal Island to Chinese Frontier: The Development of Taiwan before 1683." In *China's Island Frontier: Studies in the Historical Geography of Taiwan*, pp. 3–28. Ed. Ronald G. Knapp. Honolulu: University Press of Hawaii, 1980.

Hsü Ch'eng-li 徐承禮. *Hsiao-t'ien chi-chuan* 小腆紀傳. TW, no. 138, in 6 vols. 1963.

Hsü Ch'ung-hsi 許重熙. *Chiang-yin shou-ch'eng chi* 江陰守城記. In CNW, vol. 3.

Hsü Fang-lieh 徐方烈. *Che-tung chi-lüeh* 浙東紀略. In *T'ung-shih*, vol. 7.

Hsü Fu-yüan 徐孚遠. *Chiao-hsing che-kao* 交行摘稿. In TW, no. 123. 1961.

Hsü Shih-p'u 徐世溥. *Chiang-pien chi-lüeh* 江變紀略. In CNW, vol. 3.

Hsü Tzu 徐鼐. *Hsiao-t'ien chi-nien fu-k'ao* 小腆紀年附考. TW, no. 134, in 5 vols. 1962.

Htin Aung, Maung. *A History of Burma*. New York: Columbia University Press, 1967.

[Hu Ch'in-hua 胡欽華], attrib. Teng K'ai 鄧凱. *Ch'iu-yeh lu* 求野錄. In *Ming-chi pai-shih ch'u-pien*, ch. 17.

———. *T'ien-nan chi-shih* 天南紀事. (Manuscript in the Pei-ching Library.)

Hu Nai-an 胡耐安. "Ming-Ch'ing liang-tai t'u-szu" 明清兩代土司, *Ta-lu tsa-chih* 大陸雜誌, 19.7 (Oct. 15, 1959): 1–8.

Hua T'ing-hsien 華廷獻. *Min-shih chi-lüeh* 閩事紀略. In TW, no. 239. 1967.

———. *Min-yu yüeh-chi* 閩游月記. In *Ching-t'o i-shih*, unnumbered volume.

Huang Chang-chien 黃彰健. "Tu Ch'ing Shih-tsu shih-lu" 讀清世祖實錄. In Huang's collected articles, *Ming-Ch'ing shih yen-chiu ts'ung-kao* 明清史研究叢稿, pp. 594–612. T'ai-pei: Commercial Press, 1977.

———. "Tu *Ming-shih* Yü Ying-kuei, Chieh Ch'ung-hsi, Fu Ting-ch'üan san-jen chuan" 讀明史余應桂, 揭重熙, 傅鼎銓三人傳, *Ming-shih yen-chiu chuan-k'an* 明史研究專刊, 1 (July 1979): 170–72.

Huang Chung-ch'in 黃仲琴 and Hsia T'ing-yü 夏廷棫. "Chin-men Ming chien-kuo Lu Wang mu" 金門明監國魯王墓, *Kuo-li Chung-shan ta-hsüeh yü-yen li-shih hsüeh yen-chiu-so chou-k'an* 國立中山大學語言歷史學研究所周刊, 6.69 (Feb. 1929): 2805–08.

Huang Ch'un-yüeh 黃淳耀. *Huang T'ao-an hsien-sheng ch'üan-chi* 黃陶菴先生全集. Ed. Ch'en Ying-k'un 陳應鯤. Pao-an, preface of 1761.

Huang Hsiang-chien 黃向堅. *Huang hsiao-tzu hsün-ch'in chi-ch'eng* 黃孝子尋親紀程. In *Pi-chi hsiao-shuo ta-kuan*, orig. vol. 421.

Huang K'ai-hua 黃開華. *Ming-shih lun-chi* 明史論集. Hongkong: Ch'eng-ming ch'u-pan she, 1972.

Huang, Ray. "Fiscal Administration during the Ming Dynasty." In *Chinese Government in Ming Times*, pp. 73–128. Ed. Charles O. Hucker.

———. "Military Expenditures in Sixteenth Century Ming China," *Oriens Extremus*, 17 (1970): 39–62.

———. "Ni Yüan-lu: 'Realism' in a Neo-Confucian Scholar-Statesman." In *Self and Society in Ming Thought*, pp. 415–49. Ed. W. T. de Bary. New York: Columbia University Press, 1970.

———. *Taxation and Governmental Finance in Sixteenth-Century Ming China*. Cambridge: Cambridge University Press, 1974.

———. *1587: A Year of No Significance*. New Haven: Yale University Press, 1981.

———. "The Liao-tung Campaign of 1619," *Oriens Extremus*, 28.1 (1981): 30–54.

Huang Tao-chou 黃道周. *Huang Chang-p'u wen-hsüan* 黃漳浦文選. TW, no. 137, in 3 vols. 1962. Selections from *Huang Chang-p'u chi* 集. Ed. Ch'en Shou-ch'i 陳壽祺. N.p., 1830.

Huang Tien-ch'üan 黃典權. *Nan-Ming ta-t'ung li* 南明大統曆. T'ai-nan: Ching-shan shu-lin, 1962.

Huang Tsung-hsi 黃宗羲 [attrib.]. *Chou-shan hsing-fei* 舟山興廢. In *Li-chou i-chu hui-k'an* 梨洲遺著彙刊, vol. 2. T'ai-pei: Lung-yen ch'u-pan she, 1969.

———. *Hai-wai t'ung-ch'i chi* 海外慟淒記. In *Li-chou i-chu hui-k'an*, vol. 2.

———. [attrib.]. *Jih-pen ch'i-shih chi*, 日本乞師記. In *Li-chou i-chu hui-k'an*, vol. 2.

———. *Ming-i tai-fang lu* 明夷待訪錄. Repr. of *Szu-pu pei-yao* 四部備要 ed. T'ai-pei: Chung-hua shu-chü, 1974.

———. *Szu-ming shan-sai chi* 四明山塞記. In *Li-chou i-chu hui-k'an*, vol. 2.

Huang Yü-chai 黃玉齋. "Ming-Cheng k'ang-Ch'ing te ts'ai-cheng yü chün-hsü te lai-yüan" 明鄭抗清的財政與軍需的來源, *T'ai-wan wen-hsien* 台灣文獻, 9.2 (June 1958): 17–32.

———. "Ming Cheng Ch'eng-kung te k'ang-Ch'ing yü Jih-pen" 明鄭成功的抗清與日本, *T'ai-wan wen-hsien*, 9.4 (Dec. 1958): 99–126.

———. "Ming Cheng Ch'eng-kung pei-fa san-pai chou-nien te chi-nien" 明鄭成功北伐三百週年的紀念, *T'ai-pei wen-wu* 台北文物, 7.4 (Dec. 1958): 123–28; 8.1 (April 1959): 122–28; 8.2 (June 1959): 116–24; and 8.3 (Oct. 1959): 146–52.

———. "Cheng Ch'eng-kung shih-tai yü Jih-pen Te-ch'uan mu-fu" 鄭成功時代與日本德川幕府, *T'ai-wan wen-hsien*, 13.1 (March 1962): 114–34.

———. "Ming Yung-li Ti feng Chu Ch'eng-kung wei Yen-p'ing Wang k'ao" 明永曆帝封朱成功爲延平王考. In *T'ai-wan wen-wu lun-chi* 台灣文物論集, pp. 87–94. Ed. T'ai-wan sheng wen-hsien wei-yüan hui 台灣省文獻委員會. T'ai-pei, 1966.

———. "Hung-kuang ch'ao te chien-li" 弘光朝的建立, *T'ai-wan wen-hsien*, 18.1 (March 1967): 88–115.

———. "Hung-kuang ch'ao te shih-lüeh" 弘光朝的史略, *T'ai-wan wen-hsien*, 18.3 (Sept. 1967): 92–118.

———. "Hung-kuang ch'ao te peng-k'uei" 弘光朝的崩潰, *T'ai-wan wen-hsien*, 18.4 (Dec. 1967): 150–77.

———. "Ming-chi san ta-ju yü Yung-li Ti" 明季三大儒與永曆帝, *T'ai-wan wen-hsien*, 19.4 (Dec. 1968): 62–86.

———. "Ming Lung-wu Ti yung-li te ching-wei" 明隆武帝擁立的經緯, *T'ai-wan wen-hsien*, 20.2 (June 1969): 128–55.

———. "Ming Lung-wu Ti te cheng-lüeh" 明隆武帝的政略, *T'ai-wan wen-hsien*, 20.4 (Dec. 1969): 142–70.

———. "Ming Lung-wu Ti yü shang-shu Huang Tao-chou" 明隆武帝與尚書黃道周, *T'ai-wan wen-hsien*, 21.1 (March 1970): 67–102.

———. "Ming Lung-wu Ti yü Shao-wu" 明隆武帝與紹武, *T'ai-wan wen-hsien*, 21.2 (June 1970): 68–105.

Hucker, Charles O. "The Tunglin Movement of the Late Ming Period." In *Chinese Thought and Institutions*, pp. 132–63. Ed. John K. Fairbank. Chicago: University of Chicago Press, 1957.

———. *The Censorial System of Ming China*. Stanford: Stanford University Press, 1966.

———. "Governmental Organization of the Ming Dynasty." In *Studies of Governmental Institutions in Chinese History*, pp. 57–124. Ed. John L. Bishop. Harvard-Yenching Institute Studies, no. 23. Cambridge, Mass.: Harvard University Press, 1968.

———. "Hu Tsung-hsien's Campaign against Hsü Hai, 1556." In *Chinese Ways in Warfare*, pp. 273–307. Ed. Frank Kierman, Jr.

Hucker, Charles O., ed. *Chinese Government in Ming Times: Seven Studies*. Studies in Oriental Culture, no. 2. New York: Columbia University Press, 1969.

Hummel, Arthur, ed. *Eminent Chinese of the Ch'ing Period*. 2 vols. Washington, D.C.: Library of Congress, 1943.

Hung Ch'eng-ch'ou 洪承疇. *Hung Ch'eng-ch'ou chang-tsou wen-tz'u hui-chi* 章奏文册彙輯. Comp. Humanities Division of the Graduate School,

National Pei-ching University 國立北京大學研究院文史部. Shang-hai: Commercial Press, 1937.

I Songgyu 李成珪. "Shantung in the Shun-chih Reign: The Establishment of Local Control and the Gentry Response." Originally published in Korean, *Seouldae Dongyang sahak kwa nonjip* 서울大東洋史學科論集, 1 (1977). Translated into Japanese by Yamane Yukio 山根幸夫 and Inada Hikedo 稲田英子, in *Mindaishi kenkyū* 明代史研究, 6 (1979): 25–47. Translated from the Japanese into English by Joshua Fogel in *Ch'ing-shih wen-t'i*, (1) 4.4 (Dec. 1980): 1–34; and (2) 4.5 (June 1981): 1–31.

Ishihara Michihiro 石原道博. *Minmatsu Shinsho Nihon kisshi no kenkyū* 明末清初日本乞師の研究. Tokyo: Fuzambō, 1945.

———. "Tei Seikō to Shu Shunsui" 鄭成功與朱舜水, *T'ai-wan feng-wu* 台灣風物, 4.8–9 (Sept. 1954): 11–28.

———. "Chō Kōgen no kōnan kōhoku keiryaku" 張煌言の江南江北経畧, *T'ai-wan feng-wu*, 5.11–12 (1955): 7–53.

Iwami Hiroshi 岩見宏. "Mindai no minsō to hokuhen bōei" 明代の民壮と北辺防衛, *Tōyōshi kenkyū* 東洋史研究, 19.2 (Oct. 1960): 156–74.

Iwao Seiichi. "Japanese Foreign Trade in the 16th and 17th Centuries," *Acta Asiatica*, 30 (1976): 1–18.

Jäger, Fritz. "Die letzen Tage des Kü Schï-sï," *Sinica*, 8.5–6 (1933): 197–207.

[Juan Min-hsi 阮旻錫], pseud. Lu-tao tao-jen 鷺島道人. *Hai-shang chien-wen lu* 海上見聞錄. TW, no. 24. 1958.

Juan Yüan 阮元 et al., comps. *Kuang-tung t'ung-chih* 廣東通志, 334 ch. N.p., 1864.

Kanda Nobuo 神田信夫. *Heiseiō Go Sankei no kenkyū* 平西王呉三桂の研究. Meiji daigaku bungakubu kenkyū hōkoku, Tōyōshi 明治大学文学部研究報告, 東洋史, monograph no. 2. Tokyo: Meiji University, 1952.

K'ang Fan-sheng 康范生. *Fang chih-nan lu* 倣指南錄. In *Ching-t'o i-shih*, unnumbered volume.

Kao Yü-t'ai 高宇泰. *Hsüeh-chiao-t'ing cheng-ch'i lu* 雪交亭正氣錄. TW, no. 286, in 2 vols. 1970.

Kawagoe Yasuhiro 川越泰博. "Mindai kaibō taisei no un'ei kōzō—sōsei ki o chūshin ni" 明代海防体制の運営構造―創成期を中心に, *Shigaku zasshi* 史学雑誌, 81.6 (1972): 28–53.

Kawaguchi Chōju 川口長孺. *T'ai-wan Cheng Shih chi-shih* 台灣鄭氏紀事. TW, no. 5. 1958.

Kawakatsu Mamoru 川勝守. "Minmatsu Nankin heishi no hanran—Minmatsu no toshi kōzō ni tsuite no ichi sobyō" 明末南京兵士の叛亂―明末の都市構造についての一素描. In *Hoshi hakase taikan kinen Chūgokushi ronshū* 星博士退官記念中国史論集, pp. 187–207. Yamagata: Commemorative Volume Committee, 1978.

Keene, Donald. *The Battles of Coxinga: Chikamatsu's Puppet Play, Its Background and Importance*. London: Taylor's Foreign Press, 1951.

Kierman, Frank, Jr., ed. *Chinese Ways in Warfare*. Harvard East Asian Series, no. 74. Cambridge, Mass.: Harvard University Press, 1974.

Ko-ming yüan-yüan 革命遠源. 2 vols. Chung-hua min-kuo k'ai-kuo wu-shih-nien wen-hsien 中華民國開國五十年文獻, 1st series. T'ai-pei: Special Publication Committee, 1963.

Ku Ch'eng 顧誠. "Lun Ch'ing-ch'u she-hui mao-tun" 論清初社會矛盾, *Ch'ing-shih lun-ts'ung* 清史論叢 (Institute of History, Chinese Academy of Social Science, Pei-ching), no. 2 (1980): 139–57.

——. "Ming-tai te tsung-shih" 明代的宗室. In *Ming-Ch'ing shih kuo-chi hsüeh-shu t'ao-lun-hui lun-wen chi*, pp. 89–111.

Ku Yen-wu 顧炎武. *Sheng-an (Huang-ti) pen-chi* 聖安(皇帝)本紀. In TW, no. 183, vol. 1. 1964.

Ku Ying-t'ai 谷應泰. *Ming-shih chi-shih pen-mo* 明史紀事本末. In *Kuo-hsüeh chi-pen ts'ung-shu* 國學基本叢書, vol. 375. T'ai-pei: Commercial Press, 1968.

Kuan Wen-fa 關文發. "Shih-lun Ming-ch'ao nei-ko chih-tu te hsing-ch'eng ho fa-chan" 試論明朝內閣制度的形成和發展. In *Ming-Ch'ing shih kuo-chi hsüeh-shu t'ao-lun-hui lun-wen-chi*, pp. 45–65.

Kuang-tung Antiquities Exhibition Committee 廣東文物展覽會, ed. *Kuang-tung wen-wu* 廣東文物. 3 vols. Hongkong: Chung-kuo wen-hua hsieh-chin hui, 1941.

K'un-ming Wu-ming shih 昆明無名氏 [pseud.]. *Tien-nan wai-shih* 滇南外史. In *Ming-chi shih-liao ts'ung-shu*, vol. 10.

Kuo Ying-ch'iu 郭影秋. *Li Ting-kuo chi-nien* 李定國紀年. Shang-hai: Chung-hua shu-chü, 1960.

Kuo Yüan 郭垣. *Chu Shun-shui* 朱舜水. T'ai-pei: Cheng-chung shu-chü, 1964 [1937].

Ku-ts'ang-shih Shih-ch'en 古藏室史臣 [pseud.]. *Hung-kuang shih-lu ch'ao* 弘光實錄鈔. In CNW, vol. 8.

Kuwabara Jitsuzō 桑原隲藏. "Min no Hō Tenju yori Rōma hōō ni sōtei seshi bunsho" 明の龐天壽より羅馬法皇に送呈せし文書, *Shigaku zasshi* 史学雑誌, 11.3 (March 1900): 338–49; and 11.5 (May 1900): 617–30.

Lai Chia-tu 賴家度. "1645-nien Chiang-yin jen-min te k'ang-Ch'ing tou-cheng" 一六四五年江陰人民的抗清鬥爭. In *Ming-Ch'ing shih lun-ts'ung*, pp. 195–214. Ed. Li Kuang-pi.

Lai Chia-tu and Li Kuang-pi 李光璧. "Shan-tung Yü-yüan ch'i-i chün k'ang-Ch'ing shih-chi ch'u-t'an" 山東榆園起義軍抗清史迹初探. In *Chung-kuo nung-min ch'i-i lun-wen chi* 中國農民起義論文集, pp. 288–94. Pei-ching: San-lien shu-chü, 1958.

Lai Yung-hsiang 賴永祥. "Ming Cheng fan-hsia kuan-chüeh piao" 明鄭藩下官爵表, *T'ai-wan yen-chiu* 台灣研究, 1 (1956): 79–101; 2 (1957): 47–78.

Lei Liang-kung 雷亮功. *Kuei-lin t'ien-hai chi* 桂林田海記. In *Ming-chi shih-liao ts'ung-shu*, vol. 9.

Levenson, Joseph R. *Confucian China and Its Modern Fate: A Trilogy*. Berkeley: University of California Press, 1968.

Li Chen-hua 李振華. "Ming-mo hai-shih san-cheng Ch'ang-chiang shih k'ao" 明末海師三征長江事考, *Ta-lu tsa-chih* 大陸雜誌, (1) 6.9 (May 15, 1963): 1–5; (2) 6.10 (May 31, 1963): 18–22.

———. *Chang Ts'ang-shui chuan* 張蒼水傳. T'ai-pei: Cheng-chung shu-chü, 1967.

Li Chieh 李介. *T'ien-hsiang-ko sui-pi* 天香閣隨筆. In *Pi-chi hsiao-shuo ta-kuan*, orig. vol. 286.

Li Chieh 黎傑. "Nan Ming Kuang-tung san-chung shih-chi k'ao" 南明廣東三忠史蹟考, *Chu-hai hsüeh-pao* 珠海學報, 3 (June 1970): 162–73.

Li Chien-erh 李健兒. "Ch'en Tzu-chuang nien-p'u" 陳子壯年譜. In *Kuang-tung wen-wu*, II: 516–50. Ed. Kuang-tung Antiquities Exhibition Committee.

Li Ch'ing 李清. *Nan-tu lu* 南渡錄. (Unexamined work.)

———. *San-yüan pi-chi* 三垣筆記. In *Chia-yeh-t'ang ts'ung-shu* 嘉業堂叢書, vols. 67–69. Repr. in *Chung-hua wen-shih ts'ung-shu* 中華文史叢書, vol. 83. T'ai-pei: Hua-wen shu-chü, 1969.

Li Hsüeh-chih 李學智. "Ch'ung-k'ao Li Chen-hua hsien-sheng 'Ming-mo hai-shih san-cheng Ch'ang-chiang k'ao'" 重考李振華先生「明末海師三征長江考」, *Ta-lu tsa-chih* 大陸雜誌, 7.11 (Dec. 15, 1953): 7–8; and 7.12 (Dec. 31, 1953): 21–27.

Li Kuang-ming 黎光明. "Ming-mo Ch'ing-ch'u chih Szu-ch'uan" 明末清初之四川, *Tung-fang tsa-chih* 東方雜誌, 31.1 (Jan. 1934): 171–81.

Li Kuang-pi 李光璧. "Chi Hou-Ming cheng-fu te k'ang-Ch'ing tou-cheng" 記後明政府的抗清鬥爭, *Li-shih chiao-hsüeh* 歷史教學, 2.3 (Sept. 1951): 26–28.

———. "Nung-min ch'i-i chün tsai Ch'uan-O ti-ch'ü te lien-Ming k'ang-Ch'ing tou-cheng" 農民起義軍在川鄂地區的聯明抗清鬥爭. In *Chung-kuo nung-min ch'i-i lun-wen chi* 中國農民起義論文集, pp. 295–306. Pei-ching: San-lien shu-chü, 1958.

Li Kuang-pi, ed. *Ming-Ch'ing shih lun-ts'ung* 明清史論叢. Wu-han: Hu-pei jen-min ch'u-pan she, 1957.

Li Kuang-t'ao 李光濤. "Lun Chien-chou yü liu-tsei hsiang-yin wang-Ming" 論建州與流賊相因亡明, CYYY, 12 (1947): 193–236.

———. "Hung Ch'eng-ch'ou pei-Ming shih-mo" 洪承疇背明始末, CYYY, 17 (1948): 227–301.

———. *Ming-chi liu-k'ou shih-mo* 明季流寇始末. Nan-kang: Institute of History and Philology, Academia Sinica, 1965.

———. *Ming-Ch'ing shih lun-chi* 明清史論集. 2 vols. T'ai-pei: Commercial

Press, 1971. Articles cited therein: "Ch'ing-jen yü liu-tsei" 清人與流賊,
I: 349–57; "Do-er-kun Shan-hai-kuan chan-i te chen-hsiang" 多爾袞
山海關戰役的眞相, II: 443–48; "Li Ting-kuo yü Nan-Ming" 李定國與
南明, II: 591–614.

Li Kuang-t'ao, ed. and annot. *Ming-Ch'ing tang-an ts'un-chen hsüan-chi* 明清檔案
存眞選集. 3 vols. Nan-kang: Institute of History and Philology, Academia
Sinica, 1959–75.

Li Lung-wah. "The Control of the Szechwan-Kweichow Frontier Regions
during the Late Ming: A Case Study of the Frontier Policy and Tribal
Administration of the Ming Government." Ph.D. diss., Australian
National University, 1978.

Li Lü-an 李履庵. "Kuan-yü Ho Wu-tsou, Wu Jui-lung shih-chi chih yen-chiu"
關於何吾騶伍瑞隆史蹟之研究. In *Kuang-tung wen-wu*, II: 612–44. Ed.
Kuang-tung Antiquities Exhibition Committee.

Li Shih-hsiung 李世熊. *K'ou-pien chi* 寇變記. In *Ch'ing-shih tzu-liao* 清史資料,
vol. 1. Comp. Ch'ing History Section, Institute of History, Chinese
Academy of Social Sciences 中國社會科學院歷史研究所清史研究室.
Pei-ching: Chung-hua shu-chü, 1980.

Li T'eng-yüeh 李騰嶽. "Cheng Ch'eng-kung te szu-yin k'ao" 鄭成功的死因考,
Wen-hsien chuan-k'an 文獻專刊, 1.3 (Aug. 1950): 35–44.

Li T'ien-yu 李天佑. *Ming-mo Chiang-yin Chia-ting jen-min te k'ang-Ch'ing tou-
cheng* 明末江陰嘉定人民的抗清鬥爭. Shang-hai: Hsüeh-hsi sheng-huo
ch'u-pan she, 1955.

Li Wen-chih 李文治. *Wan-Ming min-pien* 晚明民變. Shang-hai: Yüan-tung t'u-
shu kung-szu, 1948.

Liang Ch'i-ch'ao 梁啓超. "Huang Li-chou, Chu Shun-shui ch'i-shih Jih-pen
pien" 黃梨洲朱舜水乞師日本辨, *Tung-fang tsa-chih* 東方雜誌, 20.6 (March
1923): 54–56.

Liao Han-ch'en 廖漢臣. "Cheng Shih shih-hsi chi jen-wu k'ao" 鄭氏世系及
人物考, *Wen-hsien chuan-k'an* 文獻專刊, 1.3 (1950): 54–64.

———. "Cheng Chih-lung k'ao 鄭芝龍考, *T'ai-wan wen-hsien* 台灣文獻,
10.4 (Dec. 1959): 63–72; and 11.3 (Sept. 1960): 1–15.

———. "Lu Wang k'ang-Ch'ing yü erh-Chang chih wu-kung" 魯王抗清與
二張之武功, *T'ai-wan wen-hsien*, 11.1 (March 1960): 81–105.

———. "Yen-p'ing Wang tung-cheng shih-mo" 延平王東征始末, *T'ai-wan
wen-hsien*, 12.2 (June 1961): 57–84.

———. "Yen-p'ing Wang pei-cheng k'ao-p'ing" 延平王北征考評, *T'ai-wan
wen-hsien*, 15.2 (June 1964): 47–74.

Lieberman, Victor B. "Europeans, Trade, and the Unification of Burma,
c. 1540–1620," *Oriens Extremus*, 27.2 (1980): 203–26.

———. "Provincial Reforms in Toung-ngu Burma," *Bulletin of the School of
Oriental and African Studies*, 43.3 (1980): 548–69.

———. "The Transfer of the Burmese Capital from Pegu to Ava," *Journal of the Royal Asiatic Society of Great Britain and Ireland*, 1980, no. 1, pp. 64–83.

Lighte, Peter R. "The Mongols and Mu Ying in Yunnan—At the Empire's Edge." Ph.D. diss., Princeton University, 1981.

Lin Ch'ao-tung 林朝棟. "Cheng Ch'eng-kung k'o-T'ai ch'ien T'ai-Hsia chih chien te ching-wei" 鄭成功克台前台厦之間的經緯, *T'ai-nan wen-hua* 台南文化, 5.2 (July 1956): 91–98.

[Lin Shih-tui 林時對]. *Ho-cha ts'ung-t'an* 荷牐叢談. In TW, no. 153. 1962.

[Liu Chai 劉茝]. *Shou-Mien chi-shih* 狩緬紀事. (Unexamined work.)

Liu Chia-chü 劉家駒. "Shun-chih nien-chien te t'ao-jen wen-t'i" 順治年間的逃人問題. In *Ch'ing-chu Li Chi hsien-sheng ch'i-shih-sui lun-wen chi* 慶祝李濟先生七十歲論文集, II: 1049–80. T'ai-pei: Ch'ing-hua hsüeh-pao she, 1965–67.

Liu Chien 劉健. *T'ing-wen lu* 庭聞錄. TW, no. 248. 1968.

Liu Hui 劉輝 et al., comps. *Shih K'o-fa p'ing-chia wen-t'i hui-pien* 史可法評價問題彙編. Hongkong: Yang-k'ai shu-pao kung-ying she, 1968.

Liu, Joseph. "She Ke-fa (1601–1645) et le contexte politique et social de la Chine au moment de l'invasion mandchoue." Ph.D. diss., Université de Paris, 1969. (Unexamined work.)

Liu Pin 劉彬. "Chin Wang Li Ting-kuo lieh-chuan" 晉王李定國列傳. In *Tien-ts'ui* 滇粹, pp. 52a–58b. 1909 lithograph ed. Repr. Hang-chou: Ku-chiu shu-tien, 1981.

Liu Ts'ui-jung 劉翠溶. "Ch'ing-ch'u Shun-chih K'ang-hsi nien-chien chien-mien fu-shui te kuo-ch'eng" 清初順治康熙年間減免賦稅的過程, CYYY, 37.2 (1967): 757–77.

Liu Tsung-chou 劉宗周. *Liu Tzu ch'üan-shu* 劉子全書. Repr. of Tao-kuang edition in *Chung-hua wen-shih ts'ung-shu* 中華文史叢書, part 7. T'ai-pei: Hua-wen shu-chü, n.d.

Liu Ya-tzu 柳亞子. *Huai-chiu chi* 懷舊集. Shang-hai: Keng-yün ch'u-pan she, 1947.

———. [pseud. Nan Shih 南史]. "Chi-Ming szu-ti shih-fa k'ao" 季明四帝諡法考, *Ta-feng pan-yüeh k'an* 大風半月刊, 78 (Nov. 1940): 2534–35.

Lo Hsiang-lin 羅香林. "Lang-ping lang-t'ien k'ao" 狼兵狼田考, *Kuang-chou hsüeh-pao* 廣州學報, 1.2 (April 1937): not serially paginated.

———. "Hsiang-kang hsin fa-hsien Nan-Ming Yung-li szu-nien so-tsao ta-p'ao k'ao" 香港新發現南明永曆四年所造大砲考, *Wen-shih hui-k'an* 文史薈刊, 1.1–2 (June 1959).

Lo, Jung-pang. "The Decline of the Early Ming Navy," *Oriens Extremus*, 5 (1958): 149–68.

———. "Policy Formulation and Decision-making on Issues Respecting Peace and War." In *Chinese Government in Ming Times*, pp. 41–72. Ed. Charles O. Hucker.

Lou Tzu-k'uang 婁子匡. "Cheng Ch'eng-kung ch'uan-shuo te t'an-t'ao" 鄭成功傳說的探討, *Wen-shih hui-k'an* 文史薈刊, 2 (Dec. 1960): 47–69.

———. "Cheng Ch'eng-kung tan-sheng ch'uan-shuo chih yen-chiu" 鄭成功誕生傳說之研究, *Ta-lu tsa-chih* 大陸雜誌, 22.8 (April 1961): 22–25.

———. "Cheng Ch'eng-kung shih-shih ch'uan-shuo yü shih-chieh t'ung-hsing ku-shih pi-chiao yen-chiu" 鄭成功逝世傳說與世界同型故事比較研究, *T'ai-wan wen-hsien* 台灣文獻, 12.1 (March 1961): 25–31.

———. "Ts'ung min-su-hsüeh shang k'an Cheng Ch'eng-kung te feng-kung wei-yeh" 從民俗學上看鄭成功的豐功偉業, *Hsin chien-she* 新建設, 2.3 (Sept. 1961): 61–69.

Lou-tung Wu-ming-shih 婁東無名氏 [pseud.]. *Yen-t'ang chien-wen tsa-chi* 研堂見聞雜記. TW, no. 254. 1968.

Lu Ch'i 陸圻. *Hsien-yen* 纖言. In CNW, vol. 4.

[Lu K'o-tsao 魯可藻]. *Ling-piao chi-nien* 嶺表紀年. Microfilm of undated manuscript. National Central Library, T'ai-pei.

Lu Shih-i 陸世儀. *Chiang-yu chi-pien* 江右紀變. Appended to the *Hsing-ch'ao lu* 行朝錄 in *Shao-hsing hsien-cheng i-shu* 紹興先正遺書, sec. 4, vol. 48. Ed. Hsü Yu-lan 徐友蘭. K'uai-chi, 1894.

Lung Wen-pin 龍文彬. *Ming hui-yao* 明會要. 2 vols. Pei-ching: Chung-hua shu-chü, 1956.

Ma, Feng-ch'en. "Manchu-Chinese Social and Economic Conflicts in Early Ch'ing." In *Chinese Social History*, pp. 333–51. Ed. E-tu Sun and John de Francis. Washington, D.C.: American Council of Learned Societies, 1956.

Ma Shao-ch'iao 馬少僑. "Ming-mo Wu-kang jen-min te fan fan-i tou-cheng" 明末武岡人民的反藩役鬥爭. In *Ming-Ch'ing shih lun-ts'ung*, pp. 135–44. Ed. Li Kuang-pi.

McMorran, Ian. "The Patriot and the Partisans: Wang Fu-chih's Involvement in the Politics of the Yung-li Court." In *From Ming to Ch'ing*, pp. 136–66. Ed. Jonathan Spence and John E. Wills, Jr.

Maejima Shinji 前嶋信次. "Tei Shiryū shōan no jijō ni tsuite" 鄭芝龍招安の事情について, *Chūgoku gakushi* 中国学誌, I (1964): 141–70.

Mai Shao-lin 麥少麟. "Min-tsu ying-hsiung Chang Chia-yü" 民族英雄張家玉. In *Kuang-tung wen-wu*, II: 588–611. Ed. Kuang-tung Antiquities Exhibition Committee.

Man-yu Yeh-shih 漫遊野史 [pseud.]. *Hai-chiao i-pien* 海角遺編. In *Yü-yang shuo-yüan* 虞陽說苑, part A, vol. 2. N.p., 1917.

Mao I-po 毛一波. "Shu Lu Wang chih szu yü Cheng Ch'eng-kung shou-wu shih" 書魯王之死與鄭成功受誣事, *Wen-hsien chuan-k'an* 文獻專刊, 4.3–4 (Dec. 1953): 9–10.

———. "Cheng Ch'eng-kung yü Chang Ts'ang-shui" 鄭成功與張蒼水, *T'ai-wan feng-wu* 台灣風物, 4.4 (April 1954): 4–10.

———. "Lu Wang k'ang-Ch'ing yü Ming Cheng kuan-hsi" 魯王抗清與明鄭關係, *T'ai-wan wen-hsien* 台灣文獻, 11.1 (March 1960): 60–74.

————. "Che-Min kung-an yü Nan-ao kung-an" 浙閩公案與南灣公案, *T'ai-wan wen-hsien*, 11.1 (March 1960): 75–80.

————. "Nan-Ming wu-ch'en Cheng Ts'ai te shih-chi" 南明武臣鄭彩的事跡, *Min-chu p'ing-lun* 民主評論, 12.14 (July 1961): 14–18.

————. *Nan-Ming shih-t'an* 南明史談. T'ai-pei: Commercial Press, 1970.

————. "Cheng Ch'eng-kung kuan-chüeh k'ao" 鄭成功官爵考, *T'ai-wan feng-wu*, 23.4 (Dec. 1973): 5–6.

Mao, Lucien, trans. "A Memoir of a Ten Days' Massacre in Yangchow," *T'ien Hsia Monthly*, 4.5 (May 1937): 515–37.

Martinus, Martin. *Bellum Tartaricum, or the Conquest of the Great and Most Renowned Empire of China*. English translation from the original Latin. London: John Crook, 1654.

Meilink-Roelofsz, M. A. P. "Aspects of Dutch Colonial Development in Asia in the Seventeenth Century." In *Britain and the Netherlands in Europe and Asia*, III: 56–82. Ed. J. S. Bromley and E. H. Kossmann. New York: Macmillan, 1968.

Meng Cheng-fa 蒙正發. *San-Hsiang ts'ung-shih chi* 三湘從事記. In *Pi-chi hsiao-shuo ta-kuan* 筆記小說大觀, series 10, vol. 3. T'ai-pei: Hsin-hsing shu-chü, 1975.

Meng Sen 孟森. *Ming-Ch'ing shih lun-chu chi-k'an* 明清史論著集刊. Repr. T'ai-pei: Shih-chieh shu-chü, 1965.

Michael, Franz. *The Origin of Manchu Rule in China*. Baltimore: Johns Hopkins University Press, 1942.

Ming-chi pai-shih ch'u-pien 明季稗史初編. Ed. Liu-yün Chü-shih 留雲居士 [pseud.]. T'ai-pei: Commercial Press, 1971. Published under earlier title, *Ming-chi pai-shih hui- 彙 pien*, by the Shang-hai t'u-shu chi-ch'eng chü, 1896.

Ming-chi shih-liao ts'ung-shu 明季史料叢書. Ed. Cheng Chen-to 鄭振鐸. Shang-hai: Sheng-tse yüan, 1944.

Ming-Ch'ing shih kuo-chi hsüeh-shu t'ao-lun-hui lun-wen chi 明清史國際學術討論會論文集. Ed. conference secretariat. T'ien-chin: T'ien-chin jen-min ch'u-pan she, 1981.

Ming-Ch'ing shih-liao hui-pien 明清史料彙編. Comp. Shen Yün-lung 沈雲龍. 83 vols. Yung-ho, T'ai-wan: Wen-hai ch'u-pan she, 1967–73.

Ming-shih 明史. In *Jen-shou pen erh-shih-wu shih* 仁壽本二十五史, vols. 835–934. T'ai-pei: Erh-shih-wu shih pien-k'an kuan, 1956.

Mitamura Taisuke 三田村泰助. *Shinchō zenshi no kenkyū* 清朝前史の研究. Kyoto: Tōyōshi kenkyū kai, 1965.

Mori Masao 森正夫. "Jūshichi seiki no Fukken Neikaken ni okeru Kō Tō no kōso hanran" 十七世紀の福建寧化縣における黄通の抗租反乱, *Nagoya daigaku bungakubu kenkyū ronshū* 名古屋大学文学部研究論集, *Shigaku* 史学 series, 20 (1973): 1–31; 21 (1974): 13–25; and 25 (1978): 25–65.

————. "1645-nen Taisōshū Sakeichin ni okeru Uryūkai no hanran ni tsuite"

一六四五年太倉州沙溪鎮における烏龍會の反乱について. In *Naka-yama Hachirō kyōju shōju kinen Min-Shin shi ronsō* 中山八郎教授頌寿記念明清史論叢, pp. 195–232. Tokyo: Ryōgen shoten, 1977.

―――. "Minmatsu no shakai kankei ni okeru chitsujo no hendō ni tsuite" 明末社會関係における秩序の變動について. In *Nagoya daigaku bun-gakubu sanjisshūnen kinen ronshū* 名古屋大学文学部三十周年記念論集, pp. 135–59. Nagoya: Nagoya University, 1979.

Mote, Frederick. "The Growth of Chinese Despotism: A Critique of Wittfogel's Theory of Oriental Despotism as Applied to China," *Oriens Extremus*, 8 (1961): 1–41.

―――. *The Poet Kao Ch'i, 1336–1374.* Princeton: Princeton University Press, 1962.

―――. "The T'u-mu Incident of 1449." In *Chinese Ways in Warfare*, pp. 243–72. Ed. Frank Kierman, Jr.

―――. "The Transformation of Nanking, 1350–1400." In *The City in Late Imperial China*, pp. 101–53. Ed. G. Wm. Skinner. Stanford: Stanford University Press, 1977.

Nakayama Hachirō 中山八郎. "Hanto ni okeru bempatsu no mondai—Shinsho no bempatsu rei shikō o chūshin to shite" 漢土に於ける辮髪の問題—清初の辮髪令施行を中心として, *Chūgokushi kenkyū* 中国史研究, 5 (1968): 1–24.

Nan-yüan Hsiao-k'o 南園嘯客 [pseud.]. *P'ing-Wu shih-lüeh* 平吳事略. In CNW, vol. 14.

Nathan, Andrew J. "A Factionalism Model for CCP Politics," *China Quarterly*, 53 (Jan.–March 1973): 34–66.

[Nederlandsche Oost-Indische Compagnie], trans. Murakami Naojirō 村上直次郎. *Deshima Rankan nisshi* 出島蘭館日誌. 3 vols. Tokyo: Bunmei kyōkai, 1939.

Ng Chin-keong, "The Fukienese Maritime Trade in the Second Half of the Ming Period—Government Policy and Elite Groups' Attitudes," *Nanyang University Journal*, 5.2 (1971): 81–100.

―――. "A Study of the Peasant Society of South Fukien, 1506–1644," *Nanyang University Journal*, 6 (1972): 189–212.

Nieuhoff, John [Jan Nieuhof]. *An Embassy from the East India Company of the United Provinces to the Grand Tartar Cham Emperor of China*. Trans. John Ogilby. Menston: Scolar Press, 1669.

Number I Historical Archive of China 中國第一歷史檔案館 (formerly the Ming-Ch'ing Archive Section of the Palace Museum 故宮博物院明清檔案部), comp. *Ch'ing-tai tang-an shih-liao ts'ung-pien* 清代檔案史料叢編. Series. Pei-ching: Chung-hua shu-chü. Vol. IV, 1979. Vol. VI, 1980.

Nunome Chōfū 布目潮渢. "Minchō no shoō seisaku to sono eikyō" 明朝の諸王政策とその影響, *Shigaku zasshi* 史学雑誌, (1) 55.3 (March 1944): 1–32; (2) 55.4 (April 1944): 50–87; (3) 55.5 (May 1944): 23–73.

Oxnam, Robert B. *Ruling from Horseback: Manchu Politics and the Oboi Regency, 1661–1669*. Chicago: University of Chicago Press, 1975.

P'an Chen-ch'iu 潘鎮球. "Ming-tai pei-pien chün-chen chi wei-so te peng-k'uei" 明代北邊軍鎮及衞所的崩潰, *Ch'ung-chi hsüeh-pao* 崇基學報, 7.1 (Nov. 1966): 90–100.

Parsons, James B. "The Culmination of a Chinese Peasant Rebellion: Chang Hsien-chung in Szechwan, 1644–46," *Journal of Asian Studies*, 6.3 (May 1957): 387–400.

———. *Peasant Rebellions of the Late Ming Dynasty*. Association for Asian Studies. Monographs and Papers, no. 26. Tucson: University of Arizona Press, 1970.

Pelliot, Paul. "Michel Boym," *T'oung Pao*, ser. 2, 31.1–2 (1935): 95–151.

P'eng Kuo-tung 彭國棟. "Nan-Ming Chung-Yüeh kuan-hsi shih-hua" 南明中越關係史話. In *Chung-Yüeh wen-hua lun-chi* 中越文化論集, II: 256–66. T'ai-pei: Chung-hua wen-hua ch'u-pan shih-yeh wei-yüan hui, 1956.

P'eng P'u-sheng 彭普生. "Li Tzu-ch'eng pei-hai jih-ch'i t'an-k'ao" 李自成被害日期探考, *Ku-kung po-wu-yüan yüan-k'an* 故宮博物院院刊, 1980, no. 3 (Aug.): 35–39.

P'eng Sun-i 彭孫貽. *Hu-hsi i-shih* 湖西遺事. In *Shih-yüan ts'ung-shu* 適園叢書, vol. 107. Ed. Chang Chün-heng 張鈞衡. Wu-hsing, 1913–17.

———. *P'ing-k'ou chih* 平寇志. Repr. of early K'ang-hsi edition. National Library of Pei-p'ing, 1931.

Pi-chi hsiao-shuo ta-kuan 筆記小說大觀. 500 vols. Shang-hai: Chin-pu shu-chü, Republican period. Repr. T'ai-pei: Hsin-hsing shu-tien, 1960.

Rawski, Evelyn Sakakida. *Agricultural Change and the Peasant Economy of South China*. Cambridge, Mass.: Harvard University Press, 1972.

Rossabi, Morris. "Muslim and Central Asian Revolts." In *From Ming to Ch'ing*, pp. 170–99. Ed. Jonathan Spence and John E. Wills, Jr.

Roth, Gertraude. "The Manchu-Chinese Relationship." In *From Ming to Ch'ing*, pp. 4–38. Ed. Jonathan Spence and John E. Wills, Jr.

Rudolph, Richard C. "The Real Tomb of the Ming Regent, Prince of Lu," *Monumenta Serica*, 29 (1970–71): 484–95.

Saeki Tomi 佐伯富. "Min-Shin jidai no minsō ni tsuite" 明清時代の民壯について, *Tōyōshi kenkyū* 東洋史研究, 15.4 (March 1957): 33–64.

Sakai, Robert K. "The Ryukyu (Liu-ch'iu) Islands as a Fief of Satsuma." In *The Chinese World Order*, pp. 112–34. Ed. John K. Fairbank. Harvard East Asian Series, no. 32. Cambridge, Mass.: Harvard University Press, 1968.

Sansom, George. *A History of Japan, 1334–1615*. Stanford: Stanford University Press, 1961.

———. *A History of Japan, 1615–1867*. Stanford: Stanford University Press, 1963.

Satō Fumitoshi 佐藤文俊. "Minmatsu shūhan ōfu no daitochi shoyū o meguru ni, san no mondai—Rō ōfu no baai" 明末就藩王府の大土地

所有をめぐる二、三の問題—潞王府の場合. Part I in *Kimura Masao sensei taikan kinen tōyōshi ronshū* 木村正雄先生退官記念東洋史論集, pp. 235–57. Tokyo: Kyūko shoen, 1976. Part II in *Mindaishi kenkyū* 明代史研究, 3 (Dec. 1975): 23–41.

Shang Hung-k'uei 商鴻逵. "Ming-Ch'ing chih chi Shan-hai-kuan chan-i te chen-hsiang k'ao-ch'a" 明清之際山海關戰役的眞相考察, *Li-shih yen-chiu* 歷史研究, 1978, no. 5 (May): 76–82.

Shao T'ing-ts'ai 邵廷采. *Szu-fu-t'ang wen-chi* 思復堂文集. In *Shao-hsing hsien-cheng i-shu* 紹興先正遺書, sec. 4. Ed. Hsü Yu-lan 徐友蘭. Repr. T'ai-pei: Hua-shih ch'u-pan she, n.d.

Shen Hsün-wei 沈荀蔚. *Shu-nan hsü-lüeh* 蜀難敘略. In *Pi-chi hsiao-shuo ta-kuan*, orig. vol. 220.

Sheng Ch'eng 盛成. "Shen Kuang-wen yü Ming Szu-tsung chi nan-tu chu-wang" 沈光文與明思宗及南渡諸王, *Hsüeh-shu chi-k'an* 學術季刊, 4.3 (March 1956): 42–73.

Sheng Ch'ing-i 盛清沂, Wang Shih-lang 王詩琅, and Kao Shu-fan 高樹藩. *T'ai-wan shih* 台灣史. Ed. Lin Heng-tao 林衡道. T'ai-chung: T'ai-wan sheng wen-hsien wei-yüan hui, 1977.

Shigeta Atsushi 重田德. *Shindai shakai keiji shi kenkyū* 清代社會經濟史研究. Tokyo: Iwanami shoten, 1975.

Shih K'o-fa 史可法. *Shih Chung-cheng Kung chi* 史忠正公集. In *Kuo-hsüeh chi-pen ts'ung-shu szu-pai chung* 國學基本叢書四百種, vol. 313. T'ai-pei: Commercial Press, 1968.

Shih Wan-shou 石萬壽. "Lun Ming Cheng te ping yüan" 論明鄭的兵源, *Ta-lu tsa-chih* 大陸雜誌, 41.6 (Sept. 1970): 20–29.

———. "Lun Cheng Ch'eng-kung pei-fa i-ch'ien te ping-chen" 論鄭成功北伐以前的兵鎮, *Yu-shih hsüeh-chih* 幼獅學誌, 11.2 (June 1973): independently paginated.

———. "Lun Cheng Ch'eng-kung pei-fa i-hou te ping-chen" 論鄭成功北伐以後的兵鎮, *T'ai-wan wen-hsien* 台灣文獻, 24.4 (Dec. 1973): 15–26.

———. "Ming Cheng te chün-shih hsing-cheng tsu-chih" 明鄭的軍事行政組織, *T'ai-wan wen-hsien*, 26.4–27.1 (Dec. 1975–March 1976; double issue): 50–66.

Shih Yang-sui 石暘睢. "Nan-Ming ch'ien-lu" 南明錢錄, *T'ai-wan feng-wu* 台灣風物, 11.4 (1962): 46–47.

Shimizu Taiji 清水泰次. *Mindai tochi seido shi kenkyū* 明代土地制度史研究. Tokyo: Daian, 1968.

Shore, David H. "Last Court of Ming China: The Reign of the Yung-li Emperor in the South (1647–1662)." Ph.D. diss., Princeton University, 1976.

Shu I 舒翼. "Shih K'o-fa Yang-chou szu-nan k'ao" 史可法揚州死難考, *Kuang-ming jih-pao* 光明日報, History sec., Sept. 17, 1959.

So, Kwan-wai. *Japanese Piracy in Ming China during the Sixteenth Century.* [East Lansing, Mich.]: Michigan State University Press, 1975.

———. "Grand Secretary Yan Song (1480–1566?): A New Appraisal." In

Essays in the History of China and Chinese-American Relations, pp. 1–39. East Asian Series, Occasional Paper no. 7. East Lansing, Mich.: Asian Studies Center of Michigan State University, 1982.

Spence, Jonathan, and John E. Wills, Jr., eds. *From Ming to Ch'ing: Conquest, Region, and Continuity in Seventeenth-Century China*. New Haven: Yale University Press, 1979.

Steensgaard, Niels. *The Asian Trade Revolution of the Seventeenth Century: The East India Companies and the Decline of the Caravan Trade*. Chicago: University of Chicago Press, 1973.

Struve, Lynn. "A Sketch of Southern Ming Events Affecting the Canton Delta Area." Paper presented to the Canton Delta Seminar, Hongkong University. April 1973.

———. "Uses of History in Traditional Chinese Society: The Southern Ming in Ch'ing Historiography." Ph.D. diss., University of Michigan, 1974.

———. "Ambivalence and Action: Some Frustrated Scholars of the K'ang-hsi Period." In *From Ming to Ch'ing*, pp. 324–65. Ed. Jonathan Spence and John E. Wills, Jr.

———. "The Hsü Brothers and Semiofficial Patronage of Scholars in the K'ang-hsi Period," *Harvard Journal of Asiatic Studies*, 42.1 (June 1982): 231–66.

Su Mei-fang 蘇梅芳. "Ch'ing-ch'u ch'ien-chieh shih-chien chih yen-chiu" 清初遷界事件之研究, *Li-shih hsüeh-pao* 歷史學報 (National Ch'eng-kung University 國立成功大學, T'ai-wan), 5 (July 1978): 367–425.

Su T'ung-ping 蘇同炳. "Lu Wang shih Liu Chung chih Hang-chou shu-ch'ü wang-fei chi ch'i tzu an" 魯王使劉忠至杭州贖取王妃及其子案, *T'ai-wan wen-hsien* 台灣文獻, 20.3 (Sept. 1969): 111–17.

———. "Yen-p'ing wang yü Yen-p'ing chün-wang chih cheng p'ing-i" 延平王與延平郡王之爭平議, *T'ai-wan wen-hsien*, 24.2 (June 1973): 10–13.

———. "Yu Ch'ung-chen liu-nien te Liao-lo hai-chan t'ao-lun tang-shih te Min-hai ch'ing-shih chi Ho-Cheng kuan-hsi" 由崇禎六年的料羅海戰討論當時的閩海情勢及荷鄭關係, *T'ai-pei wen-hsien* 台北文獻, 42 (Dec. 1977): 1–39.

Su Wei 蘇蔦. *Ming Su chüeh-fu shih-lüeh* 明蘇爵輔事略. Tung-kuan, 1919. (Unexamined work.)

Sun Chin-ming 孫金銘. *Chung-kuo ping-chih shih* 中國兵制史. [T'ai-pei]: Yang-ming shan-chuang, 1960.

Szu-ma Kuang 司馬光. *Tzu-chih t'ung-chien* 資治通鑑. In *Szu-pu ts'ung-k'an, shih-pu* 四部叢刊, 史部, vols. 99–178. Shang-hai: Commercial Press, 1922?

Tada Ōkuma 田大熊原. Trans. Shih Wan-shou 石萬壽. "Kuo-hsing-yeh te teng-lu T'ai-wan" 國姓爺的登陸台灣, *T'ai-pei wen-wu* 台北文物, 44 (June 1978): 111–21.

Tai Li 戴笠 and Wu I 吳殳. *Huai-ling liu-k'ou shih-chung lu* 懷陵流寇始終錄. In *Hsüan-lan-t'ang ts'ung-shu* 玄覽堂叢書, *hsü-chi* 續集, vol. 12. Nan-ching, 1947.

Ta-Ming hui-tien 大明會典. Repr. in 5 vols. of 1587 edition. T'ai-pei: Tung-nan shu-pao she, 1963.

Tamura Jitsuzō 田村實造. "Minchō no kampō to gin no mondai 明朝の官俸と銀の問題. In *Tōhō gakkai sōritsu nijūgo shūnen kinen tōhō gaku ronshū* 東方学會創立二十五周年記念東方学論集, pp. 475–94. Tokyo: Tōhō gakkai, 1972.

T'an Ch'ien 談遷. *Kuo-ch'üeh* 國榷. Coll. and ed. Chang Tsung-hsiang 張宗祥. 6 vols. Pei-ching: Ku-chi ch'u-pan she, 1958.

――――. *Tsao-lin tsa-tsu* 棗林雜俎. In *Pi-chi hsiao-shuo ta-kuan*, orig. vol. 25.

Tani Mitsutaka 谷光隆. "Mindai no kunshin ni kansuru ichi kōsatsu" 明代の勳臣に関する一考察, *Tōyōshi kenkyū* 東洋史研究, 29.4 (1971): 66–113.

Teng K'ai 鄧凱. *Yeh-shih lu* 也是錄. In *Ming-chi pai-shih ch'u-pien*, ch. 18.

Toby, Ronald P. "Reopening the Question of *Sakoku*: Diplomacy in the Legitimation of the Tokugawa Bakufu," *Journal of Japanese Studies*, 3.2 (Summer 1977): 323–63.

――――. *State and Diplomacy in Early Modern Japan: Asia in the Development of the Tokugawa Bakufu*. Forthcoming, Princeton University Press.

Tsao Kai-fu. "K'ang-hsi and the San-fan War," *Monumenta Serica*, 31 (1974–75): 108–30.

Ts'ao Yung-ho 曹永和. "Ho-lan yü Hsi-pan-ya chan-chü shih-ch'i te T'ai-wan" 荷蘭與西班牙佔據時期的台灣. In *T'ai-wan wen-hua lun-chi* 台灣文化論集, vol. 1, pp. 105–22. Ed. Lin Hsiung-hsiang 林熊祥 et al. T'ai-pei: Chung-hua wen-hua ch'u-pan shih-yeh wei-yüan hui, 1954.

Tu Nai-chi 杜乃濟. *Ming-tai nei-ko chih-tu* 明代內閣制度. T'ai-pei: Commercial Press, 1967.

Tu Yin-hsi 堵胤錫. *Tu Wen-chung Kung chi* 堵文忠公集, 10 ch.; *nien-p'u* 年譜, 1 ch.; *fu-lu* 附錄, 1 ch. N.p., 1887.

T'ung-shih 痛史. Comp. Le-t'ien Chü-shih 樂天居士 [pseud.]. Shang-hai: Commercial Press, 1911–12. Repr. in 14 vols. T'ai-pei: Kuang-wen shu-chü, 1968.

Ueda Noboru 上田信. "Minmatsu Shinsho Kōnan no toshi no 'burai' o meguru shakai kankei" 明末清初江南の都市の「無頼」をめぐる社会関係, *Shigaku zasshi* 史学雑誌, 90.11 (Nov. 1981): 1–35.

Ura Ren'ichi 浦廉一. "Ka'i hentai kaisetsu―tōsen fūsetsugaki no kenkyū" 華夷變態解説―唐船風説書の研究. In *Ka'i hentai*, vol. 1, separately paginated. Comp. Hayashi Shunsai.

Van Kley, Edwin J. "News from China: Seventeenth-Century Notices of the Manchu Conquest," *Journal of Modern History*, 45.4 (Dec. 1973): 561–82.

Wada Sei. "Some Problems Concerning the Rise of T'ai-tsu, Founder of the Manchu Dynasty," *Memoirs of the Research Department of the Tōyō Bunko*, 16 (1957): 35–73.

Wakeman, Frederic, Jr. "Localism and Loyalism during the Ch'ing Conquest of Kiangnan: The Tragedy of Chiang-yin." In *Conflict and Control in Late Imperial China*, pp. 43–85. Ed. Frederic Wakeman and Carolyn Grant. Berkeley: University of California Press, 1975.

———. "The Shun Interregnum of 1644." In *From Ming to Ch'ing*, pp. 43–87. Ed. Jonathan Spence and John E. Wills, Jr.

[Wan Yen 萬言]. *Ch'ung-chen ch'ang-pien* 崇禎長編. In *T'ung-shih*, vol. 1.

Wang Chin-hsiang 王進祥. *Chu Shun-shui p'ing-chuan* 朱舜水評傳. T'ai-pei: Commercial Press, 1976.

Wang Ch'ung-wu 王崇武. "Pa Yung-li Ti chih Wu San-kuei shu" 跋永曆帝致吳三桂書, *Tung-fang tsa-chih* 東方雜誌, 43.9 (May 1947): 37–41.

———. *Ming ching-nan shih-shih k'ao-cheng kao* 明靖難史事考證稿. Special publication of the Institute of History and Philology, Academia Sinica, no. 25. Shang-hai: Commercial Press, 1948.

Wang Fu-chih 王夫之. *Yung-li shih-lu* 永曆實錄. In *Ch'uan-shan ch'üan-chi* 船山全集, vol. 12. Ed. Chang Ping-wen 張秉文. T'ai-pei: Ta-yüan wen-hua fu-wu she, 1965.

Wang Hsien-ch'ien 王先謙, P'an I-fu 潘頤福, Chu Shou-p'eng 朱壽朋, comps. *Shih-erh-ch'ao tung-hua lu* 十二朝東華錄, 509 ch. T'ai-pei: Wen-hai ch'u-pan-she, 1963.

Wang Hsien-te 王賢德. "Minmatsu dōran ki ni okeru gōson bōei" 明末動亂斯における鄉村防衛, *Mindai shi kenkyū* 明代史研究, 2 (1975): 26–49.

Wang Hsiu-ch'u 王秀楚. *Yang-chou shih-jih chi* 揚州十日記. In CNW, vol. 2.

Wang Kuang-fu 汪光復. *Hang-hsieh i-wen* 航澥遺聞. In *Ching-t'o i-shih*, un-numbered volume.

Wang Pao-hsin 王葆心. *Ch'i-Huang szu-shih-pa chai chi-shih* 蘄黃四十八砦紀事. Repr. T'ai-pei: Chung-hua shu-chü, 1966.

Wang Tsung-yen 汪宗衍. *Tu Ch'ing-shih kao cha-chi* 讀清史稿札記. Hongkong: Chung-hua shu-chü, 1977.

Wang Yi-t'ung. *Official Relations between China and Japan, 1368–1549*. Harvard-Yenching Institute Studies, no. 9. Cambridge, Mass.: Harvard University Press, 1953.

Wang Yü-ch'üan 王毓銓. *Ming-tai te chün-t'un* 明代的軍屯. Pei-ching: Chung-hua shu-chü, 1965.

Wei Hung-yün 魏宏運. *Shih K'o-fa* 史可法. Shang-hai: Hsin chih-shih ch'u-pan she, 1955.

Wei Yung-chu 魏永竹. "Cheng Ch'eng-kung nan-hsia ch'in-wang chih t'an-t'ao" 鄭成功南下勤王之探討, *T'ai-wan wen-hsien* 台灣文獻, 33.1 (March 1982): 131–39.

Weithoff, Bodo. *Chinas dritte Grenze: Der traditionelle chinesische Staat und der küstennahe Seeraum*. Wiesbaden: Otto Harrassowitz, 1969.

Wen Jui-lin 溫睿臨. *Nan-chiang i-shih* 南疆逸史. Shang-hai: Chung-hua shu-chü, 1960.

Weng-chou Lao-min 翁洲老民 [pseud.]. *Hai-tung i-shih* 海東逸史. In TW, no. 99. 1961.

Wilhelm, Hellmut. "Ein Briefwechsel zwischen Durgan und Schi Ko-Fa," *Sinica*, 8.5–6 (1933): 239–45.

Wills, John E., Jr. *Pepper, Guns, and Parleys: The Dutch East India Company and China, 1662–1681.* Cambridge, Mass.: Harvard University Press, 1974.

———. "Maritime China from Wang Chih to Shih Lang." In *From Ming to Ch'ing*, pp. 203–38. Ed. Jonathan Spence and John E. Wills, Jr.

Wu Chih-ho 吳智和. "Ming-tai te chiang-hu tao" 明代的江湖盜, *Ming-shih yen-chiu chuan-k'an* 明史研究專刊, 1 (July 1978): 107–37.

Wu Chi-hua 吳緝華. "Ming Jen-Hsüan shih nei-ko chih-tu chih pien yü huan-kuan ch'ien-yüeh hsiang-ch'üan chih huo" 明仁宣時內閣制度之變與宦官僭越相權之禍, CYYY, 31 (1960): 381–403.

———. "Lun Ming-tai fei-hsiang yü hsiang-ch'üan chih chuan-i" 論明代廢相與相權之轉移, *Ta-lu tsa-chih* 大陸雜誌, 34.1 (Jan. 1967): 6–8.

———. *Ming-tai she-hui ching-chi shih lun-ts'ung* 明代社會經濟史論叢. 2 vols. T'ai-pei: T'ai-wan Student Bookstore, 1970. Articles cited therein: "Lun Ming-tai shui-liang chung-hsin chih ti-yü chi ch'i chung-shui chih yu-lai" 論明代稅糧重心之地域及其重稅之由來, I: 33–73; "Ming Ch'eng-tsu hsiang pei-fang te fa-chan yü nan-pei chuan-yün te chien-li" 明成祖向北方的發展與南北轉運的建立, I: 155–73; "Lun Ming-tai tsung-fan jen-k'ou" 論明代宗藩人口, II: 237–89.

———. "Ming-tai tsui kao chün-shih chi-kou te yen-pien" 明代最高軍事機構的演變, *Nan-yang ta-hsüeh hsüeh-pao* 南洋大學學報, 6.1 (1972): 144–54.

———. "Contraction of Forward Defenses on the North China Frontier during the Ming Dynasty," *Papers on Far Eastern History* (Research School of Pacific Studies, Australian National University), 17 (March 1978): 1–13.

Wu Han 吳晗. "Ming-tai te chün-ping" 明代的軍兵. In *Tu-shih cha-chi* 讀史箚記, pp. 92–141. Pei-ching: San-lien shu-tien, 1956.

Wu Mi-ch'a 吳密察. "Cheng Ch'eng-kung cheng-T'ai chih pei-ching—Cheng Shih cheng-ch'üan hsing-ko chih k'ao-ch'a" 鄭成功征台之背景—鄭氏政權性格之考察, *Shih-i* 史譯, 15 (Sept. 1978): 24–44.

Wu Shan-chia 吳山嘉, comp. *Fu She hsing-shih chuan-lüeh* 復社姓氏傳略. Repr. in *Ming-Ch'ing shih-liao hui-pien*, vol. 73.

Wu Wei-yeh 吳偉業. *Sui-k'ou chi-lüeh* 綏寇紀略. In *Shih-liao ts'ung-pien* 史料叢編, vols. 21–24. T'ai-pei: Kuang-wen shu-chü, 1968.

Wu Ying-chi 吳應箕. *Ch'i-Chen liang-ch'ao p'o-fu lu* 啓禎兩朝剝復錄. In *Kuei-ch'ih hsien-che i-shu* 貴池先哲遺書. Ed. Liu Shih-heng 劉世珩. Kuei-ch'ih, 1920.

———. *Lou-shan-t'ang chi* 樓山堂集. Shang-hai: Commercial Press, 1935.

Yamawaki Teijirō. "The Great Trading Merchants, Cocksinja and His Son," *Acta Asiatica*, 30 (1976): 106–16.

Yang Hsüeh-ch'en 楊學琛. "Kuan-yü Ch'ing-ch'u te 't'ao-jen fa'—chien-lun

Man-tsu chieh-chi tou-cheng te t'e-tien ho tso-yung" 關於清初的「逃人法」—兼論滿族階級鬥爭的特點和作用 , *Li-shih yen-chiu* 歷史研究, 1979, no. 10 (October): 46–55.

Yang K'uan 楊寬. "1645-nien Chia-ting jen-min te k'ang-Ch'ing tou-cheng" 一六四五年嘉定人民的抗清鬥爭. In *Ming-Ch'ing shih lun-ts'ung*, pp. 215–25. Ed. Li Kuang-pi.

Yang Te-en 楊德恩. *Shih K'o-fa nien-p'u* 史可法年譜. Ch'ang-sha: Commercial Press, 1940.

Yang Te-tse 楊德澤. *Yang chien pi-chi* 楊監筆記. In *Yü-chien-chai ts'ung-shu* 玉簡齋叢書. Ed. Lo Chen-yü 羅振玉. Shang-yü, 1910.

Yang Ying 楊英. *Yen-p'ing Wang hu-kuan Yang Ying ts'ung-cheng shih-lu* 延平王戶官楊英從征實錄 [orig. title *Hsien Wang* 先王 *shih-lu*]. Repr. of incomplete manuscript. Pei-p'ing: Institute of History and Philology, Academia Sinica, 1931.

Yang Yün-p'ing 楊雲萍 [Yang Yu-lien 友濂]. "Cheng Ch'eng-kung fen ju-fu k'ao" 鄭成功焚儒服考, *T'ai-wan yen-chiu* 台灣研究, 1 (June 1956): 31–37.

———. "Nan-Ming shih-tai yü Liu-ch'iu chih kuan-hsi te yen-chiu" 南明時代與琉球之關係的研究, *Shih-hsüeh hui-k'an* 史學彙刊, 2 (Aug. 1969): 173–87.

———. "Nan-Ming shih-tai yü Jih-pen te kuan-hsi" 南明時代與日本的關係, *Chung-kuo li-shih hsüeh-hui shih-hsüeh chi-k'an* 中國歷史學會史學集刊, 6 (May 1974): 1–17.

———. "Nan-Ming Hung-kuang shih-tai te chi-ke wen-t'i" 南明弘光時代的幾個問題 , *Chung-kuo li-shih hsüeh-hui shih-hsüeh chi-k'an* 中國歷史學會史學集刊 . 7 (May 1975): 157–78.

———. "Nan-Ming Lu chien-kuo shih-chi te yen-chiu" 南明魯監國事蹟的研究, *Chung-kuo li-shih hsüeh-hui shih-hsüeh chi-k'an*, 8 (May 1976): 33–61.

———. "Nan-Ming Yung-li shih-tai te yen-chiu" 南明永曆時代的研究, *Chung-kuo li-shih hsüeh-hui shih-hsüeh chi-k'an* 中國歷史學會史學集刊, 9 (April 1977): 59–88.

———. "Chi hsin-te Nan-Ming ch'ien-pi" 記新得南明錢幣, *Ch'ien-pi t'ien-ti* 錢幣天地, 2.1 (Jan. 1978): 3–7.

Yao Ming-ta 姚名達. *Liu Chi-shan hsien-sheng nien-p'u* 劉蕺山先生年譜. Shang-hai: Commercial Press, 1937.

Yasuno Shōzō 安野省三. "'Kokō juku sureba tenka taru' kō" 「湖廣熟すれば天下足」考. In *Kimura Masao sensei taikan kinen tōyōshi ronshū* 木村正雄先生退官記念東洋史論集, pp. 301–09. Tokyo: Kyūko shoen, 1976.

Yeh Meng-chu 葉夢珠. *Hsü-pien sui-k'ou chi-lüeh* 續編綏寇紀略. Preface 1688. N.p.: Tsun-wen-ko, 1911.

Yen Erh-mei 閻爾梅. *Yen Ku-ku ch'üan-chi* 閻古古全集. Ed. Chang Hsiang-chih 張相之. N.p., 1911.

Yen Hsü-hsin 顏虛心. "*Ming-shih* Ch'en Pang-yen chuan p'ang-cheng"

明史陳邦彥傳旁證. In *Kuang-tung wen-wu*, II: 551–87. Ed. Kuang-tung
   Antiquities Exhibition Committee.

Yin 隱 [pseud.]. "Ming Kuei Wang chih Wu San-kuei shu" 明桂王致吳三桂書,
   T'ien-chin i-shih pao 天津益世報, Shuo-yüan 說苑 sec. April 24–26, 1937.

Ying T'ing-chi 應廷吉. *Ch'ing-lin hsieh* 青燐屑. In *Ming-chi pai-shih ch'u-pien*,
   ch. 24.

Ying-Ki, Ignatius. "The Last Emperor of the Ming Dynasty and Catholicity,"
   Bulletin of the Catholic University of Peking, 1 (1925): 23–28.

Yü I-tse 余貽澤. *Chung-kuo t'u-szu chih-tu* 中國土司制度. Ch'ung-ch'ing:
   Cheng-chung shu-chü, 1944.

Glossary–Index

Where twentieth-century place names differ from Ming place names, they follow the latter in parentheses.

Aborigines. *See* Native peoples and chieftains
Ai Nan-ying 艾南英
Ai Neng-ch'i 艾能奇, 144, 243n30
Aisinga 愛星阿, 175, 176, 177–78
Ajige 阿濟格, 52 (map), 53, 64
A-mi 阿迷 (K'ai-yüan 開遠)
An Lu-shan 安祿山
An-ch'ing 安慶 (Huai-ning 懷寧)
An-hai 安海
An-huei 安徽
An-jen 安仁 (Yü-chiang 餘江)
An-lung 安龍, 152, 153
Annam 安南 (northern Vietnam), 152, 244n44
An-ning 安寧
An-p'ing 安平
An-shun 安順
Assistance for the emperor, problem of, 2, 82, 156, 195; in Ming times, 7–9, 9–11; Hung-kuang, 19–20, 27, 30, 33–34; Lu, 80; Lung-wu, 82; Yung-li, 129, 133, 167, 170–71, 174
Ava 阿瓦

bakufu 幕府
Bandits: Shan-tung, 40, 49; Chiang-nan, 64; Chiang-hsi, 68, 69–70; in triprovincial region, 85–98; Kuang-tung, 100, 101, 121, 122, 123; Fu-chien, 111, 246n71; Kuang-hsi, 143
Bhamo 八莫
Bolo 博洛, 52 (map), 75, 90, 95, 103, 244n40
Boym, Michael, 241n17
Burma, 167, 170–75, 176–77. *See also* Campaigns, Ch'ing; Yung-li, regime

Calendars, official, 115, 126, 128, 192, 241n16
Campaigns
—Ch'ing: on Shen-hsi, 51–53; on Chiang-nan, 52–58; on Hang-chou, 59; on Che-chiang, 95–97, 114–15; on Fu-chien, 97–98; on Chiang-hsi, 98–99; on Liang-Kuang, 99, 101–04, 130–41, 142–43, 228n29; on Hu-kuang, 102 (map), 104, 106–07, 139–40; against Cheng Ch'eng-kung, 166, 181, 189; on Yün-Kuei, 167–69; on Burma, 175–76, 176–77, 178
—Ming: by Lung-wu forces, 85, 90–91, 97; by Sun K'o-wang and Li Ting-kuo, 147–49, 154, 172. *See also* Cheng Ch'eng-kung
Ch'a Mountain 茶山
Ch'a-ling 茶陵
Chang Chia-yü 張家玉, 84, 123, 124
Chang Chieh 張捷, 31
Chang Chü-cheng 張居正, 9, 10, 241n16
Chang Hsien-chung 張獻忠, 67, 139, 146; in Hu-kuang, 15, 70, 99, 144, 228n31; in Szu-ch'uan, 37, 144; lineage, 152, 238n47
Chang Huang-yen 張煌言, 186, 187, 188, 193
Chang K'uang 章曠, 72, 73, 106
Chang Kuo-wei 張國維, 78, 79, 80
Chang Ming-chen 張名振, 108, 109, 186, 230n56, 231n65; under Regent Lu, 113, 114, 115; under Cheng Ch'eng-kung, 162, 182, 183
Ch'ang Pass 長關 (Ta-ling Pass 大嶺隘)
Chang Shen-yen 張慎言, 28
Chang Sun-chen 張孫振, 208n71

Yü-lin 鬱林
Yün-hsi, Prince of 鄖西王, 230n48
Yün-nan 雲南, 144–46, 154, 169–70, 172, 174, 175, 178
Yün-nan Fu 雲南府 (K'un-ming 昆明), 145, 146, 153–54, 169, 178

Yün-yang 鄖陽 (Yün-hsien 縣)
Yü-shan 玉山
Yü-yao 餘姚

Zeelandia, Castle, 191, 192